LIBRARY OF HEBREW BIBLE /
OLD TESTAMENT STUDIES

428

Formerly Journal for the Study of the Old Testament Supplement Series

Editors
Claudia V. Camp and
Andrew Mein

Founding Editors
David J.A. Clines, Philip R. Davies and David M. Gunn

Editorial Board
Richard J. Coggins, Alan Cooper, John Goldingay, Robert P. Gordon,
Norman K. Gottwald, John Jarick, Andrew D.H. Mayes,
Carol Meyers, Patrick D. Miller

CONTENDING FOR JUSTICE

Ideologies and Theologies of Social Justice in the Old Testament

WALTER J. HOUSTON

t&t clark

Published by T&T Clark
A Continuum imprint

The Tower Building   80 Maiden Lane
11 York Road   Suite 704
London SE1 7NX   New York, NY 10038

www.tandtclark.com

British Library Cataloguing-in-Publication Data
A catalogue record for this book is available from the British Library

ISBN 0–567–04373–8 (hardback)

Typeset by RefineCatch Ltd, Bungay, Suffolk
Printed on acid-free paper in Great Britain by MPG Books Ltd., Bodmin, Cornwall

To Fleur

CONTENTS

Preface   xi
Acknowledgements   xv
Abbreviations   xvii

Chapter 1   1
TEXTS AND CONTEXTS   1
1. Introduction   1
  1.a. The Author's Context   1
  1.b. Studies of Social Justice in the Old Testament   3
  1.c. Biblical Justice in Christian Tradition and Today 4
  1.d. The Hermeneutical Problem   5
2. A Proposal for our Method   11
3. Selecting the Objects of Study   16

Chapter 2   18
THE ANCIENT SOCIAL CONTEXT   18
1. Explaining the Evidence   18
2. Rent Capitalism   21
3. 'Ancient' Class Society   25
4. The Tributary State   33
5. The Patronage System   41
6. Conclusion   47

Chapter 3   52
OPPRESSION AND THE PROPHETS   52
1. Interpreting the Prophets   52
2. Amos   58
  2.a. The Message of the Book of Amos   58
  2.b. Perceiving Oppression in Amos   61
    2.b.1. The Victims   61
    2.b.2. The Oppressors   63
    2.b.3. The Acts of Oppression   65
    2.b.4. The Law and the Prophet   69
  2.c. The Paradox of Amos   71

3. Surveying the Prophets 73
4. Micah 75
5. Isaiah 77
6. Jeremiah 80
7. Ezekiel 84
8. Oppression in the Prophets 86
   8.a. The Victims 86
   8.b. The Oppressors 87
   8.c. The Acts of Oppression 88
      8.c.1. Bloodshed 88
      8.c.2. Violence and Coercion 90
      8.c.3. Extortion, Unjust Gain 90
      8.c.4. Loss of Freedom 91
      8.c.5. Perversion of Right 92
      8.c.6. Indulgence at the Expense of the Poor 92
9. The Justice of YHWH 93
10. Conclusions 96

Chapter 4
JUSTICE AND THE PATRON 99
1. Introduction 99
2. Ezekiel 18 100
3. Exodus 22.21 (Hebrew 20)–23.12 105
4. Proverbs 117
5. Job 126
6. The Virtue of Justice 131

Chapter 5
JUSTICE AND THE KING 134
1. Introduction 134
2. Criticism of Monarchy? 135
3. The Royal Ideology 138
4. Psalm 72 and the Ideology of Royal Justice 138
5. The Theme of Social Justice in the Royal Traditions 150
6. Expecting the Just King 152

Chapter 6
JUSTICE AND THE PEOPLE 160
1. Visions of Justice in the Prophets 160
   1.a. Introduction 160
   1.b. Visions of Justice in Isaiah 161
   1.c. Justice in the Vision of Ezekiel 163
   1.d. A Vision of Justice in Zephaniah 166
   1.e. Interpreting Utopia 167

2. The Just Society in the Torah 168
   2.a. The Torah as a Whole 168
   2.b. Deuteronomy 173
      2.b.1. The Context of Composition 173
      2.b.2. General Provisions 177
      2.b.3. The Third-Year Tithe 178
      2.b.4. The Release of Debts 179
      2.b.5. The Release of Slaves 185
      2.b.6. Deuteronomy, Class and Community 187
   2.c. The Law of Jubilee in the Holiness Code 189

Chapter 7 203
THE GOD OF JUSTICE 203
1. Introduction 203
2. Impartial and Partial Justice 204
3. Social Affinities 213
   3.a. Patronage 213
   3.b. Kingship 215
   3.c. Synthesis 217
4. Ideological Functions 218
5. Reflections for Today 221

Chapter 8 226
THE OLD TESTAMENT: A RESOURCE IN CONTENDING FOR JUSTICE 226
1. Old Testament Justice in Today's World 226
2. Embodying the Justice of God 229

Bibliography 231
Index of References 253
Index of Semitic Words 263
Index of Authors 265
Subject Index 269

PREFACE

This work has been many years in the making. My very reason for first moving into the Old Testament field about 1978 was my perception that there was richer material here than in the New Testament for Christians with a commitment to the public sphere to reflect on and be inspired by. When I was invited to become one of the founder members of Scripture, Theology and Society (now the Bible and Society Group) in 1985, I was fired by our annual conversations and stimulated to start thinking systematically about such problems as I tackle here. Like other members, I wrote some short pieces for private circulation and discussion in the group, and some of the thinking in those has found its way into the present work. But the initial stimulus to conceive something like the work that lies before you came with the invitation to give a course of lectures to the Vacation Term for Biblical Study at Oxford in the summer of 1994. I began to collect material for it in the sabbatical generously given me in my last term on the staff of Westminster College, Cambridge, in 1993. Those who were present at the Vacation Term may recognize the four lectures they heard, even in this greatly altered and expanded form, in Chapters 1 and 2, 3, 5 and 6; Chapters 4 and 7 are entirely new. I am grateful to the officers of the Vacation Term for the opportunity they gave me to present my thought in something approaching ordered form, and I also thank the members for their stimulating questions and discussion.

I would never have believed it could take so long for the work thus launched to be fitted out for publication, but besides the normal duties of academic posts, several factors delayed the work, including obligations to complete work undertaken on commission, and the move to my present very demanding post in 2000. Without further periods on sabbatical granted me by Northern College, Manchester, in the autumn of 1997, and by Mansfield College in 2003 and 2005, the work would never have seen the light of day. I offer my sincere thanks to the Senatus of Westminster College, the Governors and Principal of Northern College, and the Governing Body of Mansfield College, for affording me the time I needed to complete the work.

I am indebted to T&T Clark International for taking the book to the point of publication, and I express my thanks here to David Clines for giving consideration to my initial outline as an offering for Sheffield Academic Press, to Philip J. Law for accepting the work on behalf of the new management, to Andrew Mein for encouraging its publication, and to the staff of T&T Clark International.

Several portions of the work, or closely related essays, have been read in earlier forms to different learned bodies: besides Scripture, Theology and Society already mentioned, the Ehrhardt Seminar in the Department of Biblical Studies at Manchester University, the Sheffield Biblical Studies Department Seminar, the Sheffield Colloquium on the Bible in Ethics, the Oxford Old Testament Seminar, and the Society for Old Testament Study. I owe them a great deal not only for their comments on what they heard from me, but more generally for other people's papers that I have heard in their company, their lively discussions and their friendship.

Several parts of the work have been previously published in a variety of places, and they appear here, in revised and usually abbreviated form, with the permission of the publishers in all cases, for which I thank them. Details are given in the acknowledgments which follow this preface, and the precise places in the book where they appear (in some cases divided between different parts of the book) are noted in the footnotes.

I owe more than I can say to my wife Fleur, the companion of my life and constant stimulus to my thought, who has commented on parts of the work when time has permitted, and helped to compile the indexes, but more generally has made it possible for me to work in agreeable and helpful conditions. My first book was dedicated to the memory of my parents. This one, my second, is dedicated to my living wife with love and gratitude.

A word is probably required on the use of language in the book. For some years now it has been *de rigueur* in works in theology and the humanities generally to avoid the use of gendered language in reference both to humanity and to God. Some who pick up this volume may be offended to find it used in both ways in the greater part of the book. This is a carefully considered choice and arises from no contempt for so-called 'political correctness', which in my view is simply politeness in a world which accepts, if it does not properly realize, equality between women and men. However, most of this book consists of exegesis of texts from the Hebrew Bible and makes an attempt to present the force of their rhetoric in their social context. As I argue in my first chapter, these texts are intended to sway people in particular social situations. They therefore inevitably reflect the patriarchal character of society at the time, and to strip out the scandal of their genderedness is to misrepresent them. This certainly applies to language about God as much as about people. YHWH was a male God, there is no getting round it. Therefore when I am speaking about YHWH/Elohim as a character in the biblical text, I refer to him with masculine pronouns. When (more rarely) I am speaking of God as an object of faith at the present day, I have avoided them. If any reader finds places where, on this account, the use of the masculine pronoun is inappropriate, I would be grateful if s/he would bring them to my attention, in the hope that a reprint might give the opportunity to correct them.

Undoubtedly the work could still be improved in many ways, but after so long a gestation it is high time for the child to be born. I send it forth praying for the blessing of God to be upon it and all who read it.

Walter J. Houston

28 May 2005

ACKNOWLEDGEMENTS

Parts of this work appeared in earlier forms as follows, and thanks are owed to the respective publishers, or their successors, for permission to publish them here:

Part of Chapter 1, §2, with Chapter 6, §2.b.4, 5, 6 in ' "Open your Hand to your Needy Brother": Ideology and Moral Formation in Deut. 15: 1–18' in John W. Rogerson, Margaret Davies and M. Daniel Carroll R. (eds.), *The Bible in Ethics* (JSOTSup, 207; Sheffield: Sheffield Academic Press, 1995), pp. 296–314. Permission granted by Continuum.

Part of Chapter 2, §4, with Chapter 5, §4, in 'The King's Preferential Option for the Poor: Rhetoric, Ideology and Ethics in Psalm 72', *BibInt* 7 (1999), pp. 341–67. Permission granted by E.J. Brill.

Chapter 6, §2c, in 'What's Just about the Jubilee?', *Studies in Christian Ethics* 14.1 (2001), pp. 34–47. Permission granted by Sage Publications.

Part of Chapter 4, §4, in 'The Role of the Poor in Proverbs', in J.C. Exum and H.G.M. Williamson (eds.), *Reading from Right to Left: Essays on the Hebrew Bible in Honour of David J.A. Clines* (JSOTSup, 373; Sheffield: Sheffield Academic Press, 2003), pp. 229–40. Permission granted by Continuum.

ABBREVIATIONS

AB	Anchor Bible
ABD	*Anchor Bible Dictionary*
AHDO	*Archives d'histoire du droit oriental*
ATD	Das Alte Testament Deutsch
BASOR	*Bulletin of the American Schools of Oriental Research*
BBB	Bonner biblische Beiträge
BCE	Before the common era
BDB	Francis Brown, S.R. Driver and Charles A. Briggs, *A Hebrew and English Lexicon of the Old Testament* (Oxford: Clarendon Press, 1907).
BETL	Bibliotheca ephemeridum theologicarum lovaniensium
BHS	*Biblia Hebraica Stuttgartensia*
BHT	Beiträge zur historischen Theologie
Bib	*Biblica*
BibInt	*Biblical Interpretation*
BKAT	Biblischer Kommentar: Altes Testament
BN	*Biblische Notizen*
BWANT	Beiträge zur Wissenschaft vom Alten und Neuen Testament
BZAW	Beihefte zur *ZAW*
CBQ	*Catholic Biblical Quarterly*
CH	Code of Hammurabi
COT	Commentaar op het Oude Testament
DCH	David J.A. Clines (ed.), *A Dictionary of Classical Hebrew* (8 vols.; Sheffield: Sheffield Academic Press, 1993–)
EdF	Erträge der Forschung
ET	English translation
ETR	*Etudes théologiques et réligieuses*
EvQ	*Evangelical Quarterly*
EvT	*Evangelische Theologie*
FAT	Forschungen zum Alten Testament
FRLANT	Forschungen zur Religion und Literatur des Alten und Neuen Testaments

FzB	Forschung zur Bibel
HALOT	Ludwig Koehler and Walter Baumgartner *et al.*, *The Hebrew and Aramaic Lexicon of the Old Testament* (5 vols.; trans. and ed. M.E.J. Richardson; Leiden: Brill, 1994–2000).
HCOT	Historical Commentary on the Old Testament
HKAT	Handkommentar zum Alten Testament
HMSO	Her Majesty's Stationery Office
HTR	*Harvard Theological Review*
HUCA	*Hebrew Union College Annual*
ICC	International Critical Commentary
JB	Jerusalem Bible
JBL	*Journal of Biblical Literature*
JNES	*Journal of Near Eastern Studies*
JPS	Jewish Publication Society
JPSV	Jewish Publication Society Version
JSOT	*Journal for the Study of the Old Testament*
JSOTSup	JSOT Supplement Series
JTS	*Journal of Theological Studies*
KAT	Kommentar zum Alten Testament
KJV	King James Version
LCL	Loeb Classical Library
LXX	Septuagint
MSS	manuscripts
MT	Masoretic Text
NCB	New Century Bible
NICOT	New International Commentary on the Old Testament
NIDOTTE	Willem A. VanGemeren (ed.), *New International Dictionary of Old Testament Theology and Exegesis* (5 vols.; Grand Rapids: Zondervan, 1997)
NIV	New International Version
NRSV	New Revised Standard Version
NS	New Series
NZST	*Neue Zeitschrift für Systematische Theologie*
OBO	Orbis Biblicus et Orientalis
OBT	Overtures to Biblical Theology
OTG	Old Testament Guides
OTL	Old Testament Library
PEQ	*Palestine Exploration Quarterly*
PW	August Friedrich von Pauly and Georg Wissowa (eds.), *Real-Encyclopädie der klassischen Altertumswissenschaft* (Stuttgart: Metzler, 1894–)
RB	*Revue biblique*
REB	Revised English Bible

RSO	*Rivista degli studi orientali*
RV	Revised Version
SB	Sources bibliques
SBL	Society of Biblical Literature
SBLDS	SBL Dissertation Series
SBLMS	SBL Monograph Series
Sheb.	*Shebi'ith*
SJOT	*Scandinavian Journal of the Old Testament*
SOTSMS	Society for Old Testament Study Monograph Series
SVT	Supplements to Vetus Testamentum
SWBA	The Social World of Biblical Antiquity
TDOT	G.J. Botterweck and H. Ringgren (eds.), *Theological Dictionary of the Old Testament*
ThWAT	G.J. Botterweck and H. Ringgren (eds.), *Theologisches Wörterbuch zum Alten Testament* (Stuttgart: W. Kohlhammer, 1970–)
UF	*Ugarit-Forschungen*
VT	*Vetus Testamentum*
WBC	Word Biblical Commentary
WdF	Wege der Forschung
WMANT	Wissenschaftliche Monographien zum Alten und Neuen Testament
ZAR	*Zeitschrift für Altorientalisches und Biblisches Recht*
ZAW	*Zeitschrift für die alttestamentliche Wissenschaft*
ZDPV	*Zeitschrift des deutschen Palästina-Vereins*
ZThK	*Zeitschrift für Theologie und Kirche*

Chapter 1

Texts and Contexts

1. *Introduction*

The object of this work is to attempt to understand texts concerned with
social justice in the Old Testament, or Hebrew Bible,[1] as discourse with a
persuasive purpose in identifiable social situations in ancient society. It is
undertaken in the conviction that the Bible has something to say on the
subject which is meaningful and worth hearing in the modern world; and on
the other hand that what this enduring message is can only be properly
discerned after recognizing and allowing for the particular interests of
classes and other groups which are invariably expressed in the texts. My
purpose in this chapter is to give some account of these two convictions.

The scope of the book is defined by the issue of class, that is, of unequal
relations between groups within society which arise from its economic structure. Other issues, of race, gender, civil rights, and so forth, are bound up
with this one, as is too often not recognized today; for example in the UK
black people of Caribbean origin, as a result of the structure of the UK's
capitalist economy, tend to have more poorly paid jobs than whites and are
more likely to be unemployed. Situations in the world of the Old Testament
may be comparable, so that, for example, the plight of aliens, widows and
orphans cannot be separated from the question of the poor, though we shall
see that the texts distinguish 'the poor' from other marginal groups.[2]

1.a. *The Author's Context*

What people make of what they read depends on their context, experience
and standpoint, as is now widely acknowledged, and what they write reflects
their commitments in life. This is the truth which lies behind black theology,

---

1. Because the presuppositions of this work lie in Christian theology, I generally prefer the
expression 'Old Testament' to 'Hebrew Bible' or any other alternative, but this is not an
exclusive choice.
2. Below, pp. 62–63.

feminist hermeneutics and liberation theology. It is fair to the reader of this book to make clear from what experience and commitments the writer comes to its writing. I am British and was born in 1942; and I inherit, especially from my mother's family, a political culture that might be described as left of centre. I therefore grew up in a society that, like most others in Europe, had taken a conscious decision to confront 'the five giant evils' of want, disease, ignorance, squalor and idleness,[3] was moving towards greater equality, and had placed the major public services in public hands, while still retaining political and social freedom. In the late 70s the labour movement seemed about to gain the huge victory of workers' power in industry. There was still huge inequality on a global scale, but this seemed to be beginning to be tackled. The welfare states of Europe offered a model to which newly independent states in the 'Third World' could aspire. I remain convinced that equality is essential to social justice: equality as R.H. Tawney understood it, not mathematical equality of wealth, but the end of class distinctions in access to resources of every kind. Like him, I have 'faith in the possibility of a society in which a higher value will be set on human beings, and a lower value on money and economic power, when money and power do not serve human ends'.[4]

In 1979 we awoke as it were from a dream. The 'Thatcherite' backlash, the backlash of capitalism directed by the ideology of neo-liberal economics, had begun. It has led to increasing inequality, a trend which has not been reversed, despite measures taken by the Labour government since 1997 to help the poorest. Deeper and more analytical thought was needed about the realities of economic and political power, and serious action was required to return our society to something approaching justice. In the world at large the backlash is expressed in the ferocious shock treatment meted out to the post-communist societies of Eastern Europe, and the demands made by the IMF on poor countries struggling with international debt, insisting on privatization, trade liberalization and the reduction of welfare budgets, measures which all damage the livelihoods of the poorest people in those poor countries and make it easier for international capital to extract profit from them.[5]

Those who are deeply convinced of the injustice of these developments have attempted to fight them in various ways. But for Christians like myself this has not been enough. We are convinced that God has an intention for society, and we have turned for support to the Bible, and often specifically to the Old Testament, with its passionate words against oppression and in favour of care for the poor. We have, many of us, seen there an assurance

---

3. Beveridge 1966 (1942): 170.
4. Tawney 1964: 40.
5. See Stiglitz 2002.

that God is on the side of the poor and powerless, and have found an understanding of the just society which, we believe, it would be worthwhile for even our non-believing neighbours to hear. I myself was drawn into a group of biblical scholars, calling ourselves first Scripture, Theology and Society and later the Bible and Society Group, who set it as our goal to work out the relevance of the biblical text to present-day society. We still meet, and the group has continued to be a valuable stimulus to my thought and work.

1.b. *Studies of Social Justice in the Old Testament*

This issue has of course been the subject of a large number of works of scholarship and theology.[6] A detailed survey of the field is not aimed at here,[7] but from work in book format in recent years it is worth mentioning the concise but meaty survey by Léon Epsztein, *Social Justice in the Ancient Near East and the People of the Bible*, which begins with the ancient Near East and proceeds with a survey of earlier work on the subject before giving a brief survey of material from the Hebrew Bible, concentrating on the laws. Epsztein's bibliographies are comprehensive and valuable, but the work is now over twenty years old. The little book by Bruce Malchow, *Social Justice in the Hebrew Bible*, is a helpful introduction for the lay person. A more substantial work by Enrique Nardoni, *Los que buscan la justicia*, which appeared in 1997, and has recently been translated into English, includes the ancient Near East and both Testaments. This is written from a Latin American Roman Catholic point of view, and is intended as a textbook for colleges and lay Bible study groups. Works with a narrower focus and intended for a more academic audience include, first, Chris Wright's thesis on the relation of God, people and land. The picture of ancient Israel in this book depends more on biblical idealization than on sociological probability. Second, there is Moshe Weinfeld's book arguing for the close comparability of state measures for social justice over the whole ancient Near East, including Israel. This will be drawn on at various points in the present work.

But the most comprehensive book now available is *The Social Visions of the Hebrew Bible* by David J. Pleins.[8] This is structured as an introduction to the Hebrew Bible (unlike the Catholic Nardoni, Pleins covers the Hebrew canon only), and its coverage is comprehensive, with at least some treatment of every book; for this reason the areas of social theology and ethics

---

6. Works referred to in this paragraph: Epsztein 1986; Malchow 1996; Nardoni 2004; Weinfeld 1995; Wright 1990.

7. For the period up to 1983, see Epsztein 1986: 45–82, 149–73. For more recent work, the most convenient source may be Wright 2004: 415–40.

8. Pleins 2001.

covered stretch wider than the single issue of justice between rich and poor dealt with here. Pleins' main object is to demonstrate the variety of voices to be heard in the Hebrew Bible when understood against their social background, in the hope that this will give pause to those inclined to simplify 'the message of the Bible'. In this I am entirely at one with him; but as will be seen, I am most concerned to uncover the contradictions, or at least tensions, within single texts or groups of texts. There is therefore ample room for a book with a sharper focus and more intensive study of some texts. Further, although Pleins emphasizes the importance of the social background for understanding the Hebrew Bible, and points to the difficulty of reconstructing it,[9] he does not deal with it in a systematic way, as I attempt to do in the next chapter. It will be seen that I am in disagreement with Pleins on a number of points, but I have made no attempt to track his views on everything or engage in polemic with him.[10]

1.c. *Biblical Justice in Christian Tradition and Today*[11]

Examples can be found throughout Christian history of the understanding that the Old Testament has contemporary relevance in the social field. To take just one example, Calvin expounded the laws of the Torah as developments of the principles of the Ten Commandments, and most of those of interest here he grouped under the eighth, 'you shall not steal'. He distinguished between those which had absolute authority for Christians, including, for example, the laws against delay in paying wages, and the 'political' laws, that is those which applied to the polity of Israel, such as the debt remission and jubilee laws. But even here he argued that there were underlying principles which could not be ignored in any nation. The laws against usury were 'political' in so far as they were not applied to loans to foreigners, outside the commonwealth; but it was quite wrong for Christians to charge interest to the poor.[12] For Christians in recent centuries with a personal or class commitment to fight against social injustice, the words of the prophets have taken their place as their inspiration alongside the teaching of Jesus. This is true, for example, of the American 'Social Gospel' movement at the beginning of the last century,[13] and of Christian trade unionists in Britain.

In our own day, it is the liberation theology movement in Latin America that has led the way in developing the use of the Bible as a resource for

---

9. Pleins 2001: 5–7.
10. On one issue I have previously done so (Houston 2003).
11. For an overview of Christian approaches to the ethical use of the Old Testament, with an annotated bibliography of modern works, see Wright 2004: 387–440.
12. Calvin 1852–1855, IV, 110–79. Cf. Wright 2004: 394.
13. See below, p. 97.

Christian communities 'of the base', or as we would say, the grass roots, communities of the poor struggling against profound exploitation and injustice. In this movement, at least in principle, 'the poor become the subjects of their own history', and the privileged readers, as well as subjects, of the Bible text.[14] Classically, liberation theology takes the Bible as a whole as proclaiming the God who has a preferential option for the poor, and emphasizes those aspects of the text that can be read as proclaiming *liberation* for the poor: hence the title of Gutiérrez's seminal work *A Theology of Liberation*,[15] and the name the whole movement has acquired.

A number of writers in this tradition are specialist biblical exegetes, and have expounded the biblical text extensively from this point of view; for example José Severino Croatto[16] and Carlos Mesters. Essays covering a range of positions, some by writers from Latin America and other parts of the two-thirds world, may be conveniently found in the important collection *The Bible and Liberation*, edited by Norman Gottwald and Richard Horsley.[17] Possibly the earliest, and also one of the most provocative, was José Porfirio Miranda, with his work *Marx and the Bible*.[18] It devotes its main attention to the Bible, and takes justice rather than liberation as its main theme, though in fact Miranda's assertion of the intervention of God in history for justice is the equivalent of liberation in Gutiérrez. In Miranda's view, anyone who understands the Bible as it means to be understood—and it is only those whose interest is in the continuance of oppression who will not—cannot fail to see that to know God means to respond to the cry of the oppressed and that the kingdom of God means the coming of justice on earth.

1.d. *The Hermeneutical Problem*

It is often argued that the huge differences between the society and culture of the biblical world and our own rule the Bible out of court as an authority for us. The assumptions made by the writers and the values that they embraced are too remote from us. The Bible was written in a community where the great majority of the population lived in small towns or villages and engaged in agriculture, where for most people the work unit was the family, where professions were inherited, where slavery was taken for

---

14. The interpretation of the Bible by ordinary people as a vital part of this movement is described and reflected on by the biblical scholar Carlos Mesters: Mesters 1989 and 1993.

15. Gutiérrez 1988 (original first edition 1971).

16. Croatto 1981, 1987.

17. Gottwald and Horsley 1993. See also Rowland and Corner 1990.

18. Miranda 1977 (original 1971). Despite his title, Miranda does not employ a Marxist methodology in his exegesis of the text (contrast Mosala, below, pp. 8–9); but rather argues that the essential critique of oppression is the same in the Bible and in Marx (not the Marxists!).

granted, where women took no part in public life and the whole family was under the authority of the paterfamilias. Cyril Rodd entitles his book on Old Testament ethics *Glimpses of a Strange Land*.[19] Not only is the landscape alien to us, we only get glimpses of it, as through narrow windows in a tower. The vast difference between any plausible reconstruction of the economic system of ancient Israel and Judah and modern international capitalism will become obvious in the next chapter. This might suggest, as Rodd indeed argues, that the Old Testament has nothing relevant to say about our own situation.

And yet real and fruitful communication between the past, however remote, and the present is a fact, which is the subject of the theorists of the 'new hermeneutic', especially Gadamer.[20] They have introduced us to the ideas of 'world' and 'horizon' as terms in that science. ' "World" can be defined as "the total set of perception and participation in which we exist, the locus of historical being".'[21] And to have a 'horizon' means to have a standpoint from which one can observe in its true proportions all that lies within one's world.[22] Each historical period, and every text, has its horizon and lies within a world. The true understanding of a work of the past, as Gadamer sees it, involves not only 'transposing ourselves into the historical horizon' to listen to it in its proper context, but allowing that horizon to merge or fuse with the horizon of our own world by making adjustments in our understanding, so that we find ourselves with a new, broader horizon within which to understand ourselves and our own world.[23]

Miranda sees little difference between the two horizons. 'The capitalism criticized by Marx is only the last link (we hope) in a long chain of oppressions.'[24] He pays little attention to the precise circumstances and character of oppression in the Bible: it is sufficient that it is oppression that succeeds in extracting profit from the exploited poor. This condition is uniform in every age, and the struggle against it is one and the same; from which it is not to be concluded that there is no hope of an end to it: the hope of a just world is precisely what the Bible offers.[25] According to Miranda, and to the liberation theologians in general, what prevents people from hearing what the Bible is saying is not that they live in a different *cultural* world from that of the Bible, but that they do not stand *morally* where the Bible stands, on the side of the poor and the oppressed. Effectively the same position is

19.   Rodd 2001.
20.   Gadamer 1989; cf. also Clines 1976: 54–55.
21.   Clines 1976: 54, quoting Doty 1972: 42.
22.   Gadamer 1989: 302–03.
23.   Gadamer 1989: 305.
24.   Miranda 1977: xviii. Cf. Jameson 1981: 19–20.
25.   Miranda 1977: xviii, and passim.

taken up by Tim Gorringe in *Capital and the Kingdom*.[26] Chapter after chapter deals with systems and ideas that have only the faintest echo in the Old Testament; yet Gorringe is able to begin there and repeatedly to appeal to the Bible for the ethical values with which to challenge the modern capitalist system.

And of course in traditional Christian thought the cultural distance of the Bible has never been seen as a problem, because the Bible has been seen as the Word of God: not a series of documents arising from and reflecting the interests and beliefs of people within a particular ancient society, but a word spoken from above and beyond them, certainly speaking *to* them, but equally speaking to us.

But at the heart of my argument in this book is the perception that the Bible does not stand outside, above or at a distance from the world in which it came into existence. The Bible is a collection of documents that come directly out of that world, and were written by people contending for justice in that world—or failing to do so. They do not simply represent different individual voices in ancient Israel. Scholarship has always accepted this; but far less account has been taken of the fact that many of the voices represent different social classes and interest groups in the society of ancient Israel and Judah. We ought in particular to take account of the fact that almost all, if not all, of the writers of the Bible would have come from the upper-most strata of society. Writing was not a widespread skill in the ancient world. Even if some ordinary peasants or working people could write, or could get the services of a professional scribe to write for them,[27] they would not have had the leisure or the inclination, still less the necessary education in the art of composition and the polished style, to have composed the works in our Old Testament. If Amos is described as a shepherd, so and with the same word is Mesha king of Moab:[28] it certainly does not entitle us to think of Amos as a simple rustic, even if he is not himself responsible for the composition of his book, which points to a mind of considerable educa-tion and sophistication as its author. That does not mean we cannot hear the voices of the poor and humble in the pages of the Old Testament, only that what we hear is at second hand, filtered through the minds and pens, and doubtless affected by the attitudes and interests, of the upper classes.

Taking account of this, many recent writers who stand broadly in the liberationist tradition have adopted a hermeneutic of suspicion. In their

---

26. Gorringe 1994.

27. As presumably happened with the Yavneh Yam ostracon (G.I. Davies 1991: 76–77 (no. 7.001).

28. Amos 1.1 (cf. 7.14); 2 Kgs 3.4: both use *nōqēd*, and the NRSV is misleading in distinguishing between them.

view, the Bible is largely the work of dominant groups in society, 'elites', to use their favourite word, and represents their ideology; it arises out of class conflict and such conflicts are inscribed in it in a way which generally favours the dominant class.

This is the standpoint of the South African scholar Itumeleng Mosala.[29] Mosala was writing *Biblical Hermeneutics and Black Theology in South Africa* in the period immediately before the end of white rule, when the approach of liberation theology was being widely taken up by black theologians involved in the liberation struggle. On the whole these writers—they include such well-known figures as Desmond Tutu and Allan Boesak—held a relatively conservative view of the authority of the Bible. It was the Word of God, and it was the Word of God that called for the liberation of the oppressed.[30] The Gospel was for all: applied to the oppressed black people of South Africa it meant liberation. Mosala employs a Marxist conceptual frame to criticize this approach. It turns the Bible into something beyond history and beyond the struggles of history, which is 'merely' contextualized by such as Boesak.[31] Anyone who is involved in the struggle of the oppressed black working class, as those on both sides of this argument were, should know that history is the site of class struggle, and so are the products of history such as texts. 'The Bible is rent apart by the antagonistic struggles of the warring classes of Israelite society in much the same way as our world is torn asunder by society's class, cultural, racial and gender divisions.'[32] While there are some texts that support the oppressed and their human rights, there are others that do not, because they represent the standpoint of the oppressors, such as the story of the dispossession of the native inhabitants of Canaan by the Israelites. This is why the rulers of apartheid South Africa were able to claim the support of the Bible for their own dispossession of black South Africans. 'My contention is that the only adequate and honest explanation is that not all of the Bible is on the side of human rights or of oppressed and exploited people.'[33] What is more, where there is a text which genuinely recalls the point of view of the oppressed people, this is frequently co-opted by the elite into a structure supporting their own position: thus the theme of the Exodus, the deliverance from slavery, is used in Isaiah 40–55 to express the yearning of the Jerusalem elite for Zion, the capital of their rule; and in the book of Micah, to which Mosala devotes a

---

29.   See Mosala 1989 (two chapters are reprinted in Gottwald and Horsley 1993, 51–73, 264–95). Also characteristic of this position are the works of Gottwald himself, Pixley, and many others.

30.   According to Mosala (1989: 14–15), this was due to the influence of the black American writer James Cone, a pioneer in black theology.

31.   Mosala 1989: 20.

32.   Mosala 1989: 16.

33.   Mosala 1989: 30–31. Cf. Gottwald 1992, Prior 1997, and below, pp. 206–10.

lengthy analysis, the few texts denouncing the oppressors are enfolded in a structure expressing the desire of the former rulers of Judah for the destruction of their enemies, who are not the enemies of the oppressed peasants.[34]

In Mosala's view, a responsible hermeneutics requires the oppressed not to claim the ideology of the oppressor as the Word of God; but not simply to pick and choose the texts which appear supportive either. Rather, the oppressed working class should identify in the texts the same struggle (essentially) as they are themselves engaged in, and be enabled by their own struggle to take sides in the biblical struggle, and vice versa.[35]

There is a problem here which is not unique to Mosala. It is that there is little evidence for anything that could be called class struggle in ancient Israel and Judah. The labour movement as we understand it is the child of modern capitalist society. Mosala's reading of the story of Cain and Abel as a veiled elite condemnation of violent peasant resistance is hardly convincing.[36] The people in Neh. 5.1 'cry out' against their creditors, but the cry is channelled through the governing authorities. It might be possible to understand Exodus 5 as a realistic picture of a failed labour negotiation. Could this kind of thing have happened in forced labour gangs in Judah? At all events, none of the material we shall be examining suggests such a background. Like peasantries throughout most of history, it seems likely that the peasantry of ancient Israel and Judah suffered passively for the most part and resisted in ways they could hide from their oppressors.[37] The category of 'struggle' is thus inappropriate to the material, but those of oppression and dependency are not. This scarcely makes it irrelevant to modern social situations. It also follows, as will become very evident by the end of our study, that the authentic voice of the oppressed poor is not to be found in the Hebrew Bible. At most, we hear voices that are sympathetic to the poor and indignant at their oppression. But this also does not make it irrelevant.

Although Mosala and those he is in dispute with were on the same side in the struggle against apartheid, and more generally the liberation theologians and such writers as Mosala and Gottwald could be regarded as broadly sharing a political stance, it is clear that there is a wide gulf between them on the hermeneutical question.

Admittedly, there are important points of agreement between them. They agree that, as I asserted at the outset of this discussion, the reader's

---

34. Mosala 1989: 20; 101–53. The chapters on Micah are examined in detail below, pp. 56–57.
35. Mosala 1989: 11.
36. Mosala 1989: 33–37.
37. Cf. Scott 1985.

standpoint is a key to his or her view of the text. They argue that the objectivity of the scholarly interpreter is an illusion. Croatto devotes a monograph to hermeneutics with the title *Biblical Hermeneutics: Toward a Theory of Reading as the Production of Meaning*.[38] However, they would equally agree that there are right and wrong ways of reading the text. The reader can only read the text rightly by standing at the right viewpoint. For Miranda, the idea that the Bible has different meanings which are equally acceptable 'has been promulgated by conservatives to prevent the Bible from revealing *its* own subversive message'.[39] For Mosala the historical context of the text determines the way in which it should be understood and appropriated: 'the category of social struggle necessitates a historical-critical starting point'.[40]

Because they agree on this point, what they disagree on is even more fundamental. Is the Bible, taken as a whole and ignoring differences in detail, a witness to the God of justice who delivers the oppressed and saves the poor; or is it in the first place an expression of the attitudes and interests of the oppressors and the locus of the class struggles of ancient Israel and Judah? To some extent this is a matter of how one chooses to view the text. It is clear that Boesak and Tutu on the one hand and Mosala on the other have different theological starting points, and both views can point to persuasive evidence. But it is not entirely a matter of choice; some degree of objectivity is attainable, since some questions are to a degree answerable. What moral attitudes are in fact expressed in the texts, and how realistically do they relate to the social situation? How do the texts present the social, economic and historical situation? Whose view of that situation do they offer? Do they contain contradictions, pointing perhaps to an attempt to subsume the interests of different classes in the one discourse?

Such are the questions that I will attempt to answer in this book. It is not hard to show that the texts are social products reflecting the views and interests of groups within society. And, as I have already suggested, the mere fact that they are written products perpetuated by institutional means shows that these groups must have been in ruling and influential positions in society. If the voice of God does indeed address the Bible's readers, it is not from above or outside the social struggle, but from within it, and it must be sought for and discerned among the conflicting human voices to be heard within the Bible's pages.[41]

---

38. Croatto 1987.
39. Miranda 1977: 36.
40. Mosala 1989: 35.
41. This paragraph is slightly adapted from my essay on Deut. 15.1–18, Houston 1995: 296.

2. *A Proposal for our Method*

How should we go about our task? Terry Eagleton argues that discourse needs to be studied from the point of view of its effects. A text is not simply a text, simply words on paper, but is an act of communication, an activity with a purpose within a complex of relationships. The classical study of rhetoric is appropriate to all texts, since all have a persuasive purpose and are 'largely unintelligible outside the social purposes and conditions in which they were embedded'.[42]

However, the rhetorical study of biblical texts is far from straightforward. None of the basic data—the text's situation, speaker, audience, or persuasive purpose—can be taken for granted. Redaction, often multiple, or dramatic setting, complicates the question of authorship. The situation in which a text makes meaning in the first place is the world it constructs for itself, and for its hearers and readers. Its persuasiveness depends to a large extent on the persuasiveness of the social world it constructs. We may be able to some extent to estimate how truthful a picture it conveys, as well as the interests of possible authors, by our own analysis of the real social world, that is the configuration of social forces which may have given rise to the text. The next chapter will attempt to evaluate various proposals for describing sociologically the oppressive class relationships observable from the eighth century BCE onwards in Israel and Judah, and later studies will appeal to its results.

Yet not all audiences would necessarily evaluate the text's persuasiveness in the same way as we do. We cannot, of course, always be certain of the intended or actual audience of a text: some texts, such as psalms, may have always been intended to be overheard by a circle wider than the explicit addressees.[43] But we should always reckon with the fact that people have perceptions of justice or injustice which depend on their traditions and the concrete situation rather than on supposedly objective measures of exploitation, which we cannot calculate in any case. They may and usually do go beyond a reckoning of material costs and benefits.

Hans G. Kippenberg gives the example of the land-reform decree of the former Communist government of Afghanistan.[44] It was not dissimilar from those laws freeing the peasant from the power of the landlord which were welcomed by French, Russian and Chinese peasants with open arms, and which played a very important part in the early success of the respective

---

42. Eagleton 1996: 179. In popular and journalistic usage, 'rhetoric' has a pejorative sense, of speech that is empty or deceptive. But here it simply means speech that is designed to persuade.

43. See below, p. 139.

44. Kippenberg 1983: 75; Houston 1995: 300-301.

revolutions in those countries. In Afghanistan, the decree raised great resentment, and played a significant part in the failure of the revolution there, with effects that endure to this day. Why? Because in the tribal society of Afghanistan, peasants did not perceive their landlords as exploiters but as protectors: their rent was reckoned to be fair exchange for a guarantee of protection from bandits or rival warlords, and for help in bad times. Kippenberg comments that the Marxist definition of exploitation as an objective fact ignores what the patron contributes to the relationship between himself and his client, which is unquantifiable, but may make all the difference between the perception of a relationship as legitimate and as illegitimate. 'Legitimacy is called into question if the conditions of exchange deteriorate for the dependents', and this occurs particularly when they are threatened with proletarianization (that is, with ceasing to be independent producers), or with enslavement.

A text may be seen to represent the point of view of one group or class, or to be the result of negotiation between more than one.[45] In either case it will have an *ideological* aspect: that is to say, it represents or symbolizes social relationships in a way which advances the interests of a group or harmonizes the conflicting interests of more than one. 'Ideology' is a word with such varying meanings that it may sometimes confuse rather than enlighten. The sense in which I use it, as I have just defined it, is close to Marx's use. Ideology is not necessarily false or misleading, though it often is; but it always seeks to depict or symbolize social relationships in a way which conceals or justifies, or takes as an unquestionable given, the dominant position of one group.

It may be that some texts originated with individuals who were to an extent detached from the interests of their class. After all, we are aware that this is possible in modern society: academics are more likely than bankers to criticize the way the economy is organized. This may be true of parts of the prophetic collections, which, as we shall see, may have originated close to the governmental and temple elites, and yet functioned as their conscience.[46] However, this does not explain why such material, originating perhaps in the conscience of an individual, should have been preserved and disseminated by social groups whose interests seem to be threatened by them—as they must have been, and as is demonstrated by an analysis such as Mosala has performed on Micah or Coote on Amos.[47]

If such texts, then, represent the interests, or at least the viewpoint, of elite groups, it must be asked how it is that there is such strong sympathy for

45. See further below, pp. 172–3.
46. Below, Chapter 3.
47. Mosala 1989: 101–53; Coote 1981. See below, pp. 53–58.

the poor in them, denunciations of oppression and legal measures in their favour—sufficient even for Mosala to detect sympathetic voices, and for Miranda and liberation theologians generally to see the Bible as a book that is essentially on the side of the poor. There are a number of possible answers. One, which applies to much of the prophetic material, is that the denunciation of the oppressive practices of people who were long dead was perfectly safe for their descendants. 'The word of YHWH[48] which came to Micah of Moresheth in the days of Jotham, Ahaz and Hezekiah' was no threat to the leaders of the Second Temple community, and could indeed sustain their reputation if they were seen to be interested in disseminating it.

Another answer is given by Marvin Chaney, who attributes the frequency of measures of debt easement to the fact that the governing circles were riven by faction, as has happened throughout history in societies of a similar type.[49] Three kings of Judah died by assassination, and the throne of Israel was constantly in contention. A faction that had recently come into power and was seeking to consolidate itself against its opponents would seize on such a measure both to gain support from the peasantry and to damage the wealth and standing of their opponents, who would have been the main beneficiaries of peasant debt.[50] Some of Chaney's examples are speculative, but the case of Nehemiah is quite clear, from Nehemiah's own account (Nehemiah 5). The 'nobles and officials' whom he publicly accused and browbeat into giving up their gains were his opponents in the political and diplomatic struggle. The public outcry against their activities as creditors gave him a convenient excuse (if he had not stirred it up himself) to score a victory over them. In a similar way, it would often have been to the advantage of the kings to get the better of their rivals by appearing before the public as the defenders of the poor, whatever exploitative activities they themselves may have been guilty of. What went for measures of debt relief might go equally for prophetic denunciation. Royal patronage of prophecy enabled other power centres in society to be undermined by denouncing their oppressive activities.

Although these answers are partly true, they do not go deep enough. The historian and political philosopher Michael Walzer discusses a related question: where do social critics (such as the Hebrew prophets) get the moral standards from that they use to criticize their own society?[51] The answer is,

---

48. I use this representation of the divine name (except in quotations) rather than 'Yahweh', which I judge may be offensive to some; and rather than the English versions' 'the LORD', which obscures the fact that it is a proper name.

49. Chaney 1991. See below, pp. 79, 82–83.

50. Chaney 1991: 129–30.

51. Walzer 1987: 40–42. I am grateful to Raymond Plant for drawing my attention to this work.

they get them from the traditions of their own culture, largely disseminated by intellectuals in the service of their ruling elites. And if it seems strange that such people should provide the ammunition for their own critics, it is very easily explained. Walzer turns to Marxist writers, particularly to Gramsci with his theory of hegemony, that is, the dominance of one class over others. The class that claims to direct society must, in order to make good their claim, present themselves as guardians of the common interest. They have to set standards for themselves:

> . . . they have to make a case for the ideas they are defending among men and women who have ideas of their own. 'The fact of hegemony', Gramsci argues, 'presupposes that one takes into account the interests and tendencies of the groups over which hegemony will be exercised, and it also presupposes a certain equilibrium, that is to say that the hegemonic groups will make some sacrifices of a corporate nature.'[52]

In other words, any enduring ideological expression of the leadership of a class in society will always carry with it concessions to the subordinate classes, and in particular will contain moral ideas that are acceptable to them. It is essential to any ideology that it should claim to be universally and unquestionably true, a claim that cannot be made good if it contradicts fundamental moral (and theological) ideas of the people.[53] But this carries the consequence that the leadership of the dominant group may be criticized and contested in the light of its own ideology if it fails to act in accordance with such ideas; and further that a text in which it expresses its ideology may be deconstructed through the contradiction between the moral ideals and the safeguards to the dominant class's position which will be found in the same text. There are clear examples of this in the Hebrew Bible, as we shall see.[54]

Ideological texts are often, perhaps always, utopian, as Fredric Jameson argues.[55] This certainly seems to be true of the Bible, which contains a number of utopian visions of society, including Psalm 72 and Deut. 15.4–8, as well as many in the prophets. The above argument shows why: if a social order is to be publicly defensible, it must appear to be governed by the moral aspirations of every class. On the other hand, Karl Mannheim in *Ideology and Utopia*[56] distinguishes between ideology and utopia: both are ideas 'incongruent with reality', but an ideology does not threaten the status quo however sincerely it may be believed, for example the ideal of chivalry which was supposed to govern the conduct of the knightly class in the Middle

---

52. Walzer 1987: 41, citing Gramsci 1975: I, 461, as translated in Mouffe 1979: 181.
53. Walzer also refers to Marx and Engels 1947: 40–41. Cf. Jameson 1981: 86–87.
54. Below, pp. 138–50, 179–87, and earlier in Houston 1999 and 1995.
55. Jameson 1981: 281–99.
56. Mannheim 1936: 173–75.

Ages; but a utopia 'breaks the bonds of the existing order' and actually serves to bring a new order into being. It is hardly possible to say that any of the biblical utopias bring a new order into being in any ordinary political sense; but we can surely distinguish between a utopian representation of current realities and a utopian vision of the future. The latter does not serve to justify the existing social order: on the contrary, it undermines it by admitting its inadequacy. Such are some of the visions in the prophets.

My central contention in this book is that knowing the social roots of the Bible's ideas and language of social theology and morality and the social ends which they serve enables us to discriminate among them, and to recognize those with roots deeper than the needs of the moment and the interests of the hegemonic class. These cannot be falsified by the uses to which they are put. As readers we may take a critical attitude to such uses, but we may at the same time use the ideas to criticize our own society as far as they are applicable and throw them into the political and ethical debates around the issue of the just society. This is not what Mosala rejects as 'the escapist option of textual selectivity, an option that simply rejects as irrelevant those parts of the text that seem unsupportive of one's cause and accepts as the "Word of God" those parts that appear supportive'.[57] For it is precisely in the challenge that such ideas as community, generosity, equality, liberation of slaves, crushing of oppression, return to the ancestral land, however utopian, offer to the practice of oppression within the biblical text itself that their significance lies as pointers to justice in our world today.

It is obviously central to almost all ideologies of justice in the Old Testament that God acts to establish or preserve justice and righteousness. If some wisdom texts do not mention the action of God explicitly, they certainly assert the unbreakable connection between injustice and disaster on the one hand, and righteousness and blessing on the other. If the writers perceive that they do not live in a just society, at least they live in a just world. The world, or to put in theological terms, God's creation, is ordered and therefore exhibits justice; disorder and injustice exacts its price from those responsible, as the world asserts its true nature—or God protects it. Exactly what is meant by justice will be part of our investigation. The same perception can be seen to underlie the preaching of the prophets and of Deuteronomy.[58] On the other hand, its problematic character is explored in Job and Ecclesiastes. Thus an ideological analysis of rhetoric about justice in the Old Testament is not complete without analysing the *theology* which is at its heart.

This will affect the way in which we can understand the texts theologically

---

57. Mosala 1989: 11.
58. That all parts of the Old Testament depend on an understanding of creation as order is argued by H.H. Schmid (Schmid 1973).

today. In laying out an understanding of the way Christians may use Scripture in the face of post-modern ways of understanding texts, Francis Watson affirms that we must continue to understand the text to give access to reality.[59] I would want to understand the reality to which the texts studied here give access as one that is not only past but also present. In human terms this is the effort in all ages by those seized by the love of justice to establish it in truth. Theologically, I would suggest, it can be understood as the action of God to create a just, peaceful and blessed human community. The utopias of the Bible describe this community and point to this action of God to create it. In the Gospels it is called the Kingdom of God. In the Old Testament a wide variety of expressions are used: the book of Isaiah speaks of Zion, or alternatively of righteousness, the Psalms of the poor inheriting the land, Leviticus of the jubilee, Deuteronomy of Israel's total obedience, and so on. The text is not to be identified with this action of God, but it arises out of the work for justice that it sets off. The same work is going on today, wherever the Gospel, the good news of God's righteousness, is truly preached. The theological interpreter's task is first to identify the part played by the text within the work for justice, and then to liberate its critical and constructive potential for our own day.

To sum up, each text can be understood:

a) as a rhetorical unit, a piece of speech or writing with a purpose of persuasion;
b) within a social context, therefore ideologically;
c) as nevertheless appealing to society as a whole and therefore maintaining and defining certain ethical values, within a certain theological framework;
d) theologically, by developing the critical and constructive potential of the text for the interpreter's situation.

This scheme is an ideal: it need not and will not be applied rigidly to every text examined, but for those that are given extended treatment it expresses the aspects that will be generally be brought out.

3. *Selecting the Objects of Study*

Which texts should we look at in this study? The issue of social justice is a theme in most parts of the Old Testament, and is dealt with in distinctive ways in the various genres: we may read denunciation and oracles of judgment, and also utopian promises, in the prophets; moral exhortation in the laws; objective comments on life in Proverbs; passionate prayer in the

---

59. Watson 1994: 292–93.

Psalms. Even in narrative, where the subject is generally less prominent, we have the story of how a people resident in Egypt as aliens were put to forced labour and delivered by their God. It has a defining importance because of the frequency with which it is referred to in the rest of the Old Testament. There are in addition the stories of Joseph's manipulation of famine relief to reduce the Egyptian peasantry to dependence on the state (Gen. 47.13–26),[60] and of the judgment on Ahab for his use of judicial murder to seize a subject's inheritance (1 Kings 21).

It is the strength of Pleins' study that it interrogates every part of the canon and every genre of material on its 'social vision'. The present study aims to be intensive rather than comprehensive in its coverage. Many important texts have had to be left on one side. I particularly regret that I have been unable to deal with the Psalms as they deserved. The texts dealt with mostly concern class relationships explicitly. However, in Chapter 7, which deals with YHWH as the just God, I have surveyed a large number of texts which for the most part are not specifically concerned with justice for the poor. The importance here lies in the contrast between different ideas of justice, one of which is applied to YHWH's care for Israel rather than for the poor as such. The focus of this book on ideas and ideologies of justice in society means that we shall come to this point at the end of our inquiry rather than, as often, at the beginning: I am concerned to see how the justice of God is understood in terms of the available models in contemporary society, and their ideological significance.

I have already mentioned that Chapter 2 will attempt to evaluate socio-logical models for the process of social change in which Old Testament texts on social justice and injustice originated. This will help us in understanding how the ideologies of the text are related to reality. Chapter 3 shows how the prolonged social crisis, with its growing exploitation and inequality, described in the previous chapter is seen in prophetic texts: it is an analysis of injustice as perceived within the ideological framework of those texts. Chapter 4, which deals with how justice is understood at the level of indi-vidual action, shows from texts in Ezekiel, the law and wisdom that the prophetic response relies on a widespread understanding of what justice in society demands. The following two chapters, moving to the level of the state or nation, study utopian responses to social injustice: Chapter 5 deals with the justice expected of the king, and Chapter 6 with proposals and visions in the Torah (Deuteronomy and the Holiness Code) and the prophets. How thought and action at the present day may be enriched by our study is sketched in the concluding chapter.

60. See the analysis of this text by Watson 1994: 60–77.

Chapter 2

THE ANCIENT SOCIAL CONTEXT

1. *Explaining the Evidence*

How then are we to discover and describe, in a way which will illuminate the texts, the social forces which gave rise to oppression in ancient Israel and Judah? This is a historical task, and a historian needs evidence. Our evidence consists, on the one hand, of texts, of which all but an insignificant fraction are those of the Hebrew Bible, and on the other of archaeological remains. But all of this evidence, however valuable, is uncertain, fragmentary and disputed, and none of it gives clear information about social relationships and conflicts. Any information of that kind that there may be in the texts is bound to be distorted by the *parti pris* of the writers. Some refuse to use the biblical evidence on just those grounds, as well as the fact that it is mostly much later than the events; others trust it implicitly.[1] Most scholars, including this one, stand somewhere in between; we believe there are ways of discriminating between reliable and unreliable testimony. However, this does not give us anything like certainty in historical reconstruction. And for the purposes of this study there is an obvious danger of circular argument, if, wanting to establish an objective context for our texts against which to estimate their ideological distortions, we can only do it by appealing to those texts themselves.

In any case, for our purposes we need to be able to write not so much a precise chronological history of events as an account of the kind of things that were going on at a general period of history. Our focus is not on year-by-year detail but on the *longue durée*. Though texts may be difficult to date, they are unquestionably evidence of a real social situation at some date.

It would seem reasonable to suppose that in any society the relations of rich and poor might become a subject of discourse at the time when they became problematic or critical. Now the writings in which the issue is first raised in a critical way present themselves as having originated with

---

1. The literature on so-called 'minimalism' is extensive; for a convenient entrée see Grabbe 1997.

prophets—Amos, Isaiah and Micah—who, according to the same writings, were all active at about the same time, in the middle or second half of the eighth century BCE. These books are editorial creations of the Second Temple period, but some of their contents bear marks of having originated much earlier, in fact in the eighth century.[2] It is at this very time that archaeologists find clear signs of the rising power and economic activity of the Judaean state.[3] The kingdom of Israel had attained similar dominance over its population more than a century earlier, under Omri, and the legend of Naboth's vineyard in I Kings 21 sets the ideal scene of the clash of royal power and ancestral property rights under his son Ahab. At the same time we find the rising pressure of the Assyrians demanding tribute, invading the Levant and reducing its little states to subjection. These two developments taken together would have provided the ideal conditions for the kind of economic distress that these prophetic texts tell us of, as we shall see below.

In other words, textual and archaeological evidence converge to suggest the likelihood of growing social tension from the ninth century in Israel and the eighth in Judah.[4] The movement of these tensions was cut short in each case by the fall of the kingdom and the deportation of its ruling classes. But we have very clear evidence of their re-appearance, perhaps in an exacerbated form, in Second Temple Judah. The circumstantial, though of course self-interested, account of Nehemiah (Nehemiah 5) gives us a clearer picture of the process of deprivation of the peasantry than can be found in the rhetoric of the prophets; Isaiah 56 suggests that actual destitution was common in early Second Temple Jerusalem, while Job 24 draws a picture of rural misery that could be paralleled from some parts of the Two-thirds World today. And what we know of the Persian drive to extract revenue from the provinces of their empire would lead us to expect exactly such consequences—depending also of course on the unwillingness of the more powerful among their subjects to share the burden rather than divert it to the shoulders of the weak.

There can thus be little doubt that social classes were formed in ancient Israel and Judah and that their relationship suffered from a tension marked by exploitation on one side and immiseration on the other; and a rough chronology of the development can be sketched.

But to say as much as this is only to say that the social history of ancient Palestine was marked by the same broad characteristics as that of every other civilized country in the world. It would appear that the price of technical and cultural advance is always the exploitation of one class by another. What interests the social historian, and what must interest us if we

---

2. See Houston 2004: 142–45.
3. See Hopkins 1996.
4. I argue this case in detail in Houston 2004.

are to establish the context of biblical rhetoric on the subject with any accuracy, is to draw out far more detail: what the 'contending classes' were, in what ways exploitation took place, how the socio-economic formation might be described at different points of its history.

These questions have been answered in a variety of ways, and the literature on the subject is by now quite extensive. In the history of Israel, with its grudging supply of evidence, the tendency has been to propose models based on better-known parts of history or on contemporary social research. The majority of writers have tended to propose a single model and assess the evidence rather tendentiously and selectively to make sure that it fits. Only a few have examined several models and compared their value. These include Rainer Kessler, whose book concerns the last two centuries of the kingdom of Judah, and Gunter Fleischer, in his monograph on Amos.[5] The problem remains that the evidence is fragmentary, ambiguous and itself tendentious, so that it will not necessarily support one model without ambiguity. In any case all models in the social sciences are simplifications arrived at by bracketing out the particularities from a number of actual cases to be left with what they have in common. The hypothesis that it will also fit an additional case must reckon, even it is successful, with particularities that will set limits to our ability to draw deductions from it.

The relationship of classes within a society is not a fact that admits of a simple cause-and-effect explanation; it is an aspect of an entire social system, embracing economics, politics and culture, all in constant flux. We need a model comprehensive enough to include all these, and the available evidence in all these fields needs to be examined for the degree to which it fits the models on offer. Some explanations of social relationships in ancient Israel and Judah suffer from their lack of comprehensiveness; they could be described as one-dimensional. An extreme example is the attempt of the economist Morris Silver in his book *Prophets and Markets* to depict the late monarchic period as one of an emerging market economy.[6] Silver's argument leaves out of account all the social conventions, social pressures and moral understandings which determine action in a real society as distinct from an economic model. He is also mistaken in supposing there was a genuine free market in land in ancient Israel and Judah. The market operated under many restraints: see, for example, Jer. 32.7, 9, and compare Lev. 25.24–25. This is not to say that no markets of any kind existed. There is evidence that the fluctuation of prices under the influence of supply and demand was understood: see, for example, 2 Kgs 7.1, 16, where the price of grain falls sharply as a result of the raising of the siege of Samaria and the looting of the Aramaean camp. But such evidence only exists

5.   Kessler 1992; Fleischer 1989.
6.   Silver 1983.

for commodity markets. Nothing supports Silver's hypothesis of capital markets, and this probably applies at all periods.

The literature seems to me to offer four major competing models that are sufficiently broad and comprehensive to be considered seriously. These are the 'rent capitalism' theory of Oswald Loretz and Bernhard Lang; Hans Kippenberg's theory of 'ancient class society' (*antike Klassengesellschaft*), which has had little exposure in English-language scholarship up to now; the theory of the tributary state of Norman Gottwald and his school, which is dominant in much American scholarship; and the theory recently proposed by Ronald Simkins, developing suggestions of Niels Peter Lemche, of Israel as a patronage society. Each of these draws its comparative material from a different area. Loretz depends on the geographer H. Bobek, who coined the expression 'rent capitalism' for the structures he found in mid-twentieth-century Iran, and Lang extends the comparison only to the neighbouring states of Iraq and Syria. A much wider range of modern states in many parts of the world exhibits the workings of the patronage system, according to the work by Eisenstadt and Roniger relied on by Simkins. The idea of the tributary or Asiatic mode of production goes back to Marx's study of the great Asian kingdoms of India and China, but recent scholarship on the Hebrew Bible has preferred to work with our knowledge of states nearer in time and place in ancient Mesopotamia and Egypt. Kippenberg presupposes that similar socio-economic developments took place in the mid-first millennium BCE in a great swathe of territory stretching from Italy to Iran; but any detailed knowledge of them relies mainly on the evidence of Athens and Rome. One factor in the evaluation of these theories as they relate to ancient Israel and Judah is to ask how closely these societies resemble those from which the theories are largely drawn.

2. *Rent Capitalism*

In an accessible and much-published article in English, Lang gives a brief account of this theory and applies it to the book of Amos. A peasant society is not self-subsistent, but dependent on 'a propertied, educated and merchant élite often resident in towns and always monopolizing control of public affairs'.[7] These draw income from the peasants, and Lang distinguishes between the various titles by which this may be done, the *patrimonial*, *prebendal* and *mercantile* systems. Under the patrimonial system, holdings are family possessions inherited from generation to generation. In the prebendal system, the holdings or 'prebends' are awarded to high civil

---

7. Lang 1985: 85.

or religious officials as a source of income in place of a salary. In the mercantile system, they are freely bought and sold on the market.

According to Lang, it is the last of these which in the (modern) Near East takes the form of 'rent capitalism'.[8] The system has as its basic purpose to skim off 'the largest possible portion of the agricultural produce as a regular income', and its chief features are these. The peasant's frequent pressing need for credit makes him (or rarely her) in due course dependent on a creditor, usually a townsman, who becomes the owner of part or all of the peasant's land, while the peasant becomes in effect the owner's bondsman or even serf. Another trio of distinctions indicates the different types of relationship between peasant and landlord: *patronage*, *partnership* and *exploitation*.[9] Patronage, in which the owner takes some responsibility for the welfare of the dependents and does not attempt to maximize his return in bad times, is frequently attested in the Hebrew Bible, and it will occupy much of our attention later on; Lang cites Job 29 and the role of the kinsman exemplified in Jeremiah 32. The term 'partnership' covers share-cropping systems such as the *métayage* common in Southern Europe. In these the owner's return is large, but the risk is shared with the cultivator. There is little evidence for such a system in the Hebrew Bible. What the book of Amos denounces is obviously an exploitative relationship, in which there is no personal relationship between the two sides, but rather mutual mistrust and suspicion, and in which the owning class ensures that they always get their full return. Coote, following Wolf, adds to Lang's description the important detail that 'rent' may be exacted not simply for the cultivation of the land, but separately for every factor of production—water, tools, seed, draught animals and so forth.[10]

The cultural aspects of the system are not to be overlooked. They include the disdain for manual labour shown by the possessing classes, which creates their need for an income which they have not worked for; the stagnation of traditional culture in the countryside among the fellaheen who have scarcely enough to live on, as against the flowering of the arts, literature, philosophy and so on in the towns; and the stagnant and undeveloped nature of technology and the economy.

Lang has no difficulty in demonstrating that many of these features are exemplified in the book of Amos, and other prophetic books as well.[11] The

8. Lang 1985: 86. See Wolf 1966: 50–57. Coote (1981: 29) associates rent capitalism with prebendal domain in ancient Israel. Coote's account is confused and relies on insufficient evidence. It is true that a system of rent capitalism does not require mercantile domain, but the trend will always be towards a mercantile system. In any case, as Wolf emphasizes (1966: 56), what is decisive is not the form of domain but the way in which it is used by the power-holders.

9. Lang 1985: 87.

10. Coote 1981: 29–31; Wolf 1966: 55–56.

11. Lang 1985: 90–96.

rich Amos criticizes are city dwellers: Samaria is mentioned several times; Micah offers even more decided criticism of the cities. Archaeological evidence would tend to support the idea that the class division was also a split between city and village: there is no trace of country manor houses, and the housing in country towns is fairly uniform in size, throughout the monarchic period.[12] The rich spend their time in idle luxury, mostly in feasting (but also, Lang fails to note, in cultural pursuits—Amos 6.5!), and Thorstein Veblen's *Theory of the Leisure Class* easily applies to their 'conspicuous consumption'.[13] The poor whom they exploit are peasants: they produce grain (Amos 5.11) and wine (Amos 2.8); that they may also have to buy grain from time to time (Amos 8.5) does not contradict this. The corn trade is an addition to the exploiters' sources of income from rent and interest (Amos 8.4–6). The debt-burdened peasants become serfs of the exploiters (this is how Lang interprets 'to buy the poor for silver' in Amos 8.6), and may even be sold into slavery (Amos 2.6—not normally a feature of modern rent capitalism). The harshness with which the rich treat them is characteristic of the exploitative form of rent-capitalism.

All this is undeniable; yet as Carroll R. points out in an incisive critique of Lang's essay,[14] all these features could fit into many different systems of exploitation: they are not sufficient to point decisively to one. Lang confines his attention to Amos and does not support the case by referring to any other evidence from ancient Israel; his description of rent capitalism is drawn entirely from modern societies. As he virtually admits,[15] he is unable to demonstrate what might be thought fundamental to a system of *rent* capitalism, that is, rent itself, even though he refers several times to the peasants in Amos as 'tenants' without any basis in the text.[16] In this case, even the extension of our view to all the available texts fails to provide the required evidence. Classical Hebrew appears to lack the entire suite of words relating to the institution of tenancy: 'let', 'lease', 'rent', 'landlord', 'tenant'—not one of these words has any equivalent in classical Hebrew that recognizably relates distinctively to this institution.[17] But if the institution

---

12. Holladay 1995: 391–93. It is now clear that the often cited evidence at Tell el-Farʿah as interpreted by de Vaux (1955) was misleading: see already de Geus 1982: 53–54; also Fleischer 1989: 394–401 and Houston 2004: 135.

13. Veblen 1925.

14. Carroll R. 1992: 41, see also 33.

15. Lang 1985: 98, n. 27; see Fleischer 1989: 366.

16. Lang (1985: 93) refers to Mays (1969: 90) to support the translation of Amos 5.11 as 'Because you make tenants out of the weak, and take tribute [why not "rent" to be consistent?] of corn from him'. Mays himself refers to Koehler-Baumgartner for the rendering 'make tenants of' for *bšs*. But the new *HALOT* (s.v.) gives 'exact corn tax', so also Paul 1991: 172–73 and other commentators.

17. *nōṭᵉrîm* in Song 8.11–12 (certainly a very late text) may mean 'tenants' (so NIV), but it is not a distinctive word.

of tenancy had existed in ancient Israel, we should surely be able to recognize some expressions as relating to it. Otherwise there is no trace of the institution: a contrast with post-biblical Jewish literature and the New Testament.

The characteristic form of dependency for the native-born, referred to on many occasions in the Hebrew Bible, is not tenancy but debt-bondage. But it may be that the reason why we cannot find any trace of tenancy is because the same effect was achieved by an arrangement which differed only technically: Kippenberg argues from Neh. 5.3 with Neh. 5.11 that when a peasant had mortgaged a field he was required to hand over part of the produce in repayment of the loan.[18] Given high interest rates (the prohibition of interest in the legal texts can hardly have been effective, if it was even a law in our sense), this arrangement could easily become permanent.

But there are a number of other observations which tend to cast doubt on the hypothesis that a system of rent capitalism as observed in the modern Near East was operative in ancient Israel. We have already noted the absence of a free market in land. Paradoxically, the best evidence that there was some sort of market in land comes from Lev. 25.8–34, the jubilee law, which seeks to regulate it. But I argue below[19] that this chapter is relatively late; even so it indicates the existence of traditional restraints on such sales. It must seriously be doubted whether anything approaching a mercantile system of land tenure existed at any time before the Hellenistic period, and probably not even then. And for the monarchic period we must also note the relative scarcity of money, which is a necessity for the efficient working of rent capitalism. It is likely that the introduction of coined money in the Persian period, and its increase in volume in the Hellenistic period, was what first made possible the mercantilisation of land tenure.[20]

It is also doubtless the case, as pointed out by Dearman, that in the monarchic period the state held a dominant position in the distribution of land, and had more influence in this matter than private entrepreneurs.[21] The same is likely to have been true in the colonial era as well (consider only the Zenon papyri for the Ptolemaic period). This is a point we shall be coming back to.

Interestingly, we must also note that the contempt for manual labour which Lang (somewhat stereotypically) sees as characteristic of modern Eastern elites—it is certainly true of ancient Greek aristocracies—is entirely absent from the Hebrew Bible. The book of Proverbs is remarkable for its persistent warnings against laziness, that is *physical* laziness, reluctance to

18.   Kippenberg 1983: 92.
19.   p. 32.
20.   For its relative scarcity in the Persian period itself, see Carter 1999: 268–73.
21.   Dearman 1988: 133.

work with one's hands on one's own land; and this is a book which is rightly understood to be a broadly upper-class production. Many of the heroes of the Hebrew Bible are found working as farmers or herders: Moses was a shepherd, Gideon threshed corn, and so did Boaz; Saul went looking for his father's asses; David had to be called by his father from the sheep; and Amos is variously stated to be a shepherd (Amos 1.1), a cattleherd and a dresser of sycomore figs (Amos 7.14). There was therefore in the biblical period[22] no *cultural* incentive to avoid personal labour on the land.

Lang's account also has the weakness that it simply describes a system, and then only partially. The origin of the urban exploiting class is not explained; it does not provide an account of a historical process. Loretz says explicitly that at the time of Amos the rent-capitalist system had 'for a long time been well established' in the ancient Near East.[23] It is thus difficult to use it to explain the nearly simultaneous emergence of critics of economic exploitation in Israel and Judah, or, as Kessler argues, to explain why they should have threatened imminent disaster in response to an age-old practice.[24] For this we need to look further.

3. *'Ancient' Class Society*

In this phrase 'ancient' (*antike*) has a restricted meaning: essentially it refers to classical antiquity, Greece and Rome; but Kippenberg holds that the same, or similar, social processes took place in Israel and Judah of the biblical period as more or less contemporaneously in the city states of Greece and Italy.[25] In this, as in his use of the expression *antike Klassengesellschaft* itself, he follows Marx. In what follows I shall place 'ancient' in this technical sense always in quotation marks to distinguish it from the general meaning.

Kippenberg describes a process of social and economic development. The starting-point is a society where power and social relationships are determined by kinship structures (real or fictive); where the village land is controlled as a whole by a descent group and assigned to the family units who make it up and at first re-divided regularly between them; this village society is largely self-sufficient, but what few needs it has beyond what it can produce for itself it obtains by barter directly from the craftsmen or producers. It is not an equal society: some families and clans are politically or economically privileged (Kippenberg calls these the aristocrats), but it is

22. We may take Ben Sira (Ecclus 38.24–34) as standing outside it.
23. Loretz 1975: 277.
24. Kessler 1994: 423.
25. Kippenberg 1977.

not a class society in the sense of being divided into strata with exploitative relationships between them.

It is reasonable to assume that Kippenberg is correct in (implicitly) applying this description to early Israel and Judah as well as to Greece and Italy. As most writers on the subject agree, all the evidence points to society and land tenure being organized according to patrilineal kinship structures.[26] The village was occupied by one fictive descent group (sometimes more than one) known as the *mišpāḥâ* and claiming descent from an eponymous ancestor, for example the Ephrathites of Bethlehem (1 Sam. 17.12; Ruth 1.2; the supposed ancestor is in 1 Chron. 4.4). *mišpāḥâ* is often rendered 'clan' by scholars, but in English versions of the Bible misleadingly 'family'. The real family unit was the *bêt 'āb*, for example the family of Jesse (1 Sam. 16). This is an extended family: David's brothers are older than he and would have been married with their own families. There would be a number of these more or less extended family units in the *mišpāḥâ*, and the land would be divided among them. The village was run patriarchally by the family heads, who were collectively the clan elders. Evidence that the land of the village or *mišpāḥâ* was at one time regularly re-divided between the families is limited. Micah 2.5 and Ps. 16.6 are often quoted, and Bendor adds to these Ps. 69.27–28 and Jer. 37.12.[27] That these refer to a known practice of land distribution by lot is reasonable, but they do not prove the practice of *re*distribution in existing settlements; we would expect such distribution by lot in new settlements, which archaeology shows were always being created. However, some believe such a practice may lie behind the Jubilee provisions in Leviticus 25.

S. Bendor, in the most detailed account available, emphasizes that the village was not an equal or even an egalitarian society. Power resided with the elders of the village, both individually over their own families and collectively over the whole village. Although the juridical landholding unit was the *bêt 'āb*, the living and working unit was the nuclear family: its head was allocated land and could inherit it, he worked the land with his immediate family and retainers, and in his house the produce was stored. However, the head of the extended family had the power to allocate land from its inheritance, and this could lead to sharp practical differences in wealth and power within the family.[28] Probably very often only the eldest two of a family of brothers were allocated plots, and the eldest had a clear position of primacy; other brothers lived in their compound, assisted with the work on the land, and were nourished from it, but their rights were less

26. For a detailed study see Bendor 1996, and for a convenient summary, with references, McNutt 1999: 75–98, 164–70.

27. Bendor 1996: 141–60. See also Henrey 1954; Dybdahl 1981; Osgood 1992: 282–85.

28. Bendor 1996: 129–33.

secure.[29] Widows and fatherless children (inaccurately 'orphans') had an even more precarious foothold in the family;[30] still more so the *gēr* (usually 'alien') or migrant from another place.[31] And there could well be tensions between the adult sons and their father.[32]

This account concentrates on inequality within the *bêt'āb*; but inequalities between families are equally probable. Hebrew narrative takes for granted the existence of powerful and wealthy local figures like Boaz or the Shunemite in the Elisha stories. But it is probable that powerful local families in some areas did not belong to local kinship groups in any case. One reason for this, as suggested by Alt many years ago, may have been that the early kings gave prebends to their supporters in conquered territories, who in course of time succeeded in making hereditary possessions of them.[33] Another is that even in the pre-state period regional chiefs may have arisen.[34]

To return to Kippenberg's account: he sees in the development of 'ancient' class society two opposing strands: one is the striving of the 'aristocrats' to control the land and its cultivators and their productive activity, and to appropriate their surplus product; the other is the opposition to aristocratic rule that this engenders among the peasants and other less privileged groups. The end result is a compromise including the characteristic 'ancient' institutions of private land ownership, the use of foreign captives as chattel slaves, and coined money.[35] Kippenberg sets out the transformation under three heads: transformation of land tenure, of forms of dependency, and of circulation of surplus.[36] In our account we need not go over the three aspects separately, but recount the transformation as a whole, with particular reference to developments at Athens, which is known best to us, as well as to Israel and Judah.

There are two conditions which make possible the aristocrats' encroachment. One is the end of the regular redistribution of the village lot and the conversion of families' plots into permanent heritable holdings, though these were considered normally inalienable except by inheritance, as we see from the story of Naboth (1 Kgs 21.3). Kippenberg dates this development before the end of the eighth century in both Greece and Israel. However, it may be that, if the custom of redistribution existed in Israel, arable fields

---

29. Bendor 1996: 171–90.
30. Bendor 1996: 190–94.
31. Bendor 1996: 240–44. That the *gēr* need not be from another ethnic group is implied by Bendor 1996: 229–30, 241.
32. Bendor 1996: 194–96.
33. Alt 1959a; Ben-Barak 1981.
34. Cf. Rogerson 1986; and now Miller 2005 (which I have not seen).
35. Kippenberg 1977: 34–36.
36. See the tables in Kippenberg 1977: 38, 43, 49.

continued to be redistributed for much longer: vineyards and olive groves were a different matter because of the investment put into them.[37] The other, related, condition is the liability of the individual household for loans, as distinct from the collective liability of the village as a whole, which was generally assumed by ancient empires in the collection of taxes. These two conditions together make it possible for the peasant, certainly the *bêt'āb* head if not the nuclear family head, with land at his disposal, to mortgage parcels of land for credit.

Thus the 'aristocrats' are enabled to take advantage of the peasants' chronic need for credit as a result of famine, poor harvests, and the devastation of war, by lending on the security of their land or of the persons of members of their families; as we have seen, the security could easily be forfeit. The increasing availability of money (not necessarily in coined form, which did not exist in Palestine before the Persian period) probably encouraged this development, and over-population may have made the peasants on their shrinking plots more vulnerable.[38]

At Athens in the seventh century, before the reforms of Solon, the family continued to work the land, but in effect as tenants on their own land, remitting a sixth of the produce to the aristocratic landlord; the device by which this was reconciled with the inalienability of the land was the fiction that the plot had been 'sold' on condition that it could be redeemed by the family.[39] What happened more often was that, having no security left but the persons of themselves and their families, whenever they were unable to pay the rent, they became slaves of the lord; and this might be followed by being sold into slavery abroad.[40] Evidence from everywhere in the ancient world shows that a creditor did not need to apply to a court for execution: he could seize his debtor as and when he chose.[41] It was the debtor who had to appeal to the authorities against this, and usually had small hope of success. Finley argues that the creditor's motives in lending may quite as often have been to acquire a source of labour (and, I would add, of power and honour through the amassing of clients) as to enrich himself with the interest.[42]

We are thus presented with nothing less than a deliberate striving by a privileged element in society to entrench their privilege through the exploitation, subordination and humiliation of the rest. Every aspect of this process can be paralleled from the Hebrew Bible, as Kippenberg points out, apart from the formal payment of a rent.[43] Thus we find loans on

---

37.   Lemche 1985: 196–98; Bendor 1996: 138.
38.   Fleischer 1989: 370–73.
39.   Woodhouse 1938: 97; 148–57.
40.   Aristotle 1920: §12 (1950: 79).
41.   Kippenberg 1977: 41–42; Woodhouse 1938: 67–73.
42.   Finley 1977: 180–81.
43.   Kippenberg 1977: 33–34; 1982: 56–62.

the security of land in Neh. 5.3; sale on condition of redemption in Lev. 25.24–34; loans on security of the person and consequent slavery for debt in 2 Kgs 4.1 and Neh. 5.2, 5; and probably all references to 'Hebrew' slavery imply debt as the reason – Exod. 21.1–11; Deut. 15.12–18; Jer. 34.8–22. Further, sale of members of the community is found in Amos 2.6, and Joel 3.1–8 (Hebrew 4.1–8) makes it clear they are sold abroad; compare Neh. 5.8. The most striking parallel is Neh. 5.1–5, where the three groups of protesters can be seen as in successive phases of a process of degradation: first they pledge their children, then their land, then having lost their land their children are threatened with sale.[44] The likely much earlier prophetic texts of Isa. 5.8–10, Mic. 2.1–5, and Amos 2.6 attest the same threats to the land and freedom of the poor in a more general way.[45] The Micah text most sharply accuses the rich of a deliberate programme of appropriation. Kessler emphasizes that texts such as Isa. 5.8–10 and Mic. 2.1–11 imply not an age-old pattern of abuses to which the ancient east was inured, as asserted by Loretz, but 'a fundamental transformation of society', which the prophets proclaimed could only end in disaster.[46]

Isaiah 5.8–10 has often been taken as evidence for the growth of *latifundia*, the term used by the Romans in a later but not less cruel age for large estates cleared of their indigenous cultivators and worked by foreign slaves. The archaeological evidence tells against this: Holladay shows that country towns in Israel and Judah give every appearance of remaining the dwelling places of rough equals right down to the fall of Jerusalem, with the largest houses not exceeding the norm by more than a factor of two or occasionally three, and no one- or two-room hovels.[47] So if the Isaiah text is really of the eighth century, it must be interpreted as saying, not 'you are left to *live* alone' (NRSV), but 'you alone are settled in as full citizens'.[48] The deprived original possessors continued to live in their houses and cultivate the land which had been theirs, but as slaves or, effectively, tenants, no longer as recognized proprietors with their place among the elders at the town gate.[49] Where then did the exploiters with their fine houses (Amos 3.15, etc.) live? The answer is surely: in the big city, in Samaria (as the context in Amos strongly suggests), or in Jerusalem, and maybe in a few other important

---

44. Kippenberg 1982: 56–58, reading in v. 2 '*ōr^ebîm* for *rabbîm*, with *BHS* and many.

45. Bendor argues for a quite different understanding of these texts, in which the culprits are village elders who respond to external pressures by victimizing the weakest members of the *bêt 'āb* (Bendor 1996: 207–79; for a critique, Houston 2004: 140–41). The main objection is that in other places the critique of oppression in the prophets is directed against the ruling classes; see below, pp. 63–65, 87–88. But see also below, pp. 38–40.

46. Kessler 1992: 122.

47. Holladay 1995: 392. See also n. 14 above.

48. Wildberger 1991: 188, followed by Kippenberg 1977: 33; cf. Premnath 1988.

49. Kessler 1992: 37.

regional centres such as Lachish or Shechem.[50] This is an important conclusion to which we will return.

At Athens, and very likely also in Israel and Judah, aristocratic control over the use of the land led to big changes in the agricultural economy. The production of grain was in surplus, once the tenants had been allowed their bare minimum. They had been unable as independent farmers to invest in the crops which made more efficient use of the land and were far more lucrative as exports, that is wine and oil. Now their masters did it for them, and Attica (the territory of Athens) became especially renowned as the land of the olive tree.[51] In due course, with the growth of trade and industry, Athens became a large importer of grain from the steppes of Ukraine. For Israel and Judah, the archaeological evidence indicates a rapid spread in the eighth century of installations associated with vine and olive husbandry.[52] Most peasants would be unable to invest to any great extent in this technology; Hopkins also emphasizes the importance of spreading risk for subsistence farmers, which would prohibit specialization in export crops. This, then, suggests the proprietorship or control of those with larger resources. The issue between the 'ancient' and 'tributary' views of the development is whether they were, in general, acting independently or as agents of the state.

The reaction was fierce in both Greece and Israel, and at any rate in Greece was pivotal to the development of 'ancient' society. Long-continued popular unrest at Athens was appeased by the election of Solon as archon with extraordinary powers in 594 BCE. He cancelled all existing debts, sweeping away the *horoi*, the detested pillars recording the sale of land, and freed the peasants to become once more proprietors of their land and full citizens. He prohibited loans on the security of the person in future, and used public and private funds to buy back citizens who had been sold abroad. But Solon was no revolutionary, and refused to carry out the redistribution of the land which had been urged on him. He might be seen as the archetype of the liberal reformer.[53] The demands of the peasantry had been partially fulfilled. They had got back their freedom and control of their land, though the aristocracy retained their broad acres and much of their economic power. As time went on, their land became more and more regarded as the private property of the household, though there were still legal and customary restrictions on its disposal. It is obvious that they could

---

50.   Against Kessler 1992: 37 and 124, though he notes that Jer. 6.12 (= 8.10) implies that owners of fields lived in Jerusalem, and Mic. 6.9–15 and Zeph. 1.12–13 also set oppressors in Jerusalem (he does not deal with the Northern kingdom).

51.   Woodhouse 1938: 164–65.

52.   Hopkins 1983, cf. Hopkins 1996; Eitam 1979.

53.   Aristotle 1920: §§5–6, 9, 12 (1950: 72–74, 77, 78–80); Solon's own defence is in ch. 12; see Woodhouse 1938: 167–208.

still fall into debt, and might even find it more difficult to borrow, now that they could no longer borrow on the security of the person. But other opportunities were rapidly opening up which did not depend on the land. The development of trade and markets encouraged by the spread of money and the increasing use of foreign slaves in place of the now forbidden enslavement of fellow-citizens were key marks of 'ancient' society. In time, most of the Greek world came to follow this line of evolution. It is clearly a very different situation from the stagnation of the so-called 'rent capitalist' system of the Near East. To what extent does it correspond to developments in Israel and Judah?

In the first place, the resistance against the exploitative programme of the 'aristocrats' seized on very similar themes, as Kippenberg emphasizes.[54] The prophets proclaim the justice of YHWH against oppression—as Hesiod does that of Zeus.[55] Remedies in human hands are proposed in the legal 'codes'. There is the prohibition of usury—not part of Solon's programme, but adopted at Megara about 570–60[56]—which we find in all the main Pentateuchal codes: Exod. 22.25 (Hebrew 24); Lev. 25.36–37; Deut. 23.19–21 (Hebrew 20–21). A regular cancellation[57] of debts is demanded in Deut. 15.2–3. Against debt slavery we have on the one hand the limitation of its duration to six years in Exod. 21.1–11 and Deut. 15.12–18, and on the other the exhortation in Lev. 25.39–43 that Israelite slaves should not be treated as slaves, and should be released at the jubilee. The same chapter calls for a regular return of peasant landholders to their land (Lev. 25.8–13), prohibiting outright sale of land (Lev. 25.14–17, 23).

However, evidence of the successful implementation of these laws is harder to find. Even those measures which became part of regular Jewish law, the seventh-year cancellation of debts and the prohibition of interest on loans, were ingeniously evaded.[58] Within the biblical period we are told of just two events in any way comparable to Solon's *seisachtheia*, 'shaking off of burdens'.[59] The first is the release of Hebrew slaves decreed by Zedekiah and implemented by covenant during the final Babylonian siege of Jerusalem —and immediately reversed, according to Jer. 34.8–22. The second and more important is the measures imposed by oath by Nehemiah on the

---

54. See also the useful comparative table of legal remedies in Smith 1987: 107.

55. Hesiod: *Works and Days* lines 274–85 (1990: 61; 1988: 45); Kippenberg 1977: 34.

56. Smith 1987: 107, from E. Meyer in PW 15.1: 152ff.

57. See below, pp. 180–81.

58. Cf. Mishnah, *Sheb.* 10.1.

59. Kessler argues (1992: 212–19) that the reform of Josiah (2 Kings 23) is another: the reason why Josiah imposes it by covenant, as with Zedekiah, is that the social legislation of Deuteronomy affects the interests of the independent proprietors. But without any explicit indication by the historian that Josiah implemented this social legislation, in an account which has been suspected even as it stands of tendentiousness, this evidence is difficult to use.

nobles and officials of Judah, according to his own account in Neh. 5.6–13. These included the cancellation of debts and the return of pledges, which of course included both land and persons (vv. 2–5), therefore amounting to a redistribution of (some) land and the release of slaves. Verse 12 may also imply a prohibition of lending on security in the future.[60]

But, again, there is no telling how soon things were back to normal. The Deuteronomic and Levitical authors were right to insist on the regular repetition of such measures, if only they could have found a way to impose it. There may have been other such decrees by Judaean and Israelite rulers, following the pattern of the *mīšarum* decrees of Mesopotamian kings.[61] But we know nothing of them, unless the measures now enshrined in the legal collections are their relics, and they had few lasting results.[62] Gottwald is right to emphasize how inadequate Nehemiah's measures really were, even counter-productive if they resulted in credit for the desperate peasant drying up: enough to enable him to garner support from the peasantry in his struggle with the leading classes, not enough to alter their lasting condition of subordination and exploitation.[63] Unlike sixth-century Athens, fifth-century Judah's economy was stagnating and offered little in the way of exit routes from the bleak prison of the land.

Judah steadily drifted into the Hellenistic orbit and so became part of the 'ancient', now globalized, system, with a monetized economy, private ownership of land, foreign slaves and all the rest of it (Leviticus 25 already shows the influence very clearly—every one of these institutions is implied, if only to be countered). But there is little to show that this was the result of natural internal development. It is therefore overstating the case, as Kessler rightly sees, for Kippenberg to assert that Israel and Judah underwent a transition to 'ancient' class society.[64] At most, it could be said that they went part of the way, and the development was then aborted. They certainly became class societies, but scarcely of the 'ancient' type.

There are many reasons why this should have been so. Finley considers that the failure of the Near Eastern peasantry to revolt, as the Greek and Roman ones did, so that they had to rely on the goodwill of members of the ruling class, was an explanation for the ultimate ineffectiveness of their measures, ineffectiveness, for example, in providing for the released bondservants.[65]

---

60. Gottwald 1999: 7. Cf. Yamauchi 1980.

61. For Mesopotamia, see Weinfeld 1995 passim; for Judah, Weinfeld 1995: 45–56; 1972: 153–55; Houston 1999: 354–59. The question is discussed in detail below, pp. 144–46.

62. The most likely example is Deut. 15.2, which is a quotation in its present context, as I argue below, pp. 179–80.

63. Gottwald 1999: 7–8.

64. Kessler 1992: 124.

65. Finley 1977: 191. Deut 15.13–15 is an attempt to deal with this problem: but it is pure exhortation.

However, it is hard to prove that the 'outcry' of the Jewish people in Nehemiah's time was less serious than the 'resistance' of the Athenian people in Solon's. Again, through almost the whole of the period under review, from the eighth to the fifth century, the Israelite-Jewish lands were under the direct or indirect rule of powerful empires who sucked them dry with their constant demand for tribute or tax; not to mention the devastation of the country more than once by their armies. This increased the distress of the cultivators on whom the ultimate burden fell (Neh. 5.4 expressly notes the burden of the Persian land tax), and at the same time made conditions much more difficult for any radical development of the economy which would have made it easier for relief measures to be permanently successful. Worst of all was the catastrophe of 587, the impact of which on the economy of Judah cannot be overestimated. Moreover, all the classical states in which the move to 'ancient' society took place had already got rid of their kings, and their aristocratic governments maintained only minimal bureaucracies, no professional armies, and no royal courts. The native Israelite monarchies imposed all these burdens: it was their main *raison d'être*.

4. *The Tributary State*[66]

We must therefore turn to examine the model which places all or most of the responsibility for the exploitation of the Israelite or Jewish peasant and the transformation of society on the state: first the native monarchies, then the imperial powers. This model in one form or another has attained widespread influence today, though often with admixtures of other ideas. I have entitled this section 'The Tributary State' because this is the language used by Gottwald and others who have presented the model in its purest form.

Gottwald has argued that monarchic Israel was an example of what is generally called by Marxists the 'Asiatic mode of production'; he suggests the more descriptive name 'tributary mode of production'.[67] His idea has been taken up by followers such as Chaney and Mosala.[68] For those unfamiliar with Marxist terminology, the notion of 'mode of production' should be briefly explained. This expression denotes the way in which classes in society are differently related to the means of production: for example in the capitalist mode of production, the means of production are owned and controlled by the bourgeoisie, who pay wages to the proletariat

---

66. The first five paragraphs and two sentences of this account are derived from my article Houston 1999, with some changes.
67. Gottwald 1993b: 5–9; 1993a; cf. Gottwald 2001.
68. Chaney 1986, 1993; Mosala 1989: 103–18.

to use them to engage in production. A mode of production is an abstraction: no actually existing society exhibits one mode in its purity: thus in societies that might be called capitalist, independent farmers and tradesmen and state-owned enterprises exist alongside the dominant capitalist enterprises. It is also not a purely economic idea, although the 'base' of society is seen as the economy, since it embraces the social and political relationships of classes.

The basic features of the system, as summarized by Melotti, are:

1.   There is no fully developed private ownership of land. The crown lays claim to the entire territory, and there is no clear distinction between tax and rent.

2.   The base of the system is a large number of self-sufficient village communities, who work the land in an autonomous fashion, but are compelled to hand over surpluses to state representatives in the form of taxes/rents in kind or cash or in labour on state projects.

3.   The central power's role is the commanding one. The main exploiting class, who live off the labour of the peasants, is the state bureaucracy. The main weakness of the system is the tendency for these officials to carve out independent spheres of power by means of corrupt practices.[69]

The concept corresponds fairly closely to non-Marxist economic historians' notion of the 'redistributive economy', in which goods are redistributed by the state from the producers to the state's supporters. In such an economy, private property and the market are only weakly developed.[70] It also corresponds in many respects to Gerhard Lenski's description of the 'agrarian society', most obviously in Lenski's insistence that it is the ruler and 'governing class' that receive the surplus of production, usually amounting to not less than half of the total national income; this group never represents more than two percent of the population, often less. Wealth followed power, rather than the reverse as in today's market societies.[71] However, Lenski's concept is broader, and includes many societies that would not fall into the category of the tributary state, often because the governing class was not a bureaucracy but a land-based aristocracy. The following discussion will show evidence that the concept of the tributary state is a rather poor fit for monarchic Israel and Judah. The looser notion of an agrarian society is easier to apply, but Lenski's description is drawn almost exclusively from very much larger states than these, and he appears to admit that

69.   Melotti 1977: 54; cf. Gottwald 1993a: 153–55.
70.   Cf. Carney 1973: 25.
71.   Lenski 1966: 189–296; here 228–29.

his description might need substantial qualification for 'simpler' societies.[72] He knows that it does not apply to 'maritime' societies such as the Phoenicians and the Greeks, the prime source of Kippenberg's model.[73] On the other hand, there is no question that the Persian empire fits his description very well.

In Gottwald's major theoretical discussion of this model, he emphasizes each of the factors summarized by Melotti, and states that in the Asiatic mode of production 'the state in its tribute-collecting function was the primary, and perhaps even exclusive, expropriator of the subject classes'. Even money-lending could be seen as reliant on wealth derived from taxes or crown lands, and it could even have been a state-administered activity 'assigned to persons benefitting from the public treasury'.[74]

But he is more cautious in asserting that this was fully true of monarchic Israel (he does not here discuss the Second Temple period, and presumably includes Judah under 'Israel'). Palestine should be regarded 'under one of the weaker variants of the AMP typified by a significant degree of localized agriculture that does not depend on extensive public works'.[75] He is ready to recognize a group of landholders ('latifundaries') who are not part of the state apparatus, and are developing a form of private property in land through their activities as creditors and drawers of rent. But they all 'benefited from state power'. Although their interests varied, all the exploiting groups formed a class because it was ultimately state power that enabled them all to carry on their extraction of surplus.[76]

Andrew Dearman argues verse by verse from the eighth-century prophets that the injustices which they denounce were mainly committed by the state or its agents. This suggests to him that the economy is of the redistributive type, with most of the elite in the apparatus of government.[77] The case is a strong one. Wherever Amos refers to the place of residence of the exploiters, it is Samaria (Amos 3.9, 12; 4.1; 6.1), and likewise Micah accuses the 'heads of Jacob and rulers of the house of Israel' of boiling the people up like meat in a cauldron' (Mic. 3.1–3), and of 'building Zion with blood and Jerusalem with wrong' (Mic. 3.10). The culprits in Isa. 10.1–3 who 'make iniquitous decrees' in order to despoil widows and orphans are undoubtedly state officials. Amos 5.11 is widely understood to refer to a tax levied on the grain harvest; those who collect the tax have prebends on which they build houses and plant vineyards, or else they take a corrupt rake-off from the tax.[78]

---

72. Lenski 1966: 191, n. 5a.
73. Lenski 1966: 191–92.
74. Gottwald 1993a: 155–56.
75. Gottwald 1993a: 158.
76. Gottwald 1993b: 6.
77. Dearman 1988: 9–52, 133–34.
78. Dearman 1988: 30; see above, n. 16.

Amos 7.1 shows that the crown had a prior claim on the production of hay. Isaiah includes officials among those 'grinding the faces of the poor' (Isa. 3.14–15), and Dearman argues that 'the whole tenor of verses 12–15 . . . suggests it is . . . the official status of their position which has resulted in the perceived (mis)appropriation of property'.[79] At a somewhat later time, we find Jeremiah (Jer. 22.13–19) accusing Jehoiakim of misusing the corvée for private building projects.

To this we may add the indirect evidence of archaeology for the extent of royal domination of the economy. Most salient are the ostraca found at Samaria and dating from the early-eighth century detailing quantities of oil and wine; and the storage jars for oil and wine found at numerous sites in Judah, dating from the later-eighth century, with handles stamped *lmlk* 'belonging to the king'. The latest analysis, by N.S. Fox, concludes in line with what is probably the majority opinion, that the ostraca are dockets for shipments of commodities from prebendal estates to their owners who are officials in the capital; and that the *lmlk* handles are evidence of a system of distribution in Hezekiah's reign supplying royal garrisons and other state centres either from royal estates or from taxation, perhaps in preparation for war.[80] Zwickel argues from this evidence, combined with that of buildings in various locations in late-eighth-century Judah which he interprets as estate farmsteads for the royal domains, that Hezekiah had an extensive programme of production and distribution of foodstuffs, not only for his troops and civil service, but to assist the refugees from Israel.[81]

When we come to the time of Nehemiah, there can be no question, despite the diverse social origins of the direct exploiters of the peasantry which we have examined, that the primary responsibility lies with the Persian government. Like any other government, its policy was to maximize its cash revenue from the provinces, and Nehemiah expressly mentions 'the king's tax' as the reason the peasants needed to borrow money (Neh. 5.4).[82] A few verses later he plumes himself on not drawing his governor's salary (Neh. 5.18); the implication is that this was normally a burden on the province.

Marvin Chaney goes further.[83] There was in the eighth century a systematic programme of transformation of the agricultural economy of Israel and Judah directed by the respective state apparatuses. It was a 'command

---

79. Dearman 1988: 38; cf. Chaney 1999: 109–10.
80. Fox 2000: 204–35.
81. Zwickel 1994.
82. Grabbe (2004: 193–94) considers that we have no knowledge at all of how taxes bore on the individual. This is perhaps over-sceptical.
83. Chaney 1986; 1993; 1999, relying heavily on Hopkins 1983.

economy'.[84] The process was export-led. Imports of luxury goods and strategic materials were wanted by the 'elites', and could only be paid for by exports of three main agricultural products: wheat, oil and wine, but primarily the latter two. This involved regional specialization: wheat in the lowlands and Shephelah, oil and wine in the hill country, for which he finds evidence in 2 Chron. 26.10. Most of the lowlands, he thinks, were already in the hands of the 'elite', as they had been acquired by David's conquests and could have used to reward his followers with estates. But in much of the hill-country the cultivators had to be induced or forced to abandon their traditional mixed agriculture in favour of specialization in vines and olives. This would have been achieved by a combination of differential taxes and foreclosure on loans.

Chaney's account is mainly speculative and key points need to be questioned. The use of the phrase 'command economy' implies that the entire process was systematically thought out and directed from the centre in each kingdom. But it needs to be questioned whether anyone in the ancient world could have thought in the way that this would require; and particularly questionable is the idea that tax policy would have been directed to achieve agricultural specialization. This is a modern idea. Ancient governments used taxes to raise revenue, not as an instrument of economic policy: the very idea of economic policy had never occurred to them.[85] Even modern governments rarely look twenty years into the future: but that is how long it takes for an olive tree to grow to full maturity. It is much more likely that the increase in oil and wine production, which is clearly attested, was the result of many individual decisions made for family enrichment among the larger landowners, both in gaining land and in developing it profitably. This would certainly have *enabled* the state to increase exports and therefore imports: that this was its *object* is neither proved nor likely. The only exception to this generalization would be the developments on crown lands in Hezekiah's reign, which were probably in preparation for war. This is not to deny that the landowners formed a governing class in some sense, only that they had a coherent 'economic policy'.

If production was not normally in some way planned and directed by the state, then the idea of a tributary *mode of production* is in danger of incoherence. There is no doubt about the tribute, but where is the mode of production? All states impose taxes: the mere fact of taxation is not enough to distinguish a state with one 'mode of production' from another.[86]

---

84. Chaney 1993: 254. The phrase is also used by Hopkins, e.g., 1996: 129; but he is much more cautious in describing it, and at one point pours cold water on the idea that the requisite management techniques existed (1996: 125–26).

85. Finley 1973. This is admitted by Hopkins (1996: 126).

86. Simkins 1999: 130, quoting Hindess and Hirst 1975: 197.

Lenski's broader conception is of value here. In every state falling into his category of the 'agrarian society', the taxes, tithes, rents, debt services and other exactions made from the peasants taken as a whole go to benefit, not society as a whole, but a small governing class; though it may be, as I have suggested above, that the services by way of defence, security, religious ritual and so forth which they offer are reckoned as a fair exchange.[87]

One important aspect of the 'tributary mode of production' in its classic conception relates to the weak development of private property in that system, as against the ideas of the whole land as the royal domain on the one hand and of communal ownership within the village or tribe on the other. Certainly if private property is understood in its modern sense, of property assigned to an individual and freely alienable, it would be right to say that it did not exist in ancient Israel. But neither did it exist in most ancient societies in that sense.[88] And once the permanent heritability of land was established, it was inherited within families, and in ways which exacerbated inequalities within the village.

Deuteronomy 21.15–17 assumes that the firstborn son would inherit 'a double portion'. Whether this means double any other son's share,[89] or double everyone else's shares put together, that is, two-thirds of the estate whatever the number of brothers,[90] it is a differential which in time would lead to the concentration of wealth in the senior line of a family, and the impoverishment of the others. Further, the institution of the *gᵉʾullâ*, the redemption of property within the family, was likely to have a similar effect. Based as it was on a conception of land as a family (hardly a communal) possession, its practical effect would be to concentrate property further within the wealthiest branch, and make the others dependent on it.[91]

We have already seen that there were powerful local figures in each local community, and probably in wider areas. There is further evidence about this, which casts some light on the relative power of the centre and the provinces in late-monarchic Judah. The fathers of at least three of the Judaean queen mothers cited in the archival material of Kings (2 Kgs 12.1; 22.1; 23.31; 24.18) seem to be provincial Judaeans, and another (2 Kgs 23.36) is a Galilaean, suggesting that the dynasty felt the need of making alliances with local families. The narrative of 2 Kgs 21.24, 23.30 attributes

---

87.   Above, p. 12. Cf. Lenski 1966: 296.
88.   Cf. Finley 1986.
89.   Driver 1902: 246; McConville 2002: 330.
90.   Mayes 1979: 304; Nelson 2002: 255, 260 n. 8; both referring to Zech. 13.8.
91.   Kippenberg 1982: 34. See Lev. 25.24–25: note that this does not provide that the *gōʾēl* should return the property to the original seller (see Lefebvre 2003: 196–198); cf. Jer. 32.6–12, Ruth 4—in both these cases the impoverished family member sells directly to the *gōʾēl*. The above paragraph is taken from my article Houston 1999 (357–58), with some slight changes.

the influence in the succession of Josiah and Jehoahaz, whose mothers were among these provincial Judaeans, to 'the people of the land'. It is likely that this refers to a group with a provincial power base.[92] We note that, along with the officials, Isa. 3.15 accuses the 'elders' of YHWH's people of exploitation of the poor; and the comprehensive indictment for oppression of various estates of Judaean society in Ezek. 22.23–31 gives a special place to 'the people of the land' (v. 29; cf. Jer. 34.19). Oppression in Judaean society was not a monopoly of the official class. This is the conclusion of Kessler's very detailed examination.[93]

On the other hand, we have already noted Holladay's conclusion that the material remains of those village communities, so far as we yet know them, show little sign of serious social division down to the end of the monarchies.[94] But I have argued elsewhere that Holladay may well have deduced more from the evidence than it will bear.[95] The houses in the villages were of roughly equal size, but archaeology does not show us what relations of dependency existed between their occupants. It is true that we do not find country manor houses in ancient Israel and Judah. But there may be two reasons why we do not. One is that the necessities of defence led the wealthy, like others, to live within the walls of the country towns ('cities' in our misleading translations) with their very limited space (the aristocrats in mediaeval Italy did the same). The other is the tendency of powerful members of rural society in an urban-dominated culture to base themselves in the capital for a better standard of living and to gain political influence. English aristocrats kept both a country house and a house in London and divided their time between them; in some other countries, particularly France in the eighteenth century, the rural residence was almost abandoned. It could be that in Israel and Judah many of the heads of the most powerful local families lived in the city much of the time and left the junior members of the family to run the farm. This may account for the references to the activity of the 'people of the land' in Jerusalem mentioned above.

Such people may have been attracted by offers of positions in the bureaucracy. The story of Elisha and the woman of Shunem (2 Kings 4) hints at this. She is a 'great' woman, a leading personage of the town: yet her house

92. Cf. Oded 1977: 456–458. Seitz (1989: 42–71) re-examines the question and notes that the 'people of the land' operate in Jerusalem in all the references to them in Kings: his conclusion is that they are elements of the rural population forced to migrate to the capital by invasion or for other reasons. But it is more likely they were leading members of local communities who had chosen, rather than being forced, to migrate to Jerusalem. See below.

93. Kessler 1992: 118; cf. also Fleischer 1989: 287–97. The above paragraph is reproduced with slight changes from Houston 1999.

94. Holladay 1995: 392.

95. Houston 2004: 137–38.

has no separate guest room and her husband supervises the harvest in person, like Boaz. Elisha asks her whether he could put in a word for her with the king or the army chief. Her reply shows that seeking the favour of the king implies becoming separate from her clan. 'I dwell among my own people' (2 Kgs 4.13). She reasserts her solidarity.

For the later period, Nehemiah appears to provide evidence for the same thing. The people whom he accuses of oppressive practices as creditors are described (Neh. 5.7) as *haḥōrîm wᵉhassᵉgānîm* (NRSV 'the nobles and the officials'), a phrase that occurs elsewhere in the book for leaders of Judaean society with whom he is in dialogue, and who must therefore be in Jerusalem. Now, while the *sᵉgānîm* are generally agreed to be government officials, who are the *ḥōrîm* (usually rendered 'nobles')? If it was customary for those in difficulty to apply to the powerful heads of family in their own locality (see below), and some of these abused their trust, then these must be the *ḥōrîm*. The usage is precisely that of 1 Kgs 21.8, 11, and Nehemiah's usage of the word elsewhere does not seem to tell against this. Note that the normal phrase is 'nobles of Judah'; only Jer. 27.20 refers to 'nobles of Jerusalem'. But they nevertheless lived in the capital, and had clearly become to a large extent identified with the official class.

It thus becomes clear that whether the individual exploiters of the peasants owed their power to their local base or to their place in the royal service, they formed as a whole a governing class, to use Lenski's term, which was complicit individually and collectively in the exploitation of the agricultural producers. The specific hypothesis of the tributary state cannot be made good for monarchic Israel and Judah, for the evidence points not to an all-powerful state lording it over weak egalitarian peasant communes, but rather to a relatively powerful state sharing power with local magnates. Nevertheless it remains true that it was these states, small and relatively weak though they were, that made it possible for this class to act in the way they did. They imposed a direct burden on the cultivators of the soil through tax, military service and the corvée, leading to indebtedness. They also encouraged, through the granting of prebends and through the magnetic attraction of the capital, the formation of the governing class who took advantage of the poorer peasants' difficulties in the ways we have explored. The rise of far more powerful and aggressive states in the region that brought the smaller states into imperial subjection led to an intensification of exploitation, and may explain why it is just in the eighth century, as Assyria moves into the West, first of all cutting off income from trade and then imposing huge amounts of tribute, that regular complaints against exploitation begin to be heard.[96]

96. Houston 2004: 145–47.

5. *The Patronage System*

However, we have not yet explored the precise mechanisms whereby this exploitation took place. The hypothesis of rent capitalism we found inadequate, though it clearly has elements of the truth. Ronald Simkins argues that the basic socio-economic structure ('mode of production') in monarchic 'Israel', which played an important part in the way economic surpluses were channelled and appropriated, was a system of patronage.[97] (But there is no reason to distinguish the *monarchic* period in this way: if Simkins is right, his argument will apply at all periods.)

Patron-client relationships exist in a vast range of societies. They have been studied comparatively in Gellner and Waterbury 1977, and on a broader front by Eisenstadt and Roniger 1984: Simkins depends especially on the latter. Eisenstadt and Roniger summarize the main characteristic of such relationships.[98] The relationship is a vertical one between a more powerful individual (the patron) and a less powerful one (the client).[99] It is a personal relationship, depending on face to face contact and personal trust. The patron has access to resources which the client needs and does not have direct access to, such as means of production, markets for his/her produce, money for loans or grants, jobs or influence with others who can provide them, or influence with the authorities or with the courts. In return for supplying the client with these resources, the patron expects loyalty and solidarity, support for him[100] in his political dealings, gifts from time to time of course, and labour services in some societies. There is 'a strong element of personal obligation' in these relations, which is related especially to conceptions of personal honour: that is, the patron gains honour from performing services for the client, and both he and the client are 'shamed' if he fails him, and of course the same goes for the client's obligations. The relationship is entered into voluntarily, in theory at least; typically it is based on an informal understanding which does not have a legal or contractual character, and sometimes is opposed to the laws of the country, but is nevertheless very strongly binding. Because of its vertical and exclusive character it tends to weaken horizontal relationships based on kinship or neighbourhood, particularly on the side of the client. Patrons bypass the extended family to deal directly with nuclear families; and Simkins argues that some texts in the Hebrew

97. Simkins 1999.
98. Eisenstadt and Roniger 1984: 48–49.
99. Typically the relationship is between two individuals, though there are more complex types between networks of individuals.
100. The patron is almost invariably male.

Bible reflect this downgrading of wider kinship bonds in favour of the nuclear family: this is the ideology of patronage.[101]

Eisenstadt and Roniger comment on the paradoxes of this relationship: it is highly unequal, yet it is expressed in personal terms; it is supposedly voluntary and yet has the potential for coercion and exploitation; it is marked by obligation on both sides and yet it may be illegal or 'semi-legal'.

This description should sound very familiar to any attentive reader of the Hebrew Bible. Simkins refers to the relationships between Saul and David, Elijah and Elisha, and Tiglath-Pileser and Ahaz (2 Kgs 16.5–9), and argues that the relations between king and people and Yahweh and Israel are structured in terms of patronage.[102] In this he follows N.P. Lemche, and also refers to T.R. Hobbs.[103] One famous Hebrew word, *hesed* (variously translated 'steadfast love', 'faithfulness', 'loyalty', 'goodness', 'mercy'), precisely captures the paradoxes of the patron-client relationship: it describes 'A beneficent action, performed in the context of a deep and enduring commitment between two persons or parties, by one who is able to render assistance to the needy party who in the circumstances is unable to help him- or herself'.[104] It characterizes an action fulfilling an obligation between two partners who are normally unequal—usually the action of the more powerful partner for the benefit of the less powerful—which is nevertheless represented as voluntary and to the partner's credit. As Kippenberg notes, this paradoxical voluntary obligation is only a contradiction from the point of view of a society such as modern Western society which separates institutions from personal motivation: in other words, which does not possess the institution of patronage.[105] Clearly it expresses the ideal of the patronage relationship, not necessarily its reality.

If we wish to understand how patronage might operate between ordinary people in Hebrew society, there is no shortage of examples in the texts. A simple example of how a Hebrew writer might understand patronage as working ideally in the village setting is offered by the book of Ruth. Boaz becomes Ruth's patron and indirectly Naomi's: that he eventually becomes Ruth's husband is not a normal aspect of the patronage relationship—but this is after all a story! Ruth initiates the relationship by gleaning in Boaz's field, clearly because she and her mother-in-law are more or less destitute.[106] However, according both to this story and to Lev. 19.9–10 gleaning was her right, and was of course of very limited help. She needs more than this, help

---

101. Simkins 1999: 136–38.
102. Simkins 1999: 128–29.
103. Lemche 1994, 1995, 1996, 1999; Hobbs 1997.
104. Clark 1993: 267.
105. Kippenberg 1982: 31–32.
106. Naomi, it later turns out, had some land (Ruth 4.3), but clearly would not have been in a position to use it that year (Ruth 1.22).

that the landholder must be induced to give of his own free will. She hopes that she may 'find favour' (*ḥēn*) in his sight (Ruth 2.2, 10). 'Favour' is the beneficent recognition bestowed on the prospective client by one who has been invited to be a patron. And Boaz indeed 'recognizes' Ruth, and immediately warns her to make the relationship an exclusive one on her side (Ruth 2.8). Why? I would suggest that it is in his interest as a patron to have a client obliged to him. He shows that he is worthy of trust as a patron by generously topping up the grain she is able to get by gleaning. Later he commends her *ḥesed* in not seeking a husband elsewhere (Ruth 3.10).

The element in the situation that distinguishes it from patronage in the usual sense is that Boaz is a relative of her former husband. She is not aware of this at the time she makes her approach, but Boaz of course is, and no doubt the reader is intended to understand that this accounts for his very generous reception of his client. But it cannot be deduced from this account that it was normal and expected for a hopeful client to give preference to kin in seeking a patron, in other words that the patronage system worked *with* the kinship system rather than against it.

Certainly this is not the impression given by the wisdom sayings in Proverbs, none of which counsel reliance on kinship (Prov. 17.17 might be an exception), while some express scepticism about the value of kinship ties, as in Prov. 27.10: 'do not go to the house of your brother on the day of your calamity; better a neighbour who is nearby than a brother who is far away'; or Prov. 18.24, 'there is a friend who sticks closer than a brother'. One gets the impression from these sayings that they arise from a situation where the *bêt'āb* has been disrupted by the invasions and deportations and no longer lives together.

But Proverbs is very much aware of patronage, and of its dangers, as we see from the sayings which I will discuss in Chapter 4, both those that counsel generosity, such as Prov. 21.13, 22.9, 14.21, or 28.27, and those that note the prevalence of oppression, such as Prov. 18.23 or 22.7. Admittedly, we cannot generally make out a permanent and one-to-one relationship from these sayings. Giving alms does not amount to being a patron, though acquiring a debt-slave may well be the act of a patron. But most of them emphasize the personal: it is not just a matter of giving money or a gift in kind, but of a personal relationship.

When Job (Job 29) laments his former life and describes the pre-eminent position that he used to have in his town, he presents himself as the entire town's patron, and especially the patron of its poor. 'I was a father to the poor', he says (Job 29.16), using one of the most well-rooted and widely attested metaphors for patronage, from which of course the word 'patron' itself is derived. He also characterizes himself as a king (Job 29.25, and note the allusion to Ps. 72.12 in Job 29.12). As Lemche and Simkins argue, the king is in the same way patron of his people; but there is a distinction to be drawn between the universal justice and benevolence of the king (pictured in Psalm 72) and the *particularistic* benevolence of the patron (this is a word used as a technical term by Eisenstadt and Roniger).[107]

The Pentateuchal codes generally assume a relation of patronage between their addressees and their poor neighbour, as for example in Deut. 15.1–18.[108] Deuteronomy 15.1–11 treats loans on security, and vv. 12–18 debt slavery, the next step beyond secured credit. In each case the relationship is pictured as more than a financial or employment transaction. Hamilton notes the prominence of 'somatic' imagery in vv. 7–11: words like 'heart', 'hand' and 'eye', appealing to personal compassion.[109] The prominent use of the term 'your brother' (*'āḥîkā*)[110] for the fellow-Israelite in difficulty even more clearly suggests personal relationship. The final exhortation to give the freed slave a generous send-off underlines that the relationship of master and slave, which is essentially humiliating to the slave, is ideally an opportunity for personal generosity on the part of the master: he is a patron and not just a master. But the patron in this conception gains at least as much from the relationship as the client: materially in the labour service he gets from the bondservant (pointed out in v. 18), but more importantly in the gratitude and loyalty of the client, which he may be able to cash in at a later stage, and in the respect of the community, like Job's, for his generous behaviour; besides which the Deuteronomist's promise of divine blessing (vv. 6, 10, 18) is a less necessary motivation than it seems at first sight.

It is again a patronal relationship which Lev. 25.35–43 projects between the well-to-do reader of the text and his impoverished 'brother'.[111] Lefebvre interprets the two stages of dependency as follows. He may sustain him as a sharecropper,[112] presumably on what had been his own land, with interest-free loans as required (Lev. 25.35–38), or at a deeper stage of impoverishment, when he is unable to repay and as creditor the patron would have the right to seize him as a slave, he may take him into his service[113]—but, the writer urges, not as a slave, but in the position of a hired servant, not to be driven harshly (Lev. 25.39–43). These two ways broadly correspond to the two topics in Deut. 15.1–18. The point to notice in this connection is the use in vv. 35, 39 of the expression *'immāk*, literally 'with

107. I discuss the Job passage further below, pp. 127–29. The distinction between royal and patronal benevolence will occupy us in relation to divine justice below, pp. 213–17.

108. We shall deal with this passage in more detail below, pp. 179–87.

109. Hamilton 1992: 31–34.

110. NRSV 'member of your community', 'your neighbour'.

111. NRSV here translates most misleadingly 'any of your kin'. The term certainly refers to a fellow-Israelite (cf. Lev. 25.47).

112. *métayer*—Lefebvre 2003: 242.

113. The 'sale' of v. 39 is a virtual one; no money changes hands, but the notional price extinguishes the debt (Lefebvre 2003: 275, cf. Milgrom 2001: 2220).

you', but translated 'dependent on you' by the NRSV, surely correctly.[114] The addressee is in the position of patron to the impoverished debtor, having previously made loans to him; hence he has an obligation to support him in whatever way is appropriate to his degree of hardship. He is to be thought of not simply as a creditor, with a legal hold over the debtor, but as a patron with a personal relationship with him—the text's use of 'your brother', as in Deuteronomy, implies this.

These two forms of support are appropriate to severe impoverishment. The text distinguishes between good and bad, generous and oppressive, ways in which they may be realized: loans without interest and with; servile and unservile labour. However, the patron would gain advantage even from the conduct which is approved. Even loans without interest may accumulate and compel the client to offer his labour service; and the patron, for the trifling outlay of a few loans, acquires a labourer who does not need to be paid. Despite Milgrom,[115] surely v. 40 does not imply that wages should be paid; the only distinction the text makes between service as a slave and *like* a hired man is the degree of harshness that may be used (v. 43).

This survey makes it clear that patronage is not a morally unambiguous relation. A patron purports to help his client, and usually genuinely does so. But it is to his advantage to do so, and if it were not, few would undertake the burden. And further, patronage may all too easily slip into oppression. How many patrons would heed the warning of Leviticus to charge no interest on loans and not to drive Israelite bondservants to the limit? Certainly not the rich men blamed in Proverbs. And if bondservants were no longer of value, if their service no longer paid for their keep, the temptation beckoned to realize one's investment by selling them into permanent slavery (cf. Amos 2.6, Neh. 5.8, etc., as above), rather than losing it by releasing them with a golden handshake as Deut. 15.18 exhorts. In certain economic circumstances, if times were bad for people at large, the temptation may have been too much to resist for a large number of patrons at the same time: hence if there is some evidence of economic hardship at a particular period and also of a social crisis, the prevalence of a patronage system may be enough to explain it.

Certainly, it would not be an exaggeration to say that patronage is the normal way in which the relationship between classes is conceived in the Old Testament, and we shall come across many further examples in Chapter 4.

114. But 'become dependent on you' in v. 35 is wrong: the debtor is already dependent. See Lefebvre 2003: 232–234. Cf. Milgrom 2001: 2220, following Speiser 1960: 38–9, with much support from other passages. But his 'under your authority' (cf. JPSV) is a less satisfactory translation because of its legal implications, and because as used in v. 35 it flattens the difference between the stages of destitution treated in Lev. 25.35–38 and 39–47 (Lefebvre 2003: 233–234).

115. Milgrom 2001: 2220.

In using this as evidence for the real social configuration, the difficulty lies in being certain how ideological this normality is. It is not that patronage is idealized, except in a manifestly romantic text like Ruth. The texts are quite open about the fact that patrons may behave oppressively as well as generously; for some texts in Proverbs, rich patrons may be expected to be oppressive. But it could be that the prevalence of this conception conceals other types of relationship (through taxes, for example) and the existence of more powerful oppressors than the modestly well-to-do patrons the texts seem to have in mind. In this way they may prevent the reader from grasping that the problem of oppression does not depend solely on individual greed and hardheartedness. It could also be that by invariably reminding their hearers of their responsibilities as patrons, the legal and other texts obscure the fact that they were also clients, of the king if no one else.

However, it seems that in a small state consisting of small villages, where there were no complex commercial or bureaucratic structures and where most relationships were face to face, it is simply overwhelmingly probable that patronage played a part in most contacts between unequals; and even the short survey we have undertaken here shows how it would be possible or likely for it to be a channel whereby resources might flow, contrary to the ideology of patronage, from the client to the patron and therefore towards the ruling class. Nevertheless, we do also have to reckon with more formal and impersonal modes of relationship and redistribution, though even taxes and tithes might be considered in the light of gifts to great patrons.

As I have just hinted, it is likely that everyone in such a society was either a patron or a client or both. The mass of the population, the peasant cultivators, would tend to be clients of the most powerful family locally, whether the most powerful of the village elders, a local prebendary, or a member of an ancient chiefly family. But they themselves might well find themselves approached as patrons by the very poor, landless, widows, strangers. The texts we have discussed are ambiguous as between these different situations.

Economic pressure would thus tend to flow throughout society, generally starting from the state and the great personalities of the land, on to the well-to-do peasants and village elders and from them to the poor and marginal elements. Bendor argues that the impact of external pressures would have varied according to the internal dynamic of the *bêt 'āb*. Where its tendency was towards unity, these pressures would be evenly spread and thereby successfully absorbed. Where there was hostility and tension, the tendency would be for the unit to concentrate the impact on to its weakest members: first the widow and fatherless, and then the brothers who did not have their own plots. These would be the first to be handed over as pledges to the usurer, or even sold as slaves, or forced out to become *gērîm*.[116]

116.   Bendor 1996: 188–96.

6. *Conclusion*

We are now in a position to draw together the threads of our long discussion, to weigh up the relative value of our models and to sketch the mechanism and progress of social disruption and class formation in ancient Israel and Judah from the eighth century BCE to the fifth. Our account can be brief, as we have already given the supporting facts and discussions. Each of the four models discussed has been found to offer some part of the truth, but none has been completely adequate to the facts. In what follows the elements of each of them which have survived our testing will be integrated into a single account.

We have been able to exclude a number of canvassed possibilities. Before the end of the monarchic period there was no drastic deterioration in the standard of living of the rural population, as suggested by Holladay's survey to which I have referred. This does not mean that things had not got worse for them in any respect. They could have been *socially* degraded, losing independence, rights and status, while mostly retaining their material position. There was no serious monetization of the economy before the Hellenistic period, and hence no comprehensive market economy—above all no free market in land. There was no formation of latifundia in the monarchic period at the expense of traditional landholding patterns; the royal estates discerned by Zwickel are probably in previously unsettled areas, and this may also be true of the large estates formed after the devastation of the invasions, in Israel after 722 and Judah after 587.[117] There was no central planning of the economy: the only central plan by the governing class was to get what they could out of the country.

We can safely say that traditional society had never been equal: variations in wealth can be traced back to Iron Age I, the pre-monarchic period,[118] and may, as Holladay suggests, have given rise to the move to statehood. But it was based on a kinship structure which survived this transition, though probably not, at least in its original form, the more violent shock of the invasions and deportations 300 to 400 years later.[119]

With the formation of states, the kinship structure and its economic resources came under pressure. Many people would have been attracted into the royal establishment and rewarded with lands from conquered territory, and began to form a privileged class to a large extent separated from the rural population from which some of them had been drawn—some may have been foreigners. There were demands for taxes to support this establishment, its military enterprises, its cultic provisions, and increasingly the lifestyle of its members.

117. Holladay 1995: 393.
118. Holladay 1995: 376–79.
119. Cf. Weinberg 1992: 49–61.

For some time it is possible that these expenses were met to some or a large extent by tolls on the transit trade through Palestine.[120] But towards the end of the ninth century in Israel, rather later in Judah, external pressures would have led to declining revenues from this source: pressure from Damascus and then the Assyrians' seizure of control over the trade. At the same time, it became necessary to start paying tribute to Assyria. We know that the states were in financial difficulties: there is no new monumental building from the beginning of the eighth century—so much for the Amos commentators' 'unprecedented prosperity'![121] At this point taxes levied on agricultural production must have started to increase. There may already have been pressure on the land from population increase. Some solutions had been applied to ease the pressure: forming new settlements, emigration, enlisting as mercenaries; and these certainly continued in favour for centuries.

The more prosperous families would have been able to deal with the threat by specializing in higher value crops, especially wine and oil, which they could sell or barter for grain; again the material record witnesses to this specialization. Of course, the bureaucrats' prebends had long since been set on this path. Less well-off families were in a precarious position. As they had always done in times of bad harvests, but now had to do even more often, they could apply a to better-off cousin, to the head of the *bêt'āb*, to a prosperous head of another family in the locality, or to a member of the governing class who held lands in the village. It was a high-risk strategy. A generous patron would provide them with what they needed and not press too hard for repayment. One with an eye to the main chance would take the opportunity to pile interest on the loan, to take a field or a member of the debtor's family as security or as a source of income to pay off the loan, and more, and the debtor could eventually find that he had lost his children and his land and faced debt-bondage himself. The most ruthless creditors might sell him or his family into slavery. Such exploitative methods would be more likely to be met with from patrons whose main residence was now the city. But even locally based men of power were quite likely to use their authority to satisfy creditors by seizing on the weakest links in the family for debt-slaves.

This did not mean general destitution for the rural population. Many independent producers still remained. Those who had been degraded mostly still retained effective use of their land; true, they had loan repayments or their master's cut on top of the king's tax to take out of each year's harvest, so that destitution had crept a little nearer. But what was far worse was the loss of their status in the community as men with rights in the community's

---

120. Holladay 1995: 383–86.
121. De Geus 1982: 54.

land and its judicial institutions. Those who had been sold into foreign slavery were in even worse case, but—the unaffected might comfort themselves—at least that meant less of a problem in feeding the mouths that remained.

There will always have been a stratum of the desperately poor, those whose footing in the kinship structure was insecure, such as widows and strangers, and those who had lost land or never had it, who existed as casual labourers or on charity, who sunk into temporary or permanent bondage, or who became bandits in the hills or beggars in the cities. Lenski identifies a class of what he chillingly calls 'expendables' in every agrarian society.[122] These no doubt became more numerous as social troubles increased; we have no quantitative evidence, but it is significant to observe that the social concerns of the prophets and the law change focus as time goes on. The eighth-century prophets are primarily concerned about the exploitation and deprivation of landholding citizens; in Deuteronomy we hear of hired labourers for the first time; and in Isaiah 58 and Job in the fifth century or thereabouts the concern is for the destitute. This may suggest a deepening of social distress and an actual increase in destitution.

The privileged classes on the other hand, the urban elements, the royal bureaucracy and their hangers on, and those wealthy people in the villages who had failed to say 'I dwell among my own people', and who were engaged in patronage of an often oppressive character, were able by these means to increase both their wealth and, probably more important to them, their power. They, or some of them, lived the pleasant life pictured in Amos 6 or Isaiah 5, and were able in the political turmoil of those years to call on the services of troops of clients as enforcers.

The Assyrian catastrophe at the end of the eighth century completely wiped out the privileged class of Israel, made serious inroads into that of Judah, and caused a massive decline in population everywhere.[123] Living standards would also have fallen, but depopulation would have eased pressure on the available resources. After a rise in population during the seventh century in Judah, the next pressure point would have come when foreign demands on the kingdom reappeared in Jehoiakim's reign. This we would expect to have had the same results as before. Sure enough, it is in the final years of the kingdom that protests against economic injustice again emerge in the prophecies of Zephaniah, Jeremiah, Habakkuk and Ezekiel. Ezekiel specifically denounces all the estates of the kingdom for brutal exploitation of the poor, including both those in government employ and 'the people of the land'.

---

122. Lenski 1966: 281–84.
123. Broshi and Finkelstein 1992: 55–56

The Judaean exploiting class was destroyed or removed by Nebuchadrez-zar between 597 and 582. We are told that the poorest of the people remained to till the land. Although much has been written about conflict, partly over land, between upper-class returnees in the late-sixth and fifth centuries and those who had remained, it is not clear to me that we really know anything much about it. What we do know is that a very serious situation had arisen by the time of Nehemiah, after 444 BCE. The Persian government aimed at maximum revenue extraction from all its provinces, and the 'king's tax' created serious hardship for the rural population, especially in years of bad harvest. They had trodden the time-honoured path of application to patrons for credit, and it had led, as it had always done, to loss and degradation. Lands had been lost, children forced into servitude, through the rapacity of an exploiting class consisting of government officials and wealthy landowners, who probably took the security into their possession at the point of the loan.

Nehemiah applies an instant administrative remedy, forcing the oppressors to disgorge their ill-gotten gains, and (probably) exacting a promise not to seize securities in that manner again.[124] Although Nehemiah here drew on an established legal tradition, there is no reason to suppose that his intervention had any lasting effects, any more than the existence of laws mandating similar easements had in the past. Judah continued to drift down a course of more and more severe class division, regardless of the repeated changes of government over the next five hundred years; large estates developed, some of them under state control, with their concomitant of the institution of tenancy and a rural proletariat looking for seasonal work. The liberation of the land and its people remained a shimmering hope which was part of the inspiration of the repeated revolts of the Roman years.

This reconstruction will have shown that all the mechanisms suggested in the models we have examined were operative in the process, mostly all at the same time. The trigger was generally the demands of the state for support, which could only be met out of the limited income of the rural poor. In this sense we may speak of a tributary state system, which also contributed to exploitation by the creation of a class of government functionaries who looked for support to estates which they did not themselves farm, and tended to want to increase their support from this source. They, along with the wealthiest provincial elements, tended to form an aristocracy, which sought to reduce the rural population to subjection, and carved out spheres of influence for themselves independent of the state: thus there were forces tending towards the 'ancient' mode of production as well as those tending towards the 'Asiatic' or 'tributary' mode. They operated by using and abusing the patronage system, and as they were mostly city-based and sought to

---

124.   Blenkinsopp 1988: 259; Williamson 1985: 241.

maximize their appropriation of the peasants' surpluses a rent-capitalistic system can be said to be in operation. Through it all, however, the dominant mode of production was what Gottwald calls the 'communitarian' mode of production under the control of rural families, which continued despite all vicissitudes and despite the heavy tribute it had to pay to other systems at least until the end of our period.[125]

One general conclusion of importance for our study may be drawn. Nothing in the range of social relationships canvassed in this account bears the least structural resemblance to modern capitalism. If the response to exploitation in ancient Israel and Judah is of any relevance today, it can only be at the level of moral evaluation.

125. Gottwald 1993a.

Chapter 3

OPPRESSION AND THE PROPHETS

1. *Interpreting the Prophets*

In the previous chapter I attempted to describe socio-economic developments in ancient Israel and Judah from what scholars like to think of as an
'objective' point of view. As I have already pointed out, it is well recognized
today that objectivity is a will-o'-the-wisp. We always understand things
from our own point of view, and import perhaps more than we realize of
our own sympathies and interests into the most severely academic descrip-
tions of things. All the same, we can draw a distinction between an account
which looks at the system from the outside and tries to give scientific
explanations for what is going on, however much it may be affected or even
distorted by the interests of the observer, and one which comes from the
inside, expresses how someone who is personally involved sees it, and is
unashamedly committed to one view of things. This is what the text of the
Old Testament itself offers us, and this is what we shall be dealing with from
this point on.

In the Prophets we find the social developments of these ancient kingdoms understood as the deliberate acts of groups and individuals and
judged morally in an entirely 'subjective' way. What I shall try to do in this
chapter is to examine and analyse the moral judgements on social oppression found in the prophetic literature as aspects of rhetorical structures. I
shall ask whom they see as the victims and the oppressors, and how their
judgments are related to their social and ideological commitments. We can
treat these texts as contemporary commentary from people involved in the
events, even though it is doubtful how much of the prophetic books go back
to the prophets who bear their names. For the processes of class formation
and exploitation which we have looked at covered centuries, and were as
vigorous and malign in the fifth century as they were in the eighth. Everyone
involved in the editing and transmission of the prophetic books knew what
was meant by the oppression of the poor.

But it is not easy to tell the precise historical and social situation of
particular prophetic texts. There is widespread agreement that each of the
four main collections (the twelve 'minor' prophets being viewed as one

book) is the result of a process of redaction covering anything from one to three centuries, and that the final form of each is the work of creative editors working in the Second Temple era.[1] While some claim to be able to trace this process in detail (though always disagreeing with each other about that detail!), others deny that we can know anything definite about the origins of anything in the prophetic books, and indeed nothing very much about their social background.[2] For Robert Carroll there is no strong reason to suppose that the historical Jeremiah (if there was such a person) had anything to do with the book that goes by his name; and Richard Coggins deals with Amos in a very similar way, treating it as a book of the fifth century, and refusing to identify definitely what parts of it might come from a historical prophet Amos in the eighth.[3]

An early attempt to harness redaction criticism to an ideological under-standing of the prophetic books was made by Robert Coote.[4] Coote presents the development of Amos as a three-stage cumulative process.[5] The 'A texts' (all short orally delivered oracles, for example Amos 3.9–12 or 4.1–3) announce doom for specific crimes of oppression against specific addressees. Coote sees these, and these alone, as Amos' own words. In answer to the question what effect Amos intended his words to have on the people addressed his surprising answer is 'None'. 'Amos's oracles imply no response, have no future, offer no program, and leave no room for repentance.'[6]

These texts were taken and placed in a sophisticated literary structure addressed to a more general audience by a creative editor (or two) more than a century later in the time of Josiah, who added material of his own, including Amos 1.1–8, 13–15; 2.1–3, 6a, 9–12; 3.1–8; 4.4–12; 5.4–6, 14–15, 21–27; 6.12–14; 7; 8.1–3, 8, 11–14; 9.5–6. The book as expanded had two main themes. One was the rejection of the shrine of Bethel (as in Amos 3.13–14) in the context of Josiah's claim to the territory of the former kingdom of Israel and desecration of its principal shrine. The implication was that worshippers at Bethel should come to Jerusalem instead.[7] The second was a warning directed to Jerusalem itself, to do justly to avoid the fate of those Amos addressed (as in Amos 5.14–15), 'to hold the ruling elite accountable to their professed allegiance to the fundamentals of Yahwistic justice'.[8] A further issue was the authority of the prophet (raised in Amos

---

1. See for a useful overview Collins 1993.
2. A point made emphatically by Carroll (1989), when asked to write on just that topic, as well as in his numerous works on Jeremiah.
3. Carroll 1981, 1986; Coggins 2000.
4. Coote 1981.
5. Simplifying Wolff's analysis: Wolff 1977: 106–13.
6. Coote 1981: 42–45.
7. Coote 1981: 48–53.
8. Coote 1981: 99.

3.3–8; 7.10–17), since the necessity for a response would raise this question, whereas the A-texts simply proclaim doom and would be authenticated by the event. Thus in Coote's view the book in its main substance has a clearly ideological function, to support ruling class objectives. That the second aim is as ideologically important as the first follows from what I said in Chapter 1 about the need for ideology to respond to the needs and ideals and traditions of the whole population.

There was then a second edition in the exile which placed the existing text in a new context announcing restoration, and this C-stage editor is responsible for three of the oracles in the opening section and for the conclusion of the book, 9.7–15.

Coote's main formal distinction between A and B, between proclamation of doom and exhortation to goodness, has frequently been used as a tool in redaction criticism, and it might be considered useful in detecting ideological commitments, but it needs evaluation.[9] On the face of it, exhortation implies a basic sympathy with the addressees, while condemnation implies the standpoint of someone who is distanced from them by taking the side of the oppressed. In other words, it is the difference between saying: This whole system is utterly corrupt: God will sweep it away, and saying: You should change your ways, be kind to the poor instead of oppressing them, and so avoid the judgment and preserve your society.

But do these two types of utterance really have to have different origins? May they not make sense within the same discourse? Thus, it may be argued that pronouncements of doom have an implied condition 'if you do not repent', and therefore function as warnings; the contradiction with exhortation would then be only superficial.[10] Alternatively the primary message may be one of inexorable doom, while any exhortations and warnings are either ironical or earlier messages which have been overtaken and outdated by the refusal of the people to repent.[11] But I have argued elsewhere that this is a false alternative.[12] We have no access to the intentions of the prophets; however, examples in narrative literature show that even when judgment is announced unconditionally a possible response, however unlikely, is repentance: it is not a prediction of the future. This is an issue explored by the book of Jonah. Therefore, as we cannot tell what the intention of any prophetic pronouncement might be, there is no basis for using the distinction between oracles of judgment and exhortations as a key to redaction.

There is another distinction between Coote's A texts and the book as a

---

9. See, most recently, the discussion in Möller 2003: 141–45 and the literature cited there in nn. 121, 122, 123. The dominant view in recent times has been that the pre-exilic prophets proclaimed absolute doom, so, e.g., Westermann 1967: 19; Wolff 1977: 103–106.

10. E.g. Buber 1949: 134; Fohrer 1979: 480–81.

11. So, e.g., Hunter 1982.

12. Houston 1993b; followed by Möller (2001; 2003: 142–43).

whole, and that is in their audience. Those accused of sin in the A-texts are specific groups of rich oppressors, yet the book as it stands appears to threaten the nation as a whole with punishment. In Amos 3.1 those addressed are named as 'the Israelites', and compare Amos 2.6, 'for three transgressions *of Israel*'; 4.12; 7.8; and 8.2: 'the end has come upon *my people Israel*'. This general address is a mark of the B-stage.

Daniel Carroll attempts to resolve this contradiction by arguing from the frequent passages attacking or satirizing Israel's engaging in the cult.[13] The cult offered a world-view sanctioning oppression and therefore opposed to YHWH's will, and Israel was involved in it as a whole, therefore they all shared in the guilt of the ruling class who organized it. But though it is a widespread assumption that the whole of society joined in the cult, I am not convinced that this is true for the state temples and pilgrimage shrines attacked in Amos. Could impoverished peasants, debt-burdened or enslaved or half-starved, afford lengthy journeys to take part in the pilgrimage feasts at Bethel, Gilgal, or Beersheba? They could have attended local shrines, but these could not be seen as sanctioning the state system. Either these passages too are addressed to the elite, or Coote is right and they represent the viewpoint of Jerusalem a hundred years later, concerned to eliminate all other cults.

Another approach denies that 'Israel' means the people as a whole. For Haroldo Reimer, a Brazilian scholar, the distinction drawn between culprits and victims in the judgment oracles is the key to the whole book. Amos 7.9 shows that it is the monarchy and its cult-sites that are due to be destroyed, and this is what 'my people Israel' in the previous verse really means.[14] Möller follows Reimer's lead: Amos 9.8 declares explicitly that the 'end' of 'Israel' means the end of the state and its institutions, 'the sinful kingdom', but not of the people as a whole, the 'house of Jacob'. The following verses show that those who will be destroyed are 'all the sinners of my people', that is the oppressors who have been denounced in the course of the book.[15] The solution may seem too neat, and indeed most scholars think Amos 9.8b–10 belongs to the latest part of the book, bringing in the idea of individual retribution, supposed to be typically post-exilic, to correct Amos' condemnation of Israel as a whole.[16] It does not look as if Reimer is likely to be right, but in any case the way in which judgment happens in Amos is bound to affect the people as a whole. This creates a tension which theories of redaction are powerless to resolve, and we shall consider it further shortly.

13. Carroll R. 1992: 209–10, 219, 273–77; cf. 278–306.
14. Reimer 1992: 23, 55–56, 213 and passim.
15. Möller 2003: 139–41; cf. Rudolph 1971: 277–78.
16. E.g. Jeremias 1998: 162–66.

Mosala, in his work on Micah, acknowledges his debt to Coote, but moves beyond him in an attempt to connect prophetic texts with specific social formations.[17] He groups the material in Micah into three types according to the ideology he detects in them. The framework and dominant ideology of the book represents the aspirations of the former ruling class of Judah whose pride had been humbled by exile. This includes for example most of Micah 4 and Micah 7. This corresponds in social location to Coote's Amos C, so it becomes C in Mosala's scheme. Here 'the former oppressors of peasants and casual laborers and underclasses in Judah are now seeing themselves as the oppressed in relation to their captors . . . Instead of the rich and the powerful, it is the nations and the pagans who become targets of Yahweh's judgment.'[18] Their hope centres on the restoration of Zion: but this is quite alien to the aspirations of the real oppressed working classes then and now.

But Micah also contains material very similar to Coote's A texts in Amos, where a specific audience of the ruling class is accused of specific crimes and the judgment of God is proclaimed unequivocally, for example Mic. 2.1–5. These parts are Mosala's A material. Nevertheless these texts do not contain the actual voice of oppressed people. 'The black working-class people of South Africa would experience an absence of the voice of the laboring and underclasses of Micah's Judah in these texts.'[19] These oracles, like those in Amos, are best understood as the words of a sympathetic observer of the plight of the poor.

This point is valid for all the prophetic books: in none do we hear the voice of the oppressed poor themselves, nor should we expect to: they were in no position to make their voice heard in any enduring form. At best, we have the voice of a person whose means, social position or calling frees him of dependence on the ruling class, who is then in a position to observe the suffering of the poor with sympathy; one may think of Wolff's suggestion[20] that Micah was an elder of Moresheth-gath, who was responsible for the enforcement of justice and horrified by the injustice that he observed, but could do nothing about it other than protest. His voice is then embedded in a structure created by others for different purposes.

Mosala's B texts are more precarious as a group.[21] He sees them cast in a code typical of a middle layer in society, not the exploited poor and not the ruling class, serving rulers but without direct access to power for themselves. Addressed to a general audience, not the exploiting classes specifically, they

---

17. Mosala 1989: 123–53.
18. Mosala 1989: 132. Pleins (2001: 251, etc.) detects a similar transformation in several other prophetic texts, such as Second Isaiah. The exiled elite become the 'poor and afflicted'.
19. Mosala 1989: 149.
20. Wolff 1990: 5–8.
21. Mosala 1989: 134–43: Mic. 1.5b–7; 2.6–7, 10–11; 3.1–7; 5.1, 4–6; 6.1–8, 16; 7.1–7.

'blend adaptive and oppositional elements', and the typical stance, says Mosala, is not to accuse and condemn but to warn and exhort to goodness; not precise definitions of justice, but a general call to do justice. However, inspection of the texts reveals little to hold them together, and the typical exhortation style appears only in 6.1–8. Other sections could easily be classed under A (Mic. 3.1–7) or C (5.1, 4–6). Mosala characterizes the texts as being 'shot through with contradiction', but it is easy to say a set of texts is shot through with contradiction if you have selected a set of contradictory texts. The principle of selection Mosala does not explain. Ambiguity, according to Mosala, is typical of these texts, but he finds ambiguity where I see none, as in the rhetorical questions of 3.1; 6.6–7, which according to him 'avoid clarity of statement'. In fact, a rhetorical question is a characteristic way of making a strong assertion in Hebrew. It seems Mosala, over-influenced by Coote's analysis of Amos, is reluctant to conclude, as perhaps he ought, that Micah contains few texts not classifiable in his 'A' and 'C' categories.

Although Mosala has made a bold attempt to identify the class origins of various material in the book of Micah, he does not offer an interpretation of the book as a whole, or suggest how its various parts work together, except to make the very general statement that ideology 'is a harmonization of contradictions in such a way that the class interests of one group are universalized and made acceptable to other classes'.[22] The question is, assuming that Mosala is right in saying that the final, the dominant editors of the Micah book were members of the former Judaean ruling class whose central aspiration was the restoration of their ancient stronghold of Zion, what was their purpose in including in their composition those fierce criticisms of the Jerusalem-based ruling class? And how are we to read their final production? At the moment we cannot answer these questions, but we need to bear them in mind as we proceed.

This survey should have shown that despite the confidence of Coote and Mosala in their being able to identify the different voices and standpoints in the text, or the confidence of the more traditional redaction critics such as Wolff[23] in disentangling the successive layers, and even though there cannot be much doubt that different hands over the years have contributed to the prophetic books, the scepticism of such scholars as Carroll and Coggins that we can now sort them out is justified. Different scholars are equally confident, but disagree with each other, a sure sign that the evidence is insufficient and capable of bearing different interpretations. Moreover, not only is the analysis of the prophets uncertain, but it is not the analysed and fragmented prophets that we now read. We need to be able to make sense

22. Mosala 1989: 152.
23. Wolff 1977: 106–13; 1990: 17–27.

of the books that we have, if possible, rather than their hypothetical predecessors.[24]

However much, therefore, we are convinced that the prophetic texts show a process of growth, we cannot make a convincing reading of them depend on a particular redactional analysis. My proposal is to read the prophetic collections as rhetorical wholes and to ask what, in broad outline, their persuasive purpose is. We may then be able to understand them as such as representing specific social and political positions. In that context, their contradictions are not so much undigested fragments of the social polemics of earlier generations, as essential parts of their argument which they have not succeeded in reconciling with their basic ideology. In other words, this is a deconstructive approach—which does not mean a destructive approach! It means that we aim to uncover the conflicting presuppositions of the books to free the reader to choose between them.

Although I shall deal with the prophetic books as wholes and shall not engage in wholesale redactional fragmentation, I am not concerned, as I am sure the average reader is not concerned, with marginal elements, final redactional modifications, or glosses, which do not make much difference to the overall impact of the book. I should also point out that lack of space makes it impossible to give the kind of detailed rhetorical analysis undertaken, for example, by Karl Möller on Amos.[25] I shall simply give an impressionistic sketch of each book, picking out some key points which are of importance for its ideological evaluation. The only one of the prophetic collections in which the primary concern is to present social injustice as the ground for national punishment is Amos. In all the rest that issue is one among others. Amos therefore deserves prior and special treatment in our study.

2. Amos

2.a. *The Message of the Book of Amos*

Looking at Amos as a whole, we see that it is dominated by three great series which each build up to a climax: the oracles against the nations in 1.3–2.16, culminating in the oracle against Israel from 2.6; the series of five warning judgements in 4.6–12 leading up to the call 'prepare to meet your God!' (4.12);[26] and the series of five visions in chs. 7–9, culminating in the vision of YHWH standing by the altar and announcing his intention to hunt down

24. Cf. Childs 1979.
25. Möller 2003.
26. Not a call to repent, but an announcement of judgment: clearly argued by Paul (1991: 151, n. 119); see also Hunter 1982: 121 and Polley 1989: 146–47.

his enemies to their deaths.[27] Much of the material between these series consists of judgment oracles against Israel, primarily for the oppression of the poor. Probably the series of oracles against the nations was originally five rather than eight, those against Tyre, Edom and Judah being sixth-century supplements.[28] This would mean that all three series were structured as series of five.[29] But even in its present form, the resulting structure of the book as a whole is extraordinarily impressive, and it delivers a very clear message: that after due warning given, YHWH is about to destroy the kingdom of Israel for its sins, primarily for social injustice. This is the message delivered, according to the opening of the book, by Amos of Tekoa in the reigns of Uzziah and Jeroboam.

His opening words are 'YHWH roars from Zion and utters his voice from Jerusalem' (Amos 1.2); and after announcing the imminent destruction of the 'sinful kingdom' (9.8), including, repeatedly, the doom of its prime legitimating sanctuary, Bethel, he forecasts the restoration of 'David's tottering booth' (9.11). This framing plainly suggests that the book is written from the standpoint of Jerusalem, and it is simple enough to state its immediate rhetorical object: to persuade us that the fall of Israel is willed by God for its sin and is therefore just. In the first place, this leads to the conclusion that the place of the kingdom of Israel may now be taken by the restored house of David. But that does not mean the book is a mere Judaean nationalist apologia, as suggested by Max Polley;[30] for few readers of the book, whether in ancient or in modern times, could fail to understand *themselves* as called to do justice and thereby avoid the fate of Israel. Sicre puts it powerfully: 'to deny this aspect means mutilating the text and shutting oneself off from the dynamism of the word of God'.[31] For Möller, the sole rhetorical aim of the book is to persuade Judaean hearers at some time after 722 to avoid Israel's fate.[32]

Coote's two proposals for the object of his 'B' edition and its ideological character may thus be endorsed, but they seem to belong to the book as a whole. The ruling class viewpoint of the text may be seen from the fact that

---

27. Hayes (1988: 216) and Sweeney 1995, followed by Möller (2003: 100), argue that this vision report is too unlike the others to be the climax of the series; it is rather the climax of the book, or its message of judgment. But it is not unexpected for the climax of a series to be distinctive; at the same time one can agree that it has a climactic function in the book as a whole.

28. See, e.g., Wolff 1977: 112; Barton 1980: 22–23; Coote 1981: 112–13; a minority disagrees, listed in Möller 2003: 187, n. 156.

29. Gese 1981; cf. Auld 1986: 50.

30. Polley 1989.

31. Sicre 1984: 159 (my translation).

32. Möller 2003: 119–20.

its main subject is the fate of kingdoms, rulers, capital cities and royal sanctuaries. This is apparent from the first lines. 'I shall send fire on the house of Hazael and it will consume the palaces of Ben-hadad, and I shall break the bar of Damascus and cut off the ruler from the vale of Aven' (1.4–5). As already noted, the three great series which dominate the structure of the book are concerned with the fate of Israel as a whole. Kingdoms and capitals and peoples are the concerns of rulers; and they prefer to see their peoples as undivided wholes. So far as possible, they play down and suppress conflicts of interest between tribes, classes and other groups within their society.

But set in counterpoint over this great ground bass of the fall of Israel are the individual oracles of judgment, each of which in the compass of a few verses sketches the crimes of a specific group of people and announces their punishment, often in the style of 'poetic justice',[33] the punishment symbolically 'fitting the crime'; 5.11–12 is an obvious example. These make it impossible for the book to play down the division in society. For this is the only material at the disposal of the editor that can clearly justify the fall of Israel. Even the anti-Bethel oracles do not plainly condemn Israel for frequenting the sanctuary: they are not oracles of judgment, but are hortatory or allusive. But while each judgment oracle taken by itself threatens a group of oppressors with a punishment distinctive to them and appropriate to their crimes, when taken as a group, even without the framework in which they are set, they suggest a terrible fate for the people as a whole.

For two main modes of judgment are threatened. One is earthquake (Amos 3.14–15 (?); 4.11; 8.8; 9.1, 5–6), and it hardly needs pointing out that this is quite indiscriminate in its effects. The other and more frequently mentioned is 'the sword' and deportation (Amos 2.14–15; 3.11; 5.3, 5; 6.7, 14; 7.9, 11, 17; 9.1, 4, 10, to cite only unambiguous cases). Now although the fate of deportation fell mainly on the ruling and upper classes, and it was the well-to-do and their mercenaries who fought wars, in any major conflict the citizen levies would have to be used (absolutely clear in Amos 5.3). Invasion was a disaster for everyone, and above all for the poor, who had no way of replacing the wealth lost in the devastation of fields and orchards, olive groves and vineyards, and who would succumb first to famine. What war meant for the peasant is poignantly expressed in the conclusion to the vision of peace in Mic. 4.4: 'Everyone will sit under his own vine and his own fig tree, *with no one to make him afraid*'. The threat of war as judgment is a threat levelled at the whole of society. This contradiction remains even if the book is reduced to the supposed oracles of Amos in Coote's A text.[34] None refers to disasters which can realistically be restricted

33. Cf. Barton 1979.
34. Coote 1981: 11–15.

to the elite, or even the well to do. If these oracles assume this, they are based on illusion. It is therefore futile to try to resolve the ideological tensions of the book by redactional analysis, with Coote, or by restricting the scope of the judgment, with Reimer; and we have already dismissed Carroll R.'s attempt to implicate the whole of society in the sins of the elite.

2.b. *Perceiving Oppression in Amos*

We do not learn much from the positive expression of the moral demand in Amos. Three times it is expressed as 'justice . . . righteousness' (*mišpāṭ . . . ṣᵉdāqâ*: 5.7, 24; 6.12). This pairing ('justice *and* righteousness' in prose) has been shown to refer to what we call social justice, or negatively put the elimination and avoidance of oppression and exploitation, which of course is obvious from the context in Amos in any case.[35] But this is as general and disputable an idea in ancient as in modern times. What is meant by it in Amos comes out with all clarity in the denunciations of injustice.

The significant passages here are: 2.6–16; 3.9–15; 4.1–3; 5.10–12; 8.4–7. Space does not permit a full rhetorical analysis of each of these passages, and for details of interpretation the commentaries must be consulted. Suffice it to say that each contains a denunciation of crimes leading to an announcement of judgment. It is the crimes which concern us at this point. I propose to analyse them under three heads: the victims, the oppressors, and the moral characterization of acts of oppression.

2.b.1 *The Victims*

Amos uses only the following terms to refer to the victims of oppression in these passages: three words for 'poor', two either in the singular or the plural: *'ebyôn, dāl*, and one, *'ānî/'ānāw* only in the plural,[36] and all always in the masculine; and in two places (2.6; 5.12) *ṣaddîq* (masculine singular), conventionally translated 'righteous'. In addition 'the girl', *hanna⁽ᵃ⁾râ*, in 2.7 is likely to refer to a victim of oppression, a sexually abused woman, probably a debt slave.[37] Fleischer has a thorough and valuable discussion of these words.[38]

Argument has raged over the possible distinctions between the three words for 'poor'. Fleischer argues that the detailed contexts suggest that the *dāl* (NRSV 'poor') was a poor peasant who still possessed some land, as

35. Miranda 1977: 93, with all the OT passages listed in the notes; Weinfeld 1995: 25–44.

36. *⁽ᵃ⁾nāwîm*; in 8.4 the Qere has *⁽ᵃ⁾niyyê 'āreṣ*. Any semantic distinction between these forms is a late development. See Fleischer 1989: 272–74; Gerstenberger in *TDOT* XI, 242 (*ThWAT* VI, 259).

37. So Mays 1969: 46; Fleischer 1989: 61–65. Wolff (1977: 166–67) and Paul (1991: 81–83) do not think it refers specifically to a slave.

38. Fleischer 1989: 264–83.

against the *'ebyôn* (NRSV 'needy'), who was propertyless and eked out an existence as a day labourer. *'ānî* (NRSV again 'poor') could refer to either, but connotes especially their claim on the compassion of the better off.[39] However, the distinctions are difficult to make out, and the best discussion may still be that by Milton Schwantes, using a broader range of texts.[40] He shows that although there are differences in the entire spectrum of meaning of each, and more importantly in their connotations, they may still be used synonymously, and that is how Amos seems to use them, apparently interchangeably in various combinations, and always more than one in a particular context. They all refer, obviously, to people lacking in material resources and therefore in power. However, there is a significant restriction on the use of the words, which we will come to in a moment.

Clearly *ṣaddîq* also refers to a poor man in its contexts in Amos, in each place being parallel with *'ebyôn* or *'ebyônîm*, but it is more difficult to define in context. But since the rest of 5.12b seems to indicate a judicial context, it seems likely it means there 'innocent' in a legal sense. It could mean the same in 2.6: he is sold arbitrarily although owing nothing.[41] More likely is the sense *morally* 'innocent': there may be a legal case for the sale of the debtor by the creditor or for handing him over to the creditor,[42] but his only crime is being unable to pay his debts. At any rate it does not refer to his moral standards in an absolute sense, which Amos is not interested in. Soggin suggests that its placement at the head of the whole series in 2.6–8 indicates how all the poor victims are to be viewed.[43] They all have right on their side. But Bendor's interpretation that it refers to one who 'has rights' in the family land is attractive.[44]

In that case it would link up with a point explored by Phyllis Bird: who the victims are *not*.[45] All the words used, except for 'the girl', are in the masculine, and it is true for the whole Hebrew Bible that the words for 'poor' and the word *ṣaddîq*[46] do not occur in the feminine; that does not mean that women are not *objectively* victims, but that 'even where women of the community are clearly suffering from the conditions of poverty . . . the injustice done to the poor by the rich is formulated with males in mind'.[47] It is also notable that the widow, the fatherless and the alien, the standard

---

39. Fleischer 1989: 275.
40. Schwantes 1977: 14–51, 87–99; summary 276–78. See also the relevant entries in *TDOT* and *NIDOTTE*.
41. Fleischer 1989: 279–80.
42. Bendor 1996: 232.
43. Soggin 1987: 47.
44. Bendor 1996: 246.
45. Bird 1997. I am grateful to Cheryl Exum for drawing my attention to this article.
46. Its contrary *rāšā'* only occurs in the feminine as an adjective qualifying *derek* 'way'.
47. Bird 1997: 76.

objects of compassion in Deuteronomy and many other texts, are mentioned nowhere in the book. This is also true of Micah, though Mic. 2.9 does mention women and children. Although other prophets do mention the widow and the fatherless, Bird can only find two places where they are mentioned in the same context with the (male) poor: Isa. 10.1–4 and Zech. 7.10.[48] These are the people who have *no* rights, no fixed place in the structure of the *bêt'āb*, which is why their position is precarious and why the legal texts are concerned to defend them. In Amos, one may deduce, the sole concern is for those who do have rights, that is, according to Bendor,[49] adult male (married) members of *bātê'ābôt*, heads of nuclear families. Of course their fate involves their families. 'As a householder, his entire family suffers from his economic distress, but they are not identified separately because they fall within the family system.'[50]

The one exception, as I have said, is the *na'ªrâ* of 2.7. Bird cites Nehemiah 5 for comparison as another text where the poor are defined in male terms, as the 'brothers' of Neh 5.8.[51] But here also there is mention of the people's daughters that they have had to force into debt servitude (Neh. 5.2 and especially 5.5). Bird suggests that 'when forced to give up their children into slavery, people surrendered their daughters first'.[52] But unlike the widow and the fatherless, the debt-bonded daughter was connected with a family; she had a place in the system, although she had temporarily lost it. She is not 'poor': that term is reserved for her father; but her fate is involved with his. 'The "poor" . . . are those male members of the community whose precarious economic condition puts them in danger of losing their place in the "brotherhood" of free citizens.'[53]

It may be that with the deepening of social misery and the gradual breakdown of the old kinship networks in the seventh century and later, it became more common for marginalized people to fail to find succour in their communities; hence later prophets more frequently show concern for the widow, fatherless and stranger. But it is true for all the prophetic texts that their chief concern is for those who are or once were full citizens. What was happening to heads of families marked a new and irreversible shift in the social structure. Whom does the text of Amos see as responsible for it?

2.b.2 *The Oppressors*
Clues to the identity of the oppressors are minimal. They are not identified in class terms. The word 'rich' (*'āšîr*) does not appear, nor are any described

---

48. Bird 1997: 77.
49. Bendor 1996: 123–24.
50. Bird 1997: 78.
51. Bird 1997: 74–76.
52. Bird 1997: 75.
53. Bird 1997: 78.

as 'elders' or 'officers' as in Isaiah. For the most part the text identifies them by their actions; so we frequently get them described or even addressed with participles (in Hebrew), even at the beginning of a saying, for example Amos 5.7, 12b, 18; 6.1, 13. Identifying them therefore depends largely on being able to identify their actions.

However, in Amos 3 the nations are summoned to view what is going on in Samaria (3.9), and 'the Israelites who dwell in Samaria' is repeated in 3.12; and the 'cows of Bashan' are also 'on the hill of Samaria' in 4.1. Amos 6.1 also refers to Samaria. Samaria is the capital. What is denounced here is the actions of the metropolitan aristocracy, consisting, as we have seen, of those directly involved in the royal administration together with those wealthy country landowners who had chosen to better themselves by moving to the capital; and the reference to 'winter and summer houses' and 'houses of ivory' in Amos 3.15 probably points to the royal family itself (cf. 1 Kgs 22.39).[54]

There can be little doubt that the actions referred to in Amos 5.10–12 are those of essentially the same class as Amos 3.9–4.3 point to. Whether the exactions attacked in 5.11a are taxes, rent, tithes or loan repayments, they must be exacted by those who have acquired, legitimately or not, a title to them: tax collectors, landlords, or creditors; and they can also determine by their corruptly used power the outcome of legal cases (v. 12b).

The miscreants in 8.4–7 are almost invariably referred to as corn dealers or more vaguely 'merchants'. But Marlene Fendler and Rainer Kessler make a good case that grain would normally have been supplied directly by the producers themselves to those who needed it; so that wealthy farmers and large landowners, who produced more than they needed, would have supplied the needs of the landless and those whose land did not produce enough for their families. They were in a position to profit by it in the ways denounced by the text. Thus the oppressors in this passage are in fact the same social group as are in the sights of the text in Amos 3 and 5.[55] Fleischer thinks of crown officials in charge of the grain supply, which may have been a state monopoly in urban areas.[56]

In 2.6–8 the case is less clear. The sexual abuse of a serving maid is certainly conceivable in a house of modest resources; and loans could be

---

54. Cf. Wolff 1977: 201.
55. Fendler 1973: 42; Kessler 1989. Kessler goes on to argue that v. 6a only makes sense as part of the same text with vv. 5 and 6b if one understands them as not selling grain but lending it, and so making debt slaves eventually of those who cannot pay back; so that not only are they the same people, but their object is the same: to gain power over the poor. The only difficulty with this attractive interpretation is the reference to money payment ('making the shekel great'); Kessler refers to interest payments, but the usual understanding is that interest was added to the principal and paid in the same way, in kind in this case.
56. Fleischer 1989: 192.

made by a well-to-do peasant supplementing his income with a bit of moneylending.[57] Thus Fendler's conclusion that 'neither on the side of the exploiters nor on the side of those exploited is there any question of a homogeneous class' should not be dismissed as easily as it sometimes is.[58] She makes a strong case that given differences in wealth in rural society, the pressure of taxes and interest bearing on the peasant might well drive him to mean and grasping conduct towards his poorer neighbours. However, the fact that in all the other references to exploitation in Amos the culprits are of the upper class makes it less likely that a different group is in view here.[59]

2.b.3 *The Acts of Oppression*

We come now to the heart of our inquiry. How does the text of Amos understand the conduct of the oppressors in moral terms? It is sometimes difficult, as we have seen, to identify exactly what the practices attacked are. But what is never in doubt is the attitude the text takes up towards it, the ethical judgment that it makes on it, often in the name of YHWH. Rhetorically this can be understood as the use of both *logos* and *pathos*, argument and emotion:[60] it justifies the punishment logically, but it also arouses horror at the crimes of those attacked. Since they are for the most part directly addressed, it can be seen as an attempt to arouse self-disgust, to make them understand what their acts really mean. But this is expressed in a number of different ways, using different moral categories, and it is this that I wish to explore. We shall go through the four or five passages that we have singled out, but at each point we shall bring in similar judgements that are made in subsequent places.

The announcement which introduces the indictment against Israel in Amos 2.6a is formulated identically to those at the head of all the other oracles against the nations. It accuses Israel of 'transgressions', 'rebellions', using the noun *peša'*, which indeed means 'rebellion' in a political sense,[61] and in the priestly vocabulary 'deliberate sin' against God. It expresses the idea that the acts indicted are sins against God just as much as against humanity; and in Amos 2.6 specifically that the acts of oppression detailed

---

57. However, I show below (p. 109) that the low value of the pledge does not necessarily imply a small loan.

58. Fendler 1973: 51 (my translation); and see pp. 49–52; see also Fleischer 1989: 295–96 and Pleins 2001: 370–71. Sicre's discussion (1984: 150–52) is thorough and fair.

59. Cf. my comment on Bendor's similar argument above, Chapter 2, n. 45.

60. Two of Aristotle's three categories of 'proofs' (*Rhetoric* I.2.3 [1926: 16–17]); the other, *ethos*, convincing the hearers of the character of the speaker, is also prominent in Amos, as Möller argues, 2003: 132–33.

61. I see no merit in the view of Polley 1989: 66–67, that it refers here to breach of treaty obligations. Where is the evidence that all these nations had treaties with David, or that anyone in the eighth century or later cared if they had?

in vv. 6b–8 are just as much sins against God as the war crimes in the first six oracles.[62] Amos 5.12a repeats the judgment. The acts in question have been much discussed, and a number of phrases are obscure, as the commentaries will show. However, it is widely agreed that Amos 2.6b and 8a refer to practices in connection with indebtedness. This is certain in 8a, where the technical term *ḥᵃbûlîm* is used, indicating that the garments are security (or possibly distraint)[63] for debt; while 6b very likely has to do with bondage for debt, possibly with sale into permanent slavery, as in Neh. 5.6 (cf. Joel 3.6 [Hebrew 4.6]). As I have indicated, Amos 2.7b may deal with the sexual abuse of a bondmaid. Amos 2.7a is too general to pinpoint the practices attacked; 8b appears to refer to the personal appropriation of fines, but does not indicate whether this was an accepted practice or whether the fines themselves were legitimate.

If it is difficult to tell precisely what acts are in question here, other passages in Amos are even less informative. Only 8.6, on the use of fraudulent measures in the corn trade, is crystal clear; 5.11 probably refers to taxes, and 5.12 to the corruption of the law courts. But we cannot identify with precision the practices whereby the treasuries of Samaria were filled 'with violence and rapine' (3.10), or precisely how the women of Samaria were 'exploiting the poor and crushing the needy' (4.1): perhaps through taxation, or by overdriving the workers on their private estates, or by extracting debt payments (with interest) from peasants whose vineyards or whose persons had been distrained.[64] All we can do is to recall our discussion of the general means whereby the Hebrew kingdoms became class societies, including taxation, foreclosure and enslavement. All of these practices are condemned, but it is not always possible to say which are in mind in any particular place.

In all these cases we are dealing with uses of power which from the ethical point of view of the text are abuses, but would have been regarded as acceptable in the actors' circles. Whether they were *legal* is a question probably unanswerable in the terms understood by modern societies under the rule of law. The law was made by the judges, and the judges were the class which is here under attack.[65] In any case, the text is only interested in whether they are *moral*. And this it tells us in the following ways.

We have already noted that the characterization of the victim as *ṣaddîq* stands right at the head of the first passage, once it gets down to details

---

62. So Paul 1991: 45–46.

63. Paul (1991: 83–84, with literature in n. 402) argues for this meaning rather than the usual 'taken in pledge'. Frymer-Kensky 2001 supports this.

64. Fleischer distinguishes the sense of the two half-lines: they exploit poor peasants (*dallîm*) *financially* and slaves or day-labourers (*'ebyônîm*) *physically*.

65. It is unlikely that texts like Exodus 22–23 functioned as law in our sense. See below, Chapters 4 and 6.

(Amos 2.6b). And this is of course a moral term. It does not necessarily make a moral judgment on the person to whom it is applied—the translation 'righteous' is misleading—but it does certainly imply a moral judgment of the action described. The *ṣaddîq* has rights or is in the right, and to 'sell' him or to 'persecute' him (Amos 5.12) is to wrong him, to take away his rights. In 2.6 the right that he loses is his freedom, assuming that the verse refers to a sale by the creditor. In 5.12 the context is the court of law, so that the right the poor man loses is the right to hear his case judged fairly, as a result of bribery. He is 'shoved aside in the gate' where cases are heard.

More than once it is made clear that the motivation for this is financial greed: 'for silver', 2.6; 'taking a bribe', 5.12. It is not bribery as such that is the centre of concern, but taking bribes to pervert the justice of the poor.

The first part of Amos 2.7, which NRSV translates 'they who trample the head of the poor into the dust of the earth', is difficult. We need not try to sort out all the difficulties, but will just comment on the first word, the verb which is read *haššō'ᵃpîm* in the MT. This may be translated 'who chase, who hunt down' (cf. Ps. 56.2, 3), and Fleischer goes for this understanding.[66] Others however, like the NRSV and following the lead of the LXX and the Vulgate, take it as a variant spelling of *haššāpîm*, 'who trample'.[67] In either case, we are introduced to a new moral category, that of violence, whether understood literally or figuratively. The same phrase reappears in Amos 8.4, and 'who crush the needy' in Amos 4.1 expresses a similar idea.[68] Hunting, trampling and crushing are violent actions. No doubt they are meant metaphorically; but the choice of metaphor is vital for understanding how the text views the action of the oppressors. The poor are subject to coercion at least. Where there is a disparity of power, the powerful often need not use physical violence to achieve their ends. But the ethical vision of the text, working through metaphor, uncovers the violence hidden in all coercive actions.

The word most commonly translated 'violence' in English bibles is *ḥāmās*. This frequently means physical violence and always implies 'the cold-blooded and unscrupulous infringement of the personal rights of others, motivated by greed and hate and often making use of physical violence and brutality.'[69] In Amos 3.10, as often,[70] it is linked with *šōd*, which frequently means 'devastation', but in this connection is variously understood as 'robbery' (NRSV, REB), or 'oppression' (*HALOT*). In fact the two words form a hendiadys implying violent, ruthless oppression and exploitation. In an

---

66. Fleischer 1989: 30, 57–58.
67. See, e.g., Paul 1991: 79.
68. The word in 5.11 translated 'you trample' in NRSV is now widely understood to mean 'you exact taxes'. See above, Chapter 2, n. 16.
69. *TDOT* s.v. See also Pons 1981: 30–38.
70. Jer. 6.7; 20.8; Ezek. 45.9; Hab. 1.3.

evocative phrase Amos accuses the people of Samaria of 'storing up in their strongholds *ḥāmās wāšōd'*, or as the REB puts it, '*the gains of* violence and robbery'. The capital city is a place which exists by its brutal infringements of the rights of others. Amos' phrase 'storing up' violence and oppression implies that this is how the treasuries have been filled. The wealth stored in the warehouses of the walled city of Samaria has been gained by violent oppression: its possessors have no more right to it than a gang of bandits.

The last expression in Amos 2 which appears to express a moral judgment is the phrase 'to profane my holy name' at the end of Amos 2.7. Not merely the phrase but the idea is unique in Amos, and as Wolff says is characteristic of Ezekiel.[71] It does not easily fit in with the other ideas in Amos.[72] Its background is ritual and the phraseology is priestly, which is far from characteristic of Amos, except for its ironic use in 4.4–5. It may have been inserted by an editor who understood the sexual charge in this verse as having to do with so-called 'ritual prostitution': Wolff refers to Hos. 4.14. A similar judgment is not expressed in any other prophet in relation to oppression; it is not used even by Ezekiel when he concentrates on this subject in Ezekiel 22. So it is not in any case useful for building up a broader picture of the moral assessment of social injustice.

In Amos 3.9, representatives of foreign powers are summoned to observe the 'tumult and oppression'[73] in Samaria. The first word (*mᵉhûmōt*) does not immediately suggest a moral judgment; but it fairly clearly does so in Ezek. 22.5 and Prov. 15.16, as Paul notes,[74] and his translation 'outrages' is a sound one. The second word, *ᶜašûqîm*, is a plainly ethical term and the standard word for what we are discussing: the verb *ᶜšq* invariably means to 'oppress', and the noun *ᶜōšeq* 'oppression'. It is often associated explicitly with unjust gain or the expropriation of property, and, as Fleischer argues, always implies it.[75] *ᶜšq* is linked with *gzl* 'rob' (and their respective nouns) in several texts, for example Isa. 30.12; Jer. 21.12; Mic. 2.2; and in other ways it may connote the same thing:[76] that is, obtaining property or profit by extortion, by the use of superior social—political or economic—power. In other words, it is 'exploitation'. It is a constant prophetic theme that what the rich have obtained from the poor is robbed from them. Thus when Amos in 4.1 accuses the 'cows of Bashan' of *oppressing* the poor when they demand drink of their husbands, he means that the wine has been obtained by some oppressive use of power. 'Exploiting the poor' would be an appropriate

71. Wolff 1977: 133–34, cf. 167, n. 294.
72. Despite Rudolph 1971: 144 and Paul 1991: 83, who substitute assertion for argument.
73. Abstract plurals: the natural English translation is in the singular.
74. Paul 1991: 115.
75. Fleischer 1989: 89–90.
76. Compare for example Lev. 6.2 (Hebrew 5.21); Deut. 24.14; 1 Sam. 12:3; Prov. 22.16; Mal. 3.5.

translation. Amos and the prophets generally are not interested in the legal titles by which such gains may be justified: no matter how legal, the squeezing out of surplus product is immoral.

Thus the people of Samaria, who 'store up violence and oppression in their strongholds', 'do not know how to do right ($n^e k \bar{o} h \hat{a}$)'. 'The abstract noun designates that which is . . . "straightforward, honest, just, correct".'[77] To say that this is beyond them is to say in the most general and comprehensive way that they are immoral. But the context focuses this upon their acts of oppression, of violence and exploitation.

We move to Amos 5. We have already dealt with the accusations in v. 12b; v. 10 and the general statement in v. 12a remain. Verse 10 forms a chiasm with v. 12b, both referring to 'the gate', and accusing those whose acts of oppression are detailed in v.11a, but not given a moral assessment.[78] Verse 12b deals with their actions in court, their successful denial of justice to the innocent poor, v. 10 with the attitude they take up to those who take part in the trial, which assists them in their machinations: 'they hate the arbitrator[79] and detest the honest witness'. This implies more than mere attitudes: they hate these men because they are an obstacle to their plans, and their hatred issues in conspiracy to procure an unjust verdict. But the text mentions their hatred because it brings their lack of principle to a crystalline focus: they reject all that is true, they hate everyone who expresses the truth. They are for lies instead of truth because they are for injustice and cannot admit it.

The final passage in Amos 8 includes a number of phrases we have already met with; indeed there is some merit in the view that it has been partly formulated on the basis of 2.6–8.[80] The impatience with the taboo days attributed to those addressed is not given a specific moral assessment, but it is clearly seen as an expression of their greed—more for power than for money if Kessler's argument referred to above is accepted.[81] The use of false weights and measures raises a theme familiar in the legal literature (Lev. 19.35–36; Deut. 25.13–15) and in wisdom (Prov. 16.11). Fraudulent balances are referred to, with the same phrase $m\bar{o}'z^e n\hat{e}\ mirm\hat{a}$, in Prov. 11.1; 20.23. The latter word expresses a moral judgment: 'deceit', 'fraud'.

2.b.4 *The Law and the Prophet*
It was argued by Ernst Würthwein that Amos derives all his condemnations from the law, and this was refined by Robert Bach, who shows that all the

---

77. Paul 1991: 117.
78. See above, Chapter 2, n. 16, for the sense of *bōšas^{e}kem*.
79. See Wolff 1977: 246; Paul 1991: 171.
80. Wolff 1977: 325–26.
81. n. 55.

condemnations in Amos in some way echo the 'apodictic' laws in the 'Covenant Code' (mainly in Exod. 22.18–23.19), not the 'casuistic' laws in Exod. 21.1–22.17, and even argues that one or two are aimed against the casuistic laws, by for example condemning enslavement for debt (2.6; 8.6 compared with Exod. 21.1–11).[82] Bach relied on Alt's view[83] that these two types of law are of totally different origin and that only the apodictic law is genuinely Israelite. Many followed Würthwein, if not Bach, but since the fifties, scholarship has tended, except in the most conservative circles, to revert to Wellhausen's view that the prophets are prior to the law.[84]

It is not a simple matter (simple to state, but hard to decide!) of literary priority. There can be little doubt that there is *some* relationship between Amos 2.8 and Exod. 22.26–27 (Hebrew 25–26), since the text makes it clear that the garments are being used to sleep on, therefore presumably at night. The selection of this example from a wide range of possible abuses would otherwise imply too much of a coincidence, though it is equally possible that the legal text depends on Amos. But is this an appeal to law as such, or to a moral concern expressed equally in the law and in the prophetic denunciation? Is the argument that the people are condemned because they have broken the law as such? Miranda is clear on this point: 'For the prophets the law is important only because of its content of justice . . . They base themselves on the fact of injustice, not on the fact that injustice may be legally prohibited.'[85]

I concur with this, at least as concerns Amos, and would go further. My point is that the apodictic law is not what we understand by law, but moral teaching or exhortation. In it YHWH does not define offences and prescribe penalties, but appeals to humane, or reverential (Exod. 22.28–30), feeling, or to self-respect (22.31), and warns of his judgment (22.23–24, 27).[86] Its moral appeals have the same logical structure and theological weight as those of prophecy itself. The Amos text is not accusing anyone of 'breaking the law', and as Miranda rightly says, if the prophets had wanted to do that one would have expected them to have quoted a law at least occasionally.[87] But there is no 'law' of the kind which can be 'broken'. Rather, both the prophet and the 'law' appeal to known norms of humane conduct, of 'justice and righteousness', norms which are exemplified in the 'apodictic law', but

---

82. Würthwein 1950; Bach 1957.

83. Alt 1966: 79–132.

84. E.W. Davies discusses the question in relation to Isaiah (Davies 1981), and rejects such dependence; but he does not formulate the question in the way Miranda and I do. Nor does Fleischer (1989: 317–22), who shows that no literary dependence on the Covenant Code can be demonstrated.

85. Miranda 1977: 167.

86. In the Hebrew text respectively vv. 27–29; 30; 22–23, 26.

87. Miranda 1977: 166.

cannot be limited by it. If the oppressors do not know how to act with justice and kindness, no law can compel them to do so, and they are condemned, not by the law, but by the God of justice, both in the prophet and in the 'law'. John Barton argues in a similar way in his proposal of 'natural law' as one of the sources of Old Testament ethics.[88]

We can now sum up the essence of the moral judgements made on acts of oppressors in Amos. All their actions are offences against God, but in the first place against humanity. The text is more interested in the effects on the victims than in the motives of the oppressors: no word describes them as greedy or power-mad, even though it is implied that such are their motives; we have just the one glimpse of the women of Samaria calling for drinks. Whether their victims are citizens who possess customary rights in land and in the community or are landless labourers makes little difference. They deprive them of rights if they have any, exploit them, robbing them of what little wealth they have by using their superior political and economic power, deny them justice in the courts, and finally enslave them. To this end they commit violence and reject truth and justice in the courts. Put in simple terms, they commit robbery, violence, fraud—in a word, injustice.

These texts of Amos catch in sharp focus the abuse of patronage. According to many texts there was a right and humane way to exercise the privilege of power, as we shall see in the next chapter. However, in Amos, and the prophets generally, there is no interest in defining the limits of humane conduct towards the poor, nor is there any indication whether such institutions as distraint and debt servitude, or indeed taxation and the corvée, were acceptable in themselves. All that they can see is that their effects are deadly. The poor are bought and sold, their property and goods are diverted to the use of the rich, they are drained dry of what little wealth they had. That is enough. What makes the prophetic texts distinctive and enduringly important is the clarity of their moral vision. What economists like Silver justify as necessities for economic progress they see as robbery with violence.

2.c. *The Paradox of Amos*

The powerful indictments of the oppressors in Amos continue to inspire those concerned for the rights of the poor which are being taken away from them to this day. Each of the passages we have studied can be read as a denunciation of abuses which are going on today, and as a revelation of the oppressive character of modes of production very different from that which existed in ancient Israel. The oppressed reader of Amos can and does find in the book a voice to express his or her own experience of oppression. R. Martin-Achard reports on the work on Amos by J. and F. Atger,

88.   Barton 1979; 1998: 58–76.

first worked on by an ecumenical group in Morocco, then re-read in the
night [in 1965] which fell on Casablanca when order had been restored in
the working-class areas with machine-gun fire, arrests and beatings. 'The
message of Amos . . . struck us with the force of a whip', they write. 'We
would not perhaps have heard it with such power if we had not lived here,
but it is that which has enabled us to make sense of all these events, of our
whole life in Morocco from 1957 to 1965; it has enabled us to set all that
in its true light, on a level quite different from any political, cultural or
humanistic analysis we might have tried to undertake.'[89]

But within the book of Amos itself these passages function in a rather
different way, as we have seen. They do not serve to illustrate the class
divisions opening up within Israel's society; as we have seen, the text does
not emphasize the class of the oppressors, only that of the victims. Nor is
God celebrated in this book as the deliverer of the poor (unless Amos 9.13–15
can be seen in that way, as Coote in effect argues).[90] Verbs characteristic of
this theme such as *g'l* 'redeem' or *yš'* 'save' do not occur at all; *nṣl* 'rescue'
only ironically (3.12). YHWH's response to these transgressions is to destroy Israel, with immense suffering by all classes. This, as we have already
seen, is the paradox of the book. A class confrontation is transmuted into a
national one. The oppressors are seen primarily as representatives of their
state. Amos is denounced by the custodian of the royal sanctuary of Israel
as a conspirator against the crown, and claimed by Judah as the voice of
YHWH roaring from Zion.

But the edge of the divine sword is not so easily turned. Although this is a
strong element in the book's rhetoric, others cannot be excluded. As we
have seen, it may be read as a call to justice, and it is filled with denunciations of oppression of one kind or another. It menaces the editors of the
book themselves with its power. The editors were among those whose living
depended on the extraction of taxes from the kind of small peasants whose
oppression their own text denounces. This is a contradiction of a kind more
serious than any we have so far noted. It is well expressed by Coote. 'The
very social group that Amos condemned in Samaria is now, in Jerusalem,
sponsoring the preservation of his oracles . . . Think of the long-range
planning that went into executing such a composition, the leisure time it
required, who fed, clothed and sheltered the author during his work.'[91] This
suggests, as Coote notes, the patronage required for the production of such
a work; and also the way it must have been created out of the surplus
material production of the kind of peasants whose exploitation it deplores.

But we should not conclude from this that the attack on injustice in the

89. Martin-Achard 1984: 257–58 (my translation).
90. Coote 1981: 121–27.
91. Coote 1981: 100.

book of Amos is hypocritical or insincere. It represents, we shall see as we go on, a conviction about justice in society that runs right through the Hebrew Bible and is an integral part of Hebrew culture. It is not a distinctive viewpoint of the oppressed classes—even if the rather confused references to Amos' calling[92] could show that he belonged to them—for, as we shall see in the next chapter, it is found again and again in texts which were necessarily penned in the circles of the upper class, or at least of those serving them, the scribes. We have seen how Walzer argues that hegemonic classes and their critics share a common culture.[93] As in class-divided agrarian societies in general, a widespread moral conviction of *noblesse oblige* exists among the aristocratic class, the class of patrons, even if they fail to observe it; but it is not confined to them.[94] Of course, the aristocratic attitude is not altruistic. It is essential to their position as patrons that they should be understood to be benevolent to their clients. The conduct of those denounced in Amos is outrageous on many counts: but it is *ideologically* outrageous in that it fatally undermines the supposed concord of society on which the position of the governing class rests. There may be tensions and contradictions in the book as it is, but without the condemnations of oppression it would make no sense at all; they are the indispensable basis of everything else that is said. That is precisely why their force cannot be evaded, neither in the time of Amos, nor in that of the editors, nor in our own day.

And long after the kingdom of Israel has passed into history, followed swiftly, on the scale of historical time, by the kingdom of Judah, and even serious Bible readers have difficulty in remembering the names and order of their kings, Amos is remembered, not primarily as the prophet of the fall of Israel, but as the prophet of justice for the poor, even though the structure of his text serves the former end rather than the latter. The concern for social justice has triumphed over its co-optation into an aristocratic national project, and the rhetoric of structure is deconstructed by the rhetoric of concern.

3. *Surveying the Prophets*

Space does not permit a study of each of the prophetic texts in the same detail. To a large extent, Amos will have to stand as the representative of them all. I am conscious of the truth of Sicre's comment, that 'to speak of "the social thought of the prophets" is almost as ambiguous as to speak

92. Discussed in detail by Paul 1991: 34, 247–48.
93. Above, pp. 13–14.
94. Cf. Sneed 1996. See further below, Chapter 4.

of "the symphony in the 19th century" '.[95] They do each have their own distinct emphases and approaches, but in fact, much of what we have said about Amos is true of them all. All of them, as I shall try to show, originate from upper-class social locations. This can be shown in many cases not just in the general sense that all writing was an upper-class activity, but by identifying a specific group with which the book was associated. All of them assume an upper-class audience and have the typical upper-class concern with the fate of cities and kingdoms. All of them announce war as the punishment ordained by God for their hearers, and therefore raise the problem discussed above, though *perhaps* in a less acute form, in that social injustice is only one of their concerns. They all contain ideological tensions and contradictions, but because they are associated with varying social locations, these are not the same for all of them; so we shall need to bring out the social location of each.

We should remember that all the books date in their present form from the Second Temple period, after the disaster of the fall of the capital, temple and kingdom of Judah. Looking back from the other side of the gulf, it was easy to acknowledge the guilt of the fathers, including the guilt of oppression, because it functioned as a theodicy: it explained the disaster as being the will of God rather than a meaningless happening, and that gave a reason for including the denunciations of oppressors and pronouncements of judgment against them, provided they were part of a structure which included warning for the present and hope for the future.

What we shall do is first to identify those texts that have a significant concern with social injustice and oppression, then characterize each of the books in which they are found in social terms, and finally show how they assess oppression in moral terms, as we have done with Amos, and using headings mostly derived from our study of Amos.

The most significant passages in the prophets denouncing social injustice are the following. The list is limited to those which clearly accuse people of oppressing the poor. Words for 'poor' may not necessarily be used, but it is clear in all these texts that the wrongdoing denounced is against economically weaker people. Texts where this is not clear have not been included, which means that a number of texts which may be significant in the inquiry are not mentioned here, though one or two of them may be referred to in passing later. However, each passage is given in the extent which makes it a complete rhetorical unit, which means that in some cases not all of it is concerned with this subject. I have also not included texts about oppression by foreigners and conquerors, only those which imply a split within society.

Isa. 1.21–26; 3.13–15; 5.1–7, 8–10; 10.1–4; 58.1–12.
Jer. 2.34; 5.20–29; 7.1–7; 22.13–19; 34.8–22

---

95. Sicre 1984: 43 (my translation).

Ezek. 22.1–16, 23–31; 34.1–31
Amos 2.6–16; 3.9–15; 4.1–3; 5.10–12; 8.4–7 (as dealt with above)
Mic. 2.1–5, 6–11; 3.1–4, 9–12

4. *Micah*

Micah stands next to Amos in the prominence of accusations of social oppression, but focuses on Judah (the one passage on Samaria, Mic. 1.2–7, does not mention this theme); and these two books are the only parts of the 'Book of the Twelve' which contain such material, though there is also material of limited relevance in Habakkuk, Zephaniah, and Zechariah. Although in much recent work the 'Book of the Twelve' has been treated as a redactional unity,[96] it certainly does not form a rhetorical unity.

The material in Micah is extremely diverse: it swings from some of the fiercest denunciations of oppression in the prophetic corpus (e.g. Mic. 2.1–2; 3.1–4) to assurances of restoration and dominance for Zion (e.g. Mic. 4.1–13), and back to apprehensive recognition of national sin (Mic. 7.1–10). This is what enabled Mosala to make the ideological analysis I discussed above. So we return to the question we posed there: for what purpose are the criticisms of oppression included in a composition that appears to look for a political and military restoration of the Jerusalem ruling class, and what does the composition as a whole mean?

It is vital to realize that the judgment oracles are not replaced or toned down, but incorporated: most immediately, as Jörg Jeremias shows,[97] into a structure which is as much concerned with religious sin as with social oppression (Mic. 2.10; 6.16), and which rolls together the individual judgments proclaimed by Micah (e.g. Mic. 2.5; 3.4, 6–7; 6.13–15) into a universal one (2.3–4) which threatens the nation as a whole: compare what we said about Amos. Thus Micah is seen to proclaim, already in the days of Hezekiah, the eventual fall of Jerusalem and the destruction of Judah by the Babylonians. The promise of the triumph of Zion has to be seen against that background, and as so often the last verses of the composition are the key. 'Who is a God like you, pardoning iniquity? . . . You will cast all our sins into the depths of the sea.' (7.18–20) The present humiliation of Zion is due to her sins. YHWH's judgment upon her was true, and it is proper that those sins should be remembered; but her faithful, pardoning God will restore her to a position of honour and glory among the nations. This is

96. e.g. Collins 1993: 59–87.
97. Jeremias 1971: 349–52.

the argument by which the editors of Micah seek to encourage their compatriots. One might cast against them Anselm's comment '*Nondum considerasti quanti ponderis sit peccatum*'! 'You have not yet considered the true weight of sin.' That sin was seen in their own text as 'chopping people up and boiling them in a cauldron'. What saves the book from sheer contradiction is maybe the promise to the peasant in Mic. 4.4, contrasting with the visions of military and imperial glory for Zion, and the single verse of contrition in Mic. 7.9.

The precise social circles responsible for the book are impossible to define. All we can say is that they are deeply interested in Jerusalem and its political influence, therefore must belong to a ruling-class group based, or formerly based, in Jerusalem. The deepest contradiction in the book is that this group transmits and uses as a theodicy of the fate of Jerusalem oracles which plainly announce the condemnation of such ruling circles: 'the heads of Jacob and rulers (*qᵉṣînê*) of the house of Israel' (Mic. 3.1, cf. v. 9). They 'build Zion with blood and Jerusalem with wrong' (Mic. 3.10), which presumably refers to the use of the corvée to reinforce the defences of Jerusalem, probably against the Assyrian attack. Wolff notes that the text does not refer to the victims, either here or in Mic. 2.1–2, as 'poor';[98] the concern, even more than in Amos, is for the landholding peasant under pressure from the state. Wolff also sees Mic. 2.1–2, 8–9 as referring to the commandeering of property in time of war, rather than to the machinations of creditors.[99] But McKane's detailed discussion casts doubt on this and defends the more usual interpretation, that it refers to foreclosure on mortgaged land.[100] Of course, as McKane acknowledges, the landowners thus extending their possessions would include royal officials.

The text thus rises up against its editors more powerfully even than that of Amos. One of the major injustices—if Wolff is right, virtually the only one—which prompts the fall of Jerusalem is one which is implicated in the creation of powerful fortified cities such as they see Jerusalem becoming once more. However, I do not think Mosala is right in seeing the authors of his 'C' texts as taking over the role of the oppressed in relation to their captors.[101] Such words are not used in Micah—it is much more a feature of Isaiah 40–55—and the quality of YHWH to which appeal is made is not his compassion for the poor and oppressed, but his faithful love for his people and forgiveness of their sins (Mic. 7.18–20).

---

98.   Wolff 1990: 100.
99.   Wolff 1990: 74–75.
100.   McKane 1998: 61–65; so, e.g., Hillers 1984: 33.
101.   Mosala 1989: 132.

5. *Isaiah*

The book of Isaiah is far too long and complex for it to be possible to discover a single rhetorical aim in it. However, there is a theme which runs through it like a red thread and is clearly of key significance in each of the three sections into which historical critics have divided it: that of 'Zion's final destiny', to adopt Christopher Seitz's phrase.[102] Zion in Isaiah stands not primarily for the place of the Temple, but much more for the seat of the Davidic dynasty and the mother-city of Judah and indeed of Israel.[103] It is not new to suggest that the book can be seen as originating and developing in circles very close to the Davidic house. Isaiah himself is represented as the confidant of kings; whether this is historically accurate or not, it is how the text wishes its putative author and protagonist to be seen. Key texts such as Isa. 9.2–7 (Hebrew 1–6) and Isa. 11.1–9 express a future-oriented theology of the royal house, with a particular ideology which we shall have more to say about in Chapter 5. Even in the latter part of the book, the Servant of YHWH has more of the features of a Davidic king than of a prophet or priest,[104] and of course most of Isaiah 49–54 and 60–62 and 66 is concerned with Zion. The Davidic accent may be thought to be absent in the last part of the book, so-called Trito-Isaiah; but I would maintain that even here the speaker in Isa. 61.1 is a kingly figure.[105] Pleins observes: 'While the precise context of the compilation of Isaiah will probably always remain elusive, the persistent royal hope ought to at least make us consider the possibility that the larger text emerged from the circles surrounding Jehoiachin'.[106] The book is certainly not uncritical of kings and kings' policies, but from a position of close sympathy.

If Zion is the predominant subject of the book's rhetoric, what does it seek to persuade the reader about it? Seitz argues that in Isaiah 1–39, although the dominant note is the assurance of YHWH's protection for the city even amid judgment for the people and destruction for the land, the theology is 'supple and ambiguous enough to allow even for the overrunning of Zion in 587 B.C.E., especially when this theology was seen from the perspective of the extensive Isaiah judgment tradition with which it formed an integral part'.[107] The varying fates held out for the city are closely linked to the obedience and faith of the current representative of the Davidic

---

102. Seitz 1991: title.
103. The distinctive Isaianic title for YHWH, 'The Holy One of Israel', as a title of the God worshipped at Jerusalem, surely reflects the ancient claim of Jerusalem and the house of David to rule over Israel as well as Judah as 'all Israel'.
104. So, e.g., Eaton 1979: 92–102.
105. Houston 1987; cf. Eaton 1979: 90–91.
106. Pleins 2001: 263. This can hardly be intended to refer to the book's final form.
107. Seitz 1991: 146.

house: Ahaz is not told the same thing as Hezekiah. 'Inviolability' is not, according to Seitz, the right expression for the message of Isaiah 36–37, but it is positive enough to demand the extended reflection on the disaster of 587 that we find in Isaiah 40–55. This passage seeks to persuade Zion's disheartened and demoralized community of the purpose of YHWH to restore them, now that they have served their time, and regardless of their present conduct. Isaiah 56–66 asserts that this, the righteousness of YHWH, depends for its effective expression on the righteousness of the community, seeking to persuade them both to trust in the divine righteousness and to establish it in the public square. This brings together the distinctive uses of $s^e d\bar{a}q\hat{a}$ in the two previous sections, as seen in Isa. 56.1.[108]

Yet in this book which has such a supportive relationship to the royal house of Judah and its citadel, the centre of state exploitation and the main engine of class formation, we find passages which clearly denounce oppressors of the upper and especially the official class, as in Isa. 1.23; 3.13–15; 10.1–4. Isaiah 1.23 is a scathing condemnation of the corruption of the official class of Jerusalem, evidently responsible for justice in the courts, which even the utterly unprotected fatherless and widow cannot obtain. Isaiah 3.13–15 links in a single condemnation 'elders' and 'officers': *ziqnê 'ammô w^eśārāyw*, the powerful landowners and the governing class—just as in Nehemiah 5, which uses different vocabulary. Isaiah 10.1–4 attacks 'the writers of wicked decrees', which deprive the poor of their just claims, therefore again undoubtedly the official class, probably judges giving judgment in individual cases rather than administrators issuing general decrees.[109] In fact Isa. 5.8–10 is certainly also aimed at the upper classes, despite Bendor's attempt to show it refers to village machinations,[110] simply because the whole context of Isaiah 5 is so: vv. 11–12 is obviously aimed at rich people, and v. 23 at judges, like 1.23. Chaney, however, perhaps unduly narrows 5.3, 7 in making them refer more or less exclusively to the government and even to the king personally.[111] There is no other Isaianic oracle in which the king is accused of complicity in oppression.

There are a number of considerations which make all this not unexpected. We have already noted the tradition of *noblesse oblige*, the ethical tradition that required the rich to look after the welfare of the poor who were in their power—or were their clients, which amounts to the same thing—and not to abuse their power over them for their own ends. As the head of the administration the king would have been expected to encourage his staff to follow this tradition. He was responsible for the peace and concord

---

108. Rendtorff 1993; Leclerc 2001: 133.
109. Kaiser 1983: 227.
110. Bendor 1996: 252–53.
111. Chaney 1999: 111–17.

of society, and its freedom from injustice and oppression was essential to this.[112]

John Barton shows how in 'Isaiah of Jerusalem' (by which he means essentially Isaiah 1–39),

> the essence of morality is co-operation in maintaining the ordered structure which prevails, under God's guidance, in the natural constitution of things, and the keynote of the whole system is order, a proper submission to one's assigned place in the scheme of things and the avoidance of any action that would challenge the supremacy of God or seek to subvert the orders he has established.[113]

Among these orders are the traditional structure of society. 'Folly produces a disregard for the orders in society which should mirror God's ordering of the universe, and anarchy ensues.'[114] In Isa. 3.1–7 the worst catastrophe the prophet can imagine falling on Jerusalem and Judah is the loss of its recognized leaders. In such a view, the duties of each person are closely related to their place in society. They owe fidelity and obedience to those above them—supremely to God—justice, kindness and care to those below. It is a characteristically aristocratic view of society and of ethics.

There was an equally strong and related tradition, going back to the early dynastic period in Sumer, that the king was personally responsible for defending the poor from oppression and destroying the oppressors. We shall be giving detailed attention to this in Chapter 5. We have already seen that there is limited evidence for any practical expression of this tradition in Judah.[115] None the less, the people expected it, and it comes as no surprise that a prophetic work composed in royal circles should allude to it, as in Isa. 11.1–9; again, this and similar passages in Isaiah will occupy us in more detail in Chapter 6.

Moreover such measures were to the political advantage of the royal house. We have already noted Chaney's argument that an important motive for measures of debt relief in ancient states, including Judah, would have been the factionalization of the elite.[116] What went for measures of debt relief might go equally for prophetic denunciation. Royal patronage of prophecy enabled other power centres in society to be undermined by denouncing their oppressive activities. After the exile, the Davidic house, to which I would see the authors of Trito-Isaiah as still close, was but one faction among many, but it could still have been to its advantage to point out oppression and corruption, as in Isaiah 58 and 59.

112. More on this below in Chapter 5.
113. Barton 1981: 11.
114. Barton 1981: 11.
115. Above, pp. 33–41.
116. Chaney 1991; above, p. 13.

6. *Jeremiah*

It is much easier to describe the rhetorical aim of the book of Jeremiah, for all its complexity and apparent confusion. The superscription tells us that Jeremiah prophesied 'until[117] the eleventh year of Zedekiah the son of Josiah, king of Judah, until the deportation of Jerusalem in the fifth month' (Jer. 1.3). This seems to be at odds with the contents of the book, which portray him as continuing to prophesy until after the murder of Gedaliah. But the postscript in Jeremiah 52 reverts to the fall of Jerusalem which had already been recounted in Jeremiah 39. This framing makes clear that, regardless of when his prophecies actually cease, the end towards which Jeremiah's prophesying is directed is the fall of Jerusalem, with the devasta- tion of the country and the deportation of a large part of the urban popula- tion. And it is only too obvious that this is the theme of the great mass of material in the book, for all its variety.

Structurally, the theme is presented in two halves of different character. Jeremiah 1–25 consists mainly of poetic oracles, punctuated by prose 'ser- mons', as they are generally called, and the occasional short narrative; these can be seen as giving structure to this otherwise rather formless collection.[118] The main point of both oracles and sermons, and the lessons drawn from the narratives of prophetic actions in Jeremiah 13 and 19, is to convey the clear message that Judah and Jerusalem are doomed because of their sin. Jeremiah 26–45 is given structure instead by a series of narratives. These portray the way in which the word of judgment given to Judah and Jerusalem through Jeremiah is rejected and has its way regardless. The message is the same: that doom is inescapable. This is counterpointed, how- ever, with assurances of restoration at a distant date (Jer. 29.10), partly focused on the exiles of 597 (Jer. 29.10–14), and gathered into a section in Jeremiah 30–33, which also shows a concern for the remnant of northern Israel.

When we turn to ask how the word of destruction is grounded, we find among varied material, mainly in Jeremiah 1–9, a focus in the accusation that the people 'do not know YHWH' (Jer. 2.8; 4.22; 8.7; 9.3 [Hebrew 2], 6 [Hebrew 5], 23, etc.). This theological formulation sums up the significance of a range of failings, including their ignorance or neglect of the traditions of YHWH's saving acts (Jer. 2.4–8), their turning from YHWH to other gods (Jer. 2.9–13; 3.1–5, etc.), Judah's irresponsible behaviour in inter- national affairs (Jer. 2.18–19), and the people's immorality in social and personal relationships (Jer. 4.22; 5.1–5; 9.1–9 [Hebrew 8.23–9.8]). The last category, in Laurent Wisser's study on 'social justice and the knowledge of

117. Omitting *tōm* with LXX.
118. Stulman 1998.

God in Jeremiah',[119] includes those relatively infrequent treatments of class and state oppression cited in the list above. One of these, the attack on Jehoiakim in Jer. 22.13–19, famously asserts that (for a king) to do justice and righteousness, and to judge the cause of the poor and needy 'is to know me, says YHWH' (Jer. 22.15–16).[120]

Pleins speaks of a 'blistering social critique'[121] in Jeremiah, subverted by the accumulation of later materials. There is indeed a strong and pervasive critique of social life, but Pleins misleads the reader by suggesting that this is primarily concerned with social injustice. He seeks to annex a more substantial extent of the book to its social critique by relating the pervasive critique of idolatry to it, and quotes Wisser's comment on Jer. 2.34 that 'in this passage, social injustice appears as a consequence of idolatry.'[122] Pleins explains that 'idols are sociologically understood as the concrete representation of a religiously based value system that accorded the urban establishment the primary role as powerholders chosen by the divine to govern the nation', who are then in a position to exploit the poor.[123]

There are considerable difficulties with this view. In the first place, we have to insist that sociologically speaking, *any* religious system may function to support the social and political establishment and to authorize its injustice. Yahwistic monolatry is as good as any other for this purpose, and of course not only in Amos and Isaiah but in Jeremiah itself we find penetrating criticism of the official cult of YHWH for this very reason.[124] The connection is in fact drawn most clearly in Jeremiah, in Jer. 7.8–11, and in a way which we do not find with the attacks on idolatry. And secondly, if this had been the point of the attacks on unfaithfulness and idolatry, one would expect that such a connection would be made, or at the very least that the critique of oppression would have appeared more frequently in such passages. In Jer. 2.34 the accusation of innocent blood is merely juxtaposed to the lengthy diatribe against unfaithfulness to YHWH; no connection is made explicit. And in any case, decisively, the official cult was the worship of YHWH: it was this and no other which functioned in the manner suggested. It could be argued that as YHWH is the defender of the poor and the God of justice, to oppress the poor was constructively to desert YHWH. This is theologically true, and is effectively what the text says in

---

119. Wisser 1982.
120. Robert Carroll (1986: 425–34) argues that Jer. 22.13–15a and 15b–17 were originally separate pieces which had nothing to do with kings, but have been taken together by the editors and read as a criticism of Jehoiakim (Jer. 22.18). Whether or not this is true, it is the editors' text that I am interpreting here.
121. Pleins 2001: 314.
122. Wisser 1982: 74.
123. Pleins 2001: 288.
124. Amos 5.21–24; Isa. 1.10–17; Jer. 7.1–15, 21–26.

Jer. 7.8–11; but it is not what it says in the passages on idolatry, where it says that they have deserted YHWH, not to oppress the poor, but to worship other gods.

The leading themes of Jeremiah, and its overall message that Jerusalem fell because of its people's refusal to obey YHWH, are those of the Deuteronomistic school, as represented in the book of Deuteronomy and in the Former Prophets, especially Kings. And it has long been recognized that the book as an edited work is to be associated with the Deuteronomists; the style of the prose portions makes this very clear.[125] However, this Deuteronomism is not in essence an element or layer to be attributed to a particular redactional moment in the book's history. The book as a whole, including the poetic oracles and the figure of Jeremiah himself, is part of that broad theological movement represented in the Hebrew Bible most strongly by Deuteronomy and the Deuteronomists.

Can we locate this movement on the social map? Weinfeld links it with the royal scribes. But as Patricia Dutcher-Walls shows, the book of Jeremiah itself, while it does not contradict this view, both broadens it and gives greater precision to it.[126] According to the book, Jeremiah was supported by various ruling-class elements, including 'some of the elders of the land' in Jer. 26.17, the priest Zephaniah in Jer. 29.24–29, and especially by some of the royal officials. To be more precise, Jer. 26.24 tells us that 'the hand of Ahikam the son of Shaphan was with Jeremiah' and saved his life at a time of extreme danger. Shaphan, we recall, was Josiah's secretary of state, who is said to have read him the scroll of the Torah when it was discovered in the Temple (2 Kgs 22.8–10), and Ahikam himself is said to have played a part in those events (2 Kgs 22.12). In Jeremiah 36 a number of officials are mentioned, several belonging to the family of Shaphan. All this group of officials show marked favour to Baruch and Jeremiah, and three of them urge the king not to burn the scroll (Jer. 36.25). Finally, Jeremiah is committed after the fall of Jerusalem to the care of Gedaliah, Ahikam's son, whom Nebuchadrezzar made governor of Judah (Jer. 39.14; 40.5). Whatever the historical status of these stories,[127] it is beyond question that whoever wrote them at least wished to give the impression that Jeremiah was a protégé of the house of Shaphan—and who could have wished to do so other than they themselves? The almost obsessive listing of everyone who was involved suggests an attempt to define the circle of the supporters of Jeremiah, who we can reasonably guess were also the editors of his book. Groups opposed to

---

125. For a detailed study of the vocabulary of the Deuteronomistic writings, including Jeremiah, see Weinfeld 1972: 320–65; on p. 361 he shows that Deuteronomistic clichés occur also in Jeremianic poetry.

126. Dutcher-Walls 1991.

127. Carroll expresses scepticism (R.P. Carroll 1986: 513–22, cf. 665–66).

him, including officials, are also mentioned (see Jer. 38.1). It is not too long a shot to conclude that these groups represent opposed factions within the ruling class, the latter being the pro-Egyptian element and the supporters of Jeremiah being the pro-Babylonians, as is obviously the case with Gedaliah, and a theme in the book is the counsel to submit to Babylon after 597 (Jeremiah 27–29).

It is notable that the editors report that their protégé Jeremiah himself was 'of the priests at Anathoth' (Jer. 1.1), in other words a member of the priestly house of Abiathar banished to his estate at Anathoth by Solomon, according to 1 Kgs 2.26. That is, he was a member of another faction among the privileged groups that found itself in permanent opposition. As for his patrons, though they were able to maintain their positions up to the fourth year of Jehoiakim according to Jeremiah 36, their policies were out of favour during most of the reigns of Jehoiakim and Zedekiah. They thus had plenty of incentive to patronize, edit and publish material of an oppositional character, and to use this to attribute blame after the fall of Jerusalem.

We might suggest that the book of Jeremiah, and perhaps the whole Deuteronomistic canon, originated in circles surrounding the house of Shaphan, initially perhaps at Mizpah during Gedaliah's governorship.[128] These were men of independent means, not totally dependent on the king, and able to maintain their positions under kings of different policies. They of course drew income from lands worked by others, and their earlier position had given them a considerable investment in the consolidation of the power of the state. However, as we have seen, that would not necessarily mean that they were uninterested in ideals of social justice, still less that they engaged in exploitative practices themselves, except in the absolute sense in which any reliance on the labour of others is regarded as exploitation. It is doubtful whether any Old Testament text does take this line, but this will be further explored in the next chapter.

However, the different works edited in these circles show varying attitudes towards this issue. It is an important issue for Deuteronomy,[129] but the Deuteronomistic History seems utterly uninterested in it.[130] Jeremiah occupies a middle position, with limited reference to it. The main point to note is

---

128. Cf. Albertz 1994: I.241–42, cf. II.382–87.

129. See below, Chapter 6.

130. Frick 1994. Weinfeld (1995: 46–48) refers to 2 Sam. 8.15, where David is said to have established justice and righteousness for his people; and earlier (1972: 154, esp. n. 2) he had argued that all the Judaean kings who are said to have done right in the eyes of YHWH must have issued liberative decrees. But whereas the text frequently elaborates this in cultic terms (e.g. 1 Kgs 15.12–15 on Asa) it never refers to liberative decrees or any other expression of social justice, and ignores the one such decree that we know about from another source (Jer. 34.8–9).

that Jeremiah and the Deuteronomistic History make YHWH's commandments, that is the Deuteronomic law, the standard of faithfulness to
YHWH, so that it cannot be said of Jeremiah, as we said of Amos, that the
text is not interested in obedience to the law as such: on the contrary, in the
prose portions this is repeatedly mentioned.

True, the poetic references to the oppression of the poor make no reference to commandments. But Jer. 7.3–11 is conventional and clichéd, as are
the prose sermons generally, and while the positive part in vv. 3–7 makes
reference to 'doing justice between one another' and relies on concepts of
justice rather than on commandments, the accusation in 8–11 appears to
cite the Decalogue and does not refer specifically to justice. Again, the
denunciation of the people of Jerusalem in Jer. 34.12–22 for re-enslaving
the Hebrew slaves they had bound themselves by covenant to free relies on
the quotation of Deut. 15.12 in v. 14 and the accusation of disobedience
(v. 17), and on the breach of oath ('you profaned my name', v. 16, cf. 19–20),
rather than on the injustice done to the slaves.

The judgment on injustice in the book of Jeremiah is not so much sub-
verted as subsumed into a structure centred on faithfulness to YHWH
and his commandments and covenant. In the prophecies of restoration in
Jeremiah 30–33 there appears to be a single clear reference to the theme, when
David's 'righteous branch' is said to 'execute justice and righteousness'
(Jer. 33.15), like David himself (2 Sam. 8.15).

7. *Ezekiel*

The rhetorical structure of the book of Ezekiel is very clear. It pivots upon
the report to Ezekiel in Ezek. 33.21 of the fall of Jerusalem. Up to that
point it has consistently sought to exclude any thought of escape for the city
and the inhabitants of Jerusalem and Judah, repeatedly and in varied ways
justifying the judgment upon them (Ezekiel 25–32 consist of oracles against
the nations, largely against Tyre and Egypt). From that point it proclaims
restoration, but 'not for your sake, but for the sake of my name', raising
hopes but repressing national pride. What the book sees as YHWH's will for
the restoration of the people in a reformed community cannot begin until
any remaining shreds of pride and hope in the old order have vanished.[131]
The three great vision sequences of the book, in Ezekiel 1–3, 8–11 and
40–48, picture the dynamic of this process through the image of the glory of
YHWH, which appears to Ezekiel in exile in Ezekiel 1, when he is called
to be a prophet, which he sees abandoning the temple and the city in Ezekiel
9–11, and returning in Ezekiel 43.

131. Pleins 2001: 335.

Of all the four great prophetic collections, Ezekiel is the easiest to place sociologically. Concerns, themes, vocabulary and style, as well as the explicit statement in Ezek. 1.1, place it among the circle of the Jerusalem priesthood; Ezek. 44.15 narrows this further to the family of Zadok, which provided the high priest from Solomon to Antiochus. And although it is likely that the present form of the book is the result of a redactional process, as with the other prophets, the priestly accent is distinctly traceable at every stage: in the visions, which are centred on an image of the glory of YHWH derived from the iconography of the Jerusalem temple;[132] in the oracles of judgment, which denounce the 'abominations' of the people; in the quasi-legal discourses like Ezekiel 18, which use themes and vocabulary similar to those of the Holiness Code in Leviticus;[133] and of course in the sketch of a restored polity in Ezekiel 40–48, which is centred on the temple and its ritual and limits priesthood to the Zadokites.

Like Isaiah and Jeremiah, then, Ezekiel is revealed as the work of one faction among the contestants for power in the exilic and post-exilic community, the Zadokite priesthood. The book explicitly attacks the faction which it perceives as its closest rival, the Levites (Ezek. 44.10–14), and limits the privileges of the ruler, who is called the 'prince' (*nāśî*), deliberately not 'king'.

The denunciations of social injustice and oppression in the book clearly serve this factional interest. The most important chapters in this regard are 22 and 34. The judgment of Jerusalem in Ezek. 22.1–16 focuses on the theme of bloodshed (see below, pp. 88–90), and in vv. 7–12 recites a string of accusations closely related to the Holiness Code, not all of which are in the area of social injustice. Of greater importance are Ezek. 22.23–31. This paragraph systematically lists the estates of the realm and accuses each of the acts of oppression and violence peculiar to it: the 'princes' (v. 25, following a probable textual emendation),[134] that is, the kings; the priests (v. 26), who are indeed not accused of oppression, but of violence to YHWH's teaching; the officials (v. 27); the prophets (v. 28); and the 'people of the land' (v. 29), namely the wealthy landowners.[135] If it is objected that factional interest would have omitted the priests, it should be remembered on the one hand that there were factions among the priests, as Ezekiel 44 shows, and on the other that Ezekiel also represents the exiles of 597 against the interests of those who remained under Zedekiah (Ezek. 11.14–16; 33.23–29), and though the comprehensive denunciations in Ezekiel 20–23 evidently go back into the past, Ezek. 22.26 could be taken as referring

---

132. Cf., e.g., 1 Kgs 6.23–28.
133. Zimmerli 1979: 46–52.
134. See *BHS*: *ʾašer nᵉśîʾ ehā* after the LXX in place of *qešer nᵉbîʾ ehā*.
135. See above, p. 39, n. 92.

especially to the priests in Jerusalem in Zedekiah's reign. Ezekiel 34.1–6, in a different mood, allegorically refers to the exploitative activities of the rulers, and probably also the officials, and Ezek. 34.17–22 to those of the 'people of the land'. In the course of the sketch of the reformed Israel, opportunity is again taken to criticise the kings for their rapacity. Ezekiel 45.8–9 and 46.18 imply that they had been in the habit of dispossessing people of their land; while Ezek. 46.17 seeks to prevent prebends from becoming heritable patrimonies of the official families.

This should not be taken as casting doubt on the genuineness of Ezekiel's 'commitment to the poor' underlined by Pleins.[136] There was clearly a priestly interest in discouraging the accumulation of landed wealth in a few families, who would then control the sources of priestly support through tithes, but the priests were evidently also the custodians of the theological and moral traditions which became the Torah.[137] We have already discussed this kind of ambiguity in a similar connection. It is perfectly correct to say that there is a stronger ethical commitment in the priestly tradition than it has been given credit for—Wellhausen still lives! But the evidence does not permit us to conclude that there is a greater commitment to the cause of the poor in Ezekiel than in Jeremiah. Both traditions criticize the oppression of the poor, both have an interest in doing so, but neither puts the issue in the forefront, despite their commitment to the ideal of social justice and to the religious traditions which supported it.

8. *Oppression in the Prophets*

We are now in a position to gather together and analyse the various ways in which social oppression is characterized in the prophets.

8.a. *The Victims*

We saw that in Amos the trio of the widow and fatherless and alien, those whom *traditional* society marginalized, are not mentioned as victims of oppression. The focus is on full citizens, adult males, who are being deprived of their rights. How does this issue stand in the other texts that we are now considering?

None of the others concern themselves exclusively with full citizens in the manner of Amos, but this is a concern in all of them, and the leading concern in all except perhaps Ezekiel. Isaiah 5.8–10 and Mic. 2.1–5 are explicitly concerned with the loss of land to peasant families. All of them

---

136. Pleins 2001: 336–38.
137. This issue will be discussed further below, pp. 171–72.

also refer to the oppression of widows and fatherless, though Mic. 2.9 does not use these words. Jeremiah 7.6 and Ezek. 22.7, 29 also refer to the oppression of the *gēr*, the alien. Jeremiah 34 deals with debt slaves, both male and female, in terms derived from Deut. 15.12–18. Many of these would have been children (cf. Neh. 5.2–5), and remarks made above on 'the girl' in Amos 2.7 apply also here.

A turn of phrase found in Isaiah and Micah is 'my people' or 'the poor of my people' (in Isa. 3.15 and 10.2 in the mouth of YHWH; in Mic. 2.8–9 probably not).[138] At least in Isaiah this underlines YHWH's personal relationship with and concern for those oppressed; and in the allegorical context of Ezekiel 34 'my sheep' (Ezek. 34.8–10, 22) plays the same role.

Isaiah 58 requires separate treatment because of its quite distinctive vocabulary, which probably reflects different circumstances. 'The poor' is found once (*ʿăniyyîm* Isa. 58.7), and is quite possibly a gloss,[139] and widows and the fatherless are not referred to. This exhortation is the only place in the prophets that asks for help for the destitute as well as warning against the exploitation of those who have something to be seized, if only their own labour: the poor are hungry, homeless and naked. This could reflect bleaker economic conditions in the Second Temple period; passages in Job also refer to destitution (Job 24.7–12; 30.3–8). Where exploitation is condemned, few standard terms are found. We find the oppressed described as 'crushed' (*rĕṣûṣîm*, Isa. 58.6, cf. Amos 4.1). In Isa. 58.3 the people complaining that their fasting has no effect are told 'you drive your workers (*ʿaṣṣĕbêkem*)'; some emend this word, found only here, to obtain the sense 'you press your debtors' (*ʿōbĕṭêkem*).[140] Whichever text is correct, the oppressed are identified by their relationship to the oppressors rather than as a particular group. Verse 6 may refer to debt slavery.

8.b. *The Oppressors*

We have already commented on this issue in relation to a number of the prophetic traditions. We have noted that in Isaiah 1, 3, 5 and 10 the upper classes are certainly in view, generally the ruling groups in the capital, except (probably) for the 'elders' in Isa. 3.14. Ezekiel 22 explicitly addresses all the groups in the ruling class, including the kings (so also Ezekiel 34) and the 'people of the land'. In Micah at least Micah 3 is directed to the metropolitan directors of the state exploitation of the rural (and urban?) populace.

Jeremiah 22.13–19 addresses the king, probably about the corvée and his

---

138. Wolff 1990: 82.
139. *BHS*; Whybray 1975: 215.
140. *BHS*; see Westermann 1969: 336.

abuse of workers on it. Those in view in Jeremiah 34 are those with debt-slaves, so the wealthy, including the officials and priests explicitly (Jer. 34.19). Jeremiah 5.28 is about people who are in a position to 'judge the cause' of the fatherless and the poor. This does not necessarily refer to judicial dealings, but does imply a position of power or responsibility.[141] But Jer. 2.34 and 7.1–7, unlike most of the passages in the other prophets, are not specific about those responsible, and indeed they are explicitly addressed to the people as a whole. In Jeremiah 5, 7 and 34 the sentence on the oppressors is simply an instance of the sentence pronounced by the book as a whole on the people as a whole. Thus in contrast to Amos and Micah, the condemnations of injustice in Jeremiah fit smoothly into the structure and ideology of the book as a whole. Again, in Ezekiel, while different groups are addressed, they are not given separate punishments, but grouped together to suffer the general judgment. The position in Isaiah is much closer to that in Amos and Micah, with specific oracles of judgment on specific groups; but as the structure of the book itself is much more complex, they do not clash obtrusively in the manner of Amos and Micah with the message of the book as a whole.

8.c. *The Acts of Oppression*

We now turn to an analysis of the ethical evaluation of the acts of the oppressors in the prophets by comparison with Amos.

8.c.1 *Bloodshed*
One of the commonest accusations is one that surprisingly is not found in Amos: that of murder or 'bloodshed'. 'Your hands are full of blood', YHWH tells his would-be worshippers in Isa. 1.15; the song of the vineyard in Isa. 5.1–7 ends with the pronouncement 'I looked for justice, and found bloodshed, for righteousness and found a bitter cry'. In Micah we meet 'those who built Zion on blood and Jerusalem on iniquity' (Mic. 3.10), and Jeremiah echoes this in his attack on Jehoiakim's use of the corvée to build his palace: 'your eyes and heart are set only on your own gain, and on shedding the blood of the innocent, and on committing oppression (*'ōšeq*) and crushing' (Jer. 22.17). The condemnation of Jerusalem in Ezekiel 22 centres, as we have seen, on the charge of shedding innocent blood; it is announced with the phrase 'the city of blood', and 'a city shedding blood in itself', and it contains specific accusations of murder against the 'princes' (Ezek. 22.6, 25) and officials (Ezek. 22.27). The princes are like lions and the officials like wolves tearing the prey.

---

141. Carroll notes that the division of the people is unusual in Jeremiah: R.P. Carroll 1986: 189.

Most of these passages are quite specific accusations. Exhortations, which are much more general in their address, appear in two places: Isaiah 1 and Jeremiah 7. Isaiah 1 is now often seen as an introduction to the book intended to make links with its final chapters; and the accusation of bloodshed reappears in Isa. 59.3 and Isa. 66.3. Both the beginning and the end of the book look forward to the purification of the city and its restoration in primitive innocence. We have already noted the conventionality of Jeremiah 7.

The specific accusations are mostly addressed to rulers. Ezekiel is especially specific, and Jeremiah 22 attacks a named individual; Micah is little less specific. We have already seen that the concluding charge to the song of the vineyard is considerably more so than appears at first sight. And one might expect the ruling class to be the targets of such an accusation. It is rulers who have the power of the sword. It does not seem that Israel and Judah were such lawless countries that it was possible for private landlords and creditors to murder people with impunity, and perhaps unlikely that they would have wanted to, as their object was power over their victims. Ezekiel does not make this particular accusation against the 'people of the land' (Ezek. 22.29), and, as we have seen, Amos does not make it at all. In modern Brazil, where landlords do commit murder, agriculture is less labour-intensive, selling people is more difficult, and the oppressed are more organized and more inclined to acts of resistance.

It is unlikely that these accusations are metaphorical or hyperbolic. If modern authoritarian regimes are anything to go by, people will really have died as a result of state policy. That they were killed arbitrarily and out of hand would not, of course, be the state's perception of the matter. Death on the corvée (Mic. 3.10) would be seen, or presented, as accidental. But the references to *innocent* blood point rather to judicial acts, executions for alleged crimes which could be seen in eyes suspicious of the state as miscarriages of justice.

On the other hand, accusations of innocent blood rarely if ever specify the victim, other than as 'innocent'. Judicial murder then is not presumably seen as an injustice specially directed at the poor, and a text like Ezek. 22.25 suggests what one might expect, that kings found it necessary to get people out of the way mainly to get their hands on their wealth. But Micah's complaints, and Jeremiah's against Jehoiakim, surely concern the poor.

And as with Amos, we note that the prophetic texts in general are not concerned to determine whether the process has been technically legal. Their determination of innocence is primarily moral. To shed innocent blood is simply, fundamentally and universally recognized as the foremost wrong against humanity and against God, and it is on that basis that God, in most of these passages, proclaims judgment against it. Despite the varying social locations and ideologies of the writings, they share this basic moral understanding.

8.c.2 Violence and Coercion

A related term that we have met in Amos (Amos 3.10) is *ḥāmās*, violence. The same hendiadys *ḥāmās wāšōd* 'violence and rapine' reappears in Jer. 6.7: Amos found them in Samaria, Jeremiah in the other capital city, Jerusalem. And to complete the picture, the city which in Ezekiel 22 is full of blood, is in Ezek. 7.23 full of violence.

We above linked to it a number of expressions in Amos with similar implications, literal or metaphorical, and these are of course found elsewhere also. Micah speaks of the rulers of Jacob 'chopping up my people like food for the pot, tearing the skin off them and the flesh off the bones' (Mic. 3.2–3). The occurrence in Amos of expressions like 'crushing' or 'grinding' can be paralleled particularly in Isaiah. In a justly famous phrase in Isa. 3.15, YHWH asks the 'elders and officers of his people', 'What do you mean by crushing (*tᵉdakkᵉ'û*) my people and grinding (*tiṭḥānû*) the faces of the needy?' As in Amos, it is not easy to define here in Micah and Isaiah what practices are here held up for obloquy, but they are likely to include the entire range of exploitative practices we have become familiar with. The metaphors in different ways point to the extent to which the poor are deprived of every shred of dignity and comfort. They may be left with their lives, but no more. And in Isaiah 58, the victims presumably of debt-bondage are described as 'crushed' (*rᵉṣûṣîm*, Isa. 58.6). The use of such language implies a strong sympathy with the oppressed as victims of inhuman treatment. We would expect it normally to be the subject of condemnations rather than exhortations, and indeed it is only in Isaiah 58, a chapter in other respects untypical, that we find it in an exhortation.

8.c.3 Extortion, Unjust Gain

We noted above in connection with Amos' use of the words *'šq*, 'oppress', 'exploit', and the noun *'ašûqîm* that it is a constant prophetic theme that what the rich have obtained from the poor is robbed from them. In Isa. 3.14 immediately preceding the question about grinding the faces of the poor comes the accusation, 'It is you who have devoured the vineyard; the spoil [*gᵉzēlat*, literally "what you have robbed"] of the poor is in your houses'. The same practices are seen from two points of view: they are exploitative— the poor are deprived and their creditors or rulers enriched; and they are coercive—the victims have no choice but to yield what they have. In Ezek. 22.29 the injustice of the 'people of the land' is defined thus: *'āšᵉqû 'ōšeq wᵉ gāzᵉlû gāzēl*, 'they have practised exploitation and robbery', 'the poor and needy they have oppressed (*hônû*), and the alien they have exploited unjustly' (*'āšᵉqû* again). In each case it is a question of extortion and exploitation.

Micah 2.2 again links 'rob' (*gzl*) and 'exploit' (*'šq*): 'they covet fields and rob them, houses and carry them off, and they exploit a man and his house (family), a man and his inheritance (portion).' This is the only place in the prophets where *ḥmd*, 'covet', the word used in the Tenth Commandment, is used in this sense; it is not commoner probably because it does not always have a bad meaning. Doubtless it would be possible for the foreclosing creditor or the army quartermaster (whichever is the correct interpretation) to say that the dispossession was perfectly legal. But as we have seen, these texts are not interested in legality and formalist definitions of justice. To take another's field and house, or in short his *naḥᵃlâ*, the portion of land to which he is entitled as a member of the community, is simply robbery. If we may detect here a protest against modern developments in the name of a traditional pattern of society, the main point is still a moral one: this is robbery and extortion. The 'woe' launched in Isa. 10.1–2 against the legal chicanery which deprives the poor of their property, makes a similar point: *gzl* is used here once more.

Another frequently used word, especially common in Jeremiah (Jer. 6.13; 8.10; 22.17; 51.13) is *beṣaʿ*, usually translated 'unjust gain' or 'profit'. This is the same thing from a more subjective point of view: the oppressors are accused of having their eyes on gain or pursuing profit to the exclusion of any moral considerations: 'your eyes are on nothing but your own gain', Jeremiah tells Jehoiakim (Jer. 22.17). It is used twice in Ezekiel 22: in Ezek. 22.13 it is used of Jerusalem and linked with the blood she has shed, and in Ezek. 22.27 it defines the officials' motives in behaving like wolves. The portrait of the just man in Isa. 33.15 includes the phrase 'avoiding the profit derived from oppression (*beṣaʿ maʿᵃšaqqôt*)'.

We may still ask in all these cases: what is the really important thing that the poor man has lost? What is the centre of concern? Is it the loss of livelihood, of independence, of rightful portion, of standing in the community? Or all of these things? Some light is thrown on this by our next two headings.

8.c.4 *Loss of Freedom*
Surprisingly, direct protest against enslavement for debt seems to emerge only in Amos (Amos 2.6; 8.6). But Jer. 5.26, 'they set traps and catch men', may refer to this. We have already seen that Jer. 34.8–22 depends on a legal prescription and fails to express a clear protest against debt-bondage as such, only against the treachery of the Jerusalemites in taking back the slaves they had covenanted to free.

But in Isaiah 58 the first demand for the true fast is to set people free, expressed poetically in four different ways: 'to loose unjust bonds, to undo the thongs of the yoke, to let the crushed go free, to break every yoke'. The poor are like oxen under the yoke: they must work for a master and do his bidding. The word for 'free', *ḥopšî*, is the same word used in the law regulating debt-bondage, in Exod. 21.2, 5; Deut. 15.12, 13. These people are in slavery, probably for debt, unless the protest is against slavery of any kind, which is not impossible. Presumably the law is known, but the interest is in freeing slaves, not in the observance of the law.

8.c.5 *Perversion of Right*

We return to Isaiah 10. 'Woe to you who make iniquitous decrees, writers who write trouble, to turn aside the poor from justice, to rob the humble of my people of their rights, to make widows their prey, and to despoil orphans.' What the victims of rapacious judges lose is not just money or property, it is their right, or justice (*dîn, mišpāṭ*). In many ways this lies at the heart of the prophetic understanding of oppression as a disaster for the poor, and, as in Amos, frequently expressed by phrases such as 'to turn aside' the poor, to 'pervert' their rights.

Often but not always the context is the court of law, as in Amos 5.12. This is seen as run for the benefit of the rich, who of course can bribe the judges, another common complaint, or indeed are the judges, as in Isa. 5.23: 'you acquit the guilty for a bribe, and deprive the innocent of their rights'; compare Isa. 29.21, 32.7, where such practices are to cease in the coming just society. But it is a broader context in which Jeremiah accuses the powerful of not 'judging the cause of the orphan' or 'taking the side of the poor' (Jer. 5.28). The words are the same as in Isaiah 10: *dîn* and *mišpāṭ*; but though the judicial context is one where the poor often lose their rights, the doing of justice extends well outside it. The defence of the poor and widows and orphans against oppression and exploitation, as we shall see in Chapter 5, is the responsibility of rulers, and it is carried out not only judicially but also administratively. Because it is a responsibility of government, it is the responsibility of the official class. It is they that have 'turned aside the way of the poor' and 'turned justice to poison and the fruit of righteousness to wormwood' (Amos 2.7; 6.12). The corruption of justice and administration affects all classes. But while the loss of justice for the rich may often be only an inconvenience, the loss of justice for the poor means the loss of land, livelihood, freedom, or indeed life.

8.c.6 *Indulgence at the Expense of the Poor*

That the poor have been deprived of their rights is the central issue. Far less widespread is the concern especially in Amos that rich are indulging themselves at the expense of the poor. The women of Samaria exploit the poor; the accusation is made livelier but scarcely more compelling by the misogynistic description 'fat cows of Bashan', or by adding that they have their husbands running to and from the drinks cabinet. Amos 6.1–6 is better: a portrait not just of indulgence but of complacency: 'and they are not grieved by the ruin of Joseph.' Isaiah 5.22 may be compared. Generally the Old Testament is not marked by puritanism, but by the enjoyment of the gifts of God. Injustice consists in the poor being deprived of them, not in itself in the rich enjoying them, and on the whole the prophets stick to this line.

We may conclude that in the prophetic texts judgment is normally made on social oppression not according to specific laws, nor by harking back to an imagined past or appealing to a formal ideal pattern of society, but according to moral norms which are accepted universally in all human societies of which we have knowledge, norms which the authors of these texts clearly expect their audiences to share, and which they therefore did not create. Oppression is, put simply, murder, theft, robbery, violence and perversion of justice, backed up by bribery and dishonesty. To say this is not of course to say that the condemnation of oppression is or was non-controversial. To accept such norms is one thing; to admit that they apply to one's own conduct is another, and we may assume that then as now what was done would have been defended as both legal and necessary. State oppression would have been justified by national necessity, and private exploitation by invoking the 'moral hazard' of allowing debtors to evade their responsibilities. The challenge of the prophetic texts to all readers is whether they will choose to call the actions of those who have political or economic power by the names they use themselves, or by those that the text applies to them.

9. *The Justice of YHWH*

Prophetic texts are religious texts and YHWH is the chief speaker, not least in texts on social injustice. The underlying motivation which connects these moral judgements with the condemnations they lead up to is a theological one.

The most obvious point, and the one most consistently found, is that the acts of injustice condemned in the prophets are offensive to YHWH. Predominantly, the judgements against them are formulated as words of YHWH even if in many cases the charge is a word of the prophet.[142] YHWH is the guarantor of justice, and acts to punish breaches of justice. That central theological concept in Jeremiah, knowledge of YHWH, is in several verses identified simply with the practice of justice: for example Jer. 9.6 (Hebrew 5): 'Oppression on oppression, treachery on treachery, they refused to know me'; Jer. 22.15–16: 'Your father ate and drank and did justice and righteousness; he defended the cause of the poor and needy: is not this to know me? says YHWH.' This may be compared with Jer. 9.24 (Hebrew 23): 'Let one who boasts boast of this, of understanding and knowing me, that I am YHWH, and I show faithful love, justice and righteousness on the earth'. As Wisser notes, this triad of nouns 'is rich in allusions to the beneficent interventions of YHWH in history'.[143]

---

142. Cf. Westermann 1967.
143. Wisser 1982: 238.

In the parable of the vineyard in Isa. 5.1–7, Israel-Judah is YHWH's vineyard, and he expects fruit from them. The fruit is defined (v. 7) as 'justice . . . righteousness', which we have seen means *social* justice. When the vineyard fails to produce good fruit, his response is to destroy it (5.5). In the chapter of 'woes' which follows this is made more explicit and focused. In the centre of the chapter we find the theological assertion in Isa. 5.16: 'YHWH Sabaoth is exalted by (or in) justice, and the Holy God shows himself holy in righteousness'. Isaiah 5.15–16 are often seen as an editorial expansion to the chapter;[144] but this should not obscure the fact that they are in keeping with Isaianic theology and well sum up the message of the chapter. As Thomas Leclerc has reminded us, we have here again the hendiadys 'justice . . . righteousness', which appeared as recently as Isa. 5.7 and determines the theme of the entire chapter. Consistency of interpretation demands that it should mean the same here as in v. 7: 'the absence of justice and righteousness results in human abasement while their presence results in divine exaltation'.[145] But I cannot follow Leclerc in his view that the verse presents YHWH's exaltation and sanctification as the result of the establishment of a just social order in Israel.[146] In the context, where it is God rather than human beings who acts, the meaning must be that God's nature is revealed as the one who himself does justice and righteousness (as kings ought to), destroying the oppressors. Even if it is not spelt out so clearly, the implication of texts in the other prophets is the same.

This is the point on which the logic of the rhetoric of the prophetic books pivots. YHWH destroys oppressors; the oppressors denounced in the oracles of judgment were representative of the Israelite kingdoms; this accounts, in the structure of the prophetic books as wholes, for the downfall of those kingdoms.

We found difficulty with this logic in our study of Amos. The difficulty is not the implied understanding of injustice as social. That is profoundly correct. It is rather the global character of the punishment. 'Doing justice and righteousness' ought to mean *both* destroying oppressors *and* delivering the oppressed; yet YHWH in these texts is only said to destroy oppressors. If that leads to the deliverance of the oppressed, the texts do not usually say so, and in the global act of judgment on Israel and/or Judah the oppressed will inevitably suffer along with the oppressors. It is in line with this that references to the Exodus tradition in judgment contexts rarely have a positive function: they are rather reproaches, as in Jer. 2.4–13, Amos 2.9–10 or Mic. 6.1–5.

For Miranda, this does not seem to be a problem. The prophets proclaim

---

144. See e.g. Wildberger 1991: 195, 205–07.
145. Leclerc 2001: 61.
146. Leclerc 2001: 62.

the rejection of Israel because 'Israel had frustrated the only reason for its election'.[147] Called to teach the world justice (Miranda's interpretation of Gen. 18.18-19), they instead produced injustice, as Isaiah spells out in 5.1-7. So that YHWH's punishment of Israel is for a reason quite distinctive to Israel. 'Because Israel totally failed Yahweh, the oppressed *of the whole earth* continue to "cry out" in vain.'[148] In my view this introduces an idea into the prophecies of judgment which is foreign to them. What YHWH looks for from Israel is no different from what is expected from every nation on earth, that is the doing of justice and righteousness.

This is I believe the primary and basic theological structure of the prophetic books. There are strands in the material that have a different theological structure. Amos 2.9-11 and Mic. 6.1-8 are typical of a strand that enters as a result of the Deuteronomic movement. This makes injustice not just a failure to know God, but a matter of ingratitude after all that God has done for them.

Another strand appears particularly in the prose of Jeremiah and in Ezekiel, obedience to the commandments. As we have seen, in general there is no interest in this in those passages concerned to denounce injustice. But this would not be true of Jeremiah 7 or 34, or Ezekiel 18 or 22. We have discussed Jeremiah sufficiently. In Ezekiel 18 the virtues of the righteous man and the sins of the wicked are defined in legal terms; in 22.1-13, though there is less legal language, the denunciations have an air of the comprehensive list which must bring in every recognized kind of sin, not all of them sins of social injustice, and many of them derived from the Holiness Code. These developments are not surprising in works which represent the Deuteronomistic and Priestly movements. These were movements among segments of the former ruling class who were seeking to re-establish society on the basis of law, so that it could be just and secure, but without radically changing the order of society.

The globalization of judgment in all the prophets, the use of the Exodus tradition as a reproach, and the legalizing of the accusation in exilic texts, features bound up with the functioning of the prophetic texts as theodicy in the light of the destructions of the two kingdoms, may dilute but cannot repress the compassion for the poor, the plain moral condemnation of injustice, and the sense of YHWH as the God of justice, which are the leading features of the oracles of judgment. Compassion for the poor may even be contradicted by the manner in which the judgment is conceived, but it still comes through and resounds in our own reading of the texts.

When they turn from justifying the collapse of the Israelite states to survey current conditions in Second Temple times, the theological structure

---

147. Miranda 1977: 168.
148. Miranda 1977: 169 (my italics).

is naturally quite different again. The most important passage in this regard is Isaiah 58, and this is exhortation. Rather than threatening doom it promises blessing for those who heed the exhortation (Isa. 58.9b–12): YHWH rewards the just as he punishes the unjust. The judgment depicted in the following chapter (Isa. 59.15b–20) distinguishes individuals (Isa. 59.20), but it is no clearer than it was before that the oppressed poor are to be delivered. Injustice seems no longer to be understood as a characteristic of society.

10. *Conclusions*

Generally speaking, however, injustice is treated as a social and political theme in the prophets. The oppressors are mostly classes rather than individuals, the oppressed are certainly a class, and the oppressors are representatives of their states. Nevertheless, the social criticism of the prophets is not structural criticism; they condemn the moral choices of individuals, states and classes, but have nothing to say about the positions held by individuals, the powers of the state or the legitimacy of the class structure. To put it more sharply, the prophets do not condemn the existence of poverty and wealth side by side: they condemn the way in which wealth is extracted from those who are already poor.[149] This is pure moral condemnation from those who can see what is happening and judge that what the powerful are doing is wrong. There is no call to revolution, but simply the announcement of God's judgment; no suggestions about how to put things right—that they left to others. We simply have the announcement of divine judgment on injustice—that is, inhuman, unneighbourly conduct. This may be seen as a contemporary moral judgment on Israel and Judah's transition to a class society as it actually took place. It is a judgment of what historians might see as an inevitable social transformation in its effect on people.

There are further limitations on prophetic thought which arise from its social location. It originates from privileged but sympathetic observers, convinced of God's anger against the oppressors of the poor and of the danger which threatens a society where justice is not practised. But, as Mosala points out, it is not the voice of the oppressed themselves, and cannot be read as expressing their hopes or fears. Quite the contrary: as the prophetic texts stand, any sympathy for the poor is contradicted by the violence of the judgment.

Despite all this, it is undeniable that in this literature we have a contribution of fundamental importance to the whole Judaeo-Christian tradition of social thought, and it is important, strangely enough, *because* of its limitations. Through the prophets we have learnt to understand social

149. Cf. Rodd 2001: 174.

relationships as governed by morality as interpersonal relationships are—that social relationships are moral relationships, and hence that we can speak of social *justice*. The morality in question relates to the effects of social practices on individual victims, who are always in the forefront of the prophetic denunciations; it is far removed from the utilitarianism of much modern social thinking.[150] The effects of this insight can be traced everywhere in theological writing on social affairs and in church reports, papal encyclicals and the like. Miranda, for whom love of one's neighbour is identical with doing justice for one's neighbour, and Gorringe, who privileges the prophetic strand in the biblical tradition and insists on the relevance of ethical thought to politics and economics, are in this respect quite typical.[151]

We have learnt this from the prophets, even though other parts of the Bible express the same fact. It is above all the prophets that encouraged earlier generations to believe that in the Old Testament we heard a trumpet call to social justice for Christian nations. Pleins cites Walter Rauschenbusch, the American exponent of the 'social gospel' as an example.[152] The reason may be that in the prophets, and only the prophets in the Hebrew Bible, we are given a sharp picture of a class-divided society where one class exploits the other.[153] Those who knew the bitter class division of early industrial capitalism saw here an image of the agony of their own times, and drew the conclusion that the exploitative practices of the capitalists were God-condemned equally with those 'at ease in Zion'. Their successors continue to do so as capitalism undergoes continual metamorphoses and seeks out the lowest costs and the highest returns in every part of the world. Wherever the costs, that is the wages that workers can be made to accept, are lowest we still see the raw exploitation which so angered Amos and Micah. This is the setting to which such modern writers as Miranda and Gorringe are responding.

Of course, it is not possible to derive precise principles or prescriptions from texts that prescribed nothing for their own world. Many of the practices denounced would be illegal nearly everywhere today in any case, though this does not prevent practices such as slavery, debt bondage, bribery of judges, or murder of protesters from continuing in many places. But every age develops its own legal and 'acceptable' modes of exploitation: among ours are, for example, the competitive setting of wages and commodity prices in a global market and the subsidized dumping of surplus

150. Cf. Gorringe 1994: 34–37.
151. Miranda 1977: 60–64; Gorringe 1994: 3–56.
152. Pleins 2001: 215–18.
153. We shall see in the next chapter that certain of the Proverbs point to the same fact; but there an equal number of sayings encourage the hope that charitable relationships are possible.

production. Some follow neo-liberal prescriptions, others conflict with them: the common factor is that they advantage the rich and powerful. The point of reading the prophets, as Gorringe argues, is that they teach us to assess economic practices by moral criteria that are not purely utilitarian. They arm us against those neo-liberal thinkers who have taught the leaders of the capitalist world what they want to hear: that the global economy is self-regulating and should not be interfered with, and therefore that moral considerations are irrelevant to it.[154]

The prophets remind us that economic necessity is an abstraction that ignores the fact that people suffer because other people take decisions which affect them; and that decision-makers are morally responsible and their decisions can be morally assessed. Any view or theory that lets us off that hook is itself immoral, and would be subject to the searing contempt of the prophets themselves:

> Woe to those who say evil is good and good evil,
> who make darkness light and light darkness,
> who make bitter sweet and sweet bitter (Isa. 5.20).

---

154. E.g. F.A. Hayek; cf. Gorringe 1994: 48–56.

Chapter 4

JUSTICE AND THE PATRON

1. *Introduction*

The behaviour which led to the transformation of Israel and Judah into
class societies is understood in prophetic texts simply as immorality,
offences against justice. This implies a corresponding positive idea of
what justice is, and texts which define this are even commoner in the Old
Testament. They may be seen to be based on three paradigms, the just man
(so gendered!—see below), the just king (also gendered) and the just society.
In this chapter we shall look at examples of the call for justice as addressed
to the individual (the just man). The king will claim our attention in Chapter
5, and in Chapter 6 we shall look at ideas of justice for society as a whole.
Justice is of course a social ideal, in the Bible as elsewhere; but individuals
have a responsibility to make it a reality. But which individuals?

We saw above that the adjectives *ṣaddîq*, 'just, righteous', and *rāšāʿ*,
'unjust, wicked', never occur in the feminine with reference to a female
person. Neither are they applied to children, or to any kind of marginal
person; the use of 'righteous' in Amos 2.6 is not an exception.[1] All the
paradigms of just behaviour that we shall look at assume that one is in a
position to exercise it by being free and in command of resources: typically
an adult male head of household. Proverbs 31.10–31 does provide a portrait
of a wealthy mistress of a household, who behaves with prudence and
also justice, including the use of the family stores to provide for the poor
(v. 20); but even she is not called 'just': she is *ʾēšet ḥayil*, 'a woman of
competence'.

These passages include statements of how such a man should behave
towards God, towards his superiors, and towards his equals, but an at least
equally prominent subject is how those with power or resources should
behave towards those who have less, or no, power or resources; how the
well-off should treat the poor and how the powerful should treat dependents. In other words, they are governed by the paradigm of patronage. On

---

1. Above, pp. 62–63.

the whole they assume the existence of differences in access to wealth and
social power, and do not question them. What we said of the prophets is
true of the Old Testament as a whole, as Cyril Rodd has observed: poverty
as such is not a problem for the writers; it is the oppression of the poor that
is the problem.[2] Jon Levenson notes, 'the condemnation of the oppression
of the poor by the rich in the Hebrew Bible cannot be construed as a
rejection of the very existence of the two classes . . . the identification of
justice with equality is essentially a modern phenomenon'.[3] In fact, though
it is true that no text prescribes economic equality as a working principle
and most accept the existence of rich and poor, we shall see that there are
deeper implications in some that equality may be understood as an ideal. At
all events, the concern of the texts we shall look at in this chapter is how it is
proper to use one's power. The social ideal that they project is that of a
benevolently hierarchical society. To the extent that they assume that such
a society is or may be a reality, they may be considered utopian: but it is a
Jamesonian utopia, the idealization of an existing social order. They ignore
the existence of the state, perhaps regarding it as a given about which the
individual can do nothing.

2. *Ezekiel 18*

We begin with a passage that provides a link backward to the last chapter
and forward to later discussions. For the general social context of this book
I can refer to my discussion above.[4] Here the text explicitly defines what it
means to be a just man, as an individual making personal moral decisions,
as Andrew Mein has emphasized.[5] A just man has an unjust son, and a just
grandson. In each case the appropriate reward or retribution falls on the
man himself and not on his son. The justice of the just man is defined in a
series of brief clauses (Ezek. 18.5–9). The son and grandson's characteristics are defined in corresponding fashion, in Ezek. 18.10–13 and 14–17.
There are variations of expression, but essentially vv. 10–13 negatives the
statements in vv. 5–9 and vv. 14–17 reaffirms them. We shall confine our
attention to vv. 5–9, except in one or two places where uncertainties in the
text may be illuminated by the later paragraphs.

The paragraph is structured as an inclusio: it begins 'When a man is

2. Rodd 2001: 174; above, p. 96.
3. Levenson 1993: 133.
4. Above, pp. 84–86.
5. Mein 2001: 187–88. Mein treats the chapter as an example of 'the domestication of
ethics' in the restricted sphere of moral decision left to the exiles. However, this cannot be the
whole truth, since the just man acts as a judge.

righteous . . .' and ends 'he is righteous; he shall live'. The text enclosed by these clauses fills out what it means to be righteous (or just, *ṣaddîq*). Rodd asserts that 'despite the efforts of biblical scholars to provide a rich meaning to the term, *ṣedeq/ṣᵉdāqâ* is as empty of concrete meaning as "right" or "good" in modern English'.[6] This says less than it appears to. Any abstract expression is deprived of meaning if it is deprived of its context; but that does not mean that in context it does not have concrete meaning. And here it is explicitly given such meaning. This does not bear out Miranda's assertion that the meaning of *ṣaddîq* is exhausted by the idea of social justice, but it does show that it is a very important and often dominant part of it.[7]

Of the sixteen clauses which lie within the inclusio, at least eight, the whole of v. 7 and most of v. 8, are concerned specifically with the man's relationship with those who have less power and wealth—this would be true also of v. 8b, since judges are normally the class superiors of most of those who come before them; and another four are general. The first of these, Ezek. 18.5b, 'and does justice and righteousness', we have already seen normally refers to social justice, though here, as it is a general expression introducing the whole series, it has a wider sense. The first two clauses in v. 6 could be said to deal with relationship with God, and the second two with equals, though the last is a matter of purity rather than justice. The first half of v. 9, the reference to YHWH's 'statutes and ordinances', is not simply a matter of obedience, since these statutes and ordinances concern such matters as have been referred to already in the series. Obedience to YHWH means acting with justice because that is what YHWH demands.

When we turn to Ezek. 18.7–8, we note firstly that the persons who benefit from the man's just acts are not specified, in other words there is no reference to 'the poor' or to the alien, widow and orphan. In this respect this passage differs from others that we shall examine, no doubt because of the terse style. But there can be no question that it is these who are meant. Secondly, there are many points which correspond to those raised in the oracles of judgment; the vocabulary corresponds closely with that of Ezek. 22.29, the accusation against the 'people of the land': 'commits no robbery' (*gᵉzēlâ lō' yigzōl*) of course refers to exploitation of the poor, and in v. 18 it is paired as in 22.29, and often, with 'exploit' (*'šq*); at the beginning of v. 7, as in 22.29, *ynh* 'oppress' is used. As has been frequently pointed out, the list of virtues has close parallels in the commandments of the law, especially the Holiness Code.[8] But the positive statements especially are not derived from the law, and the paragraph has its own distinct and quite Ezekielian character.

---

6. Rodd 2001: 47.
7. Miranda 1977: 96–103.
8. See Zimmerli 1979: 380.

We can classify the statements made in Ezek. 18.7–8 as follows. First, there are general statements that the man does not commit oppression or exploitation: 'he does not oppress anyone' (beginning of v. 7); 'he does not commit robbery'; and possibly belonging in the same sphere of ideas is (middle of v. 8) 'he turns his hand back from *'āwel*' (NRSV 'iniquity'; NIV 'doing wrong'; REB 'injustice'). But for Zimmerli this refers to judicial corruption, making a pair with the clause which follows: he refers to the use of the word in Lev. 19.15, 35.[9] Secondly, there are positive acts of charity to the destitute (compare Isaiah 58): 'he gives his food to the hungry and clothes the naked'. Thirdly, the issue of his conduct as a judge is addressed: 'he performs true justice between one person and another'. This indicates that the author has in mind a man of substance, a man of his own class, but not necessarily an official.[10] And fourthly, there are two highly specific commendations, both related to the practice of making loans, that is, as usual in the Hebrew Bible,[11] lending to the poor, lending for subsistence: 'he returns the debtor's pledge';[12] and 'he does not lend at discount or take his loan back with interest'.

The specificity of these statements need not surprise us, for we have already seen how central indebtedness was to the steady subjection of the peasantry to the power of the wealthy. All who observed how easily the indebted peasantry fell into the power of their creditors (bluntly stated in Prov. 22.7), and were concerned about it, would wish for some way of defending them. This is the reason for the measures proposed in Deuteronomy 15 and Leviticus 25 which we shall study in Chapter 6. But the first line of defence, it becomes evident, was in the moral education of the creditor, which all the passages we shall be looking at here are aimed at. Loans were essential to the survival of the poor peasant, and still more the landless labourer; but he was likely to be ruined by debt unless they were given on favourable terms. The two issues of pledges and usury are the standard examples of the oppressive use of the creditor's power in the Torah and in Ezekiel.

Lending at interest is not referred to, at least not explicitly, in any other prophet than Ezekiel. It has been argued that the silence of the prophets

---

9.   Zimmerli 1979: 381. See also Ps. 82.2; Job 32.10; in both cases of divine justice. But another context in which *'āwel* turns up more than once is the condemnation of false weights and measures (Lev. 19.35; Deut. 25.16; cf. Ezek. 28.18).

10.   Greenberg (1983: 325, 330) thinks of informal arbitration; but even this points to a man of prestige in the community.

11.   But see below, n. 89.

12.   The text is corrupt, but a comparison with v. 12 shows that this is what must be meant; I read with Zimmerli (1979: 370, followed by *BHS*) *ḥᵃbōl haḥayyāb yāšîb*, though *ḥayyāb* ('debtor' in Middle Hebrew) is not otherwise found in Biblical Hebrew. Greenberg (1983: 329) construes *ḥᵃbōlātô ḥôb* as the equivalent of *ḥᵃbōlat ḥōbô*, 'his debt pledge'. But this is impossible for the same reason as the MT: 'his' can only refer to the creditor, whereas pledges remained the property of the debtor (Milgrom 1976: 97–98).

'suggests some degree of compliance with the law'.[13] This is 'to make too much of an argument from silence'.[14] The voice of 'law' and instruction is of more significance than the silence of the prophets: what is repeatedly forbidden must be commonly done. A better explanation is that it was only in the sixth century that it came to be explicitly condemned.[15] There is a precise vocabulary for it, another sign that the practice was a regular one: the two clauses which I have translated very literally above refer to the two common ways in which interest was charged: by deducting from the loan when given or by adding to the repayment at the end (regular payment of interest was not known).[16] Someone borrowing a hundred measures of grain might be given eighty but expected to repay a hundred,[17] or might be given a hundred but expected to repay a hundred and twenty. In the former case, the loan was subject to *nešek*, usually translated 'interest', but which I have translated 'discount', following the REB; in the latter, to *tarbît*, 'increase'. Obviously the effect was the same in either case.

Rates of interest are set in ancient Near Eastern law codes, for example the laws of Hammurabi prescribe twenty percent on silver and thirty-three percent on grain.[18] This is the total interest payable for the duration of the loan, but often this would be less than a year, typically from seedtime to harvest. Though these are intended as limits, they will in practice have often been exceeded, even though other laws prescribe penalties for this. A rate of thirty-three percent on a capital loan of seedcorn is not too onerous if the yield on the seed is expected to be in the region of six to tenfold, as was the case in the irrigated fields of Mesopotamia, or even two to sixfold, as in the rain-fed agriculture of Palestine.[19] But if such interest rates were imposed on subsistence loans to the needy, it is only too likely that they would be unable to repay.

If so, they might then fall subject to the most oppressive aspect of ancient credit, the seizure of their security, either a field or a person, very likely their child; see once again Nehemiah 5, or 2 Kgs 4.1. The ancient Near Eastern law and custom of credit and particularly of pledges is a maze, and it is difficult to pronounce confidently on the precise application of Ezekiel's terse expression. We have a vast quantity of loan contracts from Mesopotamia, which show that every conceivable variety of custom was practised; but we

13. Gamoran 1971: 127–29.
14. Rodd 2001: 149.
15. Morgenstern 1962: 69–81, followed by Van Seters 2003: 133.
16. This is the usual interpretation, though another has been suggested on the basis of Lev. 25.37 (Loewenstamm 1969, followed by Gamoran 1971: 132). See also Milgrom 2001: 2209–10. Weil (1938: 205) has a third, which has had no takers.
17. This may be reflected in concealed form in the 'parable of the unjust steward', Lk. 16.6–7: Derrett 1970: 56–74; 1972.
18. Richardson 2000: 68–69.
19. Kippenberg 1977: 23.

are unable to say for certain which of them applied in Israel and Judah.[20] The creditor was entitled to seize a person from the debtor's family if the debt was not paid when it fell due, but this was normally only for a short period in order to compel the debtor to pay. Alternatively, contracts might specify that a person or a piece of land would come into the creditor's possession either when the loan was made or when it fell due. The produce of the property or the labour of the person would, it seems, normally be used to pay the interest on the loan ('antichretic service'), but if the debt was not paid the pledge would become the creditor's property, though often it was possible to redeem it/him/her. The Babylonian law specifying a limit of three years on debt service[21] seems to have applied only when the debtor voluntarily sold a family member or a slave for this purpose,[22] and it may be the same with the similar biblical laws with a limit of six years in Exod. 21.2–6 and Deut. 15.12–18. The law of Hammurabi was not regularly observed, and the same may well be true of the biblical ones. An insolvent debtor, like the peasants in Nehemiah 5, could well see his daughter or even the son he hoped to succeed him disappearing into permanent servitude, or his land, meagre to begin with, cut down still further or cultivated for the benefit of his creditor.

The commendation in Ezek. 18.7, 'he returns the debtor's pledge', which is intensified when we come to the grandson in Ezek. 18.16, who 'does not exact a pledge'[23] in the first place, should be seen in this context. It is usually related to Exod. 22.26–27 (Hebrew 25–26) and Deut. 24.12–13, which command the creditor to return the poor man's cloak at nightfall. This is not the most important issue in relation to pledges. Why the legal texts make an issue of it we shall discuss in relation to the Exodus text. No, Ezekiel commends the just man for not enriching himself at the expense of his poor debtor by holding on to land or family members delivered or forfeited to him, or not demanding them in the first place.[24]

Summing up then, the righteous man in his relations with the powerless refrains from taking advantage of their powerlessness to enrich himself by any means, but particularly as a creditor by imposing interest on his loans or distraining property or failing to return pledges; assists the destitute with charitable gifts; and is an honest and incorruptible judge. This text is about how the powerful man should use his power, to help the weak rather than exploiting them. It is not about his expressing solidarity with them, reducing the distance between himself and them, or making his society less class-divided. The unequal distribution of power is treated as a given.

---

20. They are conveniently summarized by Chirichigno (1993: 61–100).
21. CH 117: Richardson 2000: 78–79.
22. Chirichigno 1993: 67–72.
23. *ḥᵃbōl lōʾ ḥābāl*.
24. Cf. Milgrom 1976: 98.

Each of the men in the schematic narrative of Ezek. 18.5–18 acts as he chooses, whether justly or unjustly; he is not subject to sanctions by society. He can so act both because there is no enforceable law dealing with these issues and because he is a powerful man who appears to be subject to no informal constraints from society such as without doubt he imposes on others. The only sanction available is YHWH's sanction of life and death, and that is what the chapter is about. A society where powerful men behave as the son behaves in Ezek. 18.10–13 is intolerable. But such power might be acceptable if it is used as the father and the grandson use it, for the benefit of the powerless. Only the justice of YHWH, it appears, will ensure that it is.

The picture is certainly an artificial one, set up as a parable for rhetorical purposes. In reality such men would be subject to constraints, notably that of society's opinion, that is the sanction of shame. But that is not an absolute control, and no doubt the text is realistic in suggesting that justice is a choice which every man in such a position is free to make. That is why YHWH's judgment is itself just. Whether it is just for one man to have such power over others and therefore to have the opportunity to use it unjustly is not questioned by this text. For the wicked, that is those who abuse their power and exploit the powerless, are destroyed by YHWH's judgment. Every reader of the Old Testament knows that this claim is made by law, prophecy, psalms and wisdom, and its cumulative effect is very powerful. It is the basis of Miranda's assertion that God's intervention in history is to do away with injustice.[25] But even he does not consider whether this very claim may serve to undergird an unequal social order. We go on to look at further examples.

3. *Exodus 22.21 (Hebrew 20)–23.12*

Ezekiel's portrait of the just man is closely related to texts in the Torah, particularly the Holiness Code (Leviticus 18 and 19), but not only there. All the major codes contain much instruction on how one should behave towards the poor and powerless. As we shall see in Chapter 6, this instruction is fundamental to the image of the just society offered by the Torah, but it can also stand alone as instruction for the individual considered as a member of Israel. The so-called Book of the Covenant in Exodus 20–23 contains a relatively self-contained section largely on this theme, in which most of the major issues are raised. In this study I shall concentrate on the Exodus text, but refer to parallels in Leviticus and Deuteronomy as appropriate.

Most scholars believe that the Book of the Covenant is the oldest of the major collections of legal material, but this view has been challenged

25. Miranda 1977: 77–108.

recently by Cornelis Houtman and John Van Seters, and the latter in particular has argued for its dependence on Deuteronomy and the Holiness Code.[26] I concur with them that the simplest and most obvious account of its origin is that it never existed as a whole outside its present position, whatever the origin of the material.[27] There are many signs that it has been shaped to fit its narrative context: see Exod. 20.22; 22.21 (Hebrew 20); 23.15, as well as 23.20–33. Its present form has been created by the author of the pre-Priestly version of the Sinai narrative. Speculation about its social origins as an independent law-code, as by Crüsemann or Pleins, is therefore redundant.[28] Its origins as its stands are purely literary (and the names '*Book* of the Covenant' and 'Covenant *Code*' are misnomers).

This does not make its social roots irrelevant, but they are to be detected in its literary features. Who is the implicit addressee of the instructions? Clearly, it is the same as the subject of Ezekiel's sketch of the just man: the free adult male landholder. The justice called for here is the kind of justice which he would recognize and accept; it does not challenge his position, but it demands of him readiness to act in ways which favour the weak rather than himself. It is much more difficult to detect the social context of the authors of the text, but analogy would suggest that they lie in the upper classes; and the close relationship of the theology to Deuteronomy suggests the scribal official class, with its developing sense of nationhood.

The long speech of YHWH to Moses which begins at Exod. 20.22 consists largely of instruction for Israel's future existence as a society; only an epilogue deals with the immediate situation facing them as they enter the land. Once this is excluded, the remainder is framed at each end by instructions for the worship of YHWH. The object of the whole of the text which lies within this frame is 'the institution of a stable and livable social order marked by justice'.[29]

This long section falls into two parts sharply distinguished by the form and style of the instructions. Exodus 21.1–22.20 (Hebrew 19) consists mainly of 'casuistic law': formal legal instructions in impersonal style setting out a case and stating what should then happen: 'when X, then Y'. The instructions we are concerned with are quite different.[30] They are doubtless

---

26. Houtman 1997: 26; Van Seters 2003 (128–62 for our section; for a critique, see Levinson 2004).

27. Houtman 2000: 85; 1997: 15–16; Van Seters 2003: 27 and passim.

28. Crüsemann 1996: 109–200 (incisively criticized by Van Seters 2003: 24–26); Pleins 2001: 53.

29. Houtman 1997: 13 (my translation; the translation of what appears to be the same sentence in his commentary on Exodus [2000: 83] has 'preservation' rather than 'institution' [*Einrichtung*]).

30. The expression 'apodictic law' is not usable, because Alt (1966) applied it to all the non-casuistic material, whereas the real distinction is between legal prescriptions in whatever style and personal appeal.

what is meant by *commandments* (*miṣwôt*) when the Hebrew Bible refers to legal texts. They are addressed personally by YHWH, primarily to the individual, even where the second person plural is used. They do not state procedure for a specific situation, or prescribe penalties to be inflicted by the institutions of society: instead they set out moral standards or religious requirements and back up the moral requirements with rhetorical appeals of various kinds.

The two sections, as Houtman sees, try to achieve the goal of justice in different ways.[31] The first section offers ways of managing conflict and avoiding violence, if necessary through legal action, though generally the rules would be 'self-executing';[32] it is mainly concerned with relations between equals in a small-scale society, though it also contains important directions to ensure that people treat slaves reasonably (Exod. 21.1–11, 20–21, 26–7). The second section is concerned with 'the foundations of society' in justice. Someone may fail to behave with justice and yet cannot be brought to book 'because, juridically speaking, he has the law on his side, or because, owing to his powerful position, no one dares to tangle with him, or because his practices are done in secret'.[33] Compassion, generosity and honesty, the essential ingredients of justice in the world-view of the text, have to be a personal commitment or lifestyle. I would add two points. The first is that rules of the kind found in Exod. 21.18–22.17 (16) work well between equals if they are committed to observing them, but that when they have weaker people in their power, they will be of relatively little use. How, for example, would Exod. 21.35 help someone who owned just one head of cattle which had been killed by another? They would be left without enough money to buy a replacement. The other point is that no laws are of any use in establishing a just society unless the members of society want to behave with justice. Law has to be backed up with moral education. Justice has to be *taught* rather than enforced; and in this part of the Book of the Covenant we have the bare bones of such an education. In Deuteronomy individual laws are backed up with teaching and exhortation, so that the two styles tend to become mixed rather than lying in separate blocks as they largely do in Exodus.

The section falls roughly into the following parts. The admonition not to oppress the alien in 22.21 (Hebrew 20) is repeated in 23.9. This has some significance for the structure, but is it an inclusio marking the beginning and end of a subsection, or does it start two successive subsections?[34]

22.21–27 (20–26) Justice for the weak
22.28–31 (27–30) Duties to YHWH

---

31. Houtman 2000: 83.
32. See Jackson 2000: 82–92.
33. Houtman 2000: 83 (my translation).
34. The latter is Houtman's view: 2000: 224. Van Seters rejects both: 2003: 130.

23.1–3, 6–8 (or 9) Honesty in judgment. *Embedded in this:*
23.4–5   Honesty and helpfulness towards an enemy
23.9 (or 10)–12   Sacral laws presented as help for the weak
23.13a   Conclusion of the section

It can be seen that the section is tied together by the emphasis on concern for the weak with which it begins and ends, and especially by the emphasis on the alien or outsider, the *gēr*, which is the first and last *word* (excluding the conclusion in 13a).

Coming then to Exod. 22.21–27 (Hebrew 20–26), we see that it makes really just two main points: 21–24 (20–23) is concerned with the marginal people, the alien, the widow and the fatherless; and 25–27 (24–26) with the poor.[35] The first point is expressed in general terms: you are not to exploit, oppress or humiliate these people, who because of their lack of footing, or secure footing, in the family-based social system are vulnerable to exploitation; they cannot engage on an equal footing in the processes of reconciliation and legal action implied in the casuistic section.

Who precisely is the *gēr*? It is generally assumed that it is a non-Israelite settler in the land of Israel, and certainly that is implied by a text like Exod. 12.48. However, sociologically speaking, in a lineage-based agrarian society the immigrant from another tribe or even the next village is just as much of an outsider; this is how Weber interpreted the word, and Christoph Bultmann has argued in detail for the view that the 'alien' is the uprooted Israelite.[36] It may be that this is the original meaning, and that with the gradual dilution of the lineage-based system and the development of a sense of national identity (these tendencies are clearly observable in Deuteronomy) the word comes to be mainly applied to foreigners. But from the point of view of social marginality and economic need there is no difference.

Why does this text lay such weight on conduct towards the outsider? That we should need to ask the question, and have no clear answer, illustrates how limited our knowledge of social conditions is. But from the literary point of view, it makes sense that the Israelites so recently delivered from oppression as aliens in Egypt should be reminded, twice, of their responsibility for those similarly at their mercy in the land they are to occupy.

The words used for 'oppress' are worth a glance. The first verb in Exod. 22.21 (20) is *ynh* (Hiph.), which is found (alone) when this command appears in Lev. 19.33, and is particularly common in Ezekiel, being used three times in Ezekiel 18 and twice in Ezekiel 22; its use in Ezek. 45.8; 46.18; Lev. 25.14, 17 implies economic exploitation, doing someone out of what is their due. The second verb in Exod. 22.21 (20), used again in Exod. 23.9, *lḥṣ,*

---

35. See above, pp. 61–63, for a discussion of the distinction.
36. Weber 1952: 32–33; Bultmann 1992; cf. Crüsemann 1996: 184.

is unusual in texts concerned with social oppression, but is quite regular in describing the oppression of one nation by another, as Christiana van Houten points out.[37] This may imply that the *gēr* is here being thought of as a foreigner. And thirdly, in Exod. 22.22 (21) and 22.23 (22) the verb used is *'nh* (pi.). It is a common word, but it is not among the words used in the prophets' attacks on social oppression. It belongs to the field of ideas of honour and shame; it is the regular word for dishonouring a woman by seduction or rape, making her unmarriageable;[38] it is also commonly used with the self (*nepeš*) as the object, meaning to humble oneself before God with fasting, sackcloth and ashes and so forth. It seems to be the strongest word available for humiliating someone by physical action, reducing someone to the lowest depths, as Ellen van Wolde suggests.[39] The emphasis is thus moved away from economic exploitation to social humiliation: the warning is not to further humiliate and marginalize those whose position is already marginal. The verb is of course related to the adjective and noun *'ānî*, 'poor', someone who is on the lowest rung of the social ladder, with no honour to lose.

When we move to the poor in Exod. 22.25–26 (Hebrew 24–25), the attention is once again all on the practice of giving credit, and the same issues of interest and pledges emerge as in Ezekiel. But they are expressed differently, and need renewed attention. Translating literally: 'When you (sg.) lend silver to my people, to the poor man with you, you shall not act like a *nōše* (see below) to him; you (pl.) shall not impose interest on him; if you (sg.) really must take your neighbour's garment in pledge, you shall restore it to him before sunset.' (I deal with v. 27 [26] below.) There are a whole series of issues here, which we shall take in the order of the text.

Why is only money mentioned, when even in the more economically advanced Mesopotamia a high proportion of loans were made in kind? In Deut. 23.20 it is forbidden to raise interest on silver, foodstuffs, 'or anything on which it is customary to charge interest'; and Lev. 25.37, similarly, mentions both silver and foodstuffs. It should not be concluded from the fact that Exodus 22 only mentions money that interest on loans in kind was unobjectionable. It is characteristic even of the casuistic laws to mention only typical cases, more so this type of moral instruction.[40] And the loan of money is typical of the grasping creditor who figures later in the verse. Such a loan can only be repaid by the sale of produce (assuming a debtor who still has some land), or by giving up part of one's wages. As subsistence loans would generally be made when prices were high and

---

37. Van Houten 1991: 52, with list of texts: Exod. 3.9; Judg. 2.18; 4.3; 6.9; 10.12; 1 Sam. 10.18; Amos 6.14; 2 Kgs 13.4, 22; Jer. 30.20; Ps. 106.42.

38. The common opinion that it denotes rape in itself is wrong: see most recently van Wolde 2002.

39. Van Wolde 2002.

40. Cf. Jackson 1989: 198.

repaid when they were low, after harvest, a money loan was a heavier burden, at least for the farmer, and the creditor reaped profit from it even without imposing interest.

The phrase ' *et ' ammî ' et he 'ānî 'immāk*, 'my people, the poor man with you' is awkward. It is usually taken as equivalent to ' *et 'ᵃnî 'ammî 'immāk* 'the poor man among my people with you', but there must be a suspicion that 'my people' is a gloss added to bring this text into line with Deut. 23.19–20 (Hebrew 20–21).[41] But even with this, the Exodus text does not explicitly restrict its protection to Israelites, unlike Deuteronomy. It would be strange to do so in a context so concerned with protection for the outsider.

For *'immāk* 'with you' I need only refer to my discussion of the same word in Lev. 25.35, 39, where I approved the NRSV's translation 'dependent on you', which it does not repeat here.[42] But I see no reason why it should not apply here also. The issue is not how the subject of the instruction is to treat all or any poor people: he does not have positive duties to all and sundry. Wherever there is no universal state provision for the needy, that is in nearly all societies other than modern industrialized ones, they rely on their own particular protectors and patrons, and these will see their first responsibility as being to those who are personally dependent on them. If I might offer a parallel from the modern period: the journals of Elizabeth (Grant) Smith of Baltiboys, the wife of a nineteenth-century Irish landlord, show her strong sense of responsibility towards their own tenants; the family went without accustomed luxuries for several years in order to keep the poor of the estate alive during the famine; yet at the same time she objected to being assessed for the support of the poor in general—she felt this was subsidizing bad landlords.[43]

The question, then, is how the subject is to treat *his clients* or his poor relatives, those who have no one but himself to turn to. He has a positive responsibility to help them, as Deut. 15.7–11 emphasizes, and not to exploit them; the present text elaborates on the possibilities of exploitation.

'You shall not act like a *nōše* to him.' What was a *nōše*? NRSV's 'creditor' will hardly do: that is exactly what a lender is. REB's 'moneylender' is better, since that has the right pejorative tone in English. The word is only found five times (1 Sam. 22.2; 2 Kgs 4.1; Ps. 109.11; Isa. 50.1), and is generally pejorative, as here. The verb *nš'* and the related noun *maššā'* are commoner, usually translated simply 'lend' and 'loan' or 'debt'. However, many years ago H.M. Weil mounted a persuasive case that they all referred specifically to lending on the security of a person (as happens in 2 Kgs 4.1 and Isa. 50.1, as well as in Nehemiah 5).[44] This has not generally been accepted, but also

41. Cf. Childs 1974: 450.
42. Above, pp. 44–45.
43. Grant 1991.
44. Weil 1938.

never thoroughly refuted.[45] It is impossible to review the case here, though I will say that I can see no text in which such a meaning has to be excluded. It would certainly be appropriate here. The loan shark who will drag off the debtor's child if the debt is not repaid on time is the type of the grasping creditor that the reader is warned not to be like. As with the use of 'silver' at the opening of the verse it is typical, not exclusive. Reducing people to debt slavery is the worst, but not the only oppressive act that should be avoided by the just man.

The text goes on to mention two practices that could well lead up to the seizure of a personal security. The first is of course the charging of interest. Because this sentence is in the second person plural as against the singular on either side of it, it has often been thought that it is a later addition to the context. This could well be so; but it is an entirely appropriate one, since the charging of interest is one of the things that loan sharks do, which make it more difficult for the debtor to repay and hence more likely for the security to be seized.[46]

The second, on which the moral appeal of Exod. 22.27 (26) is hung, is being so ruthlessly insistent on having a pledge as to deprive someone with only one cloak of it even in the cold of night. Now, how could the seizure of an object of such low value serve to secure a substantial loan? This is a question which few commentators ask, probably because they fail to envisage the situation in realistic enough terms. Weil, however, argues that such a pledge has a 'probative purpose' (*un but probatoire*) like the staff, seal and chain which Judah hands over to Tamar in Gen. 38.17–18.[47] It is not intended as an equivalent to the debt, but as a guarantee that the debt will be repaid or the true security handed over. I am satisfied that Weil's argument, which is supported by many ancient Near Eastern parallels, is correct.[48] The scope of this moral teaching is broader in Deuteronomy: nothing which is essential to life should be taken (Deut. 24.6); the creditor should avoid the appearance of seizing the pledge but wait for the debtor to bring it to him (Deut. 24.10–11); such a pledge should not be demanded of a widow at all (Deut. 24.17b). But the Exodus text is already expressed in such a way as to cast doubt on the necessity of such guarantees: I have above rendered its use of the Hebrew infinitive absolute 'if you really must . . .'[49] It is something which the truly just man, taught by YHWH, will avoid.

45. Van Seters assumes it refers to lending at interest. That would make v. 25b (24b), often thought redactional, completely redundant.

46. Weil (1938: 205) argues that *nešek* always refers to 'interest' extracted from the labour of the personal security. I do not think he has made out this case.

47. Weil 1938: 202–04.

48. And therefore that Milgrom's argument (1976: 95–97) that pledges of this type are only seized when the debt falls due is not. Weil is, however, followed by de Vaux (1961: 171).

49. See Houtman 2000: 229.

In this section there are again just two 'motive clauses' or points of rhetorical support, in Exod. 22.23–24 (22–23) and 22.27 (26), though they may each contain more than one idea, as they are quite complex. What do they appeal to? Eckart Otto would find the most basic appeal in v. 27a (26a): 'For it is his only covering, it is his cloak to keep him warm; in what else can he sleep?'[50] The underlying meaning of the requirement in Exod. 22.26 (25) is 'the social necessity of the solidarity of the stronger with the weaker for the community's sake', and the appeal is 'to community consciousness as the foundation of an ethic of neighbourliness'.[51] He points to the use of 'with you' and 'neighbour' as signs that the idea of the neighbour is the basis of the moral appeal. I would not dissent from the idea of community consciousness, but these two signs point in different directions rather than the same one, in my view. 'With you', as I have argued, refers to the debtor's dependence. But 'neighbour' (*rēaʿ*) is the standard term in the casuistic laws for the person with whom the subject of the law is in relation or dispute, and implies fellow-citizenship of the community. Thus its use is a pretty broad hint that although a client may be dependent on you, the basic relationship is one of equality. But the appeal in Exod. 22.27a (26a) seems to be to plain human compassion. Not only are the poor your equals as members of the community, they have the same human needs as you in your warm comfortable bed at night.

The appeal does not stop there: as Otto points out, it is developed in a theological direction. 'If he cries to me, I will hear him, for I am merciful.' Mercy is of course precisely the virtue that is lacking in the hard-hearted creditor who refuses to return the cloak. 'As God deals with humankind, so human beings should behave towards each other.'[52]

YHWH makes the same statement (without the last clause) in Exod. 22.23 (22). Otto, following a redactional theory that sees all the clauses in the second person plural as secondary,[53] sees this verse as originally concerned with the alien, and argues that an ethic centred on a lineage-based community could not make solidarity with the alien plausible; a theological reason was needed to universalize the ethic 'and transform an ethic of "love of the nearest" into one of "love of the farthest" '.[54] At the same time it brings in the enforcement of the command by YHWH. According to Otto, Exod. 22.24 (23) is also secondary. But in the text as it stands it is clear that

---

50. Otto 1994: 84–85.
51. Otto 1994: 84 (my translation).
52. Otto 1994: 85–86.
53. Otto 1994: 23 (after Schwienhorst-Schönberger 1990).
54. Otto 1994: 85–86 (my translation: *'und ein Ethos der "Nächstenliebe" zu dem der "Fernstenliebe" transformieren'*. The German is really untranslatable, since *'der/die Nächste'* means literally 'the nearest' but usually 'the neighbour' as in the commandment to love one's neighbour.

v. 27 (26) recalls the warning which has already been uttered in vv. 23–24 (22–23). In any case, the warning of punishment is not really separable from the statement that YHWH will hear. His mercy, which Otto emphasizes as a characteristic of YHWH as the divine king, is, as he says, combined with the motif of the divine enforcement of justice. And how otherwise will YHWH enforce it than by sanctions on the unjust? This issue had long since been exhaustively discussed by Miranda, who points out the parallels between YHWH's response to Israel's oppression in Exodus 3 and his response to the oppression of the poor and marginalized in Israel in Exodus 22.[55] However, what is entirely correct in Otto's viewpoint is that anyone who will not act with justice unless coerced by YHWH has not absorbed the moral education represented by this text. In that sense, the punishment threatened by v. 24 (23) is a provision for failure.

There is a motivation attached to the repeated warning against exploit-ation of the stranger: 'for you were strangers in the land of Egypt . . . for you know the heart (*nepeš*) of the stranger (*gēr*), for you were strangers in the land of Egypt'. (Exod. 22.21 (20); 23.9.) It is an appeal to common experi-ence; in its literal sense it can only apply on the literary level: Moses who hears this speech and will relay it, and the people who hear it from him, were themselves alien settlers in Egypt and experienced the humiliation and wretchedness of oppression by unfeeling and xenophobic natives. But to the readers of Exodus the experience is a vicarious one. The experience belongs to their people as a people, and it is precisely because the stranger does not 'belong' that the Israelite, knowing the story of the Exodus, should under-stand the plight of the stranger and take care not to take advantage of it. Some consider that this motif has been introduced from Deuteronomy, where the same clause occurs at Deut. 10.19. But Deuteronomy develops it in a rather stereotyped way, usually having 'you (sg.) were *a slave* in the land of Egypt', even where the reference to slavery is not especially relevant (as in Deut. 24.18, 22). For Van Seters, who does not allow for redaction, it shows the dependence of the whole text on Lev. 19.33–34.[56]

The key points, then, which undergird the appeal for justice for the weak are these: the status of the poor *man* (not the alien, widow or orphan) as equally a member of the community; the commonality of human needs between the client and the patron; the commonality of experience between Israel and the stranger; the appeal to compassion; YHWH's compassion as the God of justice for all; YHWH's threat to intervene on the side of the weak. The just man is one who is conscious of his membership of the community and puts it before his personal advantage; is more conscious of

55. Miranda 1977: 149.
56. Van Seters 2003: 131.

his common humanity with his dependents than of his superiority and is personally concerned for them; and is conscious that this compassion is the nature and the will of his God.

In moving on now to Exod. 23.1–8, which primarily addresses the Israelite elder as a participant in the legal process, I shall only pick out those clauses that are relevant to his relations with the weak. The section as a whole is governed by the sense of society as the battleground of rival families in a struggle for honour, power and influence, which sometimes spills over into the local courts. Essentially, it warns the hearer that he is not to let his partisanship corrupt his standards of integrity and sense of common humanity, in daily life as in the courts.

The verses relevant to our inquiry are primarily 3 and 6, though 7–8 are so also in that bribery and pressure for the condemnation of the innocent are more likely to come from the well-placed, and on occasion their efforts will relate to their drive to dispossess those in their power. But it is a mistake to think that this would be the main focus of such efforts, despite Amos 5.10, 12. The drive by powerful families to increase their power is aimed at least as much at those who are rivals for power as at those over whom they may exercise it.

Exodus 23.3 is a difficult verse. 'And a poor man (*dāl*) you shall not honour (*tehdar*) in his suit.' The more usual danger to justice is that judges may favour the powerful rather than being partial to the poor. However, Lev. 19.15, in a well-balanced verse which has never been suspected of textual damage, has 'You shall not show partiality to a poor man (*dāl* again), nor shall you honour a rich (literally great, *gādôl*) man'. The expression used for 'be partial', 'show partiality' is *nś' p^enē* 'to lift the face of (someone)'; it means to show a *personal* bias to someone, to favour him because of personal connections. The phrase used for 'honour' also uses *pānîm* 'face', with the same verb as in Exod. 23.3. Both phrases therefore refer to the perversion of justice by personal favouritism. No-one, whether rich or poor, is to be favoured in this way. Considered on its own, then, the Exodus verse is not as surprising as many think;[57] but the lack of the balancing clause is surprising. Moreover, there is another difficulty. The verb is simply wrong. It means 'honour' and is invariably applied to people who are regarded as socially worthy of honour, as in Lev. 19.15.[58] The *dāl* is precisely not one of these, and Lev. 19.15 therefore uses a different expression.[59] I therefore follow

---

57. See Houtman 2000: 240–41.

58. So, correctly, Van Seters 2003: 137. Cf. Lev. 19.32 (an old man), as well as Lam. 5.12 (old men or elders), Sir. 7.31 (a priest), 46.2 (Joshua).

59. Otto's view (1994: 68) that the *dāl* is *contrasted*, as a '*Kleinbauer*', a small farmer whose class makes up the majority of the court, with the ' *ebyôn* of v. 6, who is the really poor man, is quite unconvincing: these two words are never contrasted and are sometimes in synonymous parallelism, e.g. Amos 4.1.

those[60] who consider that something has dropped out, at least the single letter *g* which distinguishes *gādōl*, 'great', from *dāl* 'poor'. Thus the verse was originally meant to say 'You shall not honour a great man when he comes to court', obviously in the sense that you are not to defer to his wealth and power so as to pervert justice. *pānîm* is not used: the issue is not the same as in Leviticus; it is not personal favour that the verse warns against, but deference to the rich because they are rich.

Its counterpart is then found in Exod. 23.6: 'You are not to pervert the justice due to your poor man when he comes to court'. Note the expression *'ebyōn^ekā* '*your* poor man', also found at Deut. 15.11. I concur with Houtman that this means not 'the poor man who is a member of your community', but (recalling 'with you' in Exod. 22.25 (24)) 'the poor man who is dependent on you'.[61] This gives a particularly sharp point to the injunction: because the poor man is in your power, it would be very easy for you to deny him justice (by giving false witness, or a false verdict) to gain some advantage, for there is nothing he would dare or be able to do about it.

I also follow Houtman (and the NRSV) in his interpretation of the end of Exod. 23.8, concerning bribes: that *dibrē ṣaddîqîm*, usually 'the words of the righteous', means 'cases of innocent people', so NRSV 'subverts the cause of those who are in the right'.[62] Often this will be poor people who are not able to offer a bribe.

The text thus recognizes how someone taking part in judicial proceedings may be swayed by the class position of himself and others. He may deny the justice due to a poor person, or indeed to anyone, by deferring to the power of the wealthy or by yielding to the temptation offered by a rich man's bribe or by a poor person's dependence on him. He is strictly to avoid this. This text again offers two motive clauses; 'for I will not acquit the guilty', Exod. 23.7; and 'for a bribe blinds those who see and subverts the cause of those who are in the right', Exod. 23.8. It appeals to the sense of justice and underlines that in pursuing strict justice one is again imitating God, whose court is incorruptible. In a set of similar injunctions in Deut. 16.19–20 there is no reference to the danger of class justice (however, see Deut. 24.17a), but there is the striking positive injunction: 'justice (*ṣedeq*), justice shall you pursue'.

Finally we come to the two 'sabbatical' commandments in Exod. 23.10–12. They fall to be considered in our study because the motives offered for them appeal to care for the poor, the slave, and the outsider, and for animals as well. This is in a way surprising, because one may presume that the original motives for the customs were religious or at least ritual.[63] The produce of

---

60. Some of them listed by Houtman, who disagrees (2000: 240–41); add now Van Seters (2003: 137).
61. Houtman 2000: 247.
62. Houtman 2000: 250; see also Childs 1974: 443.
63. Houtman 2000: 251–57 notes various interpretations.

the untilled land of the seventh year (vv. 10–11) could hardly be a serious way of providing for the poor, but it is evident that this is a rationalization of a practice with an originally quite different motive. The assistance for the poor provided by the sabbatical year is only symbolic, but it is a significant symbol. The landholder who wishes to be just gives up his claim on the land one year in seven, and it is free for whoever will to nourish themselves on it, especially the *'ebyōnîm*, who here clearly are the landless poor.

In Lev. 25.2–7 the institution is treated rather differently. The sabbatical year is a sabbath *to YHWH*, who is the landlord (Lev. 25.23); the break of cultivation recognizes his ownership. There is a similar suggestion that the land will produce food in the seventh year (Lev. 25.6–7), but here it is for the landholder and those dependent on him, not for the poor (as well as for the animals, both domestic and wild). This is of a piece with Leviticus 25's projection of a classless Israel, which we shall discuss later.[64]

Deuteronomy does not refer to any sabbatical break of cultivation, but a rather similar moralization and rationalization of old agricultural institutions, ostensibly in the interests of the socially weak, is found in the exhortations about gleaning and the forgotten sheaf in Deut. 24.19–22, and similarly in those about the corner of the field and gleaning in Lev. 19.9–10. Clearly we are dealing once again with the symbolic abandonment of absolute claim on the produce, not with a seriously intended means of support for the landless (some go so far as to speak of a 'welfare system'—systematic it is not!). As Harold V. Bennett urges, that would be problematic in a number of ways.[65] It would not be likely to be sufficient, though I would not go so far as Bennett in saying that it is likely that no produce remained after the harvest; it would be degrading to the landless to compel them to comb the fields, olive groves and vineyards for what might have been left;[66] and the arrangement throws the responsibility for support on those who were least able to afford it after tithes, taxes and debt services. However, Bennett's suggestion that the real object was to prevent the peasantry from making use of a stratagem for concealing the size of the harvest is unconvincing. It still seems to me more likely that Deuteronomy is not innovating but using moral exhortation to underpin an old custom, which the landless had probably always taken advantage of, but which may well have been breaking down under new economic pressures. Sadly, one must recognize that the degradation of the landless was a reality, and was probably not much exacerbated by gleaning. And it had always been recognized that the widow and orphan and stranger were

---

64. Below, pp. 197–98.
65. Bennett 2002: 117, 123–124.
66. Here Bennett sees more clearly than Nelson (2002: 293), who speaks of the practice as 'preserv[ing] the dignity of the poor' by obviating handouts and begging.

the responsibility of the community where they lived. That was again no innovation.

The weekly sabbath is another matter. The relief is real which is afforded by this practice to the various working people and animals who are dependent on the landholder, here represented by the ox and ass, the 'son of your female slave', and the outsider, who no doubt, not being entitled to land, largely existed in the countryside as a wage-labourer. As before these categories are typical and not exhaustive. The understanding of the sabbath as a social provision also occurs in the Deuteronomic version of the Decalogue, Deut. 5.14, and there leads to its presentation as a commemoration of the deliverance of Israel from slavery. The relief is real—but it is only relief. It is not a fundamental alteration of the social structure to eliminate dependency. The observance of the greater and the lesser rest is an essential part of the picture of the just man presented by this text, and it is significant that it is not a simply individual commitment: each of these institutions is a social observance in which the individual participates.[67] These provisions point us forward to the collective institutions we discuss in Chapter 6. Thus we find in the end that justice in its totality is not simply an individual choice, but a character of society. But it does not in this text imply equality or an elimination of hierarchy, of dependency, of masters and slaves or patrons and clients. These relationships are fundamental to the text. The issue throughout is: how am I to conduct my relationships with my dependents justly, that is, in a way embracing an understanding of myself as a member of a community, of my dependents as human beings like myself and equally members of my community, and of God as the one who exhibits, commands and enforces compassion, concern for the needs of human beings, and integrity?

4. *Proverbs*

The whole of Proverbs may be considered teaching for the individual man (again always a man) on how to live his life with integrity and success. The question of its social background has been dealt with at some length by Norman Whybray, who deals separately with the different sections of the book, marked out as they are by differences in literary form.[68] The

---

67. The sabbath year in Exod. 23.10–11 has sometimes been seen as observed at different times by different landholders, or even in different fields. But that is not the way it is interpreted in Lev. 25.1–7, and Houtman (2000: 252) along with most other recent interpreters rejects it. Hopkins (1985: 194–201) shows how it could have been observed without significant loss of production by a farmer operating a biennial rotation of grain and fallow.

68. Whybray 1990.

discourses and wisdom poems in Proverbs 1–9 clearly reflect an upper-class urban background.[69] Here there is, disturbingly, no reference whatever to relations with the poor. But Whybray argues that this section was not systematically planned to cover all aspects of life, otherwise one would hardly expect four of the ten instructional discourses to be concerned with one topic, adultery. So it may simply be an accident that there is no reference to charity to the poor. But whether this is so or not, we have the uncomfortable spectacle of one guide to upper-class morality that feels no need to advise justice to the poor.

The sentence literature (Prov. 10.1–22.16 and Proverbs 25–29) is a different matter: here admonitions to charity to the poor are frequent. Whybray sees it as reflecting the experience and values of people of a middle station in life: modest farming folk—note the many references to an agricultural setting—who are neither rich nor poor, but are constantly threatened by the danger of poverty—hence the large number of warnings of the sad fate awaiting the lazy.[70] Although they would no doubt not have been responsible for the composition of the book, it is their wisdom, expressed in pithy oral form, which has been collected by the scribes who wrote it.

This view has been effectively criticized by Michael Fox and Mark Sneed.[71] The agricultural setting is in no way dominant;[72] and the court sayings 'speak not only *about* kings and courtiers, but *to* and *for* them'.[73] Fox sees the prominence of this theme, with the reference to editorial work by 'the men of Hezekiah' in Prov. 25.1, as showing that 'the court was the decisive locus of creativity'.[74] Even if some proverbs circulated among the population, it must certainly have been among the governing cadre of the scribes, associated with the court (of the king or, later, the governor) or the temple, that they were collected and shaped. The highest level of the service would have consisted of landowners drawing income from their estates, not mere hangers-on of the ruling class but themselves members of the economic and social elite.

Sneed shows that Whybray's dependence on the content of the literature to identify its class background is misconceived. Aristocratic literature as we know it from Egypt has a wide range of interests, including much with a popular appeal; landowners are inevitably interested in agriculture; and the fact that the proverbs appear to view both rich and poor in objective terms is no guide to the standing of the authors. He quotes the Egyptian wisdom

69. Whybray 1990: 100–101; cf. Fox 1996; Sneed 1996; Pleins 2001: 452–83.
70. Whybray 1990: 31–34.
71. Fox 1996; Sneed 1996.
72. Fox 1996: 233.
73. Fox 1996: 235, quoting Prov. 16.10, 14; 25.6–7.
74. Fox 1996: 236.

writer Amenemope, who was clearly wealthy, but speaks of rich and poor in a very similar style to Proverbs:

> Better is the poor man who speaks sweet words,
> Than the rich man who speaks harshly (25.12–13).
> God loves him who cares for the poor,
> More than him who respects the wealthy (26.13–14, as in Sneed 1996: 305).

Sneed concludes that there is nothing in Proverbs which requires the authors of the sentences to be humble folk; it is perfectly possible that some of the proverbs have a popular oral origin, but 'there is no need to assume this for the bulk of Proverbs'.[75]

What audience did the authors have in mind for the sentences? The view espoused by Pleins, following a large number of writers, aligns the book as a whole with the Egyptian wisdom literature, which is clearly intended as instruction 'for aspiring court scribes and officials',[76] and is related to the theory that there were schools for their education, which has never been demonstrated. This view is doubtful for Proverbs 1–9, which never refers to a setting of court or government; and it is of almost equally dubious merit for the sentence literature, which implies a wide range of settings, from the court to the home to the farm. It is indeed centrally concerned with the public sphere, where men interact with each other, take counsel and guide their own affairs. But this is not necessarily at the highest level: the court setting pertains only to a minority of sayings. I conclude that the sentences were intended for the delight and instruction of a broad audience, largely upper-class, but not necessarily official. The ethos of the instructions in Prov. 22.17–24.22 is very similar, and the same may be said of them, as also of the last two chapters of the book.

Though the ethics of Proverbs has been alleged to be merely prudential, there is no question that there are many sentences and other forms which instruct in the virtue of justice, in the broad sense of dutiful, honest and generous relationships with others, and many of these are concerned with how one should behave towards the poor. It will be convenient to set these out together here. I will divide them into two groups: first those that comment from an ostensibly objective viewpoint on relations between rich and poor, and secondly those that state or imply a moral evaluation of different ways of behaving toward the poor.[77] Texts in the first group maintain a rhetorical distance from those responsible for oppression, and sometimes refer to them as 'rich', a description rarely found outside the wisdom

---

75. Sneed 1996: 305. The above three paragraphs are taken with omissions from Houston 2003: 230–232.

76. Pleins 2001: 456.

77. Fleischer (1989: 331–45) makes a very similar division, while adding the 'better is' sayings (Prov. 16.19; 19.1, 22; 28.6) as a third group.

literature.[78] The sentences in the second class, on the other hand, imply that the choice between justice and injustice is one open to the hearer or reader. I have not given here texts which refer to the duty of the king to defend the poor, or the reality of his oppression, since our focus here is on the justice of the patron. As usual, my translations are fairly literal and reflect the gendered character of the original. Only Prov. 31.20 refers to a woman.

Group I.

11.26: One who holds back grain is cursed by the people, but a blessing is on the head of one who sells it (or, more generally, 'who distributes it'—not necessarily by sale).

13.23: The soil of the poor (probably: *rāʾšîm* for *rāšîm*) yields much food, but it is often swept away by injustice.[79]

14.20: A poor man (*rāš*) is hated even by his neighbour, but a rich man's friends are many. (Compare Prov. 19.4.)

18.23: A poor man (*rāš*) uses entreaties, but the rich man answers harshly.

22.2: A rich man and a poor man (*rāš*) meet together (literally; NRSV 'have this in common'; McKane 'live side by side');[80] YHWH is the maker of them all (LXX 'both').

22.7: A rich man rules over poor people (*rāšîm*), and the borrower is the lender's slave.

28.3: A man who is poor (*rāš*) but exploits poor people (*dallîm*) is like beating rain which leaves no crops (or 'beating rain and famine').[81]

28.11: A rich man is wise in his own eyes, but a poor man (*dāl*) who has insight sees through him.

29.13: A poor man (*rāš*) and his oppressor (*ʾîš tᵉkākîm*) meet together (compare 22.2); it is YHWH who gives light to the eyes of both.

30.14: There is a group whose teeth are swords, whose jaws are knives, to eat up the poor (*ᶜaniyyîm*) from the earth, and the needy (*ʾebyônîm*) from among humankind.

Group II.

14.21: One who shows contempt to his neighbour is a sinner, but one who is generous (*mᵉḥônēn*) to the poor (*ᶜaniyyîm*)—happy is he.

14.31: One who exploits a poor man (*ʾōšēq dāl*) insults his Maker; but one who is generous (*ḥōnēn*) to a needy man (*ʾebyôn*) honours him.

78.	*ᶜāšîr* 'rich' is found 13 times in Proverbs, Job and Ecclesiastes and once in Ps. 49, out of a total of 23 times in the Hebrew Bible.

79.	McKane (1970: 231) offers a quite different translation: 'The tilth of grandees (*rāʾšîm*) produces an abundance of food, but it is swept away for lack of equity'.

80.	McKane 1970: 244.

81.	Inevitably this verse has caused difficulty, and it has been suggested that *rāš* 'poor' is a mistake for *rāšāᶜ* 'wicked' or *ᶜāšîr* 'rich'. McKane (1970: 629) prefers to keep the consonantal text and read it *rōš* 'chief', 'a man in authority'.

17.5: One who mocks a poor man (*raš*) insults his Maker, and one who is glad at calamity will not escape punishment.

19.17: One who is generous to a poor man (*ḥônēn dāl*) is YHWH's creditor, and he will repay him his debt in full.

21.13: One who turns a deaf ear to the cry of a poor man (*dāl*) will himself call out and not be answered.

22.9: A generous man (literally 'one with a good eye') will be blessed, because he gives of his own bread to the poor man (*dāl*).

22.16: One who exploits a poor man (*'ōšēq dāl*) to enrich himself, and gives to a rich one, will end in want.

22.22–23: Do not rob a poor man (*'al tigzōl dāl*) because he is poor, and do not crush the humble man (*'ānî*) in the gate; for YHWH will plead their cause, and despoil of life those who despoil them. [The meaning of 23b is uncertain.]

23.10–11: Do not remove an ancient landmark, or trespass on the fields of fatherless children; for their Redeemer is strong; he will plead their cause with you.

28.8: One who increases his wealth by charging interest, advance or accrued (*bᵉnešek ûbᵉtarbît*[82]), amasses it for one who is generous to the poor (*dallîm*).

28.27: One who gives to a poor man (*rāš*) will have no want, but one who hides his eyes will get many curses.

29.7: A just man (*ṣaddîq*) knows the rights of the poor (*dîn dallîm*), but an unjust man has no insight.[83]

31.20: (In the praise of the virtuous woman) She opens her hand to the poor (*'ānî*), and stretches out her hands to the needy (*'ebyôn*).

The mere reading of this catalogue should give the lie to Pleins's assertion that Proverbs launches 'a veritable attack on the poor', and that the main role they play in the book is to function as a dreadful warning of the dangers of laziness.[84] I have criticized this view in detail elsewhere, and it would take us out of our way to repeat the argument here.[85] It is perfectly true that there are many texts in the book which denounce laziness, and most of them warn that a lazy man who does not change his ways will end up on the streets, to use the modern expression. But there are none which are less than sympathetic to the actual poor, or claim that they became poor because they were lazy. The wise, if that is what we should call the authors, know better than that. The poor are simply poor; there is no need to ask why they are poor. Like so many of the texts of the Old Testament, Proverbs takes class division, the existence of poor and rich, as a given.

---

82. Qere *ûtarbît*, but in any case it overloads the line; *BHS* suggests it is a gloss.
83. McKane 1970: 257.
84. Pleins 2001: 437, 465–70, drawing on van Leeuwen (1955: 153) and Kuschke (1939).
85. Houston 2003: 232–37.

The wise are not interested in the origins of the social system, nor are they interested in changing it. But we can see from the sayings in group I that they have a very good idea of how the system works. Wealth means power (this is the meaning of the references to 'friends' too), and power is generally used arrogantly. Of that they are well aware, and despite the deadpan way in which the facts are presented, a necessary effect of the literary style, they clearly do not approve. This is shown by their frequent injunctions to their readers to make sure that they behave differently (group II).

We are now becoming familiar with the characteristic shape of depictions of just behaviour, and a brief glance at the sayings in this group shows how it is similar to and differs from those in Exodus and Ezekiel. We note first the rarity of references to the marginalized, the widow, fatherless and stranger, in contrast to the 'poor'. There is one reference to the fatherless (Prov. 23.10) and one to the widow (15.25, not given above as it does not obviously fit in either group). They are more prominent in Job, as we shall see. The *gēr* is completely absent from the book, as from eighth-century prophecy.

So far as the 'poor' are concerned, that is, as we have seen, full citizens who have inadequate resources, there is a difference in the balance of vocabulary. The predominant words for 'poor' are *dāl* (15 times) and *rāš* (14 times; a word almost peculiar to the wisdom literature),[86] but where it is a question of doing justice to the poor, in the sayings in group II, the preference is for *dāl*. *ʿānî* and *ʾebyôn* occur relatively rarely; it has been argued that, because these terms are the normal ones used when writers take the side of the poor,[87] the Proverbs writers were no 'advocates' for the poor. Pleins notes that the pairing *ʿānî / ʾebyôn*, characteristic of such advocacy, is absent from most of the book but occurs 'repeatedly' in Proverbs 30–31, while *dāl, rāš* and *maḥsôr*, typical of Proverbs 10–29, are absent from 30–31, which he therefore regards as having a separate editorial history, if not a different social background.[88] He regards the use of this different vocabulary in the bulk of the book as indicative of a different and contemptuous attitude to the poor. It seems much more in accord with the evidence to suggest that the prevalence of *rāš* is linked to the equally notable prevalence of *ʿāšîr* 'rich'—they are frequently used in antithetical parallelism—and that these are the terms used in wisdom observations. They do suggest a certain (assumed?) neutrality, and for that reason *rāš* tends to be avoided in favour of *dāl* in sentences which exhort to justice to the poor. The use of *dāl* in

---

86. 21 times in the Hebrew Bible, of which 16 are in Proverbs and Ecclesiastes.

87. It is more accurate to say that when these terms are used, the writers are taking the side of the poor (which does not exclude the use of other terms)—Schwantes 1977: 277.

88. Pleins 2001: 466. This is something of an overstatement. *ʿānî / ʾebyôn* occurs three times (Prov. 30.14; 31.9, 20); and though *rāš* does not occur, derivatives of the same root occur in Prov. 30.8–9. Note also that the pairing does not occur in Amos.

Amos is quite comparable, and certainly cannot there be set in opposition to the use of *'ānî* and *'ebyôn*.

However, the texts are too general to enable us to pinpoint the precise social situation of these poor, and probably no one situation is in view. What we can say is that they are within the power of the subject of the sentences to exploit or to help. The subject is conceived of in the position of a patron. In these group II sayings, there is very little distinct reference to lending: it is only clearly in view in 28.8, where the charging of interest is deplored, as elsewhere. Possibly foreclosing on mortgaged land is referred to in 23.10, unless it is naked land-grabbing, taking advantage of the minority of the legitimate landholder. It is possible that the generosity which is commended includes interest-free (and perhaps unsecured) lending, but 22.9 and 31.20 certainly refer to free gifts (compare Ezek. 18.7). But as both are commended in Ezekiel 18, we can perhaps assume that both are in view, in different situations, in Proverbs.[89]

We now need to analyse the moral and theological themes apparent in these sayings. Negatively, disapproval is aimed at oppression by economic exploitation, using *'šq* and *gzl*; but also at mockery and insult (14.21; 17.5). Here we see the influence of the honour-shame complex: the poor will be shamed by being insulted, and a man of honour should be above that. Again, deliberately ignoring the need of the poor is reprehensible: it is 'sealing one's ear' (21.13) or 'hiding one's eyes' (28.27); this 'somatic' language, with its emotional rhetorical punch, reappears in Deut. 15.7–11.[90] Positively, the conduct of the just man (or the good woman) consists primarily in giving, just as the unjust man takes what is not his. Again, this can be described in somatic language: the generous man is 'good of eye' (*ṭôb 'ayin*), Prov. 22.9. But more widespread is the language of honour. In 14.21, 31 and 19.17 generosity is described with participles of the verb *ḥnn* 'to show favour' (related to the noun *ḥēn*, 'favour'); the man of honour gains honour by showing favour to less powerful people, as with Boaz and Ruth in Ruth 2;[91] and clearly the appropriate way of showing favour to the poor is to give them what they need. And *ṣaddîq* 'just' (Prov. 29.7) can also be seen as a term of honour. The contrast of 'just' and 'unjust' ('righteous' and 'wicked' in most translations) is very common in Proverbs, usually expressing the standard theodicy, the doctrine of retribution; but in 29.7 it rather expresses what the difference is: it is a matter of knowledge; the just man knows what is due to the poor—which of course implies that he also puts his knowledge

89. The most frequent references to lending in Proverbs are in connection with the theme of the danger of guaranteeing loans for others: Prov. 6.1–5; 11.15; 17.18; 20.16 = 27.13; 22.26–27. This is possibly a commercial practice which has nothing to do with subsistence loans.

90. Hamilton 1992: 31–34; see below, p. 184.

91. Above, p. 43.

into effect; the unjust shows by his conduct that he does not know or does not care.

It is apparent that once again the plea for justice offers no challenge to the hierarchical nature of society: on the contrary, it appeals to it. The man who is concerned for his honour as a man of substance will 'show favour' to the poor, behave with justice and generosity to them, and refrain from gaining financial advantage from them. We have here an ethic of *noblesse oblige*, as Kovacs defines it: the wise 'are responsible and dutiful citizens who act to uphold the proper social order'.[92] And the proper social order includes the duty of the leaders of society to care for the poor as well as the duty of the poor to respect their betters. As Carol Newsom observes, 'Since the values of this moral world endorse power differentials within the society, they are also concerned to control abuses of power'.[93]

Unfortunately, as the sages are well aware (see the sayings in group I), most people put in a position of power over weaker people will fail this test: they will prefer their material advantage to their true honour. Thus the plea is backed up further by theological or cosmological considerations, and especially by the so-called doctrine of retribution. Most of the sayings in group II express some form of this. The only ones to attribute retribution explicitly to God are 19.17 and the two instructions in 22.22–23 and 23.10–11, which belong to a different genre from the rest. But when we make a comparison with the motive clauses in Exodus 22, we can see the relationship between them and not only Prov. 22.22–23; 23.10–11, but also Prov. 21.13. It is YHWH who stands in the place of the absent redeemer of the fatherless, the absent advocate of the poor man in the gate, who hears the cry of the oppressed (Exodus) and does *not* listen to the one who has refused to hear that cry himself (Prov. 21.13).

But in most of the sentences there is no explicit theology of retribution. They rather express a conviction that the world is so structured that the unjust will fail and those who create want in others will come to it themselves. On the other hand, those who are just, kind and generous will find blessing. Newsom argues in discussing the narratives presented by Job's friends, which of course make the same point, that it is not so much a matter of retribution as of the meaning of just and unjust actions in relation to reality. 'To do an act of goodness is to root oneself in reality. To commit an act of evil is to cut oneself off.'[94] A great many of the wisdom sentences contrast the fates of *ṣaddîq* and *rāšāʿ*, righteous and wicked or just and unjust. If we were to use Prov. 29.7 as a key, and substitute 'who knows the rights of the poor' and 'who does not know'

92.   Kovacs 1974: 178.
93.   Newsom 2003: 123.
94.   Newsom 2003: 124. See further p. 127.

for the key terms in these sayings, much of the book would be seen as conveying this message.

In so far as this is intended as an encouragement to just conduct and a deterrent to unjust conduct, it may or may not work. But it is better seen as a theodicy. It assures us that even when appearances are against it, the world is based on justice. The unjust, the oppressors, are restrained by the workings of a cosmos favourable to justice and unfavourable to injustice. And such a theodicy can be seen in the context of our present inquiry as ideological. If power is to be justified by the way it is used, the theodicy assures us that it cannot be used unjustly for long; the unjust will be destroyed and the just will come into their own; hence current injustice is a distortion of the order of society rather than its inevitable effect.

Assurances of this kind are not confined to the wisdom tradition. It is plain that Ezekiel 18 rests on a similar assumption; and though Exodus 22 focuses only on the negative side of the doctrine, as it is developed within the tradition of the Torah in Deuteronomy it is deployed both negatively and positively on a large scale; not only at the level of the nation as in the covenantal blessings and curses in Deuteronomy 28, but also at many points in the code on the individual level, for example in Deut. 15.10 or 24.13, 15, 19. At all these points justice is seen as something implemented by the individual, who is rewarded with blessing. But of course both Deuteronomy and the prophets envisage mass disobedience followed by mass destruction. As theodicies, as we have already seen, these rather serve to explain the destruction of society than its endurance. Proverbs is in a different position. As it is concerned exclusively with the individual, its theodicy must be played out within the lifetime of a single individual.

But this leads to a serious tension within the book of Proverbs, between the texts that we have studied. On the one hand, we are assured that the just will receive material rewards and the unjust will be deprived of them. On the other, we learn that those that rule over the poor, give them harsh answers and exploit them (Prov. 22.2 compared with 29.13), are the rich! In other words, practical experience as represented by the sayings of observation is in tension with the assurances found in the moral teaching. The unjust, it seems, grow richer, not poorer. It is of course possible to harmonize these insights. The unjust accumulate wealth by injustice, but *ultimately* they will forced to give it up. This is precisely what Zophar asserts in Job 20, and it is the pivot on which the book of Job turns, as we shall see in a moment.

There are, however, four sayings which express their understanding of a cosmos based on justice in a rather different way: Prov. 14.31; 17.5; 22.2; 29.13 root their abhorrence of oppression in the goodness of the Creator. The last two sayings emphasize that the oppressor is just as dependent on God for the common goods of life as the poor person, and the first two assert that the poor have a dignity which derives from the fact that they are creatures of God. I have suggested elsewhere that these reflections may offer a way of appropriating the understanding of justice in wisdom literature which actually undermines its support for the existing order.

> For if it is true that our common creatureliness binds us in solidarity with one another, this takes precedence over any justification for the division of society in a way which gives a few people absolute power over the rest and the choice of how to use it: the division which the wisdom teachers dumbly accept but do not attempt to justify. 'The poor man and the exploiter have one thing in common: it is YHWH who gives light to the eyes of both' (Prov. 29.13). There is then no justification for any other goods to be monopolised by the one and denied to the other.[95]

5. *Job*

The book of Job evidently reflects a similar upper-class and educated milieu to that of Proverbs; both author and implied readers belong to such circles. It is evident not so much in the fact that the hero is a very rich man, since its picture of his wealth is fanciful, but in the sophisticated style and recherché vocabulary of the poem, and in the fact that the entire discussion turns on the conduct and fate of the wealthy and powerful. Clines argues incisively that only a leisured audience could have read or appreciated it, and that wealth, poverty and class are understood from a rich man's point of view.[96] But as a work of the imagination, it has no single persuasive purpose; rather, as Newsom shows, it deploys a variety of genres and rhetorical strategies in order to examine its subject from different points of view.[97]

Despite the upper-class orientation, social justice is a key issue in the book of Job, as Walter Brueggemann has noted and Pleins has underlined, and its discussion of theodicy has to be seen in that light.[98] Clines can scarcely be correct in arguing that issues of class conflict are suppressed in the book,[99] since the argument is partly about the fate of the unjust, the oppressors of the poor. The issue we were discussing at the end of the last section is precisely that on which the dialogue turns. The dialogue in Job makes explicit the tension implicit in Proverbs, and each side of the argument, expressed in one-line sayings in Proverbs, is developed into one or two full-blown narratives. The issue comes to a head in Job 20–24, with Zophar's second speech, Job's reply, Eliphaz's third speech, and part of Job's reply, Job 24.1–17. Zophar, as I have noted, asserts that the riches

95. Houston 2003: 238–39.
96. Clines 1995: 123–33.
97. Newsom 2003.
98. Brueggemann 1994; Pleins 2001: 504–10.
99. Clines 1995: 132–33.

which are accumulated by the exploitation of the poor must be lost in short order. The wicked rejoice 'only for a moment' (Job 20.5). In a neat irony which exploits a word-play, he says of the oppressor 'his children will beg the favour of the poor (*yᵉraṣṣû dallîm*)' (Job 20.10), the same people he had 'crushed' (Job 20.19: *riṣṣaṣ . . . dallîm*). 'He swallows wealth and vomits it up again; God drives it out of his belly' (Job 20.15). And he himself cannot escape a violent death (Job 20.23–25). Eliphaz and Bildad tell similar stories.

Newsom, as we have seen, understands narratives like this as making a claim about fundamental reality, and the reason why they are convincing, not only to themselves but to society in general, is because they are 'iconic narratives' which 'encode fundamental commitments, social roles and profiles of virtue that constitute the community'. In other words, they make sense to one who tries to live a virtuous life in the kind of community they assume: 'a hierarchical, paternalistic social order based on kinship and something like a patronage system, within an honour/shame culture with a strong purity system', exactly as we have seen in Hebrew society in the course of this study.[100] Counter-narratives such as Job will produce in Job 21 and 24.1–17 do not make sense in the same way because, although they may be true, they lack the power to explain the social order in the way its participants see it, as both natural and benevolent.[101] For Job, on the other hand, they express the perception of reality he has arrived at through his own experience.

When we come to Job's great final statement in Job 29–31, with its evocation of his former life in ch. 29 and his self-exculpation in ch. 31, we are prepared for it to be expressed to a large extent in terms of his relations with his inferiors. We already know, because the narrator has assured us of it, that he is a perfectly just man, hence his statement must make it clear what the narrator, or, more precisely, what Job as presented by the narrator, understands to be justice for a man in his position. But we also know that that position had been that of a man of fabulous wealth and therefore of power and honour, so that justice for him must concern how he relates to those of less power and less honour. The statement will also show how Job conceives of the proper rooting of the social order which had given him that power and honour in the cosmic order.

Job 29 as a whole depicts a person of surpassing divine blessing and of unparalleled honour within a 'village patriarchy',[102] before whom not only his juniors but old men and persons of distinction rise and keep silence, wait for his counsel and do not venture to submit their own. His domination of

---

100. Newsom 2003: 121–25; here 122 and 123.
101. Newsom 2003: 122–23.
102. Newsom 2003: 187.

his community was absolute, like that of a king (Job 29.25). Job 29.11 states that both his words and his actions were approved: this is what his honour consists in. Those words and actions embody the norms and values of the community.[103] But when Job describes those words and actions, they are to do exclusively with justice for the poor and socially weak. We find that they are described in terms rather different from those we have so far been used to. They are in fact appropriate for someone who is describing himself in effect as the ruler of his community, 'like a king'. It is not here simply a matter of doing justice himself, but of ensuring that justice is done and rescuing people from the injustice of others. Job 31.13–23, which we shall look at below, is different because there Job is declaring his innocence of injustice. Here he is glorying in his positive doing of justice for his whole community. The justice described in Job 29.12–17 is the justice of the king rather than the justice of the patron; indeed the first verse strongly echoes Ps. 72.12, and points forward to our next chapter.

Job here recalls that he did justice for all categories of the socially weak: the poor; the widow and orphan; the disabled (Job 29.15), not often mentioned elsewhere; but possibly the terms 'blind' and 'lame' are metaphorical, meaning those socially unable to help themselves, as 'dumb' certainly is in Prov. 31.8. In v. 16 Job says that he took up the case of 'one I did not know', which probably means someone with whom he has no family or patronal ties. The only term missing is the *gēr*. All the categories of those who required help are covered by 'those who had no helper' in v. 12, and by 'the perishing' in v. 13. The typical conception of royal justice, apparent in Psalm 72 and Prov. 31.1–8, is assistance for those who cannot assert their own rights because their social position is weak or threatened through poverty or lack of a supportive social network. How this could be effective on a nationwide scale is a moot point, but it is rhetorically convincing in the case before us, where the setting is a single country town.

Job's assistance takes the form first of rescuing the oppressed from their oppressors: this point appears at the beginning and end of the section, Job 29.12, 17; v. 17 intensifies it by suggesting that force was needed. The title 'father of the needy (*'ăbî 'ebyônîm*)' implies protection. The principles of his action are expressed in the central verse, Job 29.14: as expected they are 'righteousness and justice', the justice in society which the ruler is expected to enforce.[104]

In this passage Job presents his justice as his sole claim for honour in the community, in preference to his wealth or his ancestry. There is here an important parallel with Psalm 72, where, as I shall show, the justice of the

---

103. Newsom 2003: 188–89.

104. The sense is not affected by the reversal of the usual order and the use of *ṣedeq* in place of the more usual *ṣᵉdāqâ*. Cf. Isa. 32.1.

king is the sole justification for his dominion.[105] And as with the king, his conduct is approved by God as well as the community, and results in his surpassing blessing: note the threefold naming of the deity in Job 29.2–5.

The contrast with his present experience of shame (Job 30.1–14), 'held in contempt by the contemptible',[106] is extreme: Job's relation with God and therefore with his community is out of joint. For our present purpose, the main interest of this chapter is its indication that in Job's moral world there are undeserving as well as deserving poor. He would not even put them with his dogs; they are driven out and people shout after them like a thief (Job 30.1, 5). To give *them* charity would be a breach of justice rather than an instance of it: they stand altogether outside the community in which justice is meaningful. Who precisely might fill this role in the real world, and why, is uncertain.[107]

In Job's solemn repudiation of guilt in Job 31, the context is a more everyday one. The issue here is not Job's honour, but his innocence of any sin which would justify God's attack on him. His behaviour towards inferiors here takes a very large place, though not this time the sole one: not only the continuous passage in vv. 13–23, but also the coda in vv. 38–40 is relevant—over a third of the whole chapter. In contrast to Job 29, an important issue here is Job's personal relationship to the potential victims and his responsibility for them; whereas in his recollection of his lost honour, he prided himself on interfering with the relationship between client and patron where that had descended into exploitation (Job 29.17), here it is his conduct of relationships with his own dependants which is at stake.

In Job 31.13–15 he defends his treatment of his slaves. This is striking, since the point is not always raised in texts on justice—not in Ezekiel 18, nor in Proverbs. The 'Book of the Covenant' contains important laws giving rights to slaves in its casuistic section, and this may be why master-slave relations are not treated in the teaching on justice in Exod. 22.21–27 (20–26). Slaves of course had no right to appear in court against their master; the case or complaint (*rîb*) which Job's slaves might raise with him is subject to his sole discretion. His assertion is that he has never used this discretion to reject the complaint. And the motivation which he gives, apart from fear of God's judgment, is his common humanity with his slaves, as creatures of the one God: compare Prov. 22.2; 29.13. That he had a responsibility for his slaves could be taken for granted. That that responsibility implied always taking complaints seriously, and that having the same Maker imposed that reading of his responsibility—these are points that masters could well have disputed with Job. They are a significant contribution to theological ethics.

---

105. Below, pp. 138–49.
106. Newsom 2003: 189.
107. See Albertz 1981.

Yet the legitimacy of slavery as such, which left men and women subject to the discretionary justice of one man, is not questioned.

Job 31.16–23 cover territory familiar to us. Verses 16–20 concern Job's provision for the material needs of the destitute, and probably also his poor clients, even if not destitute. It is unlikely that Job is saying that whenever he ate, every orphan in the town was invited to eat with him. Rather, v. 18 appears to underline his close relationship with the fatherless and widows in question. Habel interprets the verse in line with Job's claim in Job 29.16 that he was 'a father to the needy', and so with Job's kingly rather than patronal justice.[108] But the Hebrew of the verse is difficult, and certainty cannot be achieved. In vv. 19–20, on the other hand, he does seem to be saying that whenever he *saw* someone perishing for lack of clothing, he made sure they were clothed.

In Job 31.21–23 we are back with the administration of justice. Here Habel's view may be accepted that 'raised my hand' is a gesture of the judge, referring to 'the public act of condemnation and punishment', as in Isa. 19.16, Zech. 2.9.[109] Job's possible temptation would have been to pronounce sentence against a friendless defendant ('fatherless' as a type) at the urging of his own supporters, no doubt his lineage group and clients.

Job's final self-condemnation in Job 31.38–40 concerns his land. This would be expected, but it comes in an odd position in the speech, and what exactly it concerns is far from clear. It is not clear what kind of payment v. 39a refers to, and the idiom in v. 39b has been variously understood.[110]

In Job 31.14, 23 Job makes clear that God's just judgment, assuming that God does judge justly, would have been against him if he had acted in the ways he says he has not. But although he seems here to assume God's justice is a reality, he has been denouncing its absence for some time, not just for himself, but generally. The wicked, that is those who abuse their position in society for selfish ends, do not suffer punishment; they live a long, honoured and happy life, and go to their graves with many mourners (Job 21). But those whom they oppress live in misery and destitution—and God does nothing about it (Job 24.1–17). 'God is assaulted not for direct actions but because of the unfair, unreliable social practices and agents God sanctions.'[111] If the theodicy is unreliable, that may suggest that the social arrangements are unreliable. It is not possible to assume that patrons will be benevolent and that kings will dispense justice: such assertions are indeed directly denied by Job in the dialogue on many occasions.

---

108. Habel 1985: 435.
109. Habel 1985: 436.
110. For full discussions see Driver and Gray 1921: I, 272–273; II, 230–231; Dhorme 1967: 466.
111. Brueggemann 1994: 191.

If this is true, then the view of reality held by Job's friends, indeed Job himself in his mood in his final testimony, and the sages of Proverbs is in ruins. It cannot be assumed that the hierarchy of society is generally benign. There may be some rulers and elders like Job, but not many; and there is no divine or cosmic obstacle to the power of those who are not like him. By questioning the will of God to judge justly, the Job dialogue pulls the rug out also from under the ideological justification of a hierarchical society.

And it would not be argued, I think, that the parts of the book that follow offer any way of restoring it; except only the epilogue. But though the epilogue, as David Clines argues, deconstructs the book's earlier argument, it does not efface its impact on the reader, as he acknowledges.[112] As for YHWH's speeches, the understanding of divine justice which may be thought to emerge from them is very different from that which the friends had assumed and Job had demanded. Not all readers accept that there is any concept of justice here, but for those that do it is a justice which is not determined by human demands, and therefore no foundation for human social order in the way in which the human characters of the book conceive it.[113] Newsom indeed argues that as the distinction between moral and physical order would not have been understood in the ancient Near East, the speeches should not be seen as rejecting God's role as the source of moral order.[114] But she goes on immediately to point out that it is rather the congruence between God and the chaotic forces represented by Leviathan that the speeches highlight, and Job's 'blessed rage for order' that is humbled.

6. *The Virtue of Justice*

Two features of this paradigm of justice in its various textual forms set it apart from modern Western understandings of justice. One, which we have just been examining, is its integral reliance on a concept of cosmic order. The other is the weight given to the commitment of the individual to do justice. It is true that we have not yet looked at more communal ideas, but when we do so, in Chapter 6, we will find that none of the proposals for establishing, or, better, strengthening social justice by communal measures is expected to work on its own. The debt release in Deuteronomy 15 and the jubilee in Leviticus 25 need to be backed up by the kind of generous conduct on the part of patrons which is inculcated in the texts we have looked at here. Justice, in a word, is dependent on individual commitment; and this is

112. Clines 1990.
113. E.g. Habel 1985: 526–35; Gutiérrez 1987: 73–75, 80, 87–88; Clines 1998: 254–255.
114. Newsom 2003: 252.

of course equally true of justice as established by the king, as we shall see in the next chapter.

This contrasts with the priority given to society in Western thought about justice. Philosophers have reflected on how a society may be ordered in such a way as to promote justice, and constructed utopias as examples. Politicians also have sought to order society in such a way that it can be called just. From the point of view of this tradition it could well be argued that what is being urged in these texts is not justice but charity. This is a distinction which could not be recognized by Hebrew thinkers; *ṣeḏāqâ* comes to mean almsgiving in later Hebrew, though of course the practice of the *ṣaddîq* in Ezekiel 18, let alone the practice of Job, includes far more than simple almsgiving. As I have suggested, these are based on the personal commitment of the patron to his client, and hence imply an obligation. It is not a matter of choice in the way that we might consider dropping a coin in the beggar's mug or sending a cheque to Oxfam was, and therefore should not be given a name which might suggest this. On the other hand, it is not compulsory: the obligation arises not from external authority but from a personal commitment which is itself undertaken because the person is just. The positions taken up in the prologue to Job by both the Satan and YHWH imply that the expectation of reward does not motivate genuine justice.

On the other hand, the personal commitment to justice is not itself a free choice. It is demanded by the social position of the patron. It can be said of Old Testament society as Alasdair MacIntyre says of 'heroic' society, that 'morality and social structure are one and the same'.[115] This kind of justice can be understood as a virtue in MacIntyre's sense. According to him, a virtue receives its primary definition in terms of a human practice which offers the arena in which it may be exercised.[116] A 'practice' receives a long definition, essentially that it is 'a coherent . . . form of socially established cooperative human activity through which goods internal to that form of activity are realized'. In the case of justice in the Hebrew Bible, it is the virtue required for the practice of patronage within what I have called a 'benevolent hierarchy' and Newsom, more precisely, a 'village patriarchy'. The goods realized are those of the peace, harmony and welfare—*šālôm*— of the community. The point can be put the other way round as well. Patrons need to be just for this kind of society to flourish.

Although that kind of society and that practice may be obsolete (but not everywhere!), the idea that justice in society must depend in part on the justice of individuals, particularly individuals with power, is unlikely ever to be outdated. For every complex society that we know of has had differences

115. MacIntyre 1985: 123.
116. MacIntyre 1985: 187.

of power. Power in advanced industrial societies is distributed in radically different ways, but still unequally. We will always have rulers, even if we mendaciously call them 'leaders'! As long as this is true people with power need to be taught to use it for the benefit of those in their power, generously, kindly, humanely; they need to be taught to care particularly for those with least power, and to prefer them to those with power. In other words, there will always be practices within which some form of justice similar to this will need to be shown.

But if the cosmic validation of a patriarchal order is blown away by the Old Testament itself, the community must rely on the *regular* commitment of the powerful to exercise their power not for their own good, but for that of those who are in their power. And it seems that this cannot be relied on. Although the commitment is not too much to ask of those who have received the moral education exemplified in the texts we have studied in this chapter, there are sadly too few who learn the necesssary lesson. To rely only on them also ignores the dignity of the currently powerless and the contribution they might make to society if the responsibility for justice were more evenly shared.

The justice of the patron, therefore, justice as a gift, albeit one required as a right, top-down justice, has to be found wanting in the light of experience. The Old Testament makes two kinds of move beyond this point. One is to bring in the state, invariably personified in the king, as the guarantor of justice, the deliverer of the oppressed and the destroyer of the oppressor. The other is to propose moves for justice which are in the hands of the community and which suggest a different and possibly more bottom-up conception of society and of justice. Both of these moves have severe drawbacks in practice, as we shall see.

However, we should note at this point how the rhetorical motivation of individual justice in the texts we have studied makes use of ideas with the potential to suggest ideas of equality. For we have seen at several points appeals for support to the common humanity and creatureliness of patron and client, of rich and poor, potential oppressor and victim. 'Did not One make both of us in the womb?' 'One who mocks a poor man insults his Maker.' 'YHWH gives light to the eyes of both.' 'Your wives will be widows and your children fatherless.' The Book of the Covenant makes also a different kind of appeal, to the experience of the Exodus, which has an equal power to subvert hierarchy. The just Israelite remembers that he is a member of a community which once was settled in a foreign land and was exploited through forced labour. All of these points suggest that the man of power, however justly and generously he may use it, has no inherent claim to his position. A society could be imagined in which this potentially humiliating relationship did not exist.

Chapter 5

JUSTICE AND THE KING

1. *Introduction*

The patron-client relationship appears to be understood in the Hebrew Bible as the fundamental locus of justice and injustice, but it is set within a state structure, and this plays a highly ambiguous role. On the one hand it is objectively responsible for financial demands and pressures which led to injustice: on the other the king is seen as charged with the responsibility to protect the poor and root out oppression. The state ultimately means the king, even though it is his subordinates who carry out his policies and may bear some, or even all, of the odium for them. This ambiguity means that it is inevitable that every text which is concerned with the king in relation to social justice will be strongly ideological.

Objectively, as we have seen, there is no question that it was the royal establishment, or later the imperial government, that was responsible for much of the oppression in society.[1] We can detect two opposite ideological reactions to this fact in the Old Testament. On the one hand, there is the positive evaluation of the king as the fount of justice and defender of the poor against oppression. This obscures his role in the oppressive structures. This ideal role of the king in establishing and maintaining justice is seen especially in the Psalms and in the book of Isaiah, and there can be little doubt that these traditions stem ultimately from the Jerusalem dynastic house itself.[2] On the other, there is the suspicious or negative evaluation of kings and royal government which emerges in such texts as Deut. 17.14–20; 1 Samuel 8; 1 Kings 21; Jer. 22.1–23.6; Ezekiel 34; Hos. 8.4; Amos 7.9.

Although these groups of texts evaluate the experience of monarchy in opposite ways, they employ the same standard of evaluation. This is particularly clear if one compares Psalm 72, the leading text for the role of king

---

1. Whether any of the texts we are here concerned with (especially Psalm 72) relate to the Persian king (suggested orally to me by Philip Davies) is a question I have left unexplored. I do not regard it as probable.

2. See above, pp. 77–79, for Isaiah.

in maintaining justice for the poor, with the Jeremiah and Ezekiel texts. For both psalmist and prophet it is the function of the king 'to do justice and righteousness', and 'judge the cause of the poor and needy' (Jer. 22.15–16), to 'deliver the needy when they call, the poor and those who have no helper' (Ps. 72.12). Thus the ideological support of the monarchy relies on a conception of the monarch's role which is shared with its opponents and critics, and which sets the king as the defender of the poor against their (other!) oppressors. The aim of this chapter will be to analyse the effect of this fact on the political and social theology of the Old Testament. In the Isaiah tradition, the ideology of the monarchy becomes a theology of Messianic expectation, and the defence of the poor is a significant element in this.[3] It will be important to establish whether the main point of the expectation is the re-establishment of the independent kingdom based on Zion, which necessitates a perfunctory reference to the defence of the poor, or a truly just (and therefore utopian) society such as the historical Davidic monarchy had failed to deliver.

2. *Criticism of Monarchy?*

In fact, there is no very widespread challenge to monarchy in principle in the Old Testament. Most of the texts cited above understand the danger as being the temptation for individual kings to abuse their position, thus offering a purely moral rather than structural criticism, which is line with our findings about words of judgment in the prophets in Chapter 3.

Jeremiah 22.13–17 contrasts Jehoiakim with his father, thus implying it is a matter of moral choice: and indeed who if not the king, it might be thought, was free to choose?[4] Jehoiakim not only does not rescue the oppressed from the oppressor, he oppresses on his own account: 'Alas for the man who builds his house without righteousness (sedeq) and his roof-chambers without justice ($\mathit{mišpāṭ}$), who makes his neighbour work for nothing and does not give him his wages'. Kessler argues that there is not even a fundamental criticism of the corvée here, but that only its misuse for private purposes is attacked.[5] This is possible, but it is quite certain that the text does not fundamentally criticize monarchy. Taken as a whole, the section on the kings, Jer. 22.1–23.6, is bracketed by positive visions of monarchy, in both cases governed by the call to ensure social justice: the bright future offered to kings who 'do justice and righteousness, and deliver the robbed ($\mathit{gāzûl}$) from the power of their exploiter ($\mathit{ʿōšᵉqô}$[6])', and so on (Jer. 22.3); and

---

3. I use the term 'Messianic' simply to refer to the expectation of a revived Davidic line.
4. See above, p. 81.
5. Kessler 1992: 83.
6. *BHS*; emended from *ʿāšôq*.

the prophecy of the 'righteous branch' (Jer. 23.5), if that is the correct translation of this difficult phrase, who is to 'do justice and righteousness'.

Ezekiel 34, the parable of the shepherds, developing the metaphor in Jer. 23.1–4, offers another powerful picture of state exploitation, in vv. 1–6, but extends to private exploitation in vv. 17–22. This is a broad attack not confined to the king, or to any one king, but like prophetic criticism in general it is moral rather than structural criticism: it is important to note that like the Jeremiah passage it leads up to a positive prophecy of a king 'David' who fulfils the requirement to maintain justice.

The story of Naboth's vineyard in 1 Kings 21 is a good moral tale which is often used to illustrate the prophetic objection to the exploitative role of the monarchy. But if it is read in its context that understanding must be nuanced. Ahab and Jezebel have already been portrayed as especially wicked. See 1 Kgs 16.30: 'Ahab son of Omri did evil in the sight of the LORD more than all who were before him'; and compare the murderous hostility of Jezebel to Elijah in 1 Kgs 19.1–2. They are special cases, therefore, and readers are unlikely to generalize to a condemnation of monarchy as such, especially in view of the praise in the Former Prophets for David, Hezekiah and Josiah.

Unless perhaps they remember 1 Samuel 8. This is the only passage that appears to take the oppressiveness of royal rule as a reason to reject monarchy as such. Samuel attempts to persuade the Israelites not to call for a king, by describing what he calls *mišpaṭ hammelek*, 'the custom of the king who will reign over you', 1 Sam. 8.11–18. This passage details all the exploitative activities of royal government in turn: conscription and the corvée, the expropriation of land in order to provide prebends to the king's supporters, the tithe, the commandeering of slaves and animals. The king is a burden on his people, who exploits them for his own benefit, who oppresses rather than crushing the oppressor, who creates poverty rather than protecting the poor and creating prosperity. The climax of the passage is the warning 'you shall be his slaves'. The point of this in the Deuteronomistic History is unmistakable: to set up a king over themselves means returning of their own accord to the state they were in in Egypt (compare Deut. 17.16).

It has been argued that this text represents the feeling of the Israelite tribes at the time of the establishment of the monarchy.[7] It seems more likely that it arises from long experience of the monarchy.[8] But we should note that it is not a complaint about oppression of the poor as such. It is not the poor who possess the fields and vineyards and flocks and herds and slaves

---

7.　Crüsemann 1978: 122–27.

8.　So most, e.g McCarter 1980: 161: 'a long and bitter experience of kingship'; cf. Noth 1981: 54.

which the king might wish to appropriate, nor is it they who have the richest harvest for the tithe. The feeling that is expressed by these words is surely primarily that of the well-to-do in the land who might be the targets of royal greed and acquisitiveness; Naboth is an example. Some such people might indeed be themselves guilty of acts of oppression, and at risk from the activity of the king in defending the poor, if there were any such activity. Thus the passage is not directly concerned with the issue of relations between rich and poor, and may even be itself suspected of ideological suppression of the truth.

We might conclude that the lack of any really fundamental criticism of the state in the Old Testament suggests that its own ideological estimate of itself had been fully absorbed and accepted by those classes responsible for the composition of the texts. However, although these texts do not challenge the legitimacy of monarchy as a system of government, they ignore the royal ideology found in Isaiah and the Psalms and thus, as Carroll notes, tend to the 'desacralizing and demystification of royalty, its status and its achievements'.[9] Moreover, there are details in one or two of these passages that suggest that the ideology is not merely being ignored. When the text in Deut. 17.14–20 allows for the appointment of a king, but commands at the same time that restrictions should be imposed on him, their object is stated to be 'that his heart should not be lifted up above *his brothers*' (Deut. 17.20). 'Brother' (*'āḥ*) is a frequent word for a fellow-citizen, a fellow-Israelite, in the Deuteronomic laws. I argue in the next chapter that it has an ethical connotation, imaging relationships in the nation as those of a family, and does not simply mean 'a member of the community' (NRSV!).[10] Deuteronomy 17.14 has already required that the king should be 'one of your brothers', not a foreigner. This makes it plain that the king is in principle only one of a family of equal 'brothers': a radical questioning of the royal mythology traceable in the Psalms, which makes him the unique offspring of God (Pss. 2.7; 110.3), and gives him a privileged relationship with God, as is implied in all the royal Psalms.[11] A similar implication may be traced in Jeremiah 22. Kessler points out that Jehoiakim is accused in Jer. 22.13 of 'making *his neighbour* (*rē'ēhû*) work for him without pay', and rightly argues that the use of this word implies that the king and his impressed worker are fundamentally thought of as equals; 'neighbour' (*rēa'*) regularly appears in all the law collections as a term for the other, the fellow-citizen, in much the same way as 'brother' does in some Deuteronomic laws.[12]

We only need to move now to a look at the royal ideology favoured by the

---

9. Carroll 1986: 412.
10. Below, pp. 181–83.
11. Eaton 1986, esp. 135–65. See also below, p. 138.
12. Kessler 1992: 84.

Judaean dynasty itself to appreciate how it is undermined by this kind of observation.

3. *The Royal Ideology*

The concept of kingship in the Psalms has gone under this title in scholarship for many years. It is a complex of myth and ritual which clearly serves the function of establishing the authority of the king among his subjects, and has very close parallels in the culture of the more powerful kingdoms in the ancient Near East, from which it was doubtless mostly borrowed. It is most obviously expressed in those eleven Psalms that were identified by Gunkel as the examples of the genre 'royal psalms', Psalms 2, 18, 20, 21, 45, 72, 89, 101, 110, 132, 144;[13] many others may well be personal prayers for the king's use.[14] The main elements can be quickly sketched.[15] According to all the royal psalms, the true ruler of the kingdom is YHWH, and the king is his agent. See for example Ps. 2.2, 6, 7: he is 'YHWH's anointed'. Anointing was a rite consecrating and giving authority;[16] he is 'my king', put there by God; 'my son', originally perhaps intended more literally than Old Testament monotheism would allow; compare Ps. 110.3.[17] YHWH has committed himself to maintain the house of David on the throne (Ps. 89.3–4, 28–37 [Hebrew 4–5, 29–38], cf. 132.11–12; 2 Sam. 7.12–16). Accordingly the king can be assured of YHWH's support in battle against all enemies (Psalms 18; 20; 21; 144). In return the king will maintain the honour of YHWH (Psalm 132) and the purity and justice of his own house and realm (Psalm 101). Invested with the blessing of YHWH, his reign will be marked by peace and prosperity (Ps. 72.3, 6–7, 16–17).

4. *Psalm 72 and the Ideology of Royal Justice*[18]

For our purposes Psalm 72 is by far the most important of these Psalms, as it is the only one that makes the justice of the king as defender

---

13.   Gunkel and Begrich 1928–33: I, 140–76.

14.   Eaton 1986: 1–86; Croft 1987: 73–132. Against: Day 1992: 88–90.

15.   Cf. also Johnson 1967.

16.   De Jonge in *ABD* IV: 778–79; Day 1992: 98–99.

17.   Kraus 1993: 344–45, 350, reading *y^elidtîkā* with the LXX and many Hebrew MSS.

18.   This section is based on my article Houston 1999, from which material is used with permission. A somewhat similar treatment of Psalm 72 may be found in Jobling 1992, and my article includes a detailed evaluation of this. Broyles (1997: esp. 34–40) gives a similar interpretation of the Psalm, but without ideological criticism. The actual text I shall interpret is Ps. 72.1–17; vv.18–19 are the doxology which concludes Book II of the Psalter, and v. 20 is the colophon to the book.

of the poor and oppressed its leading theme, though others do not neglect it.[19]

In dealing with this text as rhetoric, we need to establish who the speaker and the audience are. Who is its audience? In one sense, this is obvious. It is explicitly stated in the first word: it is God; and the rhetoric of the psalm may be effectively interpreted as a plea to God. But to leave it at that would be to miss the unmistakable message that it sends to human hearers, specifically to the subjects of the king on whose behalf the prayer is uttered. It would be reasonable to see this effect as deliberately intended. But we also cannot omit the king himself from those who are to hear and reflect on these words. I shall return to this later.

The speaker is anonymous, in fact invisible. There is no use of the first person anywhere in the text. Whom, therefore, does the speaker represent? Both tradition and socio-cultural probability would suggest that this psalm, like others, represents how the dynasty itself wished to be understood. Traditional exegesis makes no bones about this. The reference to Solomon in the title, combined with the implication in the colophon (Ps. 72.20) that it is among the 'prayers of David', appears to suggest that in the view of the editors of the Psalter the Psalm should be understood as David's prayer for his son. There is in fact every probability that prayers for the king uttered in the royal temple had royal approval and expressed dynastic policy.

But is it in fact a prayer, a blessing or a prophecy? All the older and more traditional versions translate the ubiquitous 'imperfect' verbs as futures: the LXX, the Vulgate, the KJV, the RV, and more recently the Bible de Jérusalem, followed by the JB, and in great part the NIV. Most modern translations, however, as well as most modern commentators, make them largely prayers ('may he judge', etc.). However, the verbs in Ps. 72.12–14, which stand in the shadow of the conjunction *kî*, understood as 'for', at the beginning of v. 12, are generally understood as indicatives (future or present). The Hebrew *kî* may also mean 'when' or 'if', or it can be an emphatic particle ('yea', 'surely'). I take it as 'for'. Broyles's reading 'if' might be seen to fit the structure better, linking vv. 12–14 with what follows rather than with what goes before; but to make the whole of these three verses a single long subordinate clause is uncharacteristic of Hebrew poetry.[20]

Since the first verb is an imperative, and the address is to God, the most obvious reading is that the psalm is a prayer. However, in some classes of

---

19. I assume that Psalm 72 originates in the days of the Judaean monarchy, although Niehr (1986: 285) argues that the use of *mišpāṭîm* (plural) in v. 1 is exilic.

20. Broyles 1997: 27, with n. 14 (cf. also Dahood 1974: 182). Zenger (in Hossfeld and Zenger 2000: 304) translates the verbs into German as subjunctives even in vv. 12–14, taking the *kî* as an emphatic particle ('*Ja, er errette . . .*', 'Yes, may he rescue', etc.). But is there any parallel for *kî* being used in this way before volitive verbs? BDB, *HALOT* and *DCH* all only suggest that it emphasizes statements (or questions, *DCH* IV: 388a).

Hebrew verb there is a difference in spelling between the indicative and 'volitive' forms of the 'imperfect', and in the traditional Hebrew text (the MT) of this psalm there are some verbs which have been spelt as indicatives. This probably happened under the influence of the idea of the psalm as a Messianic prophecy; and it is unquestionably this prophetic conception that has accounted for the futures in traditional versions.[21] Considered as a text under interpretation, then, the psalm needs to be understood both as a prayer for the reigning king and as a prophecy of a future king. I will deal with it first as a prayer, but later we shall have to be occupied with the other reading.

How is the psalm structured? There is a number of possibilities here, all governed by the evident repetitions in the poem. Most obviously it falls into two halves, vv. 1–11 and 12–17; in each half the same themes appear. It is clear that the theme of the king's justice is the leading theme in each half. In my 1999 article I suggested that vv. 5–17 should be understood as a palis-trophe, that is a structure in which the same themes recur in forward and reverse order, ABCBA, with vv. 1–4 as a prologue sounding the main theme.[22] And this theme is also that of the central panel of the palistrophe. Whichever way one looks at it, the theme of the king's just rule emerges as structurally dominant. We can show this diagrammatically:

I	A	1–4	Just rule
	B	5	Longevity[23]
	C	6–7	Fertility of the land
	D	8–11	Universal rule
II	A¹	12–14	Just rule
	D¹	15	Universal rule; prayer for the king
	C¹	16	Fertility of the land
	B¹	17	Longevity, prayer

H.H. Schmid has shown how ancient Near Eastern conceptions of the world, not least in the Hebrew Bible, are governed by the concept of 'right-eousness' as an inclusive term for the world order stemming from creation, covering divine blessing and prosperity as well as social justice, in the main-tenance of which the king plays a key role.[24] This idea clearly governs the presentation of the prayer in Ps. 72.1–4, especially in v. 3. However, central to this order in this psalm, and certainly in these verses, is justice for the poor, their deliverance from exploitation. This is shown by the presence

---

21. Grammatical details in Houston 1999: 345, n. 5. Broyles (1997) misses the prophetic overtones in the MT.

22. For Broyles vv. 1–3 are the prologue.

23. Here we follow the LXX, along with most modern versions and commentators.

24. Schmid 1968; see further below, p. 205.

of the parallel word-pair 'justice and righteousness', which we have seen connotes roughly what we understand by social justice.[25] Prosperity for the people in general (v. 3) is included here as an aspect of the divine righteousness, and is developed further in vv. 6–7, 16. But the central divine gift, from which all else flows, is that of justice, the defence of the poor against their oppressors.[26] Verse 1 could be seen as the basic prayer developed in the whole of rest of the psalm.

The prayer proceeds to a number of petitions which would appear to be of more personal interest to the king, though as we see from other royal psalms they are an essential part of the ideology: petitions for his everlasting and universal rule take up four verses continuously in vv. 8–11.

Clearly persuasion is needed if God is to grant such blessings. Persuasion may be by rational argument or by emotive power.[27] Rational argument appears here in the syntactical structure of the poem. Broyles shows that the prayers for the king's longevity and universal power in vv. 5, 8 and 15 are expressed as consequences of those for his justice for the poor and assurance of prosperity.[28] And whether the *kî* of Ps. 72.12 is read as 'for' or 'if', it expresses a motivation. It is presented to God as an appropriate reason for allowing the king to rule over all nations.[29]

Pathos or emotion also plays a significant role in the rhetoric. I would identify it at two main points. In Ps. 72.2, the people whom the king is to judge is called 'your people' and in the parallel colon the poor are (more unusually) 'your poor, your needy or miserable ones, *ᵃniyyekā*'. God is thus reminded of his personal connection with the king's subjects. His personal commitment to the people of Israel requires him to bestow the gift of righteousness on their king for their sake.

The other main locus of emotive language is in Ps. 72.12–14, which we have already seen to be also both structurally and logically the centre of the argument. The comparatively restrained language of vv. 1–4 is here heightened in several ways. Three different words for 'poor' are used interchangeably: *'ebyôn*, *'ānî* and *dāl*. The poor man[30] is here 'crying out', and 'has no-one to help'. The king not merely helps him, but does so through 'taking pity on him'. He saves, not simply 'the poor', but *the lives* of the

25. See above, p. 61, with n. 35.

26. Detailed argument on the wording of vv. 1–4 may be found in Houston 1999: 346.

27. Aristotle, *Rhetoric* I.2.3 (1926: 16–17: *logos* or *pathos*).

28. Broyles 1997: 35–37: these verses begin with *wᵉ* plus the imperfect, which expresses a consequence in a sequence of verbs expressing requests.

29. Zenger's view of the syntax (above, n. 18) would exclude this, and to some degree so would his view that vv. 8–11 are secondary (Hossfeld and Zenger 2000: 312–13). But this does not seem to be adequately supported.

30. See above, pp. 62–63, for the argument that 'the poor person' is always a man in the Hebrew Bible.

poor', with which the phrase in the next verse 'precious is their blood in his eyes' coheres: their very lives are in danger from their unfeeling oppressors; they suffer from 'violence' (*ḥāmās*), the strongest of Hebrew words for oppression, with its connotations of violence and rapine.[31] The final verb in the section is *yig'al*, 'he shall redeem', which though it is in a sense a synonym of the other verbs has its distinct connotations. As *gō'ēl* the king takes the place of the family redeemer whom 'he who has no helper' is without. The climax is the deeply affecting 'precious is their blood in his eyes'. This emotive heightening of the language underlines the seriousness of the king's concern; the hearer—God or the king's subjects—are thus persuaded to take it seriously and so to accept more easily the claim to dominion which the prayer embodies.

A further significant aspect of the language is the way in which what is here said of the king parallels what is said of God elsewhere. YHWH's activity in 'saving' (*yš'* Hiph. and *nṣl* Hiph.) the poor is often referred to in the Psalms (e.g. Pss. 12.5 [Hebrew 6]; 18.27 [28]; 35.10; 76.9 [10]) and the speaker in psalms of lamentation sometimes appeals to God on the grounds of being 'poor and needy' (*'ānî wᵉ'ebyôn*, Pss. 40.17 [18]; 70.5 [6]; 86.1). God is in the business of redeeming lives in Ps. 69.18 (19), cf. 103.4. The expression 'precious is the blood . . .' is unique, but while 'precious is the life . . .' is not uncommon, we have one closer parallel in Ps. 116.15: 'precious in the eyes of YHWH is the death of his faithful ones'. The text thus makes it clear that the king faithfully carries out his responsibility as God's agent, and so is entitled to receive the benefits of that position.

The main rhetorical device by which the king's claim is urged is hyperbole. The prayer is for a rule unlimited in both time and space. As far as time is concerned, the words can hardly be taken literally of a single king; but, to quote Jobling,

> whether through hyperbolic rhetoric about the present king, or more 'realistically' in terms of royal succession or the king's lasting reputation (v. 17a), it is the same permanence of the system of monarchy which is evoked. Time is treated as seamless, as beginningless and endless; nothing preceded the system, or is to follow it . . . Part of the point of the 'nations' theme, perhaps, is to make a corresponding statement about space.[32]

One can sum up the impression which the psalm leaves upon the unsuspicious listener in three broad statements: Monarchy is a universal, divinely authorized system, which sustains the fertility, peace and order of the land. The king's chief concern is to act on behalf of the poor against their oppressors. And it is this concern for the poor which entitles him to reign.

31. Above, pp. 67–68, 90.
32. Jobling 1992: 100.

It is easy to see there is a moral contradiction between basing the king's rule on his protection of the poor from oppression and praying that he may receive tribute from the nations: for tribute is oppressive. It may be levied on kings, but the burden eventually falls upon those in the system who cannot shift it on to anyone else: the peasants. Of course, the contradiction is not apparent to those who share the text's ideology; for in this, it is the poor of the *people* who are to be protected, and foreign nations are fair game. Yet this only raises the contradiction in another form. Is the monarchy really universal, that is a universal *benefit*, or is it not? The truth of the matter is, of course, that it barely controls Judah, let alone Sheba and Seba and territories beyond the sea. What tribute there is has to be raised from the king's home territory, from the people to whom the text asserts that his presence is a guarantee of justice, peace and prosperity. There may be some revenue from the transit trade, but in general the king's income is at the expense of his own subjects. The concealment of this fact is the most obvious distortion of the truth that this text commits.

Recalling our analysis of the oppressive way in which the monarchy functioned, do we not then have to say that this is a self-serving account designed to persuade people that their interests coincide with those of the house of David, when in fact they do not? They wish to retain power, the people wish to be free of oppression. Fine, it is precisely in order to deal with the oppressor that kingly power exists. The psalm is designed not to reveal but to conceal social realities.

Are we therefore to say that it is all simply propaganda, lies and deceit? That the monarchy was knee-deep in the exploitation of the people and was thoroughly identified with the class interests of the exploiters? That if they threw up the odd smokescreen, claiming that they were concerned for the poor, it is hardly something to be taken seriously?

There is truth in this, but the full reality is rather more complicated. Ideology is never simply lies: it is a partial, and partisan, view of the truth. The consumers of ideology always extend beyond the class of its producers, and it has to be plausible to its consumers.[33] And the plausibility of this ideology depends in large part on expectation. All our knowledge of the ancient Near East shows that kings were expected to do justice, to protect the poor and oppressed, and there is substantial evidence to show that at least some of them tried to do so, consequently that the language of our text in this regard was likely to raise serious expectations. For details I may refer to Weinfeld, who shows the remarkable antiquity and continuity of this theme and its wide geographical spread, from the Early Dynastic period in Sumeria, through the Old Babylonian period, from which the richest

---

33. See above, pp. 13–15.

evidence emerges, to the Neo-Assyrian period and into the Levant.[34] Most importantly, evidence exists to show that the theme was not always mere propaganda, for frequently in Mesopotamia contracts are found showing that the king's decrees of liberation have to be taken into account as factors affecting the transaction.[35]

It should be added here that the king's activity in establishing social justice was not solely by means of decrees, which is the impression given by Weinfeld. The king's regular judicial activities, in which he responded to appeals and petitions, often, as in 2 Kgs 8.3–6, restoring property, or defending the rights of *personae miserabiles*, were not only at least as important as his liberative decrees, which were infrequent, but may have been the context in which the ideas of justice expressed in the decrees were developed. An inspection of the Mesopotamian law codes (so-called) will show that they contain principles of justice, which they were very likely intended to exemplify. Bernard Jackson, in a response to Weinfeld, suggests that, contrary to Weinfeld's assumption that the justice of decree tempered a purely positive law administered by the courts, the courts themselves were expected to operate according to unwritten ideas of equity, and that it is difficult to draw a sharp line between the king's administrative and judicial functions.[36]

Can it be shown that expectations that the king would act in support of justice for the poor were common currency in Israel and Judah, and, more particularly, that their kings went any way towards fulfilling such expectations by administrative or judicial action on behalf of the poor?

There is no question about the expectations. We have already noticed the stress on this function of the monarchy in the Jeremiah pericope on the kings, which mentions it three times (Jer. 22.3, 15–16; 23.5). Proverbs 31.1–9, from a different literary tradition, is equally forthright, and almost verbally identical, in defining the proper task of a king: 'Open your mouth for the dumb, for the defence of the perishing; open your mouth, give just judgment, and defend the cause of the poor and needy' (Prov. 31.8–9). And we have already seen how Job defines his own justice in royal terms: Job 29.12 closely echoes Ps. 72.12.

What about the reality? Can it be shown that Judaean kings did engage in specific judicial and administrative activity on behalf of the exploited in their kingdom? The Deuteronomistic History is clearly uninterested in the subject, and has preserved virtually no information on it.[37] We need not conclude as Frick does that this lack of interest reflects the dynasty's own

34. Weinfeld 1995.
35. Weinfeld 1995: 78, 94.
36. Jackson 1998.
37. Frick 1994.

ideology. The assumption that this history derives from the dynasty is insecure, to say the least. The prophetic texts have relatively few explicit references to kings, and they are mostly sharply critical.

Weinfeld, however, is no doubt about the matter, citing not only the Jeremiah text about Josiah, but first of all the statement in 2 Sam. 8.15 that David 'established justice and righteousness for all his people'.[38] According to Weinfeld, this refers to acts similar to the *mīšarum* acts of the Old Babylonian kings, and occurs, he assures us, 'in an official document whose authenticity is not to be doubted'. Nothing about the text suggests the genre of an official document, let alone proves it authentic; and if it were, we would have the dynasty testifying on its own behalf as in the Psalm.[39] Jeremiah's evidence is more contemporary, yet doubt must be aroused by the provenance of this book.[40] Jeremiah was supported by the family of Shaphan which was close to Josiah and probably out of favour under Jehoiakim, so that *parti pris* may be detected.

The only specific liberative decree which we are informed of from this dynasty is the liberation of Hebrew slaves under Zedekiah, narrated in Jer. 34.8–11. This act of liberation, effected by covenant, is described as a *dᵉrôr*, the word which also describes the intention of the Jubilee proclamation in Lev. 25.10, and the proclamation of the anointed figure in Isa. 61.1, and is probably derived from the Akkadian *andurārum*.[41] Terms drawn from the law in Deut. 15.12–18 and that in Lev. 25.39–46 appear in the rendition of the decree in Jer. 34.8–9, but Chavel has shown that these are likely to be scribal expansions.[42] It appears to be an isolated act rather than part of a wider-ranging liberation, and its motives can only be guessed at.

It has been argued that the parallels in vocabulary, theme and intention between the liberative measures in the Torah—the *šᵉmiṭṭâ* or debt release of Deuteronomy 15 and the Jubilee of Leviticus 25—Mesopotamian royal measures, and this act of Zedekiah's, suggest that the Torah measures have a background in occasional acts of the Davidic dynasty.[43] It may be, for example, that the jubilee presented in Leviticus 25 by a post-monarchic writer as an institution for pre-monarchic Israel originated as an occasional royal decree. This is plausible, but the evidence is highly indirect. On the other hand, we saw above that the monarchy had to reckon with powerful

---

38. Weinfeld 1995: 45–56; cf. 1972: 153–55.

39. Weinfeld 1995: 46. Weinfeld had earlier (1972: 154, esp. n. 3) argued that all the Judaean kings who are said in Kings to have done right in the eyes of Yahweh must also have issued such decrees. This is not repeated in 1995: has Weinfeld realized how precarious such an argument must be?

40. Above, pp. 82–84.

41. Lemche 1979: 22

42. Chavel 1997.

43. Lemche 1976: 56–57; Kaufman 1984: 281.

local figures who may have lived in Jerusalem, but had power bases in the countryside: 'the people of the land'.[44] From this we may argue that it was to its advantage to act to reduce the power of rich exploiters who were not directly within its own control, whether or not it actually did so.

Of course the monarchy was itself exploitative: that is the supreme fact which the Psalm distorts. But those who most keenly resented this exploitation were in all probability not the poor, whose immediate exploiters were much closer to home, but the well-to-do who possessed the wherewithal of which the dynasty could avail itself. It was in the interests of the monarchy itself to repress the exploitation of the poor by the ruling class in general; for in doing so they were cutting down to size dangerous threats to their own power. This is not a contradiction to the policy of making alliances with the local elites. One policy or the other could be followed at a particular time according to convenience. We should also note the prevalence of faction in Judaean politics at the centre.[45] In these circumstances it would clearly have been as much in the interests of the dynasty to gain support from the masses as to suppress rival centres of power.

Thus our analysis gives a certain a priori plausibility to the hypothesis that the Judaean monarchy could sometimes have acted in the ways suggested by Ps. 72.1-4, 12-14, and that social measures in the Torah like the šᵉmiṭṭâ and the Jubilee could have originated in occasional royal decrees. We have no way of knowing how consistent a policy it was. What is absent from the text is any recognition that it was the king's interest, and not solely his concern, that motivated his attempts to defend the poor.

We have thus identified two main points at which the text mystifies the true relationships between the king and his subjects. Its pathos draws attention away from the interest of the king in controlling rival centres of power. And the king's own exploitative activities are displaced on to foreign nations, so that to his own people he appears exclusively beneficent.

Jobling suggests that the kings were operating with a borrowed ideology more appropriate to a fully-fledged tributary mode of production like Egypt's or those of Mesopotamia.[46] Even if so, a text like this must certainly have served a purpose in inflating the king's dignity among his entourage and the powerful men of the kingdom. It is a truly ideological text which harmonizes the king's interests with that of his poor subjects. However, it does not give that utopian picture of a society without class division that Jameson suggests that an ideological text will tend to do.[47] Rather, in suppressing the interests of the king and his court it gives the impression that

---

44. Above, pp. 38-39.
45. Above, pp. 13, 79; Chaney 1991.
46. Jobling 1992: 116.
47. Jameson 1981: 286-91.

shalom arises from the alliance of the king with the poor against the exploiting class.

While the Psalm may have succeeded in harmonizing the interests of the poor with those of the king, it is able to do this only by making an unmistakable, if unspoken, moral point in the logic and pathos of its rhetoric: that the legitimacy of the king's claim to rule is dependent on his justice and his compassion for the poor. This is not incompatible with the doctrine of the royal psalms more generally that the king's legitimacy derives from his divine appointment. For to rule by divine appointment is to rule in order to implement the divine will, which is justice; and the first verse of the psalm implies that such justice is unattainable otherwise than by God's gift. As Brueggemann expresses it: 'The king is to do what Yahweh as king proposes to do . . . Faithful kingship mediates Yahweh's sovereignty . . . in the . . . transformation of public power in the interest of communal well-being.'[48] The implication of Ps. 72.12–14 is, further, that the king's compassion is pleasing to God.

But though this text's doctrine of legitimacy is not incompatible with the more general one, it has the potential to undermine it. In a text like Psalm 89 the Davidic covenant is eternal and unconditional (Ps. 89.18–38; cf. 2 Sam. 7.14–16). If the king fails to observe YHWH's commandments, he will be punished, but his throne will not be removed. The absolute authority of the king is unalterable, because it depends on a divine decree which is by definition unchallengeable. Psalm 72 enables us to penetrate into the inner motivation of this divine decree, to understand its purpose and the circumstances in which it may truly be regarded as implemented. A king who is not just, who does not care for the poor, who does not allow the prayer for God's righteousness to be fulfilled in himself, is not in reality God's king. By replacing the formal requirement of divine election with the material requirement of justice, this text effectively demolishes the doctrine of the divine right of kings.

It thus becomes possible to envisage the king himself as an appropriate audience for the text. A text intended to validate his rule becomes, because of its ethical foundation, a warning or challenge to it when treated as a *Fürstenspiegel*. It is possible to suppose that the policy and behaviour of certain kings could actually have been influenced by such a text, and that the policy of defence of the poor against oppression, which was in any case in their own interests, may have been strengthened by genuine conviction. And be it noted, this comes about when an ideological text is compelled to bow to public opinion or religious tradition, to include as justification for the power of the ruler a traditional conception of how rulers ought to use their power.

---

48. Brueggemann 1997: 612. Cf. Calvin 1840: III, 256.

It is scarcely surprising that with such texts in front of them some of the pioneers of Christian political theology were able to assert that against an unjust (and therefore Godless) sovereign rebellion is legitimate.[49] They were able to read this text not as ideological legitimation of the current governing power, but as a theological standard by which to test the legitimacy of any. So may we.

Another way of looking at it is to understand the psalm, like other works of the imagination, in line with Gadamer's hermeneutic, as creating a 'world' into which the reader may enter, and whose 'horizon' may then become 'fused' with that of our own.[50] But not all works are susceptible to such *Horizontverschmeltzung*. Psalm 72 is not like an escapist novel, blotting out the real world of greedy officials, extravagant courts, and compromised rulers but not having any relation to it. The world it creates is a utopia, but it does have a relation to the real world, and as a work of literature it enables us to see that world in a new light.

But is that light false or true? Does it lull us into saying: 'Well, that's all right then, the king (or president or prime minister or whoever may hold rule in our own society) is God's justice minister, and he will do the best he can for the poor', when he or she is doing nothing of the sort? Or does it rather startle us into saying, 'That is what a state which truly embodied the rule of God would be like. Is the state I live under in any way like it, and if not, what am I prepared to do about it?' The imaginative world for one prepared to take it seriously creates possibilities which did not exist on earth before. We still read it as (partially) contrary to reality, but as challenging and thereby changing reality, rather than simply concealing or distorting it.

A challenge to rulers still emerges from Psalm 72: to accept that authority is only valid when based on care for the poor; to give the humblest first claim on state resources of power and money; to renounce their claim to any of the privileges that go with authority, unless they defend the oppressed and repress the oppressor. It is a challenge never likely to be out of date. Few if any societies beyond the simple tribal stage have succeeded in eliminating inequality and exercise of authority. Anarchy is not a serious possibility: the choice is between just and unjust government.

Nevertheless, we must also recognize the limitations of the picture of justice projected by this text. What is meant by just government in this and other Hebrew texts is rooted in the structure of contemporary civil society, marked as it was by patriarchy and patronage. Essentially it is the redress of abuses. The king restores justice where the persons responsible for it have denied it. In the political thought of the Old Testament there is no concept

---

49.   Examples in O'Donovan and O'Donovan 1999: e.g. John of Salisbury, 281–282; and esp. John Ponet, 695–701.

50.   Gadamer 1989: 302–307.

of the state as a *structure* which may exhibit justice or injustice—and hence the royal apparatus can get away with real injustices while proclaiming its justice. There is nothing here which will directly illuminate modern discussions of political ethics and the tussle between right and left wing concepts of justice, though there is a superficial resemblance to John Rawls's concept that inequalities can only be justified if they are of the greatest benefit to the least advantaged.[51]

Justice is here the act of the king who protects his subjects. He delivers them when they cry, but he remains in control. He decides when justice has been breached, and how it is to be restored. Justice is still top-down. There is no hint of the idea that the poor might, to use a phrase from liberation theology, become subjects of their own history, defend *themselves* against exploitation and create a non-hierarchical society. The king remains king and in virtue of that position and all that it implies he is a burden on society.

The king's restorative justice, like the comparable measures in Mesopotamia and like the debt-remission and jubilee in the Torah, is limited to repairing the inroads made by the powerful upon the rights of the weak—cancelling debts, returning property, liberating debt-slaves. The language of the psalm gives no hint of anything beyond this. 'Crushing' the oppressor may safely be listed in the repertoire of the text's hyperbole. The idea that justice might require a permanent change in relationships between classes or in the distribution of wealth is not apparent. Dominique Charpin's comment on Mesopotamia applies here: 'The rules of the game were not changed, they simply had a new deal'.[52] The expression 'a new deal' (*une nouvelle donne*) is peculiarly appropriate, whether Charpin intended the allusion or not. For the conception behind Roosevelt's measures in the 1930s, as behind the much more limited measures offered under the same name by the Blair government in Britain from 1997, is the same as the *mīšarum* and the same as the ideal of justice in Psalm 72: to give the poor a fresh start without changing the economic system or upsetting the social order.

Charpin points out that injustice in Mesopotamia was always conceived as disorder, and justice was a return to origins, not a progress towards a future goal. This text shares the same fundamental conception. Justice and peace depend on the divine blessing of righteousness upon the present order, indeed the present ruler. Whether we find elsewhere in the Hebrew Bible the idea that true justice might involve an end to the present order and present rulers is a question which still awaits us.

51. Rawls 2001: 42–43; 61–66; and passim.
52. Charpin 1996: 113 (my translation).

5. The Theme of Social Justice in the Royal Traditions

Having opened up this theme through the examination of its leading expression in Psalm 72, we may now broaden the scope of the inquiry.[53] A look at several other texts in the Psalms and Isaiah will show that the idea of the king as the defender of the poor is taken for granted as part of the background even in texts on other subjects: it serves to legitimize his rule and to define its character. The ode in Isa. 9.2–7 (Hebrew 1–6) which looks for an end of foreign oppression through the birth or accession—with v. 6 (5) compare Ps. 2.7—of a new prince uses the phrase 'justice and righteousness', that has become so familiar to us, to characterize his rule; and Isa. 16.5 is similar. When we find Zion, the royal citadel, named as a refuge for the poor, as in Isa. 14.32, we have an example of the self-presentation of the royal house as the protector of the poor.

In the royal wedding ode Psalm 45, the singer says to the king: 'the sceptre of your reign is a sceptre of uprightness (*mîšōr*); you love righteousness (*ṣedeq*) and hate injustice (*reša'*), *therefore* God, your God has anointed you with the oil of joy above your companions' (Ps. 45.6–7 [Hebrew 7–8]). There is a delicate ambiguity in 'has anointed you' (*mᵉšāḥᵉkā*). Craigie notes that the immediate reference will be to the king's anointing for his wedding, but that it also hints at his anointing as king.[54] The implication is that the king has been chosen by God as king because of his justice.

Psalm 101 exemplifies the genre of the 'negative confession', used by the Babylonian king at the *akitu* festival; possibly it was used at a similar ceremony of renewal of the king's office at Jerusalem. The main emphasis is on the character of the people the king has around him ('in my house', vv. 2, 7). A large number of ethical terms are used, and not all can be connected directly with conduct towards the poor; but the reference to *mišpāṭ* in v. 1, which here must mean 'justice', should be taken with the assertion in v. 8 'I shall destroy all the wicked (*rišᵉ'ê*) of the land'; *rāšā'* is regularly contrasted with *ṣaddîq*, and therefore should be translated 'unjust'.[55] The king's action against oppressors is presented as a reason for his continuance in office.

Psalm 18 is a royal psalm of thanksgiving for victory. Psalm 18.20–27 (21–28) assert that YHWH's salvation of the king depends on his righteousness (or justice), and v. 27 (28) says 'you save a humble people, but haughty eyes you cast down'. This sounds moralistic, but we should not ignore the class implications of the vocabulary. The word translated 'humble' is *'ānî*, which we have seen to be one of the commonest words for 'poor' in social justice contexts. Doubtless the humble people are the people of

---

53. Cf. Jobling 1992: 108.
54. Craigie 1983: 339.
55. Miranda 1977: 96–97.

Israel (Judah), and the 'haughty eyes' are those of their enemies, but the language used hints that the victory is formed on the pattern of the defence of the poor against their native oppressors. The 'humility' of the people is their adoption of a posture before God patterned on that of the poor who cry for vindication against their oppressors.

There are a number of other Psalms of lament or thanksgiving where the vocabulary seems to suggest situations of war at one point and social oppression at another. The Psalms are often unspecific about the situations in which they might be used; however, if this vagueness extends to the class position of the speaker, we are entitled to suspect ideological obfuscation. In Psalms 9–10, the opening verses define its genre as an individual thanks-giving, and from the statement of the subject of thanksgiving in Ps. 9.3–6 (4–7) it would appear that the speaker is a national war leader, presumably the king: he celebrates victory over enemies who are nations and possess cities; the 'nations' reappear in Ps. 10.16.[56] But he also describes them as 'unjust' (*rāšāʿ* (sing.), NRSV 'wicked', Ps. 9.5 [6]), and this description is repeated in Ps. 9.16 (17), 17 (18), and entirely governs the presentation of the renewed plea in Psalm 10, where the *rāšāʿ*, the 'wicked man', in Ps. 10.2, 3, 4, 13, 15 is plainly the subject of the verbs in most of vv. 2–13. Are we to suppose that at some point the speaker's attention turns to internal oppres-sors? Much of the language would suggest this. More significant in this respect than the way the enemies are described, which is not very surprising in any circumstances, is the characterization of the victims. *ʿānî*, 'poor', 'afflicted', appears seven times, not only in Ps. 10 (Ps. 9.12 [13], 18 [19], Ps. 10.2, 9 (twice), 12, 17). We also find *ʾebyôn*, needy, Ps. 9.18 (19), and two references to the fatherless in Ps. 10.14, 18; and this Psalm has a distinctive word for the victim of oppression, *ḥēlʾkâ* or the like, which is found in Ps. 10.8, 10, 14, but nowhere else; its vocalization and meaning are uncertain, but it is usually rendered 'hapless' or 'helpless'.

Brueggemann in his provocative reading of the poem says 'This cluster of words makes clear that the speaker (and those for whom the speaker speaks) are the socially vulnerable and marginal', and argues that the identity of the enemies is unstable, which accounts for his not giving weight to the 'nations' and 'cities' in his interpretation.[57] But while it does appear that the speaker speaks *for* the socially vulnerable and marginal, it is far from clear that the speaker is so: the language surrounding the first person singular in 9.1–4, 13–15 (2–5, 14–16) suggests the contrary. I would argue, following Eaton, that the royal complaint against the foreign enemy has been expressed in

---

56. Eaton 1986: 32–33. Both Kraus (1988: 193) and Craigie (1983: 118) assume that at these points the speaker's recollection of YHWH's deeds reaches into history. This seems to be contrary to the genre of thanksgiving, which is strong precisely in the opening verses.

57. Brueggemann 1991: 4–5.

terms characteristic of social oppression, which gives it a broader appeal.[58] Brueggemann, noting how the 'wicked' normally use 'selective, self-serving speech', while their victims here compel them to express their real thoughts,[59] has perhaps not allowed for the likelihood that liturgical material for the state sanctuary will express the interests of the state, and hence the possibility that the psalm *itself* might be self-serving and ideological.

What we said about Psalm 72 can also be said of these further texts, and on a broader front: that regardless of the intention with which they may have been written, they present or presume an ideal of the king's office as one which exists primarily for the poor, which demands attention even if any particular text might have originated as mere propaganda; that they would have challenged kings, even while the dynasty reigned, to live up to that ideal; that they continue to demand to be read as teaching that power is only legitimate, only divinely authorized, if it is exercised on behalf of the powerless.

6. *Expecting the Just King*

The ideal and ideology of royal justice becomes an integral part of the longing for a restoration of Davidic rule and Israelite independence in that stream of thought which we often call 'Messianic'. Does this longing simply reflect the frustration of an erstwhile ruling elite that rule had effectively passed to others, or does it rather reflect a desire for justice itself in the face of the failure of all existing governments to provide it? Only a wide-ranging examination of a number of texts may enable us to answer that question.

As we have seen, the prophetic or Messianic reading of Psalm 72 is present already in the traditional Hebrew text, as well as being expressed by the versions and in traditional exegesis. More than one Christian Advent hymn is based on it: I think of Montgomery's 'Hail to the Lord's Anointed', and Watts' 'Jesus shall reign'. One might expect that the emphasis of the text on justice for the poor would restrict the ways in which it could be read as a Messianic prophecy, but this does not seem to be entirely borne out by such traditional readings.

However, instructive examples exist of closer readings of the psalm in which the verbs are read so far as possible as indicatives referring to the future: anciently in the LXX and in modern times in the Bible de Jérusalem (and its English version the Jerusalem Bible). The psalm thus announces the justice of the coming king's rule, the abundance of peace and prosperity in

58.   Eaton 1986: 33.
59.   Brueggemann 1991: 8–9.

his days, his worldwide and eternal rule; and then states (Ps. 72.12): *for* he rescues the needy when he cries out, the poor and the one who has no helper. Bible de Jérusalem, however, does not translate the *kî* at all, so that the announcement of the king's concern for the poor is another aspect of the goodness of his rule, but is not so clearly presented as central. The LXX, which may be taken as presenting an ancient exegetical understanding, translates it with *hoti*, 'because', and interestingly switches into the past tense for v. 12 before returning to the future in v. 13.[60] 'All the kings will worship him, all the nations will serve him, *because* he *has* rescued the destitute from the hand of the powerful,[61] and the poor man who had no helper.' Thus the psalm is still saying that the king's option for the poor is the condition of his universal rule. It is no longer presented to God as a motivation for granting him that privilege. Instead, the psalm can now be read as saying that the nations submit to him of their own accord in response to his justice. It is still saying that justice for the poor qualifies him for kingship. In this text at least the expectation of a revived kingdom is the expectation of a community of justice.

We have referred above to the Davidic prophecies in Jeremiah and Ezekiel. In these cases, although the historical context is the loss of Judaean sovereignty, the literary context makes it unambiguous that the function of the coming king is to provide the 'justice and righteousness' looked for in vain from the dynasty's historical representatives. The traditions of these books, and indeed the immediate contexts, are sufficiently antagonistic to the royal establishment to make it unlikely that these texts represent the royal ideology. Their point is not that the house of David can be relied on to provide social justice, but that in the providence of God a future Davidide may fulfil what is expected of the agent of YHWH the God of justice as former members of the house did not.

We have already seen how the book of Isaiah represents the traditions of the house of David. It is generally recognized that the Davidic traditions were carried forward after the demise of the kingdom and appear thereafter in a number of guises in this book. In Isaiah 1–39 such texts may include Isa. 9.2–7 (Hebrew 1–6); 11.1–9 and 16.4b–5. I have already briefly dealt with Isa. 9.7, which seems to be rooted in the Assyrian occupation, and with Isa. 16.4–5, which is brief and unelaborated, but also seems to predate the fall of the dynasty. There is also the prophecy or, perhaps better, meditation on true nobility in Isa. 32.1–8. This is not of the standard 'Messianic' type, and I deal with it in the next chapter.

Isaiah 11.1–9 is concerned with the just society as guaranteed by the just

60. *erusato* (aorist); *huperkhen* (imperfect).
61. LXX reads *miššôa'*, 'from a noble', in place of *mᵉšawwēa'*, 'crying out'. No difference in the consonantal text is implied.

king. It falls into two well-marked parts: Isa. 11.1–5 details the endowment and activity of the Davidic 'shoot', but he goes unmentioned in the following four verses, which give a picture of the paradise of peace resulting from the filling of the land (or earth? *'ereṣ* can mean either) with the knowledge of YHWH.

The passage is a vision of the indefinite future after the fall of the historical Davidic dynasty: 'a shoot will come forth from the stump of Jesse'.[62] Isaiah 11.2 announces the coming king's endowment by YHWH with various needful gifts, including that of 'knowledge and the fear of YHWH',[63] a theme which recurs at the end of the poem. How these gifts might be exercised is worked out entirely in the field of justice. Isaiah 11.3 says that in his judicial capacity the Messiah will not rely on superficial appearances or on what witnesses choose to tell him, but will judge according to his gift of insight; in practice this probably means, in the light of what follows, that he rejects the case put forward by the wealthy and articulate in favour of the rights of the poor and humble. In Isa. 11.4 it becomes clear that his justice means especially his justice for the poor[64] whom he defends if necessary by bringing about the death of their exploiters, the 'tyrant' or 'violent'[65] and 'unjust'. The understanding of justice and how it is achieved is identical to that in Psalm 72.[66] Whatever the supernatural endowment of the messianic king, we are very much in the real world, where there are powerful exploiters who need dealing with firmly, violently if necessary. It should not necessarily be assumed that the image of the king 'striking with the rod of his mouth' means that his words have in themselves some supernatural power to kill. But they do express the sentence of God, and thereby foreshadow the wicked ones' death.[67]

It might be questioned whether we are still in the real world in Isa. 11.6–9, where we have predatory animals acting contrary to their biological natures. However, the verses are often read simply as a poetic picture of peace and harmony. Whether they should be read literally or metaphorically is a nice

---

62. Even Wildberger, who regards Isaiah as the author of this piece, sees that these words envisage 'the overthrow of the royal family' (Wildberger 1991: 470).

63. Or possibly 'the knowledge and fear of YHWH'.

64. The parallel with *dallîm* in the first half of the verse shows that *lᵉʿanᵉwê ʾāreṣ* means not 'the meek of the earth' (NRSV) but 'the poor of the land'; but it is not necessary to emend to *laᵃniyyê* with BHS and (hesitantly) Wildberger (1991: 461); see Gerstenberger in *TDOT* XI: 242 (*ThWAT* VI: 259).

65. Reading *ʿārîṣ* for *ʾereṣ*, 'earth', which NRSV surprisingly still reads; Wildberger (1991: 461) calls the emendation 'almost universally accepted'.

66. Broyles (1997: 30–33) finds specific echoes of Psalm 72 in Isa. 11.4, and also in Isa. 9.6–7; Zech. 9.9–10 and Jer. 21.12; 22.3, 16. But apart from Zech. 9.10 (cf. Ps. 72.8) the language is specific to the subject matter rather than to Psalm 72 in particular.

67. See my discussion of the power of the prophetic word, Houston 1993b; earlier Thiselton 1974; but also the discussion in Wildberger 1991: 477–78.

question. Their full understanding can certainly not dispense with their mythical background; Gen. 1.29–30 shows that the imagination of a world free of all violence, among animals as well as human beings, could be thrown into the unknown past as easily as the unknown future. But for our purpose in this context, we might understand them as giving a picture of justice which goes beyond the simple idea of repression of exploiters by the king's coercion. Predatory animals (i.e. powerful, potential exploiters) cease to be predators; they are no longer a danger to herbivores, that is, the weak. 'They shall not cause harm or destroy'—that is what oppressors do— because 'the land shall be filled with the knowledge of YHWH'. That knowledge which according to Jeremiah (Jer. 22.16) Josiah possessed, and is the endowment of the messianic king, will be at the disposal of every person, and must be, if the problem of injustice is to be tackled at its roots. The link with the messianic prophecy implies that to address that problem successfully requires a profounder change than simply keeping oppressors in check: it requires a different kind of society with a different kind of people in it.

Whatever the date or historical background of this prophecy, it is clear that it addresses far more profound and universal questions than the future of the Jerusalem elite. It is a vision of a society free of violence and oppression, and its answer to the question how such a society might be arrived at is: through the knowledge of YHWH. Although the first part of the prophecy retains a strongly top-down idea of the just society, the second part, through the medium of metaphor and myth, looks at the question more in the round and suggests that the divine education in justice needs to be appropriated by all, not just a responsible elite. It is a radical transformation of the Davidic ideal. It is not enough for the king simply to act against exploiters, for this does not make any permanent change. The first five verses of the passage would take us no further forward than Psalm 72, still in the realm of the 'new deal'; the last four move us into Utopia, perhaps in the absolute sense of what cannot exist (even metaphorically) in any conceivable earthly world.[68]

Keeping in mind the likely social setting of the book of Isaiah in circles close to the house of David, but in this case to a house out of power, one may suggest that the purely utopian conception of what the king can achieve does not here conceal his exploitative activity, which has been compelled to cease, but expresses the aspirations of the house. No doubt if the house of David had ever regained power (the probably brief governorship of Zerubbabel hardly counts), it would have resumed its exploitation of the people. But its intentions, as so often, were no doubt of the highest!

In the second half of Isaiah, explicit Messianic prophecies cease. But the tradition continues in altered forms. Cyrus appears in Isa. 45.1 as YHWH's

68. Cf. Mannheim 1936: 173–75.

'anointed one'; the people in Isa. 55.3 are the recipients of the 'sure mercies
of David'. John Eaton has undertaken an analysis of the whole of Isaiah
40–55 and 60–62 in an attempt to demonstrate that the roots of the tradition lie in the festal and royal traditions; in particular, that the servant of
YHWH (not only in Isaiah 42, 49, 50 and 52–53, but also in 61) is a royal
figure.[69] His work seems to have made little impact on scholarship, but
detailed exegesis of some of these texts, especially of Isa. 42.1–4 (5–9),
usually shows up the royal connections even if the exegete evades their
implications. For the present purpose I will reflect just on Isa. 42.1–4 and
Isa. 61.1–2.

It is fairly obvious that the central motif defining the Servant's work in
Isa. 42.1–4 is *mišpāṭ*; it is mentioned three times in this short poem. A survey
of exegesis, as for example in Koole's commentary, shows almost as much
variety in the understanding of this word in this poem as it has in Hebrew
altogether.[70] It 'has been understood from a religio-ethical, a legal, and a
more political point of view': thus 'doctrine', 'truth', 'law', 'religion', 'judgment', or 'justice'. Koole notes that among modern exegetes the political
understanding, 'justice', 'rule', or 'just rule', has predominated, and opts for
it himself, 'since the key word indicates not so much the work of a preacher
as a kingly virtue'. He cites for this sense a large number of passages, several
of which we have looked at above. Although the verb *yôṣî* 'he will bring
forth' with *mišpāṭ* in vv. 1, 3, is often taken to mean 'proclaim', the different
verb *yāśîm* 'he will set' in v. 4 clearly indicates that the Servant is not only to
proclaim justice but to establish it. Indeed, if one has studied such texts as
Psalm 72 and Isa. 11.1–9 it is hard to escape the sense that Isa. 42.1–4 is also
a political text.

It is possible to suggest what this political text is saying about politics
without breaking one's head on the age-old crux of the Servant's identity.
Whether he is the empirical or an ideal Israel, Cyrus, a contemporary
Davidide, or a future Messiah,[71] what is said about him suggests reflection
on some of the ambiguities which we have considered above. The interpretation of v. 3a, 'a bruised reed he will not break and a smoking wick he will
not quench', is very much disputed.[72] But it could be seen in terms of the
tradition we have been looking at as pointing to his gentle compassion for
the impotent and the wretched, categories which must include the victims of
oppression. This justice he will bring to the nations, 'and the coastlands

---

69. Eaton 1979.
70. Koole 1997: 217–218.
71. For documentation of these alternatives see North 1956, and for more recent work
Haag 1985.
72. Marcus (1937: 258–59) sees the Servant himself as the bruised reed: 'A crushed reed he
may be, but one that no one shall break', etc.

await his instruction'. The emphasis here is very different from that in Psalm 72, which focuses on what the king receives from the nations rather than on what he offers to them. One of the major contradictions of Psalm 72 is thus resolved, if only in aspiration. The universal rule of YHWH's royal servant *is* a universal benefit. His justice is for the poor of the world and not merely for YHWH's own people.

However, one widely accepted contribution to the picture must be abandoned. Isaiah 42.2 has often been taken as meaning that the servant will achieve his task without loud proclamation, implying, if the figure is royal, that he renounces the standard political methods of coercion and violence. But the analysis of the vocabulary of the verse by Marcus, developed by Koole, shows that overwhelmingly it is used of crying in distress and for help.[73] Koole concludes: 'the exiles bemoan their lot but the Servant refuses to be intimidated'. The verse therefore does not contribute to the re-evaluation of the royal ideology, which is substantial enough in any case.

But when the poem was written, whether as usually held in the sixth century, or at a somewhat later date, there was no chance of any implementation of this recast ideal, and it might be considered that as with Isaiah 11 it reflects the utopian idealism of a supporter of the monarchy who was well aware of the weaknesses and contradictions of the traditional ideology; and at a distance from real power it was easy to fashion the ideal of a universal and benevolent kingdom. In the two brief periods when sovereignty has since returned to Israel, narrow nationalism has been the hallmark of the polity, and thus the vision of the servant of YHWH may be dismissed as unrealistic. Nor is it easy to find examples in the wider world of empires that truly care equally for all their subjects.

But the significance of the vision does not lie in its correspondence to historical reality. Rather, we must again treat it, like Psalm 72, as an imaginative world inviting us to enter, challenging the real world and therefore developing the potential for change. It is precisely the detachment of the setting of writing from access to political power that enables it to have this rhetorical power.

The figure that speaks in Isaiah 61 has less widely been understood as kingly; the usual view is that the prophet speaks in his own person.[74] Attention should be paid, however, to Eaton's and Koole's argument that the only parallel for the combination of anointing and the gift of the Spirit is in royal investitures (1 Sam. 10.1, 6; 16.13; 2 Sam. 23.1–2).[75] The 'last words of David' in 2 Samuel 23 are also important in showing that prophetic inspiration could be attributed to a king. This may make it easier to attribute the

73. Marcus 1937: 251–52; Koole 1997: 219–20.
74. E.g. Westermann 1969: 365–66, or more recently Blenkinsopp 2003: 220–23.
75. Eaton 1979: 90; Koole 2001: 270.

sense of mission to a royal figure—Westermann thinks it fits badly with anointing, which is always to a permanent office rather than a mission.

But what has not previously been noted, except in an obscure article of my own, is that the echoes which have been recognized of the jubilee proclamation ('liberty', 'acceptable year') may also point to a royal figure, if the argument I hesitantly accepted above is correct.[76] The vision presented here may be of a royal figure proclaiming, surely not prophetically but as an executive act, a decree, good news to the poor (*ʿanāwîm*), and the deliverance of captives as *dᵉrôr*, the liberation of the jubilee. In view of the clear signs that Isaiah 56–66 originated among a minority or excluded group, the royal tradition may here be being employed by those who could themselves be called the oppressed.[77]

There is some point in following the trajectory of the transformed royal ideology through into the New Testament, where it is of course applied to Jesus, called the Christ, the Messiah, the anointed king.[78] Both the texts just examined are cited or alluded to at key points in the Gospels. The heavenly voice at Jesus' baptism alludes to Ps. 2.7, but probably also to Isa. 42.1, most closely in Matt. 3.17, where the third person is used: 'This is my beloved son, in whom I am well pleased'. And although Psalm 72 is scarcely alluded to directly, Broyles finds in it 'a remarkable conjunction of themes that are also central to the New Testament'.[79]

More significantly for our purpose, Luke employs Isa. 61.1–2 to characterize Jesus' ministry at its outset as an exercise, I would argue, of the royal function of deliverance of the oppressed. In Lk. 4.16–21 Jesus reads Isa. 61.1–2a and then says 'Today, in your very hearing, this scripture has come true'. This can only mean that 'the one for whom it was written, the one who alone has the authority to proclaim the liberation of which it speaks, has now proclaimed it, and as the words are a legal decree bringing that liberation into effect, it is now a reality'.[80] Jesus is the anointed Servant who brings the decree of liberation and amnesty into effect.

This essentially political understanding of Jesus' ministry is developed at several points in what follows. The beatitudes and woes in Lk. 6.20–26 are an explicit proclamation of the reversal of the world's unjust social order: the kingdom of God is the establishment of 'justice and righteousness' in the traditional sense. Deliverance of prisoners begins almost at once, with the driving out of demons. Unjust political powers have only to wait: it is a mistake to think of Luke as politically complaisant; see, for example,

---

76. Houston 1987; cf. Zimmerli 1970.
77. Hanson 1975.
78. For an effect in the Qumran writings see Houston 1987: 46.
79. Broyles 1997: 39.
80. Houston 1987: 47.

13.31–35 and 18.7–8. Luke 22.24–29 (based partly on Mk 10.42–44) fore-shadows the fall of Gentile rule and the establishment of the kingdom of Jesus' followers as a kingdom of a new sort: it is the rule of those who serve, where the greatest is the servant of all.

Thus in a trajectory through successive new settings the tradition is kept alive and at the same time radically transformed. It could be said that it is only in this reversal of the customary hierarchy of kingship—and in a situation where that hierarchy was not a realistic possibility—that the purpose of kingship as seen in its ideological texts can be fulfilled. Victory over oppression can only be achieved by those who reject for themselves any opportunity to oppress. One might point to a few attempts in modern times to embody this insight, for example in the Arusha Declaration at the beginning of Tanzania's independence. But it is important not so much for any marginal possibilities of practical implementation, as for its permanent challenge to the customary arrogance of power.

Chapter 6

JUSTICE AND THE PEOPLE

If the general assumption in the ancient Near East, exemplified in Psalm 72 and messianic texts, was that the maintenance of 'justice and righteousness' in society was the responsibility of the king, it is significant that large parts of the Hebrew Bible refuse the assumption. Several texts in the prophets offer sketches of the divinely-founded just society in which the king plays either no role or not the key role in establishing justice; and the Torah, while barely acknowledging the possibility of monarchy, lays that responsibility on the people themselves. These texts are largely from the Persian period. Judah had no native king: but to regard the Persian king as the fount of justice was an evident impossibility. Popular traditions of justice in society had now to be applied by the people themselves.

1. *Visions of Justice in the Prophets*

1.a. *Introduction*

Most of the books of prophecy contrast the message of judgment, condemning the Israelite kingdoms to destruction, with a message of salvation and restoration, offering hope after the execution of judgment. In Isaiah and Ezekiel these sections are very extensive. Among the typical themes of forgiveness and spiritual renewal, the expulsion of enemies, the rebuilding of Zion, the repopulation and fertility of the land, there are some passages which sketch in the character and to some degree the constitution of the restored polity, and some points in these touch on the questions of rich and poor, the division of the land, and the elimination of oppression. Since they all look to a future to be brought in by the apparently unmediated action of God, they have a strong tendency to the utopian or ideal—and are therefore all the more valuable in illustrating what their authors understood as a just society.[1]

---

1. Isa. 32.1–8 may be read not as a prophecy but as a wisdom reflection on good government, but this does not much affect the way in which I use it here (Williamson 1995: 133–41; 1998: 264–70; Blenkinsopp 2000: 428–31).

Such passages are particularly common in the book of Isaiah.[2] The great last vision of Ezekiel (Ezekiel 40–48), with its mass of quasi-legal material, is by no means exclusively concentrated on matters of the cult; it also deals with the question of the allotment of land and the restriction of the powers of the 'prince' with regard to it. And we must also look at a few remarkable verses in Zephaniah (3.11–13) which are more radical than anything else we look at here, subverting the hierarchies which still mark the Isaianic and Ezekielian visions.

1.b. *Visions of Justice in Isaiah*

I believe we can use the expression 'just society', although it has no exact Hebrew equivalent, in that what is described in these texts is a society in which the injustices condemned in the same books are absent. Certainly in 32.1, 16–17 we find the standard pairing of 'righteousness' and 'justice' with the sense of 'social justice'; in v. 1 describing the rule of the king and his officials, and in vv. 16–17 the effect of the pouring (or revelation[3]) of the spirit from on high.

The texts with the clearest relevance to the themes of this study are: Isa. 1.26; 9.7 (Hebrew 6); 11.1–9; 16.4b–5; 29.18–21; 32.1–8, 15–20; 60.21; 61.1–4; 65.17–25. Although the book of Isaiah reveals a social location very close to the Davidic house, and many of these prophecies of a just, blessed and peaceful community are bound up with the rule of a Davidic king and were dealt with in the last chapter—Isa. 9.7; 11.1–9; 16.4b–5; 61.1–4—there are other passages that do not use this 'messianic' motif. Thus, for example, 32.15–20 connects the transformation with 'a spirit from on high'—whether this is what other texts know as the spirit of YHWH is unclear—and 65.17–25 with the creative power of YHWH; 29.19 connects it with YHWH in a more general way.

Our analysis here draws on the more substantial of these non-messianic texts: Isa. 29.17–21; 32.1–8; 32.15–20; 65.17–25; along with parallel aspects of the messianic Isa. 11.1–9.

The essential step to a just society is the elimination of the unjust, the oppressors. This is promised in so many words in 11.4 and 29.20–21. The Davidic 'shoot' will 'strike the tyrant with the rod of his mouth, and with the breath of his lips he will slay the unjust'. 29.20–21 is more specific, but like 11.4 links the benefit to the poor with the elimination of the unjust:

> the lowly will once more have joy in YHWH,
> the needy among humankind will rejoice in the Holy One of Israel;

2. Houston 1993a: 30.
3. Beuken 2000: 221.

no more the tyrant! the end of the arrogant! Those who watch their
chance for evil will be exterminated—
those who frame people when they bring a case, or lay traps for the
arbitrator, or by falsehood deny justice to the one in the right.

This passage focuses on the abuse of justice in the courts, which will cease.

Isaiah 65.17–25 is not so explicit. The dominant theme seems to be the
long lives of the people. But several points may allude to the absence of
exploiters. Isaiah 65.21–22a, 'They shall build houses and inhabit them;
they shall plant vineyards and eat their fruit . . .' in the context seems to be
related to the theme of longevity: no-one dies without enjoying the results
of their labours. But Isa. 65.21 appears to be a slightly altered and short-
ened quotation from Amos 9.14, which may account for the odd statement
that they will *eat* the fruit of their vineyards—the Amos verse has been
compressed by leaving out 'and drink their wine, and plant gardens'. And
Amos 9.14 in its turn harks back to Amos 5.11, the punishment of the
exploiters. In Isaiah too vineyards are a symbol associated with exploitation: Isa. 3.14; 5.7.[4] Again, Isa. 65.23, 'they shall not labour in vain' implies
that there is no exploiter (or invader) waiting to receive the bulk of their
harvest. And in Isa. 65.25 another quotation appears, this time from Isa.
11.6–9. Certainly in Isaiah 11, and quite likely here also, the theme of the
fierce predators, the wolf and the lion and the serpent, living at peace with
their usual prey is (at least) an image for a human community in which some
no longer prey upon the rest. But we concluded our discussion of Isa. 11.1–
9 and particularly its intriguing second part, the vision of the peaceable
kingdom, by suggesting that the implication of the way in which the messianic prophecy is extended with this vision is that simply keeping oppressors in check cannot of itself create a peaceful and just society. What is
needed is 'the knowledge of YHWH', a divine education in justice, and it is
needed by all.

Isaiah 32.1–8 reflects on this in a somewhat different way. Because the king
and his ministers (*śārîm*) rule in justice, their activity is not disastrous like
that of the *śārîm* whom Isaiah has to accuse in Isa. 3.14 of devastating the
vineyard: rather they are a protection for their people, expressed in the four
metaphors in Isa. 32.2. The meditation in Isa. 32.5–8 depends on the semantic fact, evident in English as much as in Hebrew, that words expressing class
or status come to be invested with moral connotations, owing to class preju-
dice. In English this is true of 'noble', used to translate *nādîb* in vv. 5, 8, and
it is true of *nādîb* in Hebrew. The author prophesies, or pleads, that when
someone is given that title they will behave in the way the word implies. A
nobleman should be a noble man. If someone behaves in a way that is
unbecoming to a nobleman, specifically by failing to help the needy, or by
exploiting the poor by false pretences, they should be called by the proper

4. Cf. Chaney 1999.

name—and by implication should not be given the government position that goes with the name of 'noble'. Hence the piece is concerned to urge that government cannot be said to be just if its agents behave oppressively. Obvious enough—yet the bitter experience reflected in the prophetic books is that it was more than one had come to be able to expect from the governments of Israel and Judah.

Several of the passages speak of the results of justice in society. In a context full of the language of fertility, Isa. 32.17 states explicitly: 'The effect of righteousness will be peace, and the result of righteousness quietness and trust (or security) for ever'.[5] Peace (*šālôm*) is as usual in the Hebrew Bible to be understood in a broad sense, including welfare and prosperity. The following verses expand on the theme of peace and security for a rural population; Isa. 32.19 speaks of the end of two features of the landscape that were problematic for the peasant: uncultivable brush, and the city which was responsible for exploitation.

1.c. *Justice in the Vision of Ezekiel*

We turn to Ezekiel. First let us look at the allegory of the flock and the shepherds in Ezekiel 34. Clearly this is rooted in the situation of diaspora, and the first promises, after the initial denunciation of the shepherds, is that YHWH will rescue his flock from them, search for them in the countries where they have been scattered, and gather them in their own land. This passage addressed to the shepherds concludes in Ezek. 34.16: 'The lost I will seek, and the strayed I will bring back, and the wounded I will bind up, and the sick I will heal, but the fat and the strong I will destroy; I will shepherd them in justice (*mišpāṭ*)'. The ultimate object is a community living in peace and prosperity (Ezek. 34.25–29). Essential to this is not only the gathering and healing, but also justice, initiated by the destruction of 'the fat and the strong'—the members of the community (not 'shepherds', not rulers) who have made themselves wealthy at the expense of the rest. This theme is developed in the two speeches which follow, in which YHWH directly addresses the flock, but specifically, it becomes clear, 'the fat and the strong' who have made life a misery for the rest. YHWH 'will judge between sheep and sheep': this is the *leitmotiv*, which is repeated three times, vv. 17, 20, 22, expanded on the second occasion, 'between the fat sheep and the lean sheep'. We recall that it is Ezekiel among the prophets who most explicitly, in oracles of judgement, denounces 'the people of the land', clearly distinguishing between oppression committed by the state and its

---

5. The text is in some respects unreliable, as Beuken (2000: 221–22) shows; he suggests reading *hammišpāṭ* in place of *haṣṣᵉdāqâ hašqēṭ*, so that the half-verse would read 'and the result of justice is trust for ever'. But this does not seriously affect the sense of the verse.

agents and exploitation by wealthy landowners (Ezek. 22.29). For the peaceable kingdom an end to this exploitation is as essential as just government. The latter is ensured by the appointment of 'David' as shepherd (Ezek. 34.23). At this point the allegory is more or less dropped, and it is made clear that 'David' will be the 'prince' (*nāśî*). Ezekiel has no Messianic ideology, and tends to avoid the word 'king' in this connection (but see Ezek. 37.22, 24). Otherwise, the broad themes are very similar to those in Isaiah.

The complex mélange of vision and legal genres in the final section of Ezekiel is of course based on the restored temple, and much of it is concerned with ritual matters. That these themes are not irrelevant, and indeed in the book's ideology are central, to the proclamation of a just, peaceful and blessed community, is beautifully shown in the vision of the water pouring out from beneath the threshold of the temple and going on to fertilize the Arabah and make the Dead Sea fresh (Ezek. 47.1–12). But the section also includes specific instruction on the theme of the land and its distribution, which lie at the heart of social justice. The relevant passages are Ezek. 45.1–12; 46.16–18; and 47.13–48.35. Ezekiel 44.28–31, on the perquisites of the priests, is also relevant. The boundaries of the land and their distribution among the tribes, the sanctuary, the city and the prince (Ezek. 45.1–8a; 47.13–48.29) are highly schematic. Yet within this utopian scheme are embedded some practical instructions on justice and warnings against oppression.

The priests are to have no landholding (Ezek. 44.28); their district in the land (Ezek. 45.3–4) is residential only. This is the understanding in the Torah also; but it is quite evident that in practice the more powerful priests did hold land. They are granted the normal perquisites of sacrifices and other offerings (Ezek. 44.29–30), but nothing is said about tithes, from which one may conclude that they are intended to be supported only by the offerings.

Rather analogously, nothing is said about taxes to support the princely establishment; the prince is granted a generous portion within the land (Ezek. 45.7–8a; 48.21–22), and the numerous sacrifices which he is required to bring are evidently to be taken from the produce of his own portion of land. But the text is more specific: it follows the delineation of his portion in 45.7–8a immediately with the demand 'my princes[6] shall not exploit (using *ynh hi.*) my people any longer: they shall let the house of Israel have the land according to their tribes' (Ezek. 45.8b)—a clear warning against the practices of expropriation alluded to in 1 Sam. 8.14 and 1 Kgs 21, but not elsewhere in the prophets in explicit terms, since it is unclear who the expropriators are in Isa. 5.8 and Mic. 2.1–2. The same warning is repeated

---

6. Or 'the princes of Israel', following the LXX.

more explicitly later, in Ezek. 46.18. If there remained any doubt at this point, it is removed by Ezek. 45.9: 'cease your evictions of my people'. The general exhortation in this verse: 'Enough, princes of Israel! Remove violence and oppression (*ḥāmās wāšōd*) and execute justice and righteousness' (of course more than 'do what is just and right'—NRSV) is thus given a particular point. It could be that the instructions about honest weights and measures which follow (45.10–12) have more of a connection with the context than appears at first sight: for it is likely that the corn trade in urban areas was in the hands of the state, and thus that it was a peculiar temptation of the prince to falsify weights and measures. Ezekiel 46.16–18 makes it clear that the entire princely family and the government establishment must be supported from the princely portion, and that prebends granted from it to officials are not to become hereditary. They must revert to the prince 'in the year of release (*dᵉrôr*)' (Ezek. 46.17). This is a clear reference to the Jubilee law in Leviticus 25, which we shall study below.

The conception in this text of a just society thus centres on the fair distribution of the land, equally distributed between the tribes, and one presumes, though this is not said, fairly distributed between lineages and families within the tribes. Obviously the neat parcelling out of the land between tribes which, if they still existed at all, were of vastly different sizes, is purely ideal, and nothing like this could ever have been achieved. The value lies not in the details but in the intent and the principle: that land is a resource to be fairly distributed among the people. Remarkably, Ezek. 47.22–23 takes a step seen in no other Old Testament text (there is a particular contrast with Leviticus 25): the *gērîm* are given land holdings among the tribes, treated as if they were natives. If this were ever implemented, it would eliminate the oppression of the *gērîm* at a stroke, by giving them a secure footing in the community.

The casual allusion to the 'year of release' in Ezek. 46.17 shows that behind the purely ideal distribution here in Ezekiel lie the provisions of Leviticus 25 to secure landholders against permanent land loss. These are more practical in themselves, though resting on a utopian premise, as we shall see. In addition to those, this text adds provisions intended to protect the people against state interference with their holdings. In all, therefore, the ideal in this sketch is a landholding people secure in their holdings and broadly equal in wealth and influence, except for the prince, whose powers are strictly limited, and the priests, who are excluded from economic power. It is a fine ideal, though so far from the possibility of execution that one wonders how seriously it was intended. For the priestly faction who published it, it proclaimed their concern for the security of a peasant community and their freedom from exploitation but without the burden of having to do anything about it, to put it crudely. Despite this, it remains a valid expression of this communitarian ideal. The details which make it impossible to implement in the sixth-century situation, or whenever it was composed, are of less significance if it is taken simply as the expression of an ideal and an inspiration to more practical efforts.

1.d. *A Vision of Justice in Zephaniah*

The final promise to Jerusalem in Zeph. 3.11–20 has many stereotyped elements, and in particular vv. 14–20 is a call to praise for the triumph of YHWH on her behalf, the removal of the foreign oppressors and the gathering of the exiles and restoration of the city. However, the unit immediately before this, in Zeph. 3.11–13, is rather different. It promises radical action within the community of the city: the removal of 'your proudly exultant ones', so that 'you will no longer be proud on my holy mountain'; while those who will be left, the 'remnant of Israel', will be 'a people humble and poor', *'ānî wādāl*. We here recognize two of the words for 'poor' that have accompanied us throughout this study. But the semantic field of the first of these is generally recognized to be extended in the direction of 'humble'; and in view of the context, with the removal of the proud, this meaning must be present. But it is not present alone. The fact that it is linked with *dāl* is a clear indication that while humility may be spiritual, the referent of the phrase is not a body with a purely spiritual identity. The people in question are, it appears, physically poor, and humble in that they are poor. But in consequence, the referent of 'your proudly exultant ones' also cannot have a purely spiritual identification. These are the old ruling class in Jerusalem, and they are arrogant because they are the ruling class. Zephaniah is saying something rather different from Isaiah and Ezekiel, though Isa. 29.17–21 may come close. Those books foresee the elimination of the unjust and the establishment of justice, but mostly within a renewed or restored hierarchy, cultic or political. Zephaniah appears to envisage the removal of an existing hierarchy, and the takeover of governing functions (since this is the main function of the city) by a group identified as 'the humble and poor'.

This has aroused interest in Zephaniah as a prophet on the side of the poor. Gilberto Gorgulho, for example, a Brazilian theologian, argues that in Zeph. 2.3 'the oppressed of the land' (*'anᵉwê hā'āreṣ*) are called on to build 'a social structure of the people according to the ethical values of the tribal period', 'a social order without domination, that is built on the rights and on the side of the poor.'[7] They will thereby become 'a new historical subject'.[8] Zephaniah 3.11–13 speaks of the fulfilment of their striving.[9]

But are the 'poor of the land' truly oppressed? While most commentators

---

7. Gorgulho 1991: 85.
8. Gorgulho 1991: 84.
9. Cf. also Crüsemann (2003: 146–49), who refers to the more extensive study of Weigl (1994).

see Zephaniah as a post-exilic composition based on a nucleus from Josiah's reign, Marvin Sweeney interprets the book as a whole in the Josianic context, and identifies the 'humble and poor people' with the 'people of the land' who were Josiah's supporters: the text foresees a purge of courtiers and officials who were identified with Assyrian interests, and their replacement by rural landowners.[10] But these were certainly not poor, as Sweeney acknowledges: 'the use of designations such as "humble", "lowly", "righteous", and so on is designed to assert a certain moral (and political) superiority of one party over another'.[11] The use of this vocabulary would thus be ideological: the victory of a poor and humble people would in reality be the victory of a faction denied political power hitherto, and one which would undoubtedly set up its own governing structures. I discuss this issue in greater detail below, with reference to Deuteronomy.

But even if Sweeney is correct, the implications of the way this is expressed should not be overlooked. Even if the 'poor' are not truly poor, the mere designation implies that hierarchy is unnecessary. A just society can be a society of equals living in harmony and taking no advantage of each other (Zeph. 3.13). The aspiration was of course unrealized, as can be seen from Ezek. 22.25–29, which may allude to Zeph. 3.1–4. But as a utopia expressing the ideals of the 'people of the land', if that is what it is, it remains of permanent value.

1.e. *Interpreting Utopia*

For all these visions may be described as utopian. They depict what might be, not what, in the historical circumstances, could be. All are introduced by divine power in one way or another, and ignore the limitations of human nature. But it would be a mistake to think that for that reason they could be dismissed.

The prophetic collections, as we have seen, arise from different ruling-class factions which for one reason or another were distanced from the centre of power. For each of them, the present ordering of society is unacceptable; however, their objections are not based on narrowly factional interest, but embrace the fundamental critique of injustice and thereby extend their acceptability. In each case the critique of current injustice is balanced by a vision of society as it should *and could*, in other circumstances, be justly ordered. For Karl Mannheim warns us that it is always those whose interest is in the maintenance of the existing social order who define what is impracticable in 'the real world'—that is, their own social world—and what is therefore utopian. But what is unachievable in a particular world order

10. Sweeney 2003: 188–90.
11. Sweeney 2003: 190.

is only 'relative utopia', confused with 'absolute utopia' by those whose world is bounded by the existing conditions.[12]

It is because at a deeper level these visions speak of what *is* achievable that they retain their resonance for the citizens of the twenty-first-century world. It is only a utopia that can show us our true desires and our true possibilities. Although these utopias differ slightly, they agree in one thing: that oppression is no part of them. To dismiss them all is to show that we still take oppression for granted as something natural, that it does not anger or disturb us. These visions came to people who were angered and disturbed by oppression. They all come from books which also condemn current historical oppression; whether the passages are written by the same authors or not, they are intended to go together. True, some of them may be trying to have it both ways: hierarchy *and* no oppression, still justifying power because it may be used for good. But even to these, dare we say 'You have nothing to teach me', above all those of us who have and exercise power?

2. *The Just Society in the Torah*

2.a. *The Torah as a Whole*

Most texts on this subject in the Torah make justice the individual's responsibility, as we have seen in Chapter 4. A reading of the Pentateuch as a whole, however, shows that it does have a conception of Israel as a society which is expected to maintain justice between its members, and there are at least three texts that require nationwide action to rectify economic relationships, and therefore imply a concept of *social* justice in a narrower sense. These are the third-year tithe in Deut. 14.28–29, the seven-yearly remission of debts in Deut. 15.1–3, and the jubilee in Lev. 25.8–13. Yet none of these texts gives the responsibility for the enforcement of the measures to any specific authority. They are addressed simply to the nation as 'you' (singular or plural). Deuteronomy does provide in a limited way for judicial and political authority (Deut. 16.18–20; 17.8–20), but gives no particular function to the king.

How may this be understood? And how may the Torah be characterized in the terms we have been using throughout this work, of social setting and interest and rhetorical aim?[13] It is fairly clear that in considering the social setting of the Torah we need to allow for quite distinct settings for the various documents which go to make it up. I will therefore make suggestions in the proper places about the social settings and interests represented by

---

12. Mannheim 1936: 177.
13. Recent works bearing on these questions include Crüsemann 1996; Pleins 2001: 41–91; Watts 1999.

Deuteronomy and the Holiness stratum, to which the three texts referred to belong. Here I want to speak about the Torah as a whole, in its 'final form'.

The Pentateuch is striking for the remarkable mixture of genres which it contains, above all its combination of narrative with various genres of law or instruction. The Pentateuch as a whole cannot be classified in a genre category: it is *sui generis*. Although it has been expounded from a literary point of view as a narrative,[14] no other narrative contains such vast quantities of instructional material. True, the instruction is integrated into the narrative and does not merely interrupt it: it is spoken by one or other of two characters in the narrative, YHWH and Moses. Nevertheless, rhetorically speaking it would be unsafe to conclude that their speeches exist only for the sake of the narrative, to illuminate character or to motivate plot, though they do in fact do both. It is equally possible to argue, as James W. Watts does,[15] that the narrative exists for the sake of the speeches. It presents YHWH and Moses as figures of authority and thereby underscores the authority of their instruction for Israel; and there is no question that contemporary Israel, the Jews of the Persian Empire and later, identified themselves with the Israel addressed in the Torah by YHWH or by Moses speaking under YHWH's authority. For the Torah is seen, in a text such as Nehemiah 8, as directly addressing contemporary Israel.[16]

But more needs to be said than this to understand the rhetorical force of the Torah. The chief motif through which the instruction is integrated into the narrative is that of covenant. The instructions are not simply given to Israel. Israel accepts them and is seen as being bound by them. This is clear in relation to each of the main bodies of law. In the transaction of Exod. 24.3–8 Israel solemnly commit themselves to the observance of the Decalogue and the Book of the Covenant. Although there is no similar covenant ceremony committing them to the Priestly Law, including the Holiness Code, it is clear from Lev. 26.14 that the covenant is seen as including these. The Deuteronomic law is framed by covenant: to the covenant of Horeb recalled in Deut. 5.2–22 correspond the statements of 26.16–19 and 29.1 (Hebrew 28.69) which cover the Deuteronomic law itself. In each of these texts, in its context, the commandments become the sign and instrument of Israel's commitment to the mutual relationship of YHWH and Israel, in which YHWH's part is the past redemption of Israel from Egypt and his future blessing of the nation.

---

14. E.g. Clines 1978.

15. Watts 1999: 32–60.

16. I use the religious term Israel for the nation as it is used in the Torah itself, partly because it is clear that it was understood as directing the lives not only of Jews in Judah (Yehud), but also of YHWH-worshippers wherever they lived, and was accepted as such by a great many, including some (Samaritans) who would refuse the designation 'Jews'. But it was not the everyday term for the Jewish people: see Grabbe 2004: 168–71.

The rhetorical aim of the Torah can therefore be defined as to persuade those who hear it and identify themselves as Israel that YHWH is their God and they are the people of YHWH, committed by covenant to take the instruction as determinative for their life as a people. The Torah understands Israel as the covenant people of YHWH. This is the sense in which the Torah may be understood as 'law', although it is not law in the sense in which that word is normally understood, as the utterance of a political authority who can enforce it judicially. The Torah did come to be used judicially, but it is not well suited for the purpose and always required interpretation and supplementation. The authority under which the Torah is given is that of YHWH, and it is YHWH who takes the place of the political authority that might be expected to issue and enforce law. 'Thus God plays the same rhetorical role within the text as the Persian Empire played in the political world of its compilers and first readers.'[17]

It is this overall rhetorical structure that creates a single purpose from the varied instructional material of the Torah. In its original intent, casuistic law, as in Exod. 21.2–22.17, sets out a procedure to be followed in selected or standard examples of cases, and thus by extension or analogy sets standards of justice which may be applied in a range of cases. The purpose of this genre of law, which is that of the Mesopotamian codes, is much disputed, since it has become clear that in general judges did not make reference to the codes in deciding cases, and neither in the Bible nor elsewhere are required to follow any written text as their authority.[18] It is now widely held that the codes 'constitute a scientific description of justice as a political ideal',[19] and as published by the king they are a demonstration of his justice. Commandments, such as those in Exod. 22.21 (Hebrew 20)–23.9, give moral teaching; they are even more distant from the judicial process than casuistic law. Often enough it is made clear that they can only be enforced by the God who utters them (e.g. Exod. 22.27 [26]), and in this respect they may be compared to royal decrees.

But as part of a book of *covenant* law, both genres, with others, serve to define the moral conduct, the justice and righteousness, which is expected of the covenant people, and which they are understood to have committed themselves to. The divine sanctions, the blessings and curses, which are set out in such detail in Leviticus 26 and Deuteronomy 28, show once more that God is both the authority and the enforcer of this law, that it is divine covenant law, not political law, the law of a polity. It represents the standards to which the people as a whole and every individual is supposed to be committed. Thus, although there may have been efforts, more or less

17. Watts 1999: 147.
18. See Bottéro 1992; Jackson 1989; Fried 2001.
19. Fried 2001, referring to Bottéro 1992 and others.

successful, to enforce particular provisions, every member of the covenant people was in principle understood to be responsible for exercising that justice and righteousness that the Torah demands and the covenant commits them to.

What of the social setting of the Torah? It is certainly under Persian rule that the Torah becomes, in broadly its present form, determinative for the life of Israel.[20] A theory widely accepted in recent years is that the Persians may have specifically authorized it as a codification of Jewish law, though probably at the initiative of the Jewish community.[21] But if I am right in defining the function of the Torah as covenant law as a depiction of the righteousness asked of the covenant people rather than law to be enforced by human authority, it was not the kind of 'code' that a ruling power need have had any interest in. In any case, there is nothing in the Torah that suggests the legitimacy of foreign rule over YHWH's people, quite the contrary—Deut. 17.15!—except as a punishment for breaking the covenant (Deut. 28.43). It is therefore unclear how this view, even if it were correct, would enable us to interpret the Torah. The general interest of the empire in a peaceful and well-ordered provincial community would require law of some kind, but cannot be connected with what we have in the Torah in particular.

Much more evident is the leading place taken by priestly interests in the Torah. A large and central part of the document, the major part of Leviticus and much of Numbers, is devoted to the maintenance of the cult of YHWH and the perquisites of his priests and other cult personnel. This should be no surprise, as it was the priests who established themselves as the main native authorities under Persian rule. The Jerusalem Temple was the centre of the community. It is evident that the contributions required of the community for the support of the cult were onerous.[22] In Nehemiah 10 the community subscribes to a covenant (Neh. 10.29 [Hebrew 30]), the main object of which is to commit themselves to the support of the cult, mentioning specifically most of the main contributions which are laid down in the Torah (Neh. 10.32–39 [Hebrew 33–40]), and at least one which is not—the supply of wood for the altar fire.[23] As Grabbe remarks, in connection with

20. This is generally accepted; Grabbe 2004: 331–43 gives an overview of the evidence.

21. This was argued by Frei 1996 (original edition 1984) and 2001; see Watts 2001 and Watts 1999: 138–43; but the arguments of Fried 2001 and Redford 2001, both in Watts 2001, seem weighty enough against it.

22. Certainly in the early period when it had to be supported largely by the Jews in Judah itself; it is only at a later period, perhaps well into the Hellenistic period, that we find the Temple becoming a regular place of pilgrimage for Jews from other parts of the world and receiving generous support from them.

23. The yearly third of a shekel for the regular offerings (Neh. 10.32–33 [Hebrew 33–34]) is not precisely paralleled in the Torah, but a half-shekel gift is ordained in Exod. 30.11–16. Possibly the half-shekel is a later addition to the Torah and the third is an innovation in the covenant of Nehemiah 10. The cult in the first temple would have been supported by the king.

the tithes in particular, one can deduce from the fact that 'a pledge is necessary to make sure the dues are paid' that they were 'not necessarily paid in full by all the people'—which is probably an understatement—see Mal. 3.8–10.[24]

One ideological function of the Torah is thus to claim the authority of YHWH for the demand that the community of YHWH's worshippers should support his cult personnel, as well as the cult itself. It should be remembered in connection with the support of the cult that parts of the offerings were consumed by the priests or their families; therefore any requirement for sacrifice to be offered in any situation is at the same time a source of support for the priestly caste.

Other interests have not been suppressed, but they do seem to be subordinated. Most prominent in Deuteronomy, and elsewhere, are those of the peasantry, the mass of the population, whose living was always precarious and who, as we know, were at risk of bankruptcy, loss of their land, and debt-bondage, not least in this period (Nehemiah 5). It is evident that it would be this group that would be most heavily burdened by the demands made for the support of the cult. Crüsemann has argued that the Torah emerged from a 'compromise'[25] or 'coalition' between the cult personnel and the free farmers.[26] His view has been criticized,[27] and it is scarcely supported by his quotation of the covenant of Nehemiah 10; for, as we have seen, nearly all the items concern the support of the cult and the perquisites of its personnel. Only the commitment to observe the release of debts in the seventh year (Neh. 10.32 [Hebrew 33]) would be in the interests of the farmers.

Rather than speak of supposed negotiations between social classes resulting in the present form of the Torah, it would be better to recognize, as we have done at various points in this study, that it is to the advantage of any ruling power or leading class in a community to ensure, for the sake of peace and good order, that economic and social relationships are acceptable to the bulk of the population. This means that they should be perceived as just, or sufficiently just to be acceptable, and while, as we have seen, the Torah was probably not treated as a code, the setting out of standards of justice in the covenant law book would serve to offer the assurance that the leaders of the community were committed to such standards. This would include those measures apparently aimed at reducing debt and alleviating poverty that we have in various parts of the Torah.

What matters, of course, is justice as perceived by the members of the society, rather than as we might perceive it.[28] It is possible that some

---

24. Grabbe 2004: 236.
25. Crüsemann's original word, withdrawn in 1996: 340 n. 90.
26. Crüsemann 1996: 340–343.
27. Blum 1990: 359.
28. See above, pp. 11–12; Kippenberg 1983: 75.

considered that the tithe was a fair exchange for spiritual benefits. If the tithe and other contributions were well established and recognized as fair, the covenantal demand of the Torah as a whole would be accepted as just, with the social welfare provisions intended to prevent the slide into proletarianization and enslavement balancing the heavy demands made for the sake of the cult, and the well-to-do encouraged to help the poor with zero interest loans and gifts. On the other hand, if the tithe were seen as a novel imposition threatening the security of the poorer peasant (and ten percent is indeed a heavy impost on a farmer close to the margin of subsistence), the presence of such provisions in the Torah as the prohibition of interest on loans for subsistence and the remission of loans in the seventh year would not suffice to render the Torah as a whole acceptable as a paradigm of justice, no matter how strongly it were promoted as Israel's covenant commitment. The evidence is that many Jewish farmers did not pay a tithe, or did not tithe in full. To assume, as critics such as Malachi do, that this is because they were simply careless of their religious duty, is unwarranted. They may have been unable to pay, or they may have considered the impost unjust and unacceptable.

There is thus a severe ambiguity about the Torah. Against its concern for the poor must be set the support that it offers for the material position of the leading groups in society. This applies, as we shall see, not only to the Torah as a whole, but to the various elements that go to make it up. We shall look at two of these, Deuteronomy and the Holiness Code, and within them the texts they present suggesting means of tackling social ills collectively.

2.b. *Deuteronomy*

2.b.1 *The Context of Composition*
We need to consider the same issues with regard to this book as we have just done for the Torah as a whole. To whom is it addressed, by whom and to what end? Whose interests are displayed or concealed within it, and what do they hope to persuade the hearers of? There is of course no lack of answers offered to these questions; the difficulty is to choose between them.[29] The question of the work's date, monarchic or post-monarchic, is a significant, but not necessarily decisive, issue. It would seem at first sight that it must be the key to discerning the book's ideology: whether the authors were addressing a people who could determine their own way of life or one that was under the control of foreigners would make all the difference to what

---

29. Besides the commentaries, most recently Nelson 2002 and McConville 2002, see Weinfeld 1972; Crüsemann 1996: 201–276; Albertz 1994: I, 195–231; the Leuven symposium Lohfink 1985; Lohfink 1990a, 1990b; Perlitt 1994; and the brief but suggestive sociological essays of Claburn 1973 and Knight 2000.

they could be aiming to achieve (so Perlitt 1994: 182–183). Is it a practical reform programme for a functioning state or an idealistic plan for a Utopia?

But if that is the right way of putting the question, it should be easy to decide which is true. Why is it not? On the one hand, the utopian character of the 'constitutional' provisions (Deut. 16.18–18.22) is obvious.[30] We have an optional king who neither commands the army nor judges cases, the two essential functions of the king in all ancient states; judges whose function beside the elders is unclear; hereditary priests and charismatic prophets; and no indication how any of it is supposed to work as a system. Throughout the text it is simply the people who are addressed and expected to direct complex undertakings like the seven-year debt release. This is not a constitution but a series of ideas related not by constitutional practicality, but by religious and moral principles. And the utopian character is not confined to this section, nor to texts often seen as late: as we shall see, the seven-year debt release is tacitly admitted in the text to be capable, in the world as it actually exists (Deut. 15.11!), of making things worse rather than better for the poor; the destruction of an entire city for apostasy (Deut. 13.12–18) is purely theoretical—and so on. Like the Torah of which it forms a part, Deuteronomy is aspirational rather than a concrete programme for reform: it shows what *ought* to be done rather than announcing what *will* be done. This is the main reason, in my view, for reserve in reading it as the blueprint of the 'reform' related in 2 Kgs 23.1–24.

But on the other hand, it does not follow from the utopian character of the text that it cannot be addressed to the citizens of an independent state. Perlitt's alternative is false. It all depends on the function which we attribute to such a text. Like the Mesopotamian law codes, it might well be intended to present an ideal of justice which those in positions of responsibility should strive to fulfil, rather than being merely theoretical. The sense of national pride which suffuses the text and even has to be brought down a peg—'Do not say to yourself, "My power and the might of my own hand . . ." '(Deut. 8.17)—points strongly to the current independence of the kingdom. The signs of a people demoralized by defeat, crushed and broken in spirit, or clear recognition that the curse of YHWH has fallen on the nation, is confined to the book's marginal sections which are generally recognized as belonging to a later redaction: Deut. 4.25–31; 28.47–68; 29.19–28; 30; 31.16–21. This is strong evidence against redactional theories which attribute large parts of the core of the work to exilic and post-exilic editors.[31]

The conclusion must be that this book is a utopian text addressed in the first place to citizens of the late monarchy, with some later development, of

---

30.   Nelson 2002: 213; Lohfink 1990b: 314; Perlitt 1994: 186.
31.   E.g. Veijola 2004: 2–6.

course.[32] They are encouraged to regard themselves as the chosen and holy people of YHWH, and to transform their society into one which better reflects YHWH's intention for their life. In Mannheim's terms, it is utopian rather than ideological: it does not justify the status quo, which was quite different, but aims at its transformation. But like utopian texts in general, it is likely to represent the interests and aspirations of a particular section within society.

Weinfeld shows the influence on it of the Assyrian treaties and of wisdom traditions, and suggests that the authorship lies with official scribal circles of the royal court.[33] There can be no doubt that it is the work of a group of intellectuals likely to have been mainly engaged in the civil service, but probably including elements of the priesthood. We saw earlier that the book of Jeremiah bears clear traces of its links with a faction of crown servants, and the editors of that book were obviously 'Deuteronomists', a second generation of writers following those who produced Deuteronomy. But the authors of the book did not necessarily represent only their own interests. They were engaged intellectuals working on behalf of a much broader or more powerful group. Who would they have been?

Those who are addressed by the text are evidently the free adult male farmers and landowners of Judah, who are independent and possessed of some resources, who are able to give loans and may own slaves. They do not include the poor—'the poor man' is someone else in Deut. 15.7–11. These are the 'Israel' who stand before 'Moses'. And we shall see as we go on that their position is subtly reinforced by these laws. Crüsemann argues that it is these people whose interests and aspirations are represented by Deuteronomy,[34] and he boldly identifies them with the 'people of the land' who according to 2 Kgs 21.24 placed the eight-year-old Josiah on the throne, and through him attempted to realize their religious and political ideals.[35]

However, as Crüsemann admits,[36] the group presumably responsible in reality for the installation of Josiah and the composition of the Deuteronomic programme would have been much smaller than the whole body of free landholders: certain leading elements, perhaps primarily those who had taken up residence in the capital[37]—hence their interest in centralization—working in concert with some state officials and some Jerusalem priests. Albertz, slightly differently, sees these ruling class elements as the

---

32. Linguistic and literary-historical grounds must exclude an earlier date, *pace* McConville (2002: 34–40) and other conservative critics.

33. Weinfeld 1972.

34. Crüsemann 1996: 215–22, and more broadly down to p. 275; see also Albertz 1994: I, 201.

35. Crüsemann 1996: 212–15.

36. Crüsemann 1996: 266–69.

37. See above, pp. 39–40.

directing intelligence of the movement, working through the supreme court of Deut. 17.8–13.[38] Dutcher-Walls, working from the evidence of Jeremiah, emphasizes the factional character of the movement. It would have included elements of the royal service and the priesthood and the 'people of the land', but only some of each group.[39]

It would appear that the centralization of the cult (Deuteronomy 12) and of some aspects of judicial proceedings (Deut. 17.8–13) would be of great benefit to the crown and the ruling classes in the capital, with the potential to bring in large financial revenues. Some have made of this an argument for radical suspicion of the text as an ideological apology for a stratagem of the ruling classes to increase their power and wealth.[40] It is possible, as Claburn suggests, that the motive, or one of the motives, behind this measure, was to divert the tithe revenues from powerful local interests (that these were the Levites is more speculative) to the crown. Claburn sees the Deuteronomic innovation of allowing personal consumption of the tithe (Deut. 14.23–27) as compensation to the peasants for the expense and trouble of bringing it to the central sanctuary.[41] But as he points out, following Eissfeldt, the producer and his entourage would hardly have been able to consume the tithe in the course of a few days as the text purports to require.[42] What was to happen to the rest of it is not said, but usually a tithe is a tax. In any case, we have no information whether the permission was actually implemented. This refutes Crüsemann's assumption that the permission for consumption of the tithe represents a diversion of resources *away* from the centre.[43] He has also overlooked that it would normally have been collected locally before centralization.

In line with the religious, fiscal and political drive for the centralization of the nation is the way in which the social and political assumptions and rhetoric of the book serve to undermine familial, local and traditional ways of belonging in favour of a radical, unified nationalism. One sign of this is the use of the language of family in reference to the national community, which we will look at in connection with Deuteronomy 15. Along with this goes the relative unimportance of tribal divisions, emphasized by Perlitt;[44] though he goes too far in saying that Deuteronomy does not know of any division of the people into families and lineages. It is an illuminating exaggeration, all the same. Naomi Steinberg argues that Deuteronomic family law elevates the nuclear family over the traditional authority of the

---

38. Crüsemann 1996: 266–269; Albertz 1994: I, 201–206.
39. Dutcher-Walls 1991.
40. See, e.g., Claburn 1973, Nakanose 1993, Knight 2000, Bennett 2002.
41. Claburn 1973: 16.
42. Claburn 1973: 17, n. 9.
43. Crüsemann 1996: 216–19.
44. Perlitt 1980: 51.

extended family, and that this is a method of extending state control.[45] Most important of all, cult centralization itself would have at once attenuated the power of local loyalties, and enabled the state to weld disparate local lineages into a single community through their common religious purpose.[46] This creation of national community is one of the things that is symbolized by the two scenes of covenant making in the book.

It may be objected that this strengthening of the unity of the nation and the power of the state is scarcely compatible with the apparently limited and grudging way in which kingship is viewed in the 'constitutional sketch'. Knight sees the restrictions on kingship as representing popular sentiment, while at the same time they 'serve the interests . . . of the nonroyal elites', in that they aim to ensure that they share power with the king and his servants. They are thus 'a prime example of how the new elite . . . could rewrite popular values into a generalized system of justice that might gain maximum support even though the special interests of the elite were thereby surreptitiously favoured'.[47] The deepening of national cohesion is therefore in the interest of a broader circle than merely the royal family or ruling circles of the capital. Moreover, the undermining of local bonds and loyalties was already under way, and was hastened by the social and political tumult of the previous hundred years. Deuteronomy probably as much reflects as encourages this development.

The net result of this inquiry is that Deuteronomy serves ideologically to strengthen national cohesion in the interest of a broad range of parties who identified their interests with the state, but at the same time gives support to the position of the free landholders as a whole (as we shall see in the following sections), and shows concern for the poor and marginal groups, which is the surface intention of the laws we are about to examine. All these, after all, are 'Israel' within the ideology of the book, and the unification of the nation under one God which the book aims at is best accomplished by showing everyone that it is in their interests—or at least giving that impression, even if in places we must judge that that is an illusion.

2.b.2 *General Provisions*

Deuteronomy contains a number of social provisions, mainly gathered in Deut. 24.10–22, for the benefit of either the marginal groups—the stranger, orphan and widow, and for Deuteronomy also the Levite—or the citizen forced to borrow or reduced to slavery or to the status of a hired worker. For the most part these are exhortations addressed to the individual similar to ones we have already looked at in Chapter 4: not to charge interest on loans

---

45. Steinberg 1991.
46. Albertz 1994: I, 207.
47. Knight 2000: 108.

(Deut. 23.19–20 [Hebrew 20–21]); not to act oppressively in securing pledges against loans; not to delay paying the hired worker's wages; to leave produce on the field for the marginal groups to glean; to make sure they have a portion of the sacrificial feasts at the festivals (Deut. 16.11, 14). As we have seen before, these exhortations call for generosity on the part of the creditor, employer or landowner, without suggesting any permanent change in the relationship or a radically new conception of community.

There is nothing utopian about this moral teaching, except perhaps the prohibition of interest, which it is difficult to show was ever seriously applied. But, as we shall see, this kind of moral appeal is in the end insepar-able from the Deuteronomic utopia. The motivations attached to some of the exhortations are paralleled not only in Exodus 22–23 but also in Deuteronomy 15. The patron is warned that his client has access to God, and may either bless him (Deut. 24.13) or call against him (Deut. 24.15): the patron's righteousness or guilt before God is in the hands of his client. But if he acts generously, YHWH will bless him (Deut. 16.15; 23.20 [Hebrew 21]; 24.19). The promise of blessing is attached specifically to those com-mands that ask for generosity to the poor and dispossessed, including also Deut. 14.29; 15.10, 18.[48] Such generosity must appear risky where so many perils threaten the landowner's hard-won prosperity. The blessing assures him that the risk is worth taking. This is the motivation by theodicy.

The other main motivation asks the patron to view himself and his relationships with his clients in the light of his nation's history. 'Remember that you were a slave in Egypt' (Deut. 24.18, 22). This call occurs in Deuter-onomy only to support the command to be generous to marginal people (also in Deut. 15.15; 16.12; and in the Decalogue at 5.15).[49] The patron is reminded to understand himself as one who belongs to a people that was once marginal, dispossessed and oppressed.[50] But this wording reads oddly in the context of ch. 24, which does not have to do with slavery. This suggests that there is a deliberate echo of Deut. 15.15, and perhaps of Deut. 5.15.

We find the essential social elements of Deuteronomy's utopian pro-gramme expressed in two passages early in the code: the tithe law in Deut. 14.22–29 (compare Deut. 26.12–15), and the law of debt release in Deut. 15.1–11. These both require community action to be implemented, and both are based on a rhythm of time, though on a different cycle in each case.

2.b.3 *The Third-Year Tithe*
We have already touched on the tithe law and noted Claburn's understanding of it as a means of increasing crown revenues. The tithe remains holy (Deut.

---

48. Crüsemann 1996: 225.
49. Oosthuizen 1997: 81.
50. Cf. Lasserre 1995, on Deut. 15.12–18.

26.13) and subject to traditional ritual restrictions (Deut. 26.14); it still has to be 'removed from' the producer's 'house'. While the first and second year tithes must be taken to the central sanctuary, in the third year it remains in the local community, to be given to the Levites, the strangers, the orphans and the widows—in a word, the landless and resourceless, those who are not fully integrated into the agrarian community. To give it to those who need it is in itself to sanctify it. And the blessing of YHWH will follow those who act in this way. By providing for a sharing of the benefits in this way, and assuring the farmers of the divine blessing, it appears that the writers were suggesting a mode in which the farmers might experience solidarity with the landless groups.

It is worth reflecting that it is likely that in early Israelite society the stranger (such as there were), orphan and widow, and perhaps also the Levite, would have been provided for within the extended family as a matter of course. The need for such a provision as this suggests the extent to which older community structures had broken down. This law is a modest step towards the re-creation of community.

2.b.4 *The Release of Debts*[51]
This aim is also expressed in the next passage, Deut. 15.1–11. Its utopian social vision appears both in the provision for a seven-yearly release of debts and in the rhetoric which supports it, which can be seen as another attempt to re-create a sense of community. The law on slave release in Deut. 15.12–18 can be dealt with in the same connection because, although it calls for individual rather than community action, it is enveloped in the same rhetoric.[52]

It is widely accepted that Deut. 15.1–11 is based on an older law. In Deut. 15.2 we find a formulation in the third person which marks it off from the uniform second person around it: 'Every creditor shall remit what he has lent to his neighbour (*or* 'the pledge he has against his neighbour's debt');[53] he shall not press his neighbour, his brother, because YHWH's remission has been proclaimed'. The Deuteronomic author himself would naturally

---

51.   This and the following two sections incorporate material from my essay Houston 1995.

52.   Some have thought that the same seven-year cycle as in v. 1 is meant in Deut. 15.12 (e.g. Seitz 1971: 171; Mayes 1979: 250). But this is a very difficult interpretation of the text, which is naturally understood as saying that each slave should serve for six years, not that all slaves should be released in the same year.

53.   The text, structure and meaning of this verse are all disputed; for details of the discussion see Oosthuizen 1997: 66–67; Houston 1995: 302–303 n. 3, as well as the commentaries. It is uncertain which of the two translations given above is correct; but if the pledge is to be remitted it would mean that the debt was in effect cancelled, while if it is the debt, the question whether the debt is cancelled or payment simply suspended remains open. Veijola's translation (2004: 310) is different again: 'Every creditor shall loose his hand. Whoever has lent to his neighbour, shall not . . .'

have said, 'You shall remit . . . you shall not press', as in Deut. 15.12, where the word 'master' is never used, because the master is himself being addressed throughout. Something is therefore being quoted; it is a decree requiring creditors to remit debts, and considering our discussion in the last chapter it would not be too far-fetched to conclude that it is the wording of a royal decree comparable to the decrees of *andurārum* and *mīšarum* issued by the Babylonian kings.[54] As we have seen, such decrees could have occasionally been issued by Davidic kings. This writer, however, uses this traditional wording to call for something quite different: not an occasional, but a regular release of debts, every seven years, a permanent institution. I want to suggest that it is aimed at transforming economic relationships and preventing those burdened by debt from sliding into a permanent underclass.[55]

Whether this is so depends on what is meant by 'remission' (the verb *šmṭ* and the noun *šᵉmiṭṭâ*). Is it a one year suspension of the creditor's right to repayment or the cancellation of the debt?[56] Deuteronomy 15.9 presumes that lenders may be put off by the approach of the year of release, and this seems more likely if something more than a mere suspension is meant. However, the weight of this consideration depends on the usual term of loans of this kind. If, as seems likely, repayment would normally be expected within the year, by the next harvest, then even a year's suspension would be a serious deterrent to lending, though not as serious as a cancellation.[57] A further argument for assuming a cancellation is that we have plenty of comparative material requiring the cancellation of debts,[58] but none ordaining a temporary suspension. True, all the examples of debt-cancellation we know of are irregular events, and the idea of a regular, periodic cancellation is as unexampled as that of a suspension. But if we are correct in assuming that an older decree is taken up in Deut. 15.2, it is likely to have originally referred to a cancellation, and is unlikely to have been taken up in a different sense. The decisive argument is that Jewish tradition has always taken it to refer to a cancellation; and this is consonant with the tone of the passage, which expounds the necessary conditions of a just society and not simply what can be practically achieved. In Judah around

54. Morrow 1995: 101.
55. I was of course wrong to say (Houston 1995: 302) that the basic law requires a remission every seven years. That provision is in v. 1, which is expressed in the second person.
56. Jewish tradition as far back as we can go has taken it in the sense of cancellation (Philo, *de Spec. Leg.* II 71–73 (Philo 1937: 350–53); Mishnah, *Sheb*. 10.1; cf. Driver 1902: 179). Critical opinion shifted towards this view, which is now predominant, in the twentieth century: for the nineteenth see S.R. Driver (1902: 179), who hesitantly marks the beginning of the switch. But many writers still maintain the view that a suspension is meant (Craigie 1976: 236; Wright 1984; McConville 2002: 259; Veijola 2004: 312–13). For a detailed discussion see Chirichigno 1993: 272–75.
57. So Veijola 2004: 313.
58. Weinfeld 1995: 75–96.

the turn of the eras, though the law was technically in force, it was deprived of effect by a legal device, the *prozbul* (Mishnah, *Sheb.* 10.3).

I would argue then that what we have here is no mere modest measure of relief consequent on the observance of the fallow year,[59] but a profoundly egalitarian measure calling for a total reordering of economic relationships, which when put into effect would inevitably be evaded by those whose interests were affected by it. This problem is recognized and addressed in vv. 7–11.

But before we reach that point, there are other important observations. Already in v. 2 we find the word *'āḥîw* 'his brother': literally, 'he shall not press his neighbour *and his brother*'.[60] The second noun clarifies the first. 'Neighbour' (*rēa'*) seems to be the standard legal term for the person with whom the addressee has to do: it is used in the Covenant Code and in the Decalogue, and with other terms in the Holiness Code. It is to a large extent replaced by 'your brother' in the Deuteronomic code. Here 'his brother' is added alongside it, because the writer is editing an older text; normally we find the second person singular suffix, *'your* brother'. This is the first place where it occurs, and from this point on it is used repeatedly, especially in social justice contexts. In Deuteronomy 15 it appears six times: vv. 2, 3, 7, 9, 11, 12. Three times (Deut. 15.3; 17.15; 23.20–21) it contrasts the Israelite with the foreigner; in other places, as in 15.7–11, there is a possible clash of interests with another Israelite, and calling him 'your brother' draws attention to what the addressee has in common with that person.[61]

What does this usage imply? Briefly, that they are fellow-members of a community which they are encouraged to understand as a family, in which they are linked by kinship. Lothar Perlitt has devoted an article to this usage in Deuteronomy, and much of the following is indebted to it.[62]

First, as we have noted before in other connections, the use of this word implies that the text normally has males in mind: the awkwardness of the expression in v. 12, literally, 'your brother, a Hebrew or a Hebrew woman' arises from the exceptional need to emphasize that the law applies equally to men and women (cf. v. 17b).

Secondly, does v. 3 imply that only the true-born Israelite is worthy of just treatment, as opposed to the foreigner? There is a contrast with the

---

59. As suggested by, e.g., Craigie (1976: 236).

60. NRSV 'member of the community'; REB 'fellow-countryman'. NRSV is attempting to use inclusive language, but in the process loses the emotional force of the word, as does REB.

61. For Veijola, who relies on an article by Christoph Levin (2003), this usage belongs to an exilic layer in the text (Veijola 2004: 314–15). He argues that the word breaks the syntax. But the syntactic awkwardness in vv. 2, 12, arises because the Deuteronomic author is quoting an older law; and the syntax in vv. 7, 9 is straightforward.

62. Perlitt 1980.

foreigner, but not a chauvinistic one: the contrast is with *nokrî*, the foreigner
as such, not with *gēr*, the resident alien, and it is usually thought that the
exception is intended to exclude commercial loans from the operation of
the law. The *gēr* has the same claim on the Israelite's concern as the
'brother', as Deut. 24.14 shows. Perlitt argues that the three passages that
contrast the 'brother' with the foreigner belong to a later stratum.[63] In his
view the usage is not based on the idea of the blood relationship of all the
members of the people, which (he says) has no interest for Deuteronomy;
nor is it an extension of the older cultural ideal of responsibility within the
extended family or clan.[64]

He lays stress instead on the word's emotional colouring, which emerges
very strongly in its concentration in Deut. 15.7–11. The colouring is so
much stronger than that of 'neighbour', and this makes it appropriate to use
where a strong ethical appeal is to be made to help and protect the needy.
'The (national) community of brothers arises out of the claim on the individual Israelite to see and treat his neighbour as a brother.'[65] It is a more
emotional and indeed a more religious way of saying 'your neighbour', a
way which appeals more deeply to the heart; a way of expressing 'the common humanity of those who together live out of the liberating love of
God'.[66] The appeal to brotherhood is not the result of the natural relationship of all Israelites: the relation of all Israelites as brothers (and sisters) is
the result of the law's appeal to treat each other as such.

But is Perlitt right in arguing that it is not an extension of the older
cultural ideal of responsibility within the extended family or clan? It is true
that Deuteronomy hardly ever refers to this. Deuteronomy 13.6–11 (Hebrew
7–12) makes it uncompromisingly plain that the Israelite has a higher loyalty even than that to his immediate family and his literal brothers. Whereas
in Leviticus 25 the particular responsibility of the lineage or clan is provided
for (Lev. 25.25), this is not true of Deuteronomy 15, where responsibility
is defined solely in terms of the 'brother', meaning the fellow-citizen in
general.

But all of this does not disprove that Deuteronomy is intending to depict
the relationship between members of the national community *as if it were*
an extended family or clan; indeed, it rather tends to confirm it. The text
uses language which recalls the requirements of clan redemption (Lev.
25.25). It also recalls the pragmatic fact that inequalities arose within the
lineage because of the way in which this institution worked, tending to
concentrate wealth within the senior branches and render the junior ones

63. Perlitt 1980: 42.
64. Perlitt 1980: 50–51.
65. Perlitt 1980: 37 (my translation).
66. Perlitt 1980: 42 (my translation).

dependent on them.[67] But it extends and deepens the import of the language of 'brotherhood' in two ways: by extending its range to the nation as a whole, and by implicitly pleading that 'brothers', whatever their degree of blood relationship, should genuinely act like brothers: that is, with generosity, not with hard-heartedness.

It cannot, therefore, be sufficient to define the stress of 'your brother' in purely emotional and ethical terms. It does have emotional weight, and it is used to argue for an ethical stance, but it does that in part because it defines the nation in the image of the kin-group and, conversely, redefines responsibility to kin as responsibility for fellow-nationals. Thus the idea of brotherhood, ethically central to this chapter, can be seen as the expression in a new context of a very old idea of community in which it defines the responsibility of people to those who, in the typical tribal village inhabited by members of one or a few clans, would be both neighbours and relatives.[68] Its practical expression would in many situations be very similar.

Deuteronomy 15.4–6 are a theological reflection that if Israel were truly obedient measures like this would not be required.[69] There would be no poor because of YHWH's blessing—so most translations and commentators. There is a consensus that the 'commandment' referred to in v. 5, which Israel must obey to retain the blessing, is the Deuteronomic code as a whole.[70] Somewhat differently, Morrow reads v. 4a as a prohibition: 'there is not to be a poor person among you'.[71] Whichever interpretation is adopted, the contrast with Deut. 15.11, 'the poor will never cease out of the land' (often seen as a contradiction) is sharp, and all commentators attempt to deal with it. Many scholars have attributed the verses to a later hand on stylistic grounds.[72] Yet they do express the utopian object of the law very well. Craigie, for example interprets this passage as a possibility 'contingent on the completeness of Israel's obedience', while v. 11 'is a more realistic appraisal'.[73] For Hamilton, vv. 4–6 represent the consequence of obedience, like v. 10b, while v. 11a expresses the situation that makes the law necessary.

But it is Lohfink's view that is of particular interest for us.[74] He rightly sees that the whole passage partakes of the 'utopian' character attributed to vv. 4–6. The way in which he interprets this, however, is that the text understands poverty as a temporary state arising quite naturally from, say, a bad

---

67. Kippenberg 1982: 33–41; cf. Crüsemann 1983: 93.
68. See Bendor 1996 and above, pp. 25–27.
69. So Driver 1902: 175–76.
70. E.g. REB: 'these commandments'; NRSV, 'this entire commandment'; Craigie 1976: 234: 'the whole of this code of law'.
71. Morrow 1995: 92, 94; Oosthuizen 1997: 68–69.
72. E.g. Seitz 1971: 169; Mayes 1979: 248; Veijola 2004: 315–16.
73. Craigie 1976: 237.
74. Lohfink 1990a: 47.

harvest, which is instantly eliminated by the generosity of those who have
not been affected to the same extent: so v. 11 means 'people will always be
falling into poverty', and v. 4 means 'but there will be no *class* of poor
people', provided that the command of generosity is heeded. It is an attractive view, but in the end I do not find it convincing. The tensions in the
passage are more profound. The consistent use throughout vv. 7–11 of the
term *'ebyôn*, 'poor', usually as a noun, suggests a person who has this constant characteristic. To express the idea in Hebrew of someone temporarily
falling into financial straits one would expect a verb, as in Lev. 25.35. Moreover, Deut. 15.12 assumes that there will still be people who through poverty
are going to have to go as far as selling their children into slavery. Lohfink's
idea fits Leviticus 25 much better, as we shall see.

Therefore it seems that there is a real contradiction within the passage.
The utopian object of the programme, an undivided society of equal
'brothers', is for ever to be out of reach. The text recognizes this, but urges
the hearers to constantly act *as though it were true*: the moral appeal of vv.
7–11 is based on the perception of the poor man as a brother.

The un-utopian realism of Deut. 15.7–11 lies in its highlighting in v. 9 of
the potential ineffectiveness of the law. It would choke off credit in the year
or two leading up to the year of release. The way the text deals with the
problem is not to introduce a refinement into the law but to call for a
generosity going beyond the demands of the law, and to appeal to concern
and compassion. Give loans anyway, whether you expect them back or
not! It is not your advantage you should be concerned with, but your
brother's need.

There are several points to note here. First, the repeated use of 'your
brother', more concentrated in this passage than anywhere else in Deuteronomy. Secondly, Hamilton draws attention to the repeated strategic use of
'somatic' vocabulary— 'hand' and 'heart' and 'eye': open your hand, let
there not be a villainous thought in your heart, let your eye not be evil. This
concentration of terms for parts of the body casts the relationship in intimate
terms and so intensifies the emotional power of the rhetoric.[75]

Thirdly, there is a religious appeal. It is of two kinds: the stick and the
carrot, the threat and the promise. In Deut. 15.9 we have the threat of the
poor man's appeal to God, as in Exod. 22.23–24, 27 (Hebrew 22–23, 26),
and Deut. 24.15. In Deut. 15.10 there is the promise of blessing if the
command of generosity is heeded; this refers to this specific commandment,
unlike v. 5. There is no question here of a rule that can be enforced. This is
an appeal straight to the heart. As Perlitt says of it, with this passionate
appeal *'macht man der Liebe Beine'*—'it gets love moving'.[76] The text

---

75. Hamilton 1992: 31–34.
76. Perlitt 1980: 33.

presents this as the only way of counteracting the deterrent effect of the base law, quite correctly if one grants the premise in Deut. 15.11: there will always be poor in the land.

There is a contradiction not merely between v. 4 and v. 11, but within the heart of vv. 7–11. The text presumes the continued existence of inequalities and of the patron-client relationship. There will be poor, and the addressees of the law, the 'people of the land', will be in a position to help them. The fundamental relation of dependency is not abolished. If we had temporarily to reckon with such a revolution through Deut. 15.4–6, we are rapidly disabused. Yet it is precisely this part of the text, vv. 7–11, that most urgently insists on the transformation of relationships between the dependent and those on whom they depend. As Hamilton puts it, the text places dependants 'at the center of society, not at the margins', indeed, with the power to call down the wrath of God upon the hard-hearted and close-fisted.[77] Above all, it makes them members of one family. No social revolution is assumed, after all, but there is a call for a moral revolution, which would eliminate exploitation.

Moreover, although the fundamental measure in Deut. 15.1–2 calls for community action, indeed must require the activity of the state to set up a simultaneous remission of debts, it emerges that it will be of no effect unless the hearts of individuals are touched and their moral conduct changed. What sets out to be a law for a radical economic transformation ends up as moral exhortation of a familiar type, though exceptionally powerful in its rhetorical appeal. The fate of the poor is left as usual in the hands of the well-to-do.

A similar situation emerges from the following passage, on the release of debt-slaves.

2.b.5 *The Release of Slaves*

There is a close relationship between this passage and the previous one, since both are concerned with the problem of debt. Creditors might take a family member as surety, and the debt-release provision of Deut. 15.1–2 will ensure that they cannot keep them beyond the year of release.[78] But besides this, debtors might need to sell family members into bondage to pay off debts. The text accepts that, despite the seven-year remission, this will continue.[79] In view of the use of the verb *mkr* 'sell', this seems more likely to be the situation envisaged than the offering of persons on pledge, though it

---

77. Hamilton 1992: 134.

78. Cf. Kippenberg 1983: 80.

79. Chirichigno 1993: 221–23. It is uncertain whether the verb form *yimmākēr* (ni.) should be understood as a passive 'is sold', or a reflexive 'sells himself'. Since it was most usually children who were sold (cf. Neh. 5.2 [emended], 5), the former seems more likely (cf. Lefebvre 2003: 307–14). To sell himself would be the last resort for the paterfamilias.

could also be creditors who are envisaged as selling forfeit debtors. It is likely that a law similar to Exod. 21.1–6 is here being modified.[80] Like the previous one, this law is brought home to the hearer by personal appeal to feeling for the brother (or sister!). Even at the expense of stylistic smoothness, 'your brother' is added in v. 12. The 'slave' is actually a brother. Where all are brothers, there can be no masters and slaves; and the word 'slave' is avoided until the point where the man himself volunteers for permanent slavery. The contract is not one of slavery but of the sale of one's labour for a fixed term.

Deuteronomy 15.13–15 may possibly put an old custom into words, but it could be enforced only by the pressure of public opinion, and where that failed, by appeal to 'brotherly' feeling. It is not an enforceable rule, but again relies on generosity that goes beyond the law. And like Deut. 15.7–11 this responds to a weakness in the law. It was not sufficient to provide for a fixed term of service; for released bondservants would have no recourse but to return to their families, which, with an extra mouth to feed, would be left in no better position than before. If they brought with them a substantial addition to their resources, that might make all the difference.

Here the prime religious appeal is very pertinent: the master is reminded that his own current prosperity is due solely to the divine blessing, and further to 'remember that you were a slave in Egypt and YHWH your God redeemed you'. This underlines that all are in the same boat: there can be no class divisions where everyone is a freed slave and all owe their liberty and prosperity to God. The point is essentially the same as with the language of brotherhood. Guy Lasserre points out that the master is called on not just to change his practice, but 'to redefine his concept of himself, of his property, of his relations with his slaves, of his past and of his future'![81] Also implied here may be an appeal to the imitation of God. The God whom the master serves is one who releases slaves! How can the servant of this God do less with his own servant?

Thus in this section, in an even more marked way than with the year of release, the institutional structure of dependency is retained, but the expectation is that it will be transformed by a new understanding of social relationships. There is again a hidden contradiction: the institution of

---

80. It is generally held that Deut. 15.12–18 is based directly on Exod. 21.1–11. This has been disputed by Loretz (1984: 122–65) and now by Van Seters (2003: 82–95), who offers detailed arguments for the dependence of the Exodus law on that in Deuteronomy. Although some of his arguments are well taken, it seems to me that Deut. 15.12 must be dependent on an older law of some sort for two reasons: first, the use of the term *'ibrî* 'Hebrew', which is only found here in Deuteronomy; and second, the awkwardness of the opening which points to the addition of material—clearly including the typical Deuteronomic 'your brother', and probably also *'ô 'ibriyyâ* 'or a Hebrew woman'.

81. Lasserre 1995: 489 (my translation).

debt-bondage is not abolished, yet to take the meaning of the rhetoric seriously is to see that there cannot be masters and slaves within a family of brothers.

2.b.6 *Deuteronomy, Class and Community*
It is painfully easy to deconstruct the laws of social solidarity in Deuteronomy. Their social and moral assumptions pull in opposite directions. The only social innovations suggested for the relief of poverty are the redirection of the third-year tithes and the seventh-year remission of debts. The class structure of society otherwise remains. Moral exhortation is required to encourage people to act in accordance with the reformers' utopian aims of social justice. But one finds oneself asking: if the well-to-do could be counted on to respond to such appeals, what need would there have been for legal innovations, and if not, what use would they have been? To rely on personal generosity and good will was surely to rely on precisely those qualities in social life whose absence had caused the social grievances in the first place.

But Deuteronomy's appeals are not simply appeals to individual generosity. When they are read in context we see that they are attempts to re-create a sense of community. The appeal to brotherly generosity is bound up with the inadequacy of legal changes to achieve a real change in social relationships. Was this just a failure in the specific measures offered? Does it not rather reflect a general problem in achieving and preserving social justice? The problem is this: that legal and institutional changes, even revolutionary ones, are not enough by themselves. They must be accompanied by the personal and communal commitment to their intention that Deuteronomy calls for. And that can only be achieved by moral education, by the influence of a recognized moral tradition. Here I would again refer to Michael Walzer's theory of moral tradition.[82] Whatever the inadequacies of Deuteronomy's institutional contribution, its renewal of the sense of community of Israelite tribal society in a national context is a profound contribution to the kind of moral tradition that any society aiming to be just requires; and it is there waiting to be picked up by anyone—social critic, reformer, revolutionary— bold enough to take it seriously. The evidence is that it was picked up very quickly by the compilers of the Holiness Code, who use 'your brother' five times in Leviticus 25.

The law of Deut. 15.2 may have been found impractical in the 'real world', that is the class-divided world of creditors looking for security and debtors needing cash, and so was evaded by means of the *prozbul*. But the 'brotherly' ethos inculcated by the text at a deeper level became the distinctive ideology both of Judaism as a religious community and of the early

---

82. Walzer 1987: 40–42; see above, pp. 13–14.

Christian community. It is clear in the New Testament that Christians were understood to be brothers and sisters one of another, and they can be seen to be making genuine, if unsuccessful, efforts to overcome class divisions between their members. Unfortunately, as Margaret Davies argues, the failure of New Testament writers to call on Christian masters to free their slaves, or even to adopt the restrictions on servile relationships found in Deuteronomy and Leviticus, vitiated these efforts.[83] The ideology remained to a large extent illusory.

The French revolution proclaimed as its goal 'liberty, equality and fraternity'. The history of the last two hundred years has been largely one of the promotion by rival political forces of liberty and equality. Fraternity tends to be forgotten, yet one might argue that it is the glue without which the other two must inevitably fall apart and appear to be rivals.[84] Tawney argues cogently that in industrial society greater equality must mean greater liberty for the majority rather than less: 'Freedom . . . is not only compatible with conditions in which all men are fellow-servants, but would find in such conditions its most perfect expression. What it excludes is a society where only some are servants, while others are masters.'[85] But this is an admirable expression of the ideal of fraternity. It was the ideal of the early co-operative movement in England, and was picked up from it by F.D. Maurice, who in his *Tracts on Christian Socialism* urged that it was already expressed in Christianity.[86] However, he believed that it expressed the proper relationship of master and servant rather than dissolving it. Like the New Testament writers, he does not seem to have fully realized the implications of his own ideology.

The word 'fraternity' or 'brotherhood' itself is unusable today, not only because it is gendered, but also because we have become conscious of the frequent oppressiveness and dysfunction of the family. 'Solidarity' might be a possible substitute. 'Community' has become such a wax nose of a word—very much a motto of New Labour[87]—that it is equally unusable. What is intended by the word, however, remains valid. Equality must mean the restriction, not of all liberty, but of my liberty *to dominate others*. That is, I must be coerced, *unless* I recognize my fellow-citizens as brothers and sisters. Conversely, the cry of liberty (also found in other dress: 'choice' is the favourite at the moment) must result in increasing inequality, as has happened over the last twenty-five years in Britain, unless we deepen the

    83.   Davies 1995.
    84.   Cf. Tawney 1964: 164: 'Liberty and equality have usually in England been considered antithetic; and since fraternity has rarely been considered at all, the famous trilogy has been easily dismissed as a hybrid abortion'.
    85.   Tawney 1964: 166.
    86.   Christensen 1962: 136–42.
    87.   Chapman 2005.

sense of solidarity, which has instead been eroded. Except in a totalitarian society, law depends to a large extent upon consent: therefore 'fraternity', or whatever we choose to call it, is indispensable. We need to learn that we belong together. We could do worse than learn it from Deuteronomy.

At the same time, we cannot ignore the fundamentally religious character of Deuteronomy, which is also essential to our modern quest. To believe that a just society is achievable is at a minimum to accept that the world is structured in such a way that justice is possible and will result in happiness for the society that truly lives by it. Deuteronomy is more specific: 'because of this, YHWH your God will bless you in all your works and in all you undertake' (Deut. 15.10). This God who blesses is a just God 'who maintains the rights of orphans and widows, and who shows his love for strangers by giving them food and clothing' (Deut. 10.18); who delivered Israel from slavery in Egypt. In our next chapter we shall need to examine the problems in this idea of a just God.

2.c. *The Law of Jubilee in the Holiness Code*[88]

The imagination of radical Christian theologians has been seized by the jubilee as the symbol par excellence of the social justice inculcated by the Old Testament. It is this general function rather than any specific idea in Leviticus 25 that is important in the choice. Gorringe, for example, can assume that the restoration of alienated property mandated by the jubilee law 'does away with poverty altogether', and he lays emphasis on 'the denial of absolute ownership rights to any individual on the grounds that the land belonged to God'.[89] The jubilee sets clear limits to the operation of the market, and offers the appealing vision of a repeated return to a primitive equality, every fifty years sweeping away the distortions of human community introduced and multiplied over time. It offers to the wretched of the earth a fresh start symbolized by the round figure of fifty years.

This is one reason why it is appropriate that our survey of ideas of human justice in the Old Testament should conclude with Leviticus 25. There are others. Unlike all other passages on the topic, this one explicitly addresses the problem of land loss and suggests a mechanism for regularly reversing it. Like the third-year tithe and debt release laws in Deuteronomy alone, Lev. 25.8–10 requires community action to bring a state of social justice into being, through the jubilee. But the combination of this law with the series of laws for individual execution in Lev. 25.23–55 results in the most

---

88. This section is largely a revised version of my essay Houston 2001.
89. Gorringe 1994: 116–17.

comprehensive and systematic treatment of the problem of indebtedness and land loss in the Hebrew Bible.[90]

However, it has repeatedly been dismissed as utopian in the pejorative sense that it is incapable of implementation in the 'real world'. There is no evidence that the Jubilee was ever implemented, and, it is said, every reason to suppose that it could not be.[91] If potential financiers knew in advance that it was coming, they would be encouraged to prepare for it by choking off credit in the last ten years or so of the cycle, so that the end for those in financial straits would be worse than the beginning. It would also be a strong disincentive to agricultural investment.

To what extent does this text deserve its status as an icon of justice? Its impracticality is a serious issue, but not the only one. We cannot avoid the questions which have to be asked about any text that claims, or is claimed, to mediate justice: what kind of justice does it offer and to whom; whose interests are represented by the text; what understanding of the social world does it embody, and how close is that to anything we might acknowledge as reality?

It is if anything more difficult to assign a precise social location to the 'Holiness Code' (H),[92] to which this chapter belongs, than to the Deuteronomic Code. It is usually taken for granted that it is the work of priests, as the bulk of its vocabulary is held in common with P in the narrower sense. But Milgrom shows how loosely H uses terms which have a precise ritual meaning in P.[93] Its distinct concept of holiness is particularly important: it has become a moral as well as a ritual term.[94] Does this argue for priestly composition? Joosten argues for an origin among priests in the countryside as distinct from Jerusalem.[95] This is rather speculative.

What can surely be established is the passionate interest which it expresses in every line in establishing a society committed to the values of a conservative Yahwism and a strong traditional social structure. It is these values which are expressed in the Code's central symbol of holiness. It is not unreasonable to see the deliberate expression of these values as a response to a perceived threat. In Mannheim's terms, H is the utopian expression of the

90.   The most recent, detailed and comprehensive treatment is Lefebvre 2003; it is also insightful. In English Fager 1993 is a stimulating and valuable essay, but for detailed analysis one should go to the commentaries, most recently Milgrom 2001 (much the most detailed), Hartley 1992, Gerstenberger 1996 and Levine 1989.

91.   The attempt of L.S. Fried and D.N. Freedman in Milgrom 2001: 2257–70 to demonstrate a series of celebrations of the jubilee is entirely speculative.

92.   Generally defined as Leviticus 17–26; however, see Knohl 1995 and Milgrom 2000: 1332–44, who argue for H as being the final redactional phase of P, with identifiable insertions throughout the Tetrateuch.

93.   Milgrom 1991: 36–38; 2000: 1327–30; cf. Knohl 1995: 106–11.

94.   Milgrom 1996.

95.   Joosten 1996: 92, 203–204.

conservative mentality.[96] Mannheim describes the conservative intellectual movement of the early-nineteenth century as a reaction to liberalism and the French Revolution. There was nothing comparable to these in the intellectual world of late-monarchic to early-Persian period Judah; but threats to social order are not only or even often intellectual.

Fager sees it as a reaction to the collapse of institutions in the exilic period. 'Lacking the core rituals of the temple cult, the exiles turned to ideological and philosophical foundations to reinterpret the meaning of their history and to legitimate Yahwism in the new world.'[97] But an exilic date is hardly as secure for H as Fager assumes. Serious arguments have been mounted for dates as far apart as the reign of Hezekiah (late-eighth century)[98] and the mid-Persian period, after Nehemiah in the late-fifth century.[99] I have pointed out above that Leviticus 25 betrays a historical setting at a time when the money economy had become dominant, so hardly earlier than the late Persian period.[100] But the whole time was one of political, social and economic turmoil to which religious rethinking had to be a response. There were Hebrews in exile from 732 BCE or earlier, and throughout these centuries the ancient securities could only be yearned for. A significant aspect of such ancient security was the settlement of the peasantry on their tribal lands, which was threatened or actually damaged by the economic changes we identified in Chapter 2 long before the Judaean elite was deported; and this process had since gathered strength. Analysis of Leviticus 25 itself will suggest what social groups stood to gain if the chapter's proposals were implemented. However, given that the Jerusalem priesthood eventually attained hegemony in Persian-period Judah, it is not unreasonable to suggest that this document of conservative ideology of that period may after all be their work.

Leviticus 25 is a composition consisting of two halves related in content but stylistically inconsistent. Leviticus 25.2–22 ('A') is mainly in the style of a decree: it mandates the community to take certain measures which have a universal effect. I have already suggested that it may have a background in royal decrees comparable to those of Mesopotamian kings.[101] Leviticus 25.23–55 ('B'), on the other hand, is set out as a series of four casuistic laws, detailing the way in which individuals should behave in particular situations, and it is reasonably argued that they represent three successive stages of destitution for an indebted peasant proprietor (the last two are at the

---

96. See Mannheim 1936: 206–15.
97. Fager 1993: 49.
98. Milgrom 2000: 1352–64; cf. Joosten 1996: 203–07.
99. Lefebvre 2003: 331–32.
100. Above, p. 32, cf. Carter 1999: 268–85.
101. Above, p. 146.

same stage).[102] We have seen that such laws may in part be understood as 'self-executing' rules, not applied by a court but by the parties themselves; in part they are didactic in intention, teaching standards of justice which may be applied by analogy.[103]

Section A might at first sight seem to be quite different in effect, since the *mīšarum* decrees are known to have been enforced by royal officers. But this is one of the two major points in which the jubilee law and the *mīšarum* decrees differ. The other is that the *mīšarum* decrees were issued unexpectedly, at irregular intervals, to be applied immediately, while the jubilee is to be observed at regular intervals, with the probable counter-productive effects that have frequently been suggested.

A royal decree is impersonal and enforced by royal officers; but the jubilee law is addressed to the nation in the second person and enforced solely by the covenantal justice of YHWH, as set out in Leviticus 26. But the effect of this is entirely retrospective: it is activated by the obedience or disobedience of Israel. As is usual in Pentateuchal legislation, nothing makes it clear whose responsibility it might be to implement such laws on behalf of the nation. The plain implication of the second-person formulation (both singular and plural) is that implementation was everyone's responsibility. The text, it may be suggested, projects a narrative ideal of justice rather than mandating a specific administrative procedure.

We may say that the jubilee law is *like* a royal decree in its universal scope, but in effect it is rather different. It is a standard of justice, a call to do justice. Its object is not to administer but to persuade, and in its interpretation canons of rhetoric are more significant than those of law.

This is set out in the following table.[104] Each of the five subsections, that is section A and the four laws of section B, is supported by a theological motivation. The first law in section B, that concerning the redemption of land, uniquely has its motivation placed at the beginning rather than the end. The paragraph division in the NRSV, for example, might suggest Lev. 25.23–24 are the motivating conclusion to the law of jubilee proper (section A). In fact they are the statement of principle which is placed before the law on redemption of land. The effect is to create a bridge between the two main sections, since both jubilee and redemption are mechanisms which prevent the permanent sale of land, and also to highlight it in its position at a pivotal point of the text.

---

102. Chirichigno 1993: 323–43; Milgrom 2001: 2191–92; Lefebvre 2003: 176, 246–83.
103. Above, pp. 107, 170.
104. From Houston 2001: 46. Cf. Lefebvre's translation (2003: 23–27).

Section A: the decree   2b–22
  the sabbath year   2b–7
    the jubilee   *8–13*
      basic statement   8–10
      link with sabbath year   11–12
      resumption   13
    consequence of the jubilee for   *14–17a*
  sale of land
      explication   15–16
      resumption   17a
    theological motivation: obey my   17b–19
commands!
    Appendix: a problem   20–22
Section B: casuistic laws
  redemption of property before the jubilee   *23–34*
    principle: no permanent sale; the land is mine!   23–24
    main law   25
      subcase a   26–27
      subcase b   28
    exemption: walled cities   29–30
    villages and Levites' cities not   31–34
exempt
    responsibility to impoverished fellow-citizens   *35–38*
    theological motivation   38
  sale of a person to an Israelite, don't treat as a slave *39–42*
    theological motivation   42
    addendum: aliens can be chattel   43–46
slaves
    sale of a person to an alien: *47–55*
redemption required
    theological motivation   55

Note how the points where there is the greatest likelihood of injustice creeping into the system are emphasized by warnings to 'fear your God' (Lev. 25.17, 36). Here it is non-family members who have the responsibility, whereas it is the nearest relative who must act as redeemer, and he may reasonably be expected to see it as in his own interests to do so.[105]

The structure of theological motivations projects a vision of the land of

---

105. Cf. Lefebvre's reference to Rashi: these are points where the addressee alone can judge to what extent his behaviour conforms to the spirit of the law (Lefebvre 2003: 351–52).

Israel and its law as part of a divine, cosmic system of justice, as noted by Fager and shown in detail by Lefebvre.[106] Both land and people belong to YHWH, the people having been rescued from slavery in Egypt to become his slaves or his tenants, in two different but not incompatible metaphors.[107] It is the divine master, patron, landlord, who commands just and compassionate conduct, in imitation of his own. If Israel so acts, then the land will co-operate with them and produce its bounty. If they rebel, it will rebel against them, and they will lose it.

The accusation of impracticality levelled against the law is relativized once we accept that the object is to teach justice rather than to enforce detailed regulations. If that object is not achieved, no legislation, no matter how ingenious, will achieve a just society. For the impracticality is not a matter of physical impossibility but of motivation: the allegedly 'natural' response to the approach of the jubilee will defeat its object. Although, unlike Deuteronomy 15, Leviticus 25 does not explicitly acknowledge the problem, its persuasive language implicitly recognizes it: 'do not oppress one another', when buying and selling, Lev. 25.14, 17: the implication is that the buyer will want to depress the price. He has the whip hand, because the only situation envisaged in which a sale may take place is the seller's economic need, as in Lev. 25.25. The attachment of the peasant to his ancestral land is a basic assumption of the whole chapter: he will only sell if he has to. The result of such forced sales in normal conditions is a reduction of the price below the full market value.[108]

However, as I shall show in more detail later on, the text assumes an essentially classless society, where among Israelites impoverishment and inequality are temporary accidents arising from the changes and chances of harsh physical conditions. If this type of society is presupposed, there is no reason why people should not behave in the ways that the text demands.

We are faced again with Mannheim's distinction between relative and absolute utopia: yes, in empirical Persian or Ptolemaic Judah the implementation of the jubilee was impossible, but that does not mean that it is always and everywhere impractical. The conviction of the jubilee's impracticality mainly depends on classical economics' construct of the rational subject who always behaves so as to maximize material benefit. Such a person would certainly not buy a fifty-year lease for the price of even forty-two crops, or lend his feckless neighbour food for a year at zero interest. But the rational subject does not exist: he (he always is a he) is a fantasy of Enlightenment individualism. Real people are motivated by a range of

---

106. Fager 1993: 104–05; Lefebvre 2003: 349–89.

107. See the discussions of the phrase *gērîm wᵉtôšābîm* in Lev. 25.23 in Lefebvre 2003: 235–48; 358–61.

108. Westbrook 1991: 100–101.

considerations, and especially by what is accepted as the done thing in their society and by the need to maintain the social relationships which are important to them and therefore as much in their interests as material profit. Given a society where the dominant sentiment was a conviction of the equal value of all the members, it would not be inconceivable for people to act in accordance with that, even against their material interests.

The laws of Lev. 25.23–55, and perhaps even the idea of the jubilee itself,[109] rest on traditional rural customs and institutions, and we have seen how they represent a widely accepted morality of social action. I do not find it impossible to conceive that the common sentiment in its favour would induce most well-off people who cared for their neighbours' opinion—as in an honour-oriented society everyone does—to give at least an impression of acting in accordance with it. The conviction that ancestral land is in principle inalienable is an ancient one, deeply rooted in Israelite tribal society; what this chapter attempts to do is to give it a theological basis (Lev. 25.23), and to set out means by which it may have practical effect, not in an ideal world but in the real world of the encroaching cash economy.[110]

To whom, then, are these words addressed, and whom do they concern? Who is expected to implement them, or at least to listen to them, and who may be affected by them? The formal audience here (Lev. 25.2) is the Israelites. It is Israel that must proclaim the jubilee and it is the whole people that must, each individually, return to their native place and possess once more their allotted fields. It is, however, sufficiently clear once we get down to details that it is only the secure possessors of property who are in a position to obey or disobey the law. In Lev. 25.14 an attempt is made at a balanced and reciprocal statement: 'When you sell property to your neighbour, or buy from your neighbour, do not oppress one another'. But already in the next verse the pretence that the seller is in any position to 'oppress' the buyer has been dropped: Lev. 25.15–16 are formulated exclusively from the point of view of the buyer, who is warned to ensure that the price corresponds to the number of crop years he may expect from the property before the jubilee.[111]

And as one goes through the following laws in Section B it is always and inevitably the case that the addressee, the 'thou' who is the subject of the law, is the secure proprietor who is in a position to help his 'brother' (Lev. 25.25, 35, 39, 47) who has fallen on evil days. The use of 'your brother'

---

109. Cf. Weinfeld 1995: 178 and literature noted by Houston 1999: 356 n. 19.

110. Lefebvre 2003: 395–96; he notes that the law recognizes the rights of the creditor as well as those of the debtor. Fager 1993: 115–16 regards the regular land reform as unrealizable 'in the world as its actually exists'; but doubts whether that was the intention in any case (110–11).

111. This is purely relative; there is no indication of what a just price might be absolutely; see Soss 1973.

here, meaning a fellow-Israelite whether related or not, has probably been influenced by Deuteronomy, where it is much more widespread than in the Holiness Code.[112] Redemption of land (v. 25) and persons (v. 47) was the prime responsibility of the family. But as we have seen, in the sections beginning with vv. 35 and 39, it is the creditor who is charged with responsibility for the 'brother'; a pre-existing state of dependence is implied.[113] There is a tension in the use of this motif, as in Deuteronomy: the law uses language demanding in principle that people treat each other as equals, as 'brothers', but at the same time envisages a situation of inequality, which may be expected to continue until the jubilee: this is particularly clear in vv. 35 and 40. In this context, then, justice depends as ever on the fortunate recognizing their responsibilities to the less fortunate. Justice, between jubilees, is a gift of the superior to the inferior, as we have repeatedly seen it in this study; in a word, patronage.

But the jubilee, in theory, offers a term to the situation of inequality. The chapter does not say with Deut. 15.11 that 'the poor will not cease from the land'; for the return of each man to his *ᵃḥuzzâ*, his ancestral holding (Lev. 25.41) marks the end of his state of need which required the sale of the land or of himself (vv. 28, 40, 54). Division of YHWH's people into sellers and buyers, patrons and clients, masters and servants marks the period between jubilees; at the jubilee each one returns, takes up his holding and the nation once more becomes equal. At that point the poor cease from the land.

Is this, however, a true picture of what the text envisages? Universal equality? Norman Habel, for one, is clear that it is not. 'The society is not truly egalitarian in the modern sense of the word. Laborers, servants, immigrants and urbanites are excluded from gaining the same level of social standing as landholding peasants and priests . . . the rural workers at the bottom of the order remain dependent on the landed peasant farmers.'[114]

This is not quite how the text sees it. True, it is perfectly explicit on the subject of foreign slaves, who have no right to be redeemed, and on the *gērîm*, the resident aliens, who do not possess *ᵃḥuzzâ*, so that they have nowhere to return to at the jubilee. Foreigners and *gērîm*, though not a class, since they may include masters as well as slaves, are yet a group without any of the rights of the trueborn Israelite. They may be enslaved in perpetuity, and it is implied that they may be treated harshly, unlike an Israelite (Lev. 25.46). We are also bound to notice that even among Israelites this justice only applies between adult males, who are the possessors of land. Women and children are entirely invisible in the text. No doubt Christopher Wright

112. Against Milgrom 2000: 1357. The NRSV's 'anyone of your kin' is misleading.
113. See above, pp. 44–45 and n. 114; Lefebvre 2003: 228–34.
114. Habel 1995: 112.

is correct in arguing that the subject of the law is functioning as a family head rather than as an isolated individual (see Lev. 25.41).[115] Lefebvre shows that the reason for the difference between the slave laws of Exod. 21.1–11 and Deut. 15.12–18 and that of Lev. 25.39–55 is that Exodus and Deuteronomy apply to dependants, but Leviticus to family heads.[116] But it is an uncomfortable fact that the Israelite peasant would abandon his children, particularly his daughters, to his creditors (Neh. 5.5) before he would abandon his land, let alone sell himself. Thus the justice of the jubilee is a specifically national justice which applies only between 'brothers', that is Israelite adult male landholders (and Levites).

But, on the other hand, this text does not admit the very existence of those rural Israelite workers without an ancestral holding that Habel refers to. In the real world there was doubtless a class of permanently landless labourers and permanent slaves of native origin who could show no connection with any ancestral land. But even though the text is addressed to a situation in which the traditional system of land tenure has broken down, or is breaking down, it gives the impression that there are no class divisions among Israelites. Essentially there are three social groups in the land, none of which are classes: the landholding Israelites, the *gērîm*, and the Levites. Poverty and landlessness, which are the motive of the whole system, are in this text not a condition, not a state of life, but a process, an event: 'If your brother becomes impoverished'. This is a temporary misfortune of individuals which will last at most fifty years. None of the Hebrew nouns or adjectives meaning 'poor' appears in the chapter. Nor is any exploiting class referred to, although exploitation is admitted to be a temptation (Lev. 25.14, 36–37, 39): the patrons are the addressees. But none of this corresponds to the facts at any likely period of the text's composition, as we know.

Of course, this is partly a result of the dramatic setting: 'When you enter the land I am giving you' (Lev. 25.2). The projected system of the jubilee, if it operates as intended from that moment, will prevent poverty from ever becoming the permanent lot of a class. We start from scratch and we exclude class formation from the word go. But this cannot be the whole explanation: for Deuteronomy has the same setting, yet, as we have seen, frankly admits the permanent presence of poverty in the land, among the people of Israel.

Despite constant reference to the utopianism of the chapter, attention has rarely been given to this truly, if only relatively, utopian feature. The society portrayed in Leviticus 25 was not a reality. But a society like it would be necessary for the jubilee to work. A class society would successfully resist the attempt to transform it every fifty years. For like all societies, class society has an ideology which persuades its members that it has to be like

115. Wright 1990: 124–25.
116. Lefebvre 2003: 307–14; see above, pp. 185–86.

that. In contrast, riches and poverty in Leviticus 25 are temporary accidents, and nothing hinders people's return to the original conditions. We arrive at the paradoxical conclusion that the jubilee may not be impractical, but it is utopian.

And here Jameson may be allowed to have his say.[117] This text projects a utopia, a society without class divisions (though not without ethnic, caste and gender divisions), precisely because it is an ideological text. It maintains that justice between 'brothers' is a possibility, exemplified by the proclamation of *dᵉrôr* ('liberty'), and everyone's periodic return to their *ᵃḥuzzâ* and *mišpāḥâ* (Lev. 25.10), as well as in the just and generous conduct of patrons and family members. (It should be clear, however, if only from the following chapter, that it is not saying it is a reality.) But this is only possible if class divisions are not there at the outset. This is the basic reason why the law remained a dead letter.

There have been various suggestions as to who the hidden sponsors were who would benefit from such a supposedly deceptive law. The chief suspects are the priesthood, whose rights to the tithe would not be affected by the provisions, but who had an interest in preventing the accumulation of the land in the hands of a governing elite who would then be in a position to dictate to them. Fager argues that 'the concept of Yahweh as the ultimate owner of the land ... would be advantageous to [the priests'] quest for political and economic power'.[118] It is hard to see how, especially as the chapter makes no mention of priests: it is not as if the doctrine of divine ownership made the priesthood the land agents! Another idea is that the fifty years of the jubilee are related to the fifty years of exile and the law's object is to legitimate the repossession of Judah by the exiles. Fager appears to favour this view also; Habel points out in its support that the sequel in ch. 26 promotes the 'myth of the empty land' which enjoys its sabbaths (Lev. 26.34).[119] This is impossible to disprove, but there are obvious objections even if an exilic date for the chapter is accepted. As Lefebvre notes, the context is concerned with sold, not abandoned, property, with impoverishment, not with deportation;[120] and the Near Eastern parallels also underline the economic context of measures of this kind.

But these suggestions are beside the point. I have already suggested that the intent of the text is to propose a narrative ideal of justice rather than to mandate a concrete administrative procedure in present-day Judah: to show how the justice of YHWH might in principle be implemented in the world of the cash economy. Since the law was unlikely to be implemented

117.   Jameson 1981: 281–99.
118.   Fager 1993: 62, citing Neufeld 1958: 66.
119.   Fager 1993: 61, cf. 111; Habel 1995: 113; cf. also Levine 1989: 274.
120.   Lefebvre 2003: 15.

as things stood, no one stood to 'benefit' from it, except in the general sense
that we have already noted in connection with the Torah as a whole: through
the persuasion that 'Israel', the people of YHWH, is a people among
whom YHWH has instituted justice, they might be reconciled to rather less
equitable proceedings as regards tithes and taxes.

But as with other texts that we have studied, the ideal of justice that is
projected by the text, the key values which it draws from tradition and
popular consensus, are of more significance than the ideology that it
currently subserves. I suggest that among these values are the following.

First, the proper ordering of society is to be found in the past. In this
belief Leviticus is at one with the ancient Near East generally;[121] but it
expresses the idea in a way distinctive of the Old Testament. The assumption by which it is guided is that when the Israelites entered Canaan, they
received just allocations of land; but the misfortunes of some and the
advantage taken of them by others will lead inevitably to the loss of this
original just ordering. The task of the lawgiver is to ensure that this original
justice is restored. As we have noted, this is not a progressive belief, but a
conservative one: justice is not a thing of the future to be striven towards by
eliminating the distortions and abuses of the past, as French revolutionaries
or Marxists believed, but is to be found by rescuing the old order from the
encroachments of modernity, from the dynamic forces of the market and
capital accumulation.[122] It is not necessary to this belief that the old just
order should really have existed, needless to say.

Secondly, the system values the attachment of the rural population to the
soil, and not just of the population generally to the soil in general, but of
this man or family to this piece of ground. 'Everyone shall return to his own
possession'; Naboth refuses Ahab's offer of another vineyard better than
his own, because his own belonged to his ancestors. No-one should underestimate the strength of this sentiment in any peasant population. In the
Highland clearances in the early-nineteenth century, the witnesses tell of
occasions when people had the roofs of their miserable huts burnt over their
heads rather than leave them. And the sentiment underlies the strength of
resistance to Israel from Palestinian people who were driven from the homes
of their ancestors in 1948.

Although some have argued that the jubilee has its origin in a communal
system of landholding,[123] there is no trace of this in the text, which takes
individual landholding, presumably through inheritance, for granted. But
valuing the individual's possession of his own plot on behalf of his family
is not the same thing as believing that the individual has an indefeasible

121. See above, p. 149.
122. Cf. Mannheim's typology of modern utopias, 1936: 190–222.
123. Cf. n. 109.

property right, including the right of alienation, that the community ought not to interfere with. On the contrary, the text denies this in its theory of divine ownership, and specifically denies that anyone can acquire property rights over land other than their ancestral land.

Thirdly, it is in keeping with the particularity of this attachment that poor relief is envisaged as taking place through patronage rather than through a state or even a locally organized system. To our minds leaving it to whoever has a mind to it to relieve the necessities of the poor is a hit-or-miss arrangement which comes under the heading of charity rather than justice. The Bible does not recognize this distinction; and certainly the biblical writers would find the impersonality of our system intolerable. Our studies above will have suggested that in biblical thought there is always a particular person whose responsibility it is to keep another particular person from starving, to put it no higher.[124] This finds concrete expression in the designation of the fellow-Israelite as 'your brother'; but more narrowly, the right of redemption gives not merely a right but a responsibility to the family, acting through the next of kin, to relieve a person in particular circumstances of distress.

Fourthly, these particularities in the concept of justice exclude any abstract egalitarianism. The sons of Israel are a community of equals, and none of them is permitted to acquire overwhelming wealth or power over the others; but it is does not occur to Hebrew writers to present equality of income or capital as a good. It is better for Naboth to retain the land of his fathers, however wretched it might be and however many mouths he has to feed, rather than having the land constantly redivided for the sake of equality.

What of the idea of *derôr*, 'liberty' as it is often translated, which is to be 'proclaimed to all the inhabitants of the land' (Lev. 25.10)? We have found it before in the contexts of release from slavery (Jeremiah 34) or from deportation (Isa. 61.1). It is not a right of self-determination as we conceive liberty, but is an act of deliverance from subservience to take one's place in this community of equals.

Finally, Fager is surely correct to see in the statement of YHWH's ownership of the land in Lev. 25.23 the ultimate moral basis of the Jubilee legislation, 'the cornerstone of the jubilee'.[125] And along with this principle go the theological motive clauses which declare that the Israelites, whom YHWH delivered from Egypt and to whom he gave the land of Canaan, belong to him: 'they are my slaves, whom I brought up from the land of Egypt' (Lev. 25.42, 55). The immediate object of both assertions is very similar. No-one can acquire absolute rights over YHWH's land or YHWH's people. They are in the position of tenants on his land, and cannot call it their own. As Lefebvre puts it:

124. Cf. above, p. 110.
125. Fager 1993: 116.

To be truly free and enjoy the results of the Exodus, and to be able to 'serve the Lord' in the framework of the Covenant, a land is needed, the instrument of the Creator's blessing, and a law, the expression of the wisdom of the Redeemer, the new master whom Israel is to serve. Conversely, to live according to the Law given at Sinai and so to become a 'holy people', they must be free to apply its precepts on a land free of dependency.[126]

One can distinguish here a metaphor derived from the subject matter of the chapter, and a rhetorical aim. The metaphor is of God as patron, who stands in the same relation to the people of Israel as they as individuals may from time to time stand towards their own impoverished brethren, except that this relationship is permanent. Note the echo between 'aliens and tenants', *gērîm wetôšābîm*, in Lev. 25.23 and 'an alien and a tenant', *gēr wetôšāb* in Lev. 25.35. As YHWH has graciously delivered his people from slavery in Egypt and enabled them to live before him, so they are required to deliver their own kin from slavery to live with them. In the following chapter I will develop further the implications of this metaphor.

The rhetorical aim is to persuade the audience that they have no right to appropriate for themselves what YHWH has claimed for himself. Neither land nor people is to be used for personal profit, which is what sale in perpetuity implies. 'If the land is to be used exclusively for God's purposes, it may not be used to further the economic interests of any person or class of persons. The land may not become a commodity to be bought and sold in order to enrich a few wealthy individuals.'[127] Nor, one may add, may the people. Fager neatly expresses this by saying that the land must provide the means of life, and not, through exploitation, produce the means of death.

One may now better appreciate why the text has to project a utopia. Its understanding of justice is entirely discordant with society as it currently exists: as it existed then, or as it exists now.

Does the jubilee deserve its status as an icon of justice? Let us be clear that its utopian character is no disqualification, but rather essential to this status. Practical suggestions for the improvement of society are no inspiration to work for justice: it is a vision of justice that is needed; and the jubilee provides this within a framework that is recognizably the agrarian life of ancient Judah. It makes it possible to ask: if that is what justice meant to those writers in that society, what might it mean to us in ours? Its values present a significant challenge to the present-day domination of the globalized market system. Some tie in very closely with the world-view of many Third World countries today—the attachment of families to their land, the

---

126. Lefebvre 2003: 386 (my translation).
127. Fager 1993: 117.

preference for personal models of justice, the alien nature of Enlightenment models of liberty and equality.

The most difficult questions are raised by precisely these positive aspects. The tendency of the market to deepen inequalities is challenged by the principle which Leviticus inherits from the *mīšarum* tradition, that such processes can be halted or put into reverse. The attraction of the jubilee for the debt remission campaign which took the name 'Jubilee 2000' was its promise of a new start unencumbered by debts, in full possession of one's land and person, just as severely indebted countries dream of a new start free of debt and unencumbered by structural adjustment programmes and the stranglehold of the multinationals. The jubilee suggests that it is possible to go back to the time before such evils overtook them: returning is after all its *leitmotiv*. But in that its attraction lies in this motif of reversal, returning, a golden age, it is also dangerous. The difficulty with which theologians must wrestle is that going back is not actually possible, and in any case justice does not lie in the past. The only hope of justice is in going forward to a new situation. In this respect the prophecies of a just society 'in those days', which we looked at at the beginning of this chapter, have the advantage.

However, the deepest value of the symbol lies in the assertion: 'The land shall not be subject to sale in perpetuity, since the earth is mine' (Lev. 25.23). The most crying need of our world at the present day is for the humble acknowledgement that human beings have no right to absolute possession of the earth or any part of it to do with as they wish: it belongs to a higher purpose.

Chapter 7

THE GOD OF JUSTICE

1. *Introduction*

Central to the Old Testament's teaching about justice is the claim that YHWH is the God of justice and will enforce it. We have reflected on the part played by this claim in most of the texts we have studied. Wherever the prophets denounce injustice, the purpose of doing so is to announce in the name of YHWH that the punishment of the oppressors is at hand. In most of the passages that define the characteristics of the just man, YHWH's sanction against the unjust is asserted; in Job alone the reality of such sanctions is questioned. The king exercises on earth the justice of God. The just society in the prophets arises from the power of YHWH alone, not from revolutionary human action. The action for justice required by the Torah is in obedience to YHWH's covenant.

YHWH the righteous God, the God of justice, is a commonplace of Old Testament theology, more especially in the current of liberation theology.[1] For Miranda the God of the Bible is known simply in doing justice to the poor, as Hos. 4.1–2 and Jer. 22.13–16 make clear.[2] The formula 'I am YHWH', with all its variations, always signals his intervention in favour of the oppressed, whether for Israel, as in Exod. 6.2–8, or against, as in Ezek. 5.13.[3] God's intervention in history 'has only one purpose—to serve the cause of justice, to save from injustice'.[4] He acts in response to the cry of the oppressed, as in Exod. 3.7–9. His character as a warrior is only in the service of his work as 'judge', that is, one who delivers the oppressed and punishes the oppressor, whether the war is in favour of Israel, as in Jeremiah 51, or against them, as in Jeremiah 6.

There are problems in Miranda's presentation, which we shall come to in

---

1. See for example Eichrodt 1961: 239–49; Brueggemann 1997: 233–41, 303–07; Gutiérrez 1988: 110–12; and the entire work of Miranda 1977.
2. Miranda 1977: 35–76.
3. Miranda 1977: 78–80.
4. Miranda 1977: 78.

due course. But there is clearly no need for me to repeat what has already been well said by many. What has received much less attention is how the concept of divine justice is shaped by social experience and the way in which *that* is conceived, and how it in turn reacts on the way in which social institutions are conceived. It is well recognized that all our ideas of God are analogies from human experience, and this is true also of the Bible. The biblical writers were involved in social relationships and institutions, some of which we have explored in the last two chapters, and make God comprehensible through ideas drawn from those fields. As will already have become clear, these relationships and institutions were understood ideologically; there was no neutral experience to reflect on, but right from the start experience was guided by ideas developed to justify them, and God was integrally involved in these ideologies.

I will argue in this chapter that the action of God for justice is conceived on the analogy of two central institutions in Hebrew society: kingship, which includes war, administrative action and judicial action, all of which can be used to right wrongs and deliver people from oppression; and patronage, which involves the offer of aid and protection, possibly up to and including the use of violence against oppressors. There is a large measure of overlap between the functions of these two institutions, as well as significant differences, so that when used as analogies they cannot always be distinguished. But the differences are significant enough to be associated with serious tensions within the concept of the just God. Both also create problems for our own reflection on the justice of God in a society which has rejected these institutions, or at least the ideologies by which they were justified.

2. *Impartial and Partial Justice*

It will be useful to demonstrate first that tensions do indeed exist in the concept of the justice of God. I am not here concerned with the fact that God may be understood as acting from motives other than that of justice, as in Ezekiel when YHWH asserts, 'Not for your sake am I acting but for the sake of my holy name' (Ezek. 36.22 and elsewhere)—though even here it can be argued that because YHWH has a name for justice and is only known where justice is practised, to act for YHWH's name is to act to establish justice.[5] Rather, I wish to show that even when the action of YHWH is conceived as just or directed towards justice, the concepts of justice used differ.

Rolf Knierim has pointed clearly to this fact, though his treatment is

---

5.   This in effect is Miranda's argument (1977: 81, 293–96).

extremely concise and not fully argued. In his lecture 'Justice in Old Testament Theology' he sets out no less than sixteen different aspects of justice found in the Old Testament (not all relate to the justice of God), and points out the tensions between some of them. The tension most significant for us is that between his third aspect, 'Justice as Divine Liberation of Elected Israel from Oppression by Others and as Yahweh's and Israel's Oppression of Others', and his eighth, 'Divine Justice Equally for Israel and the Nations'.[6]

The latter of these may be seen by modern readers as the less problematic. It is expressed especially in those psalms (cited by Knierim) that announce the judgment of the world 'with righteousness, and the peoples with his truth' (Pss. 96.13, cf. v. 10; 98.9). Incidentally, let us note at this point that in both these psalms YHWH is praised as king (Pss. 96.10; 98.6). In Psalm 82 Elohim (that is, YHWH) in council denounces the gods of the nations for showing favour to the unjust and thus failing to ensure justice for the poor and powerless and to deliver them from oppression. As Zenger emphasizes, this obligation is here seen as the one essential mark of deity, and the failure of the gods in it leads to their demise. Consequently, Elohim is invited by the psalmist to take over their roles (v. 8): Elohim becomes the God of all nations, ensuring justice in them all.

As is now widely recognized following the work of H.H. Schmid, when in these Psalms God is said to 'judge' the world, this implies the restoration of a cosmic model of order and harmony, resulting in or inclusive of peace and prosperity (*šālôm*);[7] this is a concept common to the whole ancient Near East, and is made concrete in the widespread myths of the ruling god's defeat of chaos, represented as a monster such as a dragon. These myths were told in Israel and are referred to in much poetic theology (e.g. Job 9.13; Pss. 74.12–14; 89.9–10 [Hebrew 10–11]; Isa. 27.1; 51.9). According to Schmid, the Hebrew name for cosmic order is *ṣᵉdāqâ*, 'righteousness'; and central to this model of order, as is quite clear from Psalm 82, is the maintenance of justice within society and the absence of oppression. This is Knierim's aspect number 14, but it does not seem clearly differentiated from number 8.[8]

With these aspects we may associate Knierim's fourth, 'Justice as Divine Judgment against Israel for Apostasy and Oppression', which scarcely needs illustration, since it is the dominant theme in most of the prophetic books.[9] For our purpose, the judgment on oppression is the more relevant. The important point is that in this YHWH is shown acting against Israel; the ties binding him to his people are not seen to forbid this. Amos 9.7 famously

---

6. Knierim 1995: 96–100, 102–103.
7. Schmid 1968.
8. Knierim 1995: 110.
9. Knierim 1995: 103; see above, Chapter 3.

asserts the impartiality of YHWH as between Israel and other nations: 'Are you not like the Cushites to me, Israelites? . . . Did I not bring Israel up from Egypt—and the Philistines from Caphtor and the Aramaeans from Kir?' On the other hand, in the same book it is assserted that the judgment on Israel is actually a consequence of those particular ties (Amos 3.1), and there are other prophetic texts which associate the judgment with YHWH's care for his people, as for example Isa. 5.1–7, the song of the vineyard.

YHWH's deliverance of Israel from oppression is not usually seen as based on any different concept of justice from this, indeed in liberation theology it is the leading paradigm of justice conceived as deliverance from oppression, as in Psalm 82. Miranda for example begins two major discussions respectively with YHWH's two announcements that he is about to liberate Israel from the Egyptians.[10] Miranda repeatedly emphasizes that whether YHWH acts for Israel or against them he acts against the oppressor and in favour of the oppressed, and solely because of the 'cry' ($s^{e^{\epsilon}}\bar{a}q\hat{a}$) of the oppressed.[11] Given the Yahwist's insistence on this 'cry', he argues on Exod. 3.7–9,

> it seems to me that we must completely exclude the possibility that Yahweh's 'descent' to 'deliver' in Exod. 3:7–9 should be attributed to the fact that it is 'my people' who cry out. The exegesis which tries to make his intervention depend completely on a promise or pact—as if God would not have intervened against injustice if he had not officially promised to do so beforehand—contradicts with this kind of positivism the deepest and most radical conviction of the Old Testament authors. For them evil is evil whether or not there have been official prohibitions; crime is crime whether or not there have been covenants or promises.[12]

And Miranda goes on to show that God in the Bible responds to the cry of the oppressed in the entire absence of any pre-existing relationship, beginning with Cain and Abel.

This is well said; yet one must respond that in that case it is hard to understand why so much is made in Exodus 3 of the fact that YHWH is 'the God of your father, the God of Abraham, Isaac and Jacob' (Exod. 3.6). The main issue, after all, is not whether God's intervention depends on a prior promise or 'covenant'.[13] It is whether, quite simply, it is motivated by the fact that Israel is 'my people'. Why should God mention the fact unless it is?

10.   Miranda 1977: 78–79 on Exod. 6.2–8; 88–89 on Exod. 3.7–9.

11.   Miranda 1977: 80–81; 127.

12.   Miranda 1977: 89.

13.   The text of Exodus as it stands makes it clear that God, in responding to the cry of Israel, 'remembered his covenant with Abraham, Isaac and Jacob' (Exod. 2.24). This however is a P text, and Miranda, writing more than thirty years ago, could not conceive of a final-form reading in which the exegesis of a J text was determined by a later P text.

And it is mentioned repeatedly. We may point to 'my people, the Israelites' in Exod. 3.10; 'the God of your fathers' in Exod. 3.13, 15, as well as in v. 16; and 'the God of Abraham, Isaac and Jacob' again in v. 15 as well as v. 16.[14] Looking forward, we find the very significant text Exod. 4.22–23, 'You shall say to Pharaoh, "Thus says YHWH, 'Israel is my first-born son, and I said to you, "Let my son go in order to serve me", and you refused to let him go. Behold, I shall slay your first-born son.' " ' Brueggemann connects with this text Hos. 11.1–3, 'When Israel was a child I loved him, and out of Egypt I called my son . . .'[15] The familial metaphor surely removes all doubt about the motivation.

But the question really becomes an issue, as Knierim underlines, if YHWH's partisanship for oppressed Israel leads to the oppression of other peoples, for in that case Miranda's argument that YHWH's action is invariably against the oppressor and for the oppressed—hence that the concept of YHWH's justice is invariably the same—cannot be sustained. Already in Exodus 3 we are told twice that YHWH will bring the Israelites up 'into the land of the Canaanites, the Hittites, the Amorites, the Perizzites, the Hivites and the Jebusites' (Exod. 3.8, 17). The question is not raised at this point, which must occur nevertheless to the critical reader, what will happen to these peoples if Israel is put in possession of their lands, and how this can be understood as just. What will happen to them is of course made abundantly clear later on, first in Exod. 23.20–33, and then especially in Deuteronomy 7, as well as in the narrative of the event itself in Joshua. Even before then we hear of the first-born of Egypt dying 'from the first-born of Pharaoh who sits on his throne to the first-born of the maid at the mill' (Exod. 11.5). Are we to suppose that the slave who grinds corn is implicated in the oppression of Israel rather than being herself a victim of oppression?

A later generation of post-colonial theologians has reacted with understandable sensitivity to the annihilation of the peoples of the land that is promised or mandated and then carried out in these texts.[16] As one might expect, Palestinians are in the forefront here, for Zionists have applied the texts directly to them;[17] but there are many others, Mosala among them.[18] The massacre is not only unjust on the face of it, indeed the word genocide

14. In common with mid-twentieth-century scholarship in general, Miranda would have regarded Exod. 3.10–15 as 'E', whereas Exod. 3.7–9, 16 was 'J'; but since then the distinction has virtually vanished, and final form readings have become commonplace.

15. Brueggemann 1997: 245.

16. It should perhaps be made clear that the following argument is not related in any way to the question of the historicity of these texts. Whether or not there really was a massacre of the indigenous inhabitants by incoming Israelites, or any conquest at all, does not affect how the texts that assert it should be understood theologically.

17. See Ateek 1989: 83–87.

18. Mosala 1989: 29–30.

is entirely appropriate, it has been used to justify later acts of dispossession and genocide of native peoples by aggressive incomers. Michael Prior documents this in great detail in respect of the treatment of native American peoples by the Spanish conquistadors in the sixteenth century, of the Bantu people by the Afrikaners in the nineteenth, and of the Palestinians by the modern Israelis in the twentieth.[19] Other examples could be cited, notably the massacres and dispossession of the Catholic (and therefore 'idolatrous') Irish by Protestant English conquerors.

The Bible does, of course, justify this annihilation, indeed there are several different justifications offered in the text. Miranda barely notices the problem, but in so far as it is above his horizon he rests his own case on just one of these, found in Deut. 9.1–6, where it is twice stated (vv. 4, 5) that YHWH will dispossess the nations of the land in favour of Israel 'not because of your righteousness ($s^e d\bar{a}q\hat{a}$), but because of the wickedness ($ri\check{s}^c\hat{a}$) of these nations'.[20] Miranda, as always, maintains that as the antonym of $s^e d\bar{a}q\hat{a}$, 'justice', $ri\check{s}^c\hat{a}$ must mean 'injustice'. YHWH's fight as the warrior God against the Canaanites is, as always in Miranda's view, to oppose injustice and to punish the oppressors. Characteristically, he fails to pursue the implications of this example, in which entire peoples are to be destroyed (so v. 3, not merely dispossessed) 'because of their injustice'. When Joshua 'left no survivor and devoted to destruction everyone who breathed' in the whole land (Josh. 10.40, cf. 11.11, 14), according to Miranda because they were oppressors, who, it may be asked, were the oppressed?[21] And Joshua, of course, is only carrying out the instructions of Moses in Deuteronomy.

Knierim analyses the various reasons given for the destruction of the Canaanites.[22] The most basic in the narrative of the Pentateuch is that very promise to the patriarchs that their descendants should possess the land— the promise dismissed by Miranda as the reason for YHWH's deliverance of Israel from Egypt. But when it is given in Genesis, 'the sins of the Canaanites play no role as a reason for that promise'.[23] The dispossession and destruction of the Canaanites are required because of their idolatry, or, more neutrally, their polytheism. This seems to be closer to the mark than Miranda's insistence on injustice as their sole sin requiring notice. Both the

19. Prior 1997.
20. Miranda 1977: 121–22.
21. A similar question may be asked about Sodom and Gomorrah, for here too Miranda (1977: 95–96) takes their 'wickedness' to be injustice (as does Ezekiel, Ezek. 16.49). He never once refers to the content of Abraham's dialogue with YHWH in Gen. 18.23–33, which makes it clear that there are less than ten 'righteous men' in Sodom. If the entire city and the people of all the Plain (Gen. 19.25) are oppressors, where are the oppressed? See Fewell and Gunn 1993: 64–67.
22. Knierim 1995: 97–100.
23. Knierim 1995: 98.

key texts in Exodus 23 and Deuteronomy 7 lay emphasis on this precise point. But Knierim notes that polytheism in itself is not the reason why these peoples must be destroyed. Israel was surrounded by polytheistic nations, but this is never a reason in itself for the judgments pronounced on them in the prophets. Rather, it is the danger presented by the Canaanites' polytheism to 'Israel's own identity and existence',[24] in that they may ensnare the Israelites into falling into their own idolatrous ways, and thus seduce them from their loyalty to YHWH. This is surely correct. The key text Deuteronomy 7 makes the point repeatedly: see Deut. 7.4, 16, 25–26, and undergirding them all Deut. 7.6, 'you are a people holy to YHWH your God . . . his treasured possession'; compare Exod. 23.24, 33; Deut. 12.29–30; Josh. 23.11–13; Judg. 2.3. In the editorial preview of the Judges narratives in Judg. 2.11–13; 3.5–7 the gods the Israelites worshipped are given explicitly Canaanite names, Baal, Astarte and Asherah. Thus, 'the reference to the sins of the Canaanites as the reason for their destruction is not a rationale for justice independent of the theology of Israel's exclusive election. It depends on and serves that theology.'[25]

This does not quite finish Miranda, for he bases his understanding of Israel's election on Gen. 18.18–19, which he interprets as implying that all the nations of the world are to be blessed through Abraham in that he and his descendants ('his house after him') are elected to teach the world 'justice and righteousness', that is, social justice. On that argument, the preservation of Israel from the temptation to worship false gods who will not create justice in place of YHWH the God of justice is essential to God's long-term plan to establish justice on earth. Miranda does not indeed argue in this way, since he does not face the problem. Moreover, his interpretation of the text is highly dubious. It is not said that the whole world will be taught 'justice and right'; the teaching extends as far as 'his house after him'; and Miranda's understanding of the Hebrew syntax is forced.[26]

Thus it seems clear that the action of YHWH for Israel to deliver them from Egypt and bring them into the land of Canaan cannot be founded on a concept of universal justice for the oppressed impartial as between one nation and another. It can only be explained on the grounds of YHWH's election of Israel as his particular people, his 'treasured possession', in that justice for Israel may and does involve oppression for others. What still has to be shown is that this latter concept is in fact a concept of justice, and is not simply injustice and immorality, as it would be in a judge or king who showed such favouritism to one person. This is where my project diverges

24. Knierim 1995: 98.
25. Knierim 1995: 98.
26. Miranda 1977: 94. He interprets the initial *kî* in v. 19 as 'because' and links it only with the last clause of v. 18. Contrast the NRSV's 'No, for'; the REB does not translate the word.

from that of Knierim, who insists that this concept must be downgraded
and indeed denied in favour of the universal justice of God which contradicts it.[27] Not that the concepts can be perfectly reconciled either, as
MacDonald suggests on the basis of Deut. 10.12—11.1.[28] This depends
partly on interpreting Deut. 7.1–6 in such a way as to deny that the election
of Israel involves the literal oppression of the Canaanites.[29] But MacDonald
is right in pointing out that in that passage of Deuteronomy universal and
particular viewpoints are brought together; I return to this below.

My argument turns largely on the usage of the Hebrew word *ṣᵉdāqâ*,
which most definitely includes action marked by this kind of partiality, but
which I will argue is an ethical term, just as much in these cases as where it
describes more impartial action. It is used to refer to YHWH's saving acts
on behalf of Israel, or his intention to save Israel, or (in the Psalms) individual worshippers, or the results of those acts. This usage is particularly
prominent in the Psalms and Deutero-Isaiah. As is generally recognized, in
most places where *ṣᵉdāqâ* and *ṣedeq* occur in Isaiah 40–66, and often in the
Psalms, the context requires that they carry some such sense as 'deliverance', 'victory', 'salvation'.[30] They frequently stand in parallel with expressions for salvation such as *yᵉšûʿâ*. But this does not mean that the words have
two (or more) entirely distinct meanings, such as 'justice' and 'salvation'.
The different senses are related, but the range of meaning of both words,
and especially *ṣᵉdāqâ*, is so extensive that it cannot be certain exactly how
any two usages are related.

When in Isa. 41.2 it is said of Cyrus that 'victory (*ṣedeq*) meets him at
every step', it would be difficult to argue that the word in some way connotes
'justice'; rather, the root meaning here is 'success', that is, being in a pragmatic rather than ethical sense 'on the right side'.[31] Similar connotations
may be detected in Isa. 48.18; 58.8; 62.1, 2; essentially these texts speak of
Israel's 'success'.[32] But does *ṣedeq/ṣᵉdāqâ* simply denote 'success' in all those
passages where words from this root are used to refer to God's saving acts
for Israel? If so, their use would not be good evidence that the actions of
God signified by them imply a concept of justice. But it is clear that this is
not so, that there is ethical content to these words. More frequently in Isaiah

27. Knierim 1995: 131–37.
28. MacDonald 2003: 214.
29. MacDonald 2003: 108–22.
30. See most modern translations, particularly the REB and NRSV; most commentaries, e.g.,
North 1964: 166; Westermann 1969: 184; cf. Baltzer 2001: 262, 265; the standard dictionaries;
and the exhaustive analysis by Krašovec (1988).
31. Krašovec 1988: 86.
32. Granted that this 'success' is the *result* of their faithfulness and justice, Krašovec
(1988: 100–101, 111–113, 121–23) too easily retains the translation '*la justice*' for *ṣedeq* and
ṣᵉdāqâ themselves.

40–66 YHWH speaks of 'my justice', *ṣidqātî* (or *ṣidqî*), along with 'my salvation', as in Isa. 46.13; 51.5, 6, 8; 56.1, etc., rather than of 'your *ṣedeq/ ṣᵉdāqâ*'. In all these passages there can be no doubt that the salvation in question is other-directed, to Israel or sometimes further afield (as in 51.5); it is not simply YHWH's own 'success', it is YHWH's action to promote the deliverance and welfare of his people (or of the whole world, but usually of Israel). I would suggest that the choice of words from the root *ṣdq* for this sense is determined by the fact that YHWH's salvation of Israel derives from his personal commitment to them, therefore it is 'right'. In relation to Israel the justice of YHWH is precisely his salvation. It is notable that Krašovec, as well as others, while insisting on the 'salvific' sense of *ṣedeq/ ṣᵉdāqâ*, does not hesitate to continue to speak of '*la justice de Dieu*'.

The alternative might be that these words are chosen to denote the success, welfare, salvation provided by YHWH (therefore 'mine') to his people, without any ethical connotation. But this latter suggestion is undermined by Isa. 45.21. Here as so often the *ṣdq* and *yšᶜ* roots appear in parallel, but rather than the abstract nouns, we find the adjective and participle, 'a just God and a saviour', *'ēl ṣaddîq umôšîaᶜ*. The sense 'giving success' would be a very improbable one for *ṣaddîq*. Even 'victorious', the REB's choice, is a sense the word never bears in reference to human beings, and it always has an ethical sense elsewhere. Far preferable is *HALOT*'s 'loyal, in the sense of helpful and faithful', which aligns this passage with such parallels as Deut. 32.4, Ps. 11.7 and Ps. 145.17. Koole, on the other hand, following Beuken, suggests that YHWH's intervention as saviour 'is because he "supports a just world order and acts accordingly" '.[33] This is defensible in the universal context of Isa. 45.20–25; but does *ṣᵉdāqâ* in Isa. 46.13, for example, mean '(establishment of) a just world order'? Koole's comment on this passage is 'In *ṣᵉdāqâ* justice is done to God and man because Yahweh establishes his order, in *tᵉšûᶜâ* God reveals himself as the Saviour from distress and people experience salvation as a liberation by God'.[34] Koole thus attempts to approximate the concept of justice in Isaiah 40–66 to that in Pss. 96.10, 13; 98.9. But in general it is directed too clearly towards Israel or Zion.

Further evidence for the ethical connotation of *ṣdq* words where they denote 'salvation' may be found from other words with which they are found in parallelism, particularly in the Psalms, which have a wider range of such words than Isaiah 40–66. There are a number of places where *ṣdq* is found with *ḥesed* (NRSV 'steadfast love'). Careful analysis of the sense of *ḥesed* in context demonstrates, in the words of Gordon Clark, that it denotes an attitude and an act stemming from it which 'may be described as a beneficent action performed, in the context of a deep and enduring

33. Koole 1997: 485.
34. Koole 1997: 518.

commitment between two persons or parties, by one who is able to render assistance to the needy party who in the circumstances is unable to help him- or herself'.[35] And while it is 'characteristic of God rather than of human beings', it is also 'a supreme human virtue, standing as the pinnacle of moral values'. Thus there can be no question that it is always an ethical term, and that it comes into play as a feature of a 'commitment between two persons and parties'. When words from the *ṣdq* family are found in the same context, and the personal commitment in question is of God to a human party, we may conclude that they are being used to denote faithful, saving action in that context. This is plainly the case at Ps. 103.17–18, where YHWH's *ṣ*ᵉ*dāqâ* is his faithful saving grace, as his *ḥesed* is his committed and compassionate action to help, towards 'those who fear him, keep his covenant and remember to perform his commandments'. At Ps. 143.11–12 the hopeful recipient of YHWH's *ḥesed* and *ṣ*ᵉ*dāqâ* is an individual, 'your servant' (vv. 1, 12), and he knows he does not deserve them (v. 2). Nevertheless, it is YHWH's 'righteousness' that he relies on, and the parallelism with YHWH's *ḥesed* shows that this righteousness or 'saving grace' arises from the commitment of a personal relationship between YHWH and his servant.

This allows us to be confident that both in the Psalms and in Isaiah 40–66, as in some other places, where YHWH's *ṣedeq*/ *ṣ*ᵉ*dāqâ* is spoken of together with his *y*ᵉ*šû*ʿ*â* (or other word denoting salvation or victory), it refers to his saving grace which is 'righteous' because it arises out of his moral commitment to his servants. To take a striking example: in Psalm 51, the sinner pleads for forgiveness on the basis of YHWH's *ḥesed* and *raḥ*ᵃ*mîm* (compassion: Ps. 51.1, Hebrew 51.3), and comes towards a conclusion (v. 14 [16]) praising God as 'my saving God' (*ᵉlōhê t*ᵉ*šû*ʿ*ātî*) and promising praise of 'your *ṣ*ᵉ*dāqâ*'. The first basis of appeal is to God's *ḥesed*, implying, as does the language of the psalm as a whole, a personal relationship; the sinner's deliverance is sought through God's righteous saving grace exercised in the context of this relationship. Here is a serious ethical concept, but neither Miranda's concept of justice delivering the oppressed nor that of a just world order is appropriate to it. But this usage of *ṣ*ᵉ*dāqâ* is in no way unusual in the Psalms: on the contrary it is perfectly standard; the only unusual feature is that the danger the speaker is in derives from his own sin rather than the hostility of others.[36]

In this concept of justice, there is no question of impartiality. It takes place in the context of commitment to a specific partner, and *parti pris* is built into it. Thus in Isa. 43.3–4 three innocent African nations, in no way implicated in Israel's oppression, are to be handed over as ransom for them,

---

35. Clark 1993: 267.
36. See, e.g., Pss. 22.31 (Hebrew 32); 31.1 (2); 40.9–10 (10–11); 71.2, 15, 24.

a parallel to the annihilation of the Canaanites in the Exodus and Settlement story. The root *ṣdq* is not used in this immediate context, but it is widespread enough in the section to make it clear that YHWH's deliverance of Israel is understood as 'just' wherever it is spoken of, including here. It is 'just' in that YHWH acts for the sake of a partner to whom he is morally committed.

This commitment is expressed in many different ways in Deutero-Isaiah: YHWH has chosen Israel (41.8, 9, etc.) and called him (41.9; 43.1, etc.), created him (43.1, 7, etc.) and redeemed him (43.1). As the theme of covenant, by which the relationship of commitment is expressed so prominently in certain parts of the Old Testament, has no salience here, I have avoided using that language. But this does not lessen the power with which the faithfulness of YHWH to an undeserving people is conveyed. The relationship is marked in the titles given to both YHWH and Israel. YHWH is Israel's Holy One (41.16, 20), redeemer (*gōʾēl*, 41.14 and constantly), Zion's husband (54.4, where 'Maker', 'Holy One' and 'Redeemer' also appear), and so forth. Israel is YHWH's servant (41.8 and frequently); Zion is his wife (54.1–8).

This discussion has shown that the relation of YHWH to his people in many parts of the Old Testament is governed by a concept of justice which is properly ethical, but because of its partiality is not the same as the concept of impartial world justice found in some other places, and is in potential tension with it. Knierim's hypothesis is confirmed.

3. *Social Affinities*

3.a. *Patronage*

It is our next task to demonstrate the affinity of this concept to the ethical norms which are conceived to govern certain aspects of social life in ancient Israel and Judah. Put simply, YHWH's justice in fulfilling his commitment to Israel, or, in the Psalms, his individual servant, is conceived on the analogy of the relationship of patron to client or *gōʾēl* to kin.

In every respect the way in which the relationship between YHWH and Israel is conceived in the Old Testament is comparable to the ideology of the relationship between patron and client among human beings—to the ideology, which of course presents an ideal, not necessarily to the reality.[37] The patron offers protection and assistance—salvation and blessing—in return for loyalty and support. Gifts are expected from the client, not as munificent as the patron's loans and grants, but fitted to the client's resources: in just the same way the human partner in the divine-human relationship offers

37. See above, pp. 42–46.

sacrifice and maintains the service of the shrine. The exclusive loyalty demanded by YHWH is paralleled in Boaz's warning to Ruth not to glean in another field (Ruth 2.8). Even the covenant, as the way in which the relationship is formally defined, has its parallel in the vassal treaties which define the relationship of patronage in the international political realm.

The parallel extends to the concept of justice involved. In analysing the sketches of the just man in the Old Testament in Chapter 4, I noted the points where such expressions as 'your poor', 'with you', are used, and suggested that they are best understood as pointing to the subject's responsibility to particular poor or marginalized people, to his clients or poor relatives. The institution of the *gō'ēl* in Hebrew society follows this general pattern. The *gō'ēl* is the nearest available kinsman; this is clear from Ruth 3.12 and Lev. 25.25, 49. His duties are to redeem persons and property that have fallen into hands outside the lineage (Lev. 25.25, 47–49), and to avenge bloodshed (Deut. 19.6). But we can be sure that these are only the visible tips of a submerged mountain of demands made by the needy on relatives in maybe only slightly better circumstances. It is taken for granted even today in most developing countries that the function of a person who has had some success in life, such as a job in the civil service, is to use it to help out struggling kin; this is a large part of the cause of the 'corruption' that these nations find so difficult to uproot—a classic modern example of the conflict between rival conceptions of morality, a personal family-based model and an impersonal one based on a rational concept of duty to society at large.

The institutions of patronage described by Eisenstadt and Roniger are different in that the patron is generally decidedly better off than the client, and that the ties between them are not related to the family and indeed cut across family ties. But they share with family ties the characteristic that they create a general moral obligation on both sides, even though they do not dictate a specific action on a particular occasion. I have already suggested that the virtue of *ḥesed* is the ideal virtue of the patronal relationship, where the patron (or the *gō'ēl*), more selflessly committed than was perhaps usual, acts to secure the life of the client without any expectation of direct reward.[38] We have seen in the use of *ḥesed* and *ṣᵉdāqâ* in parallel that the latter may also be applied to what is seen as the morally right action in such a situation.

It is a reasonable conclusion that the concept of YHWH's partial and particular justice in relation to Israel is modelled on the concept or experience of patronal justice.

---

38. Above, p. 42. But note that *ḥesed* may also be shown between equals (e.g. Gen. 40.14), or by inferior to superior (e.g. Ruth 3.10). It does not in itself imply any particular relationship of status.

3.b. *Kingship*

Against this it is obvious that one of the most widespread ways of conceiving the power of God in Israel, as in other monarchical societies, is by representing God as a king.[39] The king's justice, as we have seen, is understood to be disinterested, however far from the reality this ideological understanding may be. In the Old Testament (as also in the New) we have many references to YHWH under the title of king, and also a number of 'throne room visions' in which YHWH is physically visualized as a king on his throne surrounded by courtiers: 1 Kgs 22.19–23; Isa. 6.1–8; Ezekiel 1. In Psalm 82, less vividly depicted, the scenario is the same: 'Elohim stands in the assembly of '*ēl*; in the midst of the gods he passes judgment'. The phrase 'assembly of El', originally the name of the Canaanite supreme god, recalls the Ugaritic epics and thus makes it clear that this mythical scenario is very widespread in the ancient East. A number of Psalms, according to a widespread opinion, are 'enthronement psalms' in which YHWH's accession to kingship is celebrated as part of the main annual festival.[40] In any case they all refer to YHWH as king at significant junctures, often the beginning of the Psalm.

It is true that kingship is sometimes seen as an extended form of patronage, so that there would be no tension between these concepts on the social level.[41] And it is perfectly true that in many respects the king acts as patron of his people, while conversely a powerful patron such as Job can speak of his justice in kingly terms (Job 29.12, 17). But in general the functions and ideology of kingship are quite distinct from those of patronage, and they provide a distinct language for speaking about the justice of God.

In the first place, the king is responsible not just for the livelihood and security of some poor people and their families, against whatever dangers may threaten them, but for ensuring that justice is done to all the poor people of his kingdom without distinction or partiality; he is responsible for 'justice and righteousness' as a moral characteristic of his realm. It is also clear that ideally the king's realm is universal. Both of these points emerged very strongly from our study of Psalm 72.[42] Moreover, the king's justice consists not only, indeed not primarily, in seeing to the needs of the poor, the normal function of the patron, but of doing justice to them by delivering them from oppression and 'crushing the oppressor' (Ps. 72.1–4, 12–14; Isa.

---

39. And Tomes (2005) shows that in many respects the prayers of the Psalter are modelled on letters to kings.

40. Mowinckel 1962: I, 106–92; II, 222–50; Day 1992: 69–82; the Psalms are 47, 93, and 96–99.

41. See esp. Lemche 1994, 1996.

42. Above, pp. 138–49.

11.3–5). As we have seen, the king's administrative and judicial functions were expected to be exercised in the defence of the poor, and some Psalms hint at the necessity for military action.

It is made clear in the first verse of Psalm 72 that the king's justice is the earthly expression of the justice of God: 'Give to the king your justice, God, and your righteousness to the king's son'. And YHWH is seen to exercise all these functions and express his universal justice through them. As creator, he issues decrees (*ḥuqqîm, ḥuqqôt*) for the good ordering of his creation, which obeys them: Jer. 5.22; 31.35–36. Mythically this is expressed in the story, frequently referred to, of his victory over the sea and the sea monster, a story whose counterparts both in Babylon and in Ugarit are associated with the divine hero's assumption of the title of king over the pantheon. The title does in fact appear in the context of the allusion to the myth in Ps. 74.12–14.

YHWH's giving of laws to humanity, as his words to Noah show (Gen. 9.1–7), is not confined to Israel, over whom he has peculiar authority as their redeemer and patron. But all his legislation is given in virtue of a royal prerogative. And although his laws for Israel are given as a result of his particular redemption of his people, they are for the most part not partial laws; they are laws designed to develop in Israel the virtue of impartial justice, including the explicit injunction to judge impartially, Exod. 23.1–8; Lev. 19.15; Deut. 16.18–20, and not to oppress the alien, Exod. 22.21 (20); 23.9, and so on. They instruct Israel in the virtues which according to Deut. 10.17–18 YHWH himself shows. It is only the occasional passage which violates this impartiality by an unequal provision, unfavourable to the foreigner, such as Lev. 25.44–46; Deut. 15.3; or to particular foreigners, such as Deut. 23.3–8.

But it is especially YHWH's response to injustice among humanity that illustrates his exercise of kingly justice. It can be seen to be in a sense judicial in so far as it comes in response to a 'cry' or plea from the oppressed, but primarily administrative or military in that it involves the active repression of the oppressor. Thus YHWH is portrayed as responding to a 'cry' (*sᵉʿāqâ* etc.) in Gen. 4.10; 18.20; Exod. 2.23–25; 3.7–9; Isa. 5.7; and elsewhere. In such Psalms as 10, 58 or 94 YHWH is appealed to to destroy the unjust (*rāšāʿ*, NRSV usually 'wicked': Pss. 10.2, etc.; 58.3 [4], 10 [11]; 94.3) and deliver the oppressed poor (Ps. 10; Ps. 94.6) or the just (Ps. 58.10 [11]). In a rather different way, but very clearly, in Psalm 82, Elohim (YHWH) accuses the gods of the nations of judging unjustly and showing partiality to the unjust, and thus of failing in their task as gods, which is identical to the task of kings, to 'give justice to the poor and the orphan, to maintain the right of the humble and poor' (Ps. 82.2–3).

Miranda observes that in the Psalms and elsewhere YHWH may be portrayed as judge or warrior, but in either case there will characteristically be words defining his cause as being in favour of the poor and oppressed and against the 'unjust'.[43] He therefore presses the argument that in all such cases the context must actually be the oppression of the poor. This is to underestimate the rhetorical value of such words to complainants whose cause may be somewhat different.[44] Since the Jerusalem temple was a state sanctuary, the insistence on the 'poor and needy' status of the suppliant must often come under suspicion in this way.[45] But what gives the words their rhetorical value is evidently the understanding that one of the central concerns of the king and of YHWH is to defend the poor against oppression.

3.c. *Synthesis*

There is no absolute opposition in practice between these two concepts of divine justice. Levenson, for example, argues that God's intervention to deliver Israel in Exodus, as expressed in concentrated form in Exod. 2.23–25, includes both a particular dimension—it is YHWH's own people that YHWH takes notice of, no other—and a universal one—he hears the cry of the oppressed people independently of his remembering his covenant, and thus 'the pain of *any* slave can evoke sympathy in God'.[46]

MacDonald has shown that even though in Deuteronomy the election of Israel is 'not a universal movement by YHWH on behalf of the weak and poor ... YHWH leaves many weak and poor in the other nations outside',[47] yet even in relationship to Israel, the justice of YHWH can be conceived as kingly, impartial and universal.[48] The key passage is Deut. 10.14–19, where YHWH's universal power (v. 14) provides the background for his choice of Israel, and Israel is exhorted to submit to his authority (v. 16) in that he is 'God of gods and Lord of lords, the great, mighty and fearful *el*' (MacDonald's translation); MacDonald comments that these expressions are 'reminiscent of royal epithets ... he is the divine warrior king'.[49] The words which follow express an ideal of kingship: 'who has no partiality (*lō' yiśśā' pānîm*) and does not accept bribes, who does justice for orphan and widow and loves the alien ...' The backgrounds here are, of course, first in the king's judicial function, and then in his active administrative intervention on behalf of the poor. MacDonald feels he has to emphasize that the

43. Miranda 1977: 111–27.

44. So for example even Ps. 18 is seen by Miranda (1977: 120), on the basis of v. 28, to speak of a war for the poor against their oppressors. As we saw above, pp. 150–51, the language of poverty has been appropriated here for its rhetorical value; it is a mistake to take it literally.

45. Pss. 22.25; 25.16; 34.7; 35.10; 40.18; 69.30; 70.6; 74.19; 86.1; 88.16; 109.22; 140.13.

46. Levenson 1993: 152.

47. MacDonald 2003:158–59.

48. MacDonald 2003: 166–70.

49. MacDonald 2003: 168, following Mayes (1979: 210) and Weinfeld (1991: 438).

impartiality of the judge and the intervention on behalf of the needy 'were not perceived to be contradictions in YHWH's kingship';[50] but we have already seen that the phrase *nś' pānîm* refers to *personal* favouritism. The potential contradiction is not with YHWH's 'option for the poor', but with his exclusive option for Israel.

At this point MacDonald raises the question whether YHWH's actions on behalf of the marginalized are a universal concern under which the exodus can be subsumed. His answer, more nuanced than Miranda's and apparently without reference to his work, is that 'YHWH's claim to be God' is seen first in his election of Israel, but then *through* Israel and the care that YHWH commands them to give not only to the widow and orphan but also to the stranger. In loving the stranger, Israel will be imitating YHWH, who 'has already shown his love for the stranger by redeeming Israel . . . The concern for the orphan, widow and stranger does point in the direction of a universal concern for the marginalized, but not one that can be detached from the particularity of YHWH's elect people.'[51]

An absolute polarization of universal and particular justice is unnecessary. Nevertheless, enough has been said to show that concepts of divine justice associated both with patronage and with kingship are entertained in the Old Testament and combine, but not without significant tension, to form the picture of YHWH's justice.

4. *Ideological Functions*

It will have become apparent from this discussion that these concepts of divine justice serve important ideological functions. The patronal concept over large swathes of the Scriptures provides the nation with a god who is committed to their support, in whom it is justice to give blessing and victory against all comers; but it also provides the god with a nation committed to his support. YHWH is bound up with national identity and success; in Deuteronomy it is his oath to the fathers and his love of their descendants that accounts for their escape from Egypt and occupation of the land; it justifies the destruction of the supposed former inhabitants and therefore of anyone else who threatens the integrity of an Israel conceived as bound to the service of one god at one holy place—an Israel, therefore, more readily subordinate to central political authority.[52] In Deutero-Isaiah it enables a take on current events which makes them centred entirely on the restoration

---

50. Macdonald 2003: 169.
51. MacDonald 2003: 170.
52. Compare our discussion above, pp. 173–77.

of 'Israel' and of 'Zion', that is, the restoration of the Jerusalem-based former ruling class of Judah.[53]

Contrary to the confident view of Miranda and other liberation theologians, the Exodus is not simply an example of God's liberating justice, for it delivers Israel from oppression at the expense of other nations. However, it is quoted on a number of occasions in both Exodus and Deuteronomy as the motivation for obedience to laws enjoining the decent treatment of slaves or aliens, including the liberation of slaves (Deut. 15.15). But this is a specific application to aspects of justice that can metonymically be connected with the Exodus, not the general basis of social justice in Israel. It is rather YHWH's kingly justice that provides this.

But kingly justice clearly has its own ideological functions. Most obviously, in the monarchic period, YHWH as king guaranteed and justified the rule of the earthly king, who ruled as YHWH's vice-regent. The kingship of YHWH was probably renewed and celebrated at the same festival as that of his anointed one. Like that of his divine lord, the king's rule was, ideologically speaking, universal (Pss. 72.8–11; 89.25, 27), even though in reality it barely ever extended beyond the hill-country of Judah. The king's status as YHWH's governor on earth is set out very plainly in Psalm 2. Disobedience to the king is disobedience to YHWH: Ps. 2.10–11. Judaean kingship thus supported itself ideologically in reliance on a doctrine of universal divine kingship; in this it was no different from the dynasties of all its neighbours. This doctrine is applied to royal *justice* in particular in Psalm 72, where it is made clear that its origin is in YHWH's justice: v. 1. As I have argued, the assertion that the king exercises the justice of God for the poor serves to conceal the exploitative character of a rule which extracted tax and corvée from precisely those 'weak' and 'needy' people whom it claimed to serve.[54]

A more general ideological function may be seen to be served by all kinds of assertions that God rules the world justly, and especially by the bold assertions of God's active intervention for the poor which are so common in the Old Testament, such as Ps. 113.7–9. In so far as they are believed they may serve to reconcile the poor and those who are concerned for justice to the present injustice of the world; for this after all is seen to be a temporary condition. Even if present injustice is acknowledged, the strong assertions of YHWH's coming judgment of the world which we find in Psalms 96 and 98, not to mention the prophets, may serve to allay grievances in the expectation that they will in due course be dealt with by no human hand.

It is certainly a commonplace of social history to suggest that Christian belief in rewards in the afterlife served to induce such oppressed groups as the African-American slaves to accept their present lot. Such tenets

---

53. For this view of Deutero-Isaiah see Gottwald 1992.
54. Above, pp. 138–49.

were purposely employed to that end by some; in the English Industrial Revolution Dr Andrew Ure, quoted by E.P. Thompson, asked

> how are these disciplinary virtues [required for the efficient running of the factory] to be inculcated in those whose Godliness is unlikely to bring any temporal gain? It can only be by inculcating 'the first and great lesson . . . that man must expect his chief happiness, not in the present, but in a future state'.[55]

However, once belief in the liberating God of the Scriptures had been absorbed by the oppressed themselves, they became convinced of their own worth as persons for whom Christ had died, and this could and often did lead to radical industrial and political activism, as Thompson goes on to chronicle.[56] Moreover, the working-class struggles of those years, in which Methodists were often prominent, drew upon the Old Testament both typologically and morally; Thompson has probably underestimated the systematic character of this use.[57]

In the case of the African-American slaves it was often specifically the story of the Exodus that induced confidence in their value as persons worthy of freedom, and an emphasis on freedom in their spirituality. One may cite many of the passages on religion in the *Slave Narrative Collection*, the enormous gathering of recollections of elderly ex-slaves collected in the 1930s.[58] The well-known spiritual 'Go down, Moses' was sung by slaves on the 'Underground Railroad' on the way to freedom.[59]

> You may hinder me here, but you can't up dere,
> Let my people go!
> He sits in de hebben and answers prayer.
> Let my people go!

It was more than a century later before the same understanding of the Exodus was adopted by liberation theology in Latin America.

These examples point to the truth, which I have emphasized again and again in this study, that theological themes, even where they can be seen to have ideological functions both at the time of writing and in subsequent readings, cannot be exhausted by this. They could not function ideologically unless they expressed ideas rooted at a deeper level in the religious traditions of the people. In this case both of the concepts of divine justice we have been working with are far more than devices to provide religious justification for particular political arrangements. Both ideas are extremely widespread

55. Thompson 1968: 398, citing Ure 1835: 423–25.
56. Thompson 1968: 411–40.
57. Thompson 1968: 431–32.
58. Excerpted in Yetman 1970. Cf. Hopkins and Cummings 2003.
59. Longley 2002: 242.

in the ancient Near East. Belief in a god who is the personal supporter and
gō'ēl may well originate in personal or domestic piety, even though it is most
prominent in the political religion of kings.[60] We have found testimony to
the divine guarantor of justice for the poor in literature of various genres,
wisdom, psalm and prophecy, most of which cannot be understood as royal
propaganda.

5. *Reflections for Today*

Both biblical concepts are capable of making indispensable contributions to
the ongoing struggle for justice even today, and indeed both together are
indispensable, despite the tension between them, to enable Christians join-
ing this struggle to make a distinct contribution to it. Enlightenment concepts of social justice, both in their Marxist and liberal forms, rooted
though they ultimately are in the biblical tradition, have eviscerated it of
that which alone gives it its power: the commitment of the person, in the
beginning of God himself, to enact justice.

On the one hand, the value of faith in a God impartially committed to
justice for every nation and race is obvious, both as an inspiration and as a
promise of victory, in a time in which the struggle for justice, never divisible,
has become truly global. Through the Gospels the kingly understanding of
divine justice has become enshrined in the concept of the kingdom of God,
and while this has been subject to a great variety of interpretations in the
course of the history of the Church, its understanding as a just, peaceful
and blessed human community to be brought into being on earth has been
very influential in the twentieth century and since.

On the other hand, faith begins where the individual or the community is
seized by the knowledge that *my* God, *our* God, has graciously intervened to
save us. The old evangelical slogan, 'accept Jesus Christ as your personal
saviour', may not be biblical phrasing, but it hits a psychological nail on the
head. This is what is seen by liberation theology where it draws its strength
from the faith of the base communities. For these people, the God of the
Bible is their own God, the God who has proclaimed himself the God of the
poor, the God of the struggling and the marginalized, and acted to deliver
them. It is a modern version of the doctrine of election. It is significant that
liberation theology met much criticism from a conventional orthodoxy that
complained that it had no gospel for the rich.

It is true that a democratic age, or more accurately an age when democracy is treated as the ideal, has difficulty with the idea of God as king, and
would not even understand that of God as patron. The effect of this modern

60. Cf. Albertz 1978.

solvent of traditional theological ideas is seen, for example, in the way in which Croatto's hermeneutical treatment of Exodus makes YHWH's sovereign action to deliver Israel an interpretation after the event of a popular initiative for liberation.[61]

Interpretations of this kind appear at first sight to abandon the sense that it is *God* who acts to establish justice. Indeed, we must always face the possibility that faith in the God of justice is an illusion. Theology cannot do without a just God; but where in the real world, as distinct from the text, may God's justice be perceived? The slaves were freed, but is it possible to say that that was the work of God? The reality of God's just government of the world is questioned in the Old Testament itself. Job questions it with specific reference to the exploitation of the poor in Job 24. 'Why are times [i.e. dates for the hearing of cases] not kept by Shaddai, and why do those who know him never see his days? . . . From the city the dying groan, and the throat of the wounded cries out; but Eloah does not charge [anyone with] the outrage.'[62] Between these two accusations in vv. 1, 12, stands the most rhetorically impressive account of rural exploitation and destitution in the whole of the Scriptures, including the prophets.[63] Job's complaint is that God sees this gross violence and injustice by the landowners and takes no steps to judge them and rectify the injustice. When YHWH answers Job from the whirlwind, he ignores this complaint as he does Job's more personal ones, thus apparently confirming that he has no interest in bringing a just society into being.

David Clines has written a provocative essay on this chapter, which brings us to the heart of this question. He makes three points against Job.[64] He complains first that Job has no idea of any other way of dealing with the wicked than that God should judge and punish them: repentance, reform, education of the wrongdoer, none of them come within his purview. This overlooks the fact, sufficiently emphasized by Clines himself earlier in his essay, that Job is not talking about common criminals but about the ruling class of his society. The urgent requirement is that injustice should cease, and the only way of achieving that, by God or by human beings, is by strong action against the exploiters. Clines's later objection to the forensic terms of Job's complaint, that 'days of assize' are 'accounting after the event', and no way of running a business (Clines chooses a metaphor appropriate for his late-twentieth-century viewpoint as Job's is for his), that a good manager develops a forward-looking plan for the enterprise and good relationships

---

61. Croatto 1981.

62. Or 'pay attention to their prayer', NRSV, reading *tᵉpillâ* for *tiplâ*.

63. Clines complains that it 'glamorizes' poverty and does not see it from the inside (Clines 1995: 126–28). This is only to say that it is indeed rhetorically effective.

64. Clines 1998: 254–55.

with the staff, surely misunderstands Job's metaphor in the same way. The judgment sought by Job on behalf of the exploited is not a settling up of accounts after the event, but decisive action in the midst of the struggle against the exploiters.

Secondly, he objects to Job's 'hard-and-fast distinction between the wicked and the righteous', which is 'the morality of the school playground', and suggests that there must be shades of grey, for example 'the good ruler who is sometimes selfish and careless'. This is hardly a fair objection to this specific speech of Job, which deals with a specific social evil for which certain people are responsible, though as an objection to the ethical scheme of the book as a whole it may carry some weight.

But the point which most concerns us is Clines' third: that Job is wrong to suggest that it is God's responsibility to rectify social injustice. 'If there are rich and poor in a community, and if that is an injustice, to appeal to God to do something about it is to absolve humans of responsibility, of the rich to care for the functioning of the whole community that sustains their wealth and of the poor to unite in action against a system from which they are suffering.' It is humans who have created the problem, and it is their responsibility to solve it.[65] And in his speeches, God ignores it precisely because it is not his concern. He does maintain a universal order, 'but its principles are not balance and equity and retribution and equivalence . . . It majors on intimacy, on sustenance, on variety.'[66]

This may well be a valid interpretation of the divine speeches in Job; it may be compared with those of Habel and Gutiérrez.[67] But to suggest that, because social justice is a human responsibility (as the whole of the Bible affirms), it is therefore not God's ignores both the way in which belief in a just God actually works, by inspiring a commitment to justice in human beings, as we have just seen, and also the general biblical and theological understanding of divine action. In the book of Job, as in the Bible generally, God is seen to act in and through what happens in the affairs of humanity, as for example in the raid of the Sabaeans which deprives Job of his oxen and donkeys (Job 1.14–15). Job is not necessarily objecting that God does not take some extraordinary step to bring the exploiters to justice. He is simply objecting that they are not brought to justice by any means. If the people together found a way to achieve it, that too would be the work of God: and God, accordingly, was at work in the liberation of the American slaves.

So Job's question continues to press; it cannot be so easily turned aside. The world is in fact unjust; that is because (indeed it consists in the fact that)

65. Clines 1998: 258.
66. Clines 1998: 256.
67. Habel 1985: 526–35; Gutiérrez 1987: 73–75, 80, 87–88.

people are unjust. But if, as the Old Testament in general maintains, God is just, one would expect that to be reflected in some way in the way that people behave. And that is just what Job does not see. Yes, YHWH's answer does announce a broader vision of cosmic order, but altogether avoids the question of how human society finds its place in that.

Miranda, at the end of his book, proposes an extremely radical escape from this dilemma.[68] 'The heart of the matter is that men will not have Yahweh as their God unless they love their neighbor and achieve justice completely on the earth. God will not be God until then . . . The true God is not; he will be.' This is in a way the logical conclusion of what we have been saying. YHWH's justice is found in human justice, and cannot be known without it. For Miranda, for whom YHWH is known only in justice, YHWH is therefore absent unless justice be present.

The Old Testament itself proposes an understanding which parallels this but at the same time is profoundly different. It may be found in Isa. 56.1, which plays on the ambiguity of $s^e dāqâ$, bringing together the characteristic word-pairs of Isaiah 1–39 and 40–55, as we have seen:[69]

> Thus says YHWH: Observe justice and do righteousness ($s^e dāqâ$), for my salvation is about to come, and my righteousness/victory ($s^e dāqâ$) to be revealed.

Not only does the verse link the call to justice of Isaiah 1–39 with the proclamation of YHWH's (particular) justice in Isaiah 40–55, it 'sounds themes to be developed in [different parts of] the remainder of Third Isaiah'.[70] The verse thus has a pivotal function in the book. It has been observed that, like many passages in the following eleven chapters, it responds to the disappointment engendered by the apparent failure of Deutero-Isaiah's vision.[71] The author reasserts the vision of YHWH's righteous saving grace towards his people. It is a reality which will soon be seen; but it can only be known as a *saving* reality by a people who practise justice.

Isaiah 59.1–2 expresses a similar idea, but that chapter presents YHWH as a *deus ex machina* who appears in order to impose justice/salvation by force when he can find no human person to create it (Isa. 59.15–20); it includes both vengeance on his enemies (Isa. 59.18) and redemption for 'those in Jacob who turn from transgression' (Isa. 59.20). This and similar expressions in the final phase of the composition of the book of Isaiah (cf., e.g., Isa. 1.27–28; 65.13–15) stand at the head of the long and broad stream

---

68. Miranda 1977: 293–96.
69. Above, p. 78; Rendtorff 1993.
70. Leclerc 2001: 133, following Polan 1986.
71. Carroll 1979: 153.

of apocalyptic thought. But what real or even conceivable actualization can be found for them? How can justice be truly justice, that is just *relationships*, unless human beings voluntarily adopt it as their practice?

Ernst Käsemann asserts that apocalyptic was 'the mother of Christian theology'.[72] It is doubtless true that much in the New Testament sits easily with the thought of the God who comes in power and glory to establish the kingdom of righteousness. But like other mothers, apocalyptic cannot lay exclusive claim to the genetic inheritance of her child. If we turn back to the end of Chapter 5, we shall be reminded that the stream of thought centred on the justice and righteousness of the Davidic king is transformed in the New Testament, where Jesus is hailed as the son of David, the Messiah, the Lord's anointed, and yet renounces domination and teaches his followers to renounce it. If we follow this thread of thought in the New Testament, we may find it able to support the idea that the Messianic kingdom is a peaceable kingdom in a sense going well beyond that of Isaiah 11, a kingdom in which justice is established in peace as well as existing in peace. It is peaceable action, which certainly does not mean passivity or avoidance of conflict, which characterizes not only Jesus' own practice but the practice of his followers as well. 'My kingdom is not from this world; if my kingdom had been from this world, my followers would have fought to prevent my being handed over to the Jews' (Jn 18.36). The point is that this is the only way in which justice which is truly and fully the justice of God's new community can come into existence. It is embodied first in Jesus the Messiah, the king of justice who is yet not a king in a sense capable of being recognized by Pilate, who as the Word of God incarnate is the justice of God present in the world in both potential and act. His mission is then carried forward by his followers, and it is they who are called to embody that action of God for justice in this world that Job missed. Christians live 'by neither violence nor compromise, but by hope in the redeeming, which is to say liberating, action of the God who raised Jesus Christ from the dead'.[73]

Yet we have to recognize that it is rather seldom that the followers of Jesus have fulfilled this calling, so that, to adapt a sentence of Miranda's, 'Because [the Church] totally failed [God], the oppressed of the whole earth continue to "cry out" in vain'.[74] Is this the last thing that we are able to say about the justice of God in human society? Let us hope not. The concluding chapter will sum up how the Old Testament may assist in renewing the practice of justice by Christians.

72. Käsemann 1969: 137.
73. Gorringe 1994: 169.
74. Cf. Miranda 1977: 169.

Chapter 8

THE OLD TESTAMENT: A RESOURCE IN CONTENDING
FOR JUSTICE

The work I have done in this book should not be thought to be of relevance solely to Christians, or even other theists. Most of what we take for granted in the West by way of social morality goes back ultimately to the Old Testament. This does not mean that our society has already learnt what it needs to learn from it. It does mean that there is a cultural space here which is potentially friendly to its ideas. It is true that the theological issues which we have discussed appear to be issues primarily for those with a religious faith. But they are not esoteric matters; as Lesslie Newbigin continually argued in his later years, if the Gospel is not 'public truth' it is of little consequence.[1] In our case, it does make a difference to us all whether we live in a world where injustice can go on flourishing or in one where justice can finally be established. Nevertheless, we can make a rough distinction between moral and theological issues, which will structure this concluding chapter, a chapter of conclusions.

1. *Old Testament Justice in Today's World*

I am writing at a time when issues of social justice and the way in which they are conceived ideologically are as significant as they have ever been. The world is being ever more profoundly shaped by the economic power of monopoly capitalism, which reaches into the furthest territories and the remotest villages of the world with its mass production methods and its enticements to consume its products. This influence has not only profound economic and ecological effects, though those are serious enough, with inequality doubling and redoubling over the past few decades, and a minority of humanity enjoying luxuries that their grandparents could not have dreamt of, as the site of their production moves into economies with lower and lower wages, and global warming and destruction of habitat begins the

---

1. E.g. Newbigin 1986.

sixth great extinction of species in five hundred million years. It is degrading local cultures all over the world as Hollywood and Macdonalds provide the universally recognized icons. Most importantly for us, its power is ideological: it is able to shape the public perception of its own presence and effects. An economic system which is reducing local choices and the liberty of governments to determine their own economic policies offers 'liberty', 'free enterprise', 'choice', and any restraint on its operations is a 'burden'. Ironically, it is able to persuade people that Marxism is outmoded precisely because one of Marx's predictions is being confirmed.

In Britain under a professed social-democratic government social justice seems to have been reduced to the bloodless and uninspiring ideas of equality of opportunity and the delivery of public services, while the sense of values has been so eroded by luxury advertising that more than half of us, in a country where average real incomes are three times what they were in 1950, say that they do not have enough money for essentials.[2] This is a society which is losing its power even to recognize genuine poverty or to understand what justice requires.

However, at the same time, there is an openness in the system. Political leaders of the 'first world' insist in a way not seen before on the importance of democracy. They may then attempt to manipulate democratic processes, but the very holding of free elections offers the possibility of changing minds and raising questions about the ruling ideology. Many groups among the world's rulers are conscious of their responsibility to the world's poor and have genuine intentions to relieve poverty. 'Equality' does not seem to be a word in their vocabulary, but 'justice' is. In a situation which might otherwise seem hopelessly oppressive, this ensures that it may be possible to engage our masters on the subject of what justice really is and the commitment it demands.

Thus to contend for justice is at the same time to contend for ideology. We have seen that some of our most basic ideas of social morality began life as ideologies in situations of conflict. The situations may be different, but the moral imagination of the Old Testament still has the power to break open the ideologies of our own world. It is indeed the Old Testament's moral imagination which is its permanent contribution to the struggle for true human community. It is not laws or institutions. Inspiration may indeed be drawn from a utopian institution, as the resonance of the jubilee theme in recent years shows. But it is a mistake to conclude that such an institution, rooted as it is in a particular culture with a particular social history, is to be transplanted into one alien to it. Not even at the most abstract level could this be a realistic possibility. It is rather the moral imagination exemplified by the treatment of the jubilee theme in Leviticus 25 that may

---

2.   Clive Hamilton in Seenan 2003.

mean something for indebted communities today—the imagination of a human community with the life to resist the destructive power of the market. Nor should the Old Testament's contribution be seen as something like 'the power of the poor'. We have seen that there are few texts where this is convincingly exemplified. Justice is generally conceived as a virtue of the superior in an ordered society: it is in accord with this that God's 'preferential option for the poor'—that is, God's justice—is seen everywhere. Rather, the power of the poor is a power whereby the moral imagination of the Old Testament may be seized and put into effect.

Some of the moral lessons that the Old Testament appears to offer us are clearly unacceptable: for example, that a people may be divinely authorized to seize another people's land. If this means that we cannot be uncritical of what we read in the Old Testament, it would be a false deduction that we can have nothing to learn from the Old Testament. Indeed, it is hard to see the value of the kind of study whose object appears to be to show that that the moral values of an Old Testament text are inadequate as judged by the standards of the author. If the ethics and theology of the Hebrew Bible are invariably inferior to ours, there is no point in reading it, unless for entertainment or to provide research fodder. Being truly critical means being able to distinguish within interested discourse those ideas that transcend their ideological framing. In the course of our study, we should have learnt some criteria for this. Some of these ideas are a challenge not merely to the interests of those groups responsible for the texts but to those who read them today.

For it cannot be maintained that our world has nothing to learn from the Hebrew Bible. For example, we still need to learn the importance of what Deuteronomy calls brotherhood. Although we have developed more sophisticated institutional protections of human rights, they are valueless without the conviction learned by each member of society that we belong together. We can still learn from the anger of the prophets against what offends against human solidarity and dignity, however difficult that may be in a society where impersonal relationships are dominant. The most widespread image of righteousness in the Old Testament is of one who uses economic power to assist the powerless, rather than to enrich oneself. This may be found of little value to oppressed people seeking justice for themselves against implacable opposition. But as I have suggested, it is far from valueless in situations where the best hope of justice may be the conscience of the well to do—and that covers many, if not most, situations in our world today.

What all these images and ideas have in common is their moral character. In Chapter 3, we found that the prophetic criticism of the current social transformation was made in strictly moral terms. What was happening was murder, robbery, violence, trampling on people's rights. No part of the Bible offers anything resembling social analysis, nor could it be expected to.

And it is a moral concept which dominates all those passages which speak positively of justice. This makes the Old Testament's contribution peculiarly necessary at the present day. It is characteristic of the modern ideologies which have justified oppression in the twentieth century, and look like continuing to do so in the twenty-first, that they fail to envisage human relationships in moral terms. Although, as Miranda convincingly argues,[3] Karl Marx was inspired by a similar moral passion to the Bible, his followers justified murder, violence and oppression on the grounds that they furthered the revolution. The currently dominant neo-liberalism, as Gorringe splendidly shows, argues for an economic system which ignores human relationships and steadily destroys human customs by referring in utilitarian fashion to the value of prosperity for all, calculated in numerical terms and ignoring the qualitative value of what is offered for the thriving of human persons in community.[4]

The utopian character of many Old Testament visions of justice may be thought a problem. I well remember a meeting of Scripture, Theology and Society where Ronald Preston read a brief paper passionately dismissing Leviticus 25 as having anything useful to contribute to the search for justice in the world today. It was simply pie in the sky and was a dead letter in its own day, let alone now. But as I hope I have shown, it is a mistake to approach such texts as if any value they might have lay in some institutional embodiment. No one criticizes Isa. 11.6–9 in the same way, since no one expects lions to be able to eat straw, at least in this world, and therefore no one is disappointed to discover that they cannot. In fact, the way in which these two texts 'work' as a stimulus to the imagination may be far more similar than we at first realize, despite their unlikeness in genre, style and image. Like utopias in general, they project an image of a world of justice and non-violence which convinces us that such a thing is possible and encourages us to work towards it.

2. *Embodying the Justice of God*

Old Testament texts understand justice as being possible in this world because they accept that the cosmos is justly ordered under the rule of a just God. Where that faith is questioned, as by Qoheleth and by the speeches of Job in the wisdom dialogue of the book of Job, the questioning arises from the apparent absence of justice in the world. I have argued that if we cling to this faith despite everything, we need to understand God's justice as embodied in human justice. Apocalypticism is a dead end in theology. Thus

3.   Miranda 1977: 250–92. Cf. Gorringe 1994: 55.
4.   Gorringe 1994: 29–42.

the biblical faith in a God of justice is confirmed, for the believer, with each faltering step towards a world of justice that we observe.

Believers need to understand themselves as the vehicles of the justice of God. Social justice concerns social relationships, but it is only capable of becoming a reality through the commitment of individuals. There is a stimulus to the moral imagination of the individual felt through reading and reflecting on the Bible, which affects attitude, concern and habitus. However, such a stimulus is only effective if the individual works within a community concerned for the transformation of social life and economic relationships, and willing to work alongside those struggling for justice worldwide, primarily the victims of injustice.

In the secular world, Christians need to be prepared to work in this way within communities of many different kinds, political parties, pressure groups, trade unions, mass movements. Ideally, however, the Christian church itself should be a community committed to the establishment of God's justice in the world. As the community of the Messiah, it finds itself within the stream of tradition we explored in Chapter 5. We traced that stream down into the Gospels, where we saw the concept of power transformed. Christians acknowledge as Lord the one who came 'not to be served but to serve'. Mark places this idea in a political context. It does not happen 'among the Gentiles', but it is to be observed 'among you'. Thus the disciples of Jesus are those called in the present-day world to serve the victims of injustice by putting into practice the Bible's values of justice.

Bibliography

Albertz, Rainer
  1978 *Persönliche Frömmigkeit und offizielle Religion: religionsinterner Pluralismus in Israel und Babylon* (Stuttgart: Calwer).
  1981 'Der sozialgeschichtliche Hintergrund des Hiobbuches und der "Babylonischen Theodizee"', in J. Jeremias and L. Perlitt (eds.), *Die Botschaft und die Boten* (Neukirchen-Vluyn: Neukirchener Verlag): 349–72.
  1994 *A History of Israelite Religion in the Old Testament Period* (2 vols.; London: SCM Press).

Alt, Albrecht
  1959 *Kleine Schriften* III (Munich: Beck).
  1959a 'Der Anteil des Königtums an der sozialen Entwicklung in den Reichen Israel und Juda', in Alt 1959: 348–72.
  1959b 'Micha 2,1–5. γῆς ἀναδασμός in Juda', in Alt 1959: 373–81.
  1966 *Essays in Old Testament History and Religion* (Oxford: Blackwell).

Aristotle
  1920 *Atheniensium Respublica* (ed. F.G. Kenyon; Oxford Classical Texts; Oxford: Clarendon Press).
  1926 *The Art of Rhetoric* (ed. and trans. J.H. Freese; LCL; London: Heinemann).
  1950 *Constitution of Athens* and related texts (trans. with intro. and notes by Kurt von Fritz and Ernst Kapp; New York: Hafner).

Ateek, Naim Stifan
  1989 *Justice, and Only Justice: A Palestinian Theology of Liberation* (Maryknoll, NY: Orbis Books).

Auld, A. Graeme
  1986 *Amos* (OTG; Sheffield: JSOT Press).

Bach, Robert
  1957 'Gottesrecht und weltliches Recht in der Verkündigung des Propheten Amos', in W. Schneemelcher (ed.), *Festschrift für Günther Dehn* (Neukirchen: Buchhandlung des Erziehungsvereins Neukirchen): 23–34.

Baltzer, Klaus
  2001 *Deutero-Isaiah: A Commentary on Isaiah 40–55* (Hermeneia; Minneapolis: Augsburg Fortress).

Barton, John
  1978 'Understanding Old Testament Ethics', *JSOT* 9: 44–64.
  1979 'Natural Law and Poetic Justice in the Old Testament', *JTS* NS 30: 1–14.

1980   *Amos' Oracles against the Nations. A Study of Amos 1.3–2.5* (SOTSMS, 6;
        Cambridge: Cambridge University Press).
1981   'Ethics in Isaiah of Jerusalem', *JTS* NS 32: 1–18.
1998   *Ethics and the Old Testament* (London: SCM Press).
Ben-Barak, Z.
1981   'Meribaal and the System of Land Grants in Ancient Israel', *Bib* 62: 73–91.
Bendor, S.
1996   *The Social Structure of Ancient Israel: The Institution of the Family (Beit
        'Ab) from the Settlement to the End of the Monarchy* (Jerusalem Biblical
        Studies, 7; Jerusalem: Simor).
Bennett, Harold V.
2002   *Injustice Made Legal: Deuteronomic Law and the Plight of Widows,
        Strangers and Orphans in Ancient Israel* (Grand Rapids: Eerdmans).
Bess, S.H.
1963   'Systems of Land Tenure in Ancient Israel' (unpublished dissertation,
        University of Michigan).
Beuken, Willem A.M.
2000   *Isaiah, Part II, Volume 2: Isaiah Chapters 28–39* (HCOT; Leuven: Peeters
        ET of *Jesaja, deel II A* [Nijkerk: Callenbach, 1983]).
Beveridge, William
1966   *Social Insurance and Allied Services*, report by Sir William Beveridge (Nov.
        1942, reprinted 1966; London: HMSO Cmd 6404).
Bird, Phyllis
1997   'Poor Man or Poor Woman: Gendering the Poor in Prophetic Texts', in
        *Missing Persons and Mistaken Identities: Women and Gender in Ancient
        Israel* (Minneapolis: Fortress Press): 67–78; repr. from B. Becking and M.
        Dijkstra (eds.), *On Reading Prophetic Texts: Gender-Specific and Related
        Studies in Memory of Fokkelien van Dijk-Hemmes* (Leiden: Brill, 1996):
        37–51.
Blenkinsopp, Joseph
1988   *Ezra-Nehemiah: A Commentary* (OTL; London: SCM Press).
2000   *Isaiah 1–39: A New Translation with Introduction and Commentary* (AB, 19;
        New York: Doubleday).
2003   *Isaiah 56–66: A New Translation with Introduction and Commentary* (AB,
        19B; New York: Doubleday).
Blum, Erhard
1990   *Studien zur Komposition des Pentateuch* (BZAW, 189; Berlin: de Gruyter).
Bobek, H.
1969   'Die Hauptstufen der Gesellschafts- und Wirtschaftsentfaltung in
        geographischer Sicht', in E. Wirth (ed.), *Wirtschaftsgeographie* (WdF, 219;
        Darmstadt: Wissenschaftliche Buchhandlung): 441–85.
Bottéro, Jean
1992   'The "Code" of Hammurabi', in idem (ed.), *Mesopotamia: Writing, Rea-
        soning, and the Gods* (Chicago: University of Chicago; ET of *Mésopotamie:
        l'écriture, la raison et les dieux* [Paris: Gallimard, 1987]: 156–84.
Broshi, Magen and Israel Finkelstein
1992   'The Population of Israel in Iron Age II', *BASOR* 287: 47–60.

Broyles, Craig C.
 1997 'The Redeeming King: Psalm 72's Contribution to the Messianic Ideal', in
  C.A. Evans and P.W. Flint (eds.), *Eschatology, Messianism and the Dead
  Sea Scrolls* (Grand Rapids: Eerdmans): 23–40.
Brueggemann, Walter
 1991 'Psalms 9–10: A Counter to Conventional Social Reality', in Jobling, Day
  and Sheppard 1991: 3–16.
 1994 'Theodicy in a Social Dimension', in *A Social Reading of the Old
  Testament: Prophetic Approaches to Israel's Communal Life* (ed. Patrick D.
  Miller; Minneapolis: Fortress): 174–96.
 1997 *Theology of the Old Testament: Testimony, Dispute, Advocacy* (Minneapolis: Fortress).
Buber, Martin
 1949 *The Prophetic Faith* (New York: Macmillan).
Bultmann, Christoph
 1992 *Der Fremde im antiken Juda: Eine Untersuchung zum sozialen Typenbegriff
  <ger> und seinem Bedeutungswandel in der alttestamentlichen Gesetzge-
  bung* (FRLANT, 153; Göttingen: Vandenhoeck & Ruprecht).
Calvin, John
 1840 *A Commentary on the Psalms of David* (3 vols.; London: Thomas
  Tegg).
 1852–55 *Commentaries on the Four Last Books of Moses, Arranged in the Form
  of a Harmony* (trans. etc. C.W. Bingham; 4 vols.; Edinburgh: Calvin
  Translation Society).
Carney, T.F.
 1973 *The Economies of Antiquity: Controls, Gifts and Trade* (Lawrence, KS:
  Coronado Press).
 1975 *The Shape of the Past: Models and Antiquity* (Lawrence, KS: Coronado Press).
Carroll R., Mark Daniel
 1992 *Contexts for Amos: Prophetic Poetics in Latin American Perspective* (Sheffield: JSOT Press).
Carroll, Robert P.
 1979 *When Prophecy Failed: Reactions and Responses to Failure in the Old Testament Prophetic Traditions* (London: SCM Press).
 1981 *From Chaos to Covenant: Uses of Prophecy in the Book of Jeremiah*
  (London: SCM Press).
 1986 *Jeremiah: A Commentary* (OTL; London: SCM Press).
 1989 'Prophecy and Society', in R.E. Clements (ed.), *The World of Ancient
  Israel: Sociological, Anthropological and Political Perspectives* (Cambridge:
  Cambridge University Press): 203–26.
Carter, Charles E.
 1999 *The Emergence of Yehud in the Persian Period: A Social and Demographic
  Study* (JSOTSup, 294; Sheffield: Sheffield Academic Press).
Chaney, Marvin L.
 1986 'Systemic Study of the Israelite Monarchy', *Semeia* 37: 53–76.
 1991 'Debt Easement in Israelite History and Tradition', in Jobling, Day and
  Sheppard 1991: 127–40.

1993 'Bitter Bounty: The Dynamics of Political Economy Critiqued by the Eighth-Century Prophets', in Gottwald and Horsley 1993: 250–63.

1999 'Whose Sour Grapes? The Addressees of Isaiah 5:1–7 in the Light of Political Economy', *Semeia* 87: 105–22.

Chapman, Mark D.

2005 *Blair's Britain: A Christian Critique* (London: Darton, Longman & Todd).

Charpin, Dominique

1996 'Le "bon pasteur": idéologie et pratique de la justice royale à l'époque paléo-babylonienne', in ARGO (ed.), *Les moyens d'expressions de pouvoir dans les sociétés anciennes* (Lettres Orientales, 5; Leuven: Peeters).

Chavel, S.

1997 ' "Let my People Go!" Emancipation, Revelation, and Scribal Activity in Jeremiah 34.8–14', *JSOT* 76: 71–95.

Childs, Brevard S.

1974 *Exodus: A Commentary* (OTL; London: SCM Press).

1979 *An Introduction to the Old Testament as Scripture* (London: SCM Press).

Chirichigno, Gregory C.

1993 *Debt-Slavery in Israel and the Ancient Near East* (JSOTSup 141; Sheffield: JSOT Press).

Christensen, Torben

1962 *Origin and History of Christian Socialism 1848–54* (Aarhus: Universitetsvorlaget).

Claburn, W. Eugene

1973 'The Fiscal Basis of Josiah's Reforms', *JBL* 92: 11–22.

Clark, Gordon R.

1993 *The Word Hesed in the Hebrew Bible* (JSOTSup, 157; Sheffield: JSOT Press).

Clines, David J.A.

1976 *I, He, We and They: A Literary Approach to Isaiah 53* (JSOTSup, 1; Sheffield: JSOT).

1978 *The Theme of the Pentateuch* (JSOTSup, 10; Sheffield: JSOT Press).

1990 'Deconstructing the Book of Job', in Martin Warner (ed.), *The Bible as Rhetoric: Studies in Biblical Persuasion and Credibility* (London: Routledge 1990): 65–80. Reprinted in *What does Eve do to help? and Other Readerly Questions to the Old Testament* (JSOTSup 94; Sheffield: JSOT Press 1990): 106–23.

1995 'Why Is There a Book of Job, and What Does It Do To You If You Read It?', in *Interested Parties* (JSOTSup, 205; Sheffield: Sheffield Academic Press): 122–44.

1998 'Quarter Days Gone: Job 24 and the Absence of God', in T. Linafelt and T.K. Beal (eds.), *God in the Fray: A Tribute to Walter Brueggemann* (Minneapolis: Augsburg Fortress): 242–58.

Coggins, Richard

2000 *Joel and Amos* (NCB; Sheffield: Sheffield Academic Press).

Collins, Terence

1993 *The Mantle of Elijah: The Redaction Criticism of the Prophetical Books* (Sheffield: JSOT Press).

Coote, Robert B.

1981 *Amos among the Prophets* (Philadelphia: Fortress Press).

Craigie, Peter C.
1976 *The Book of Deuteronomy* (NICOT; Grand Rapids: Eerdmans).
1983 *Psalms 1–50* (WBC, 19; Waco: Word Books).
Croatto, José Severino
1981 *Exodus: A Hermeneutics of Freedom* (Maryknoll: Orbis Books; ET of *Liberación y libertad*)
1987 *Biblical Hermeneutics: Toward a Theory of Reading as the Production of Meaning* (Maryknoll: Orbis Books).
Croft, Steven J.L.
1987 *The Identity of the Individual in the Psalms* (JSOTSup, 44; Sheffield: JSOT Press).
Crüsemann, Frank
1978 *Der Widerstand gegen das Königtum* (WMANT, 49; Neukirchen-Vluyn: Neukirchenener Verlag).
1996 *The Torah: Theology and Social History of Old Testament Law* (Edinburgh: T&T Clark; ET of *Die Tora: Theologie und Sozialgeschichte des alttestamentlichen Gesetzes* [München: Chr. Kaiser, 1992]).
2003 'Israel, die Völker und die Armen: Grundfragen alttestamentlicher Hermeneutik am Beispiel des Zefanjabuches', in *Kanon und Sozialgeschichte: Beiträge zum Alten Testament* (Gütersloh: Chr. Kaiser): 146–53.
Dahood, Mitchell
1974 *Psalms. II. Psalms 51–100* (AB, 17; Garden City, NY: Doubleday, 3rd edn).
Davies, Eryl W.
1981 *Prophecy and Ethics: Isaiah and the Ethical Tradition of Israel* (JSOTSup, 16; Sheffield: JSOT Press).
Davies, G.I.
1991 *Ancient Hebrew Inscriptions: Corpus and Concordance* (Cambridge: Cambridge University Press).
Davies, Margaret
1995 'Work and Slavery in the New Testament: Impoverishments of Traditions', in Rogerson, Davies and Carroll R. 1995: 315–47.
Day, John
1992 *Psalms* (OTG; Sheffield: Sheffield Academic Press).
Day, John (ed.)
2004 *In Search of Pre-Exilic Israel* (JSOTSup, 406; London & New York: T&T Clark International).
Dearman, J. Andrew
1988 *Property Rights in the Eighth-Century Prophets: The Conflict and its Background* (Atlanta, GA: Scholars Press).
Derrett, J. Duncan M.
1970 *Law in the New Testament* (London: Darton, Longman & Todd).
1972 ' "Take thy bond . . . and write fifty" (Lk xvi.6). The Nature of the Bond', *JTS* NS 23: 438–40.
Dhorme, Edouard
1967 *A Commentary on the Book of Job* (London: Nelson; ET of *Le Livre de Job* [Paris: Gabalda, 1926]).

Driver, Samuel Rolles
1902   *A Critical and Exegetical Commentary on Deuteronomy* (ICC; Edinburgh: T&T Clark).
Driver, Samuel Rolles, and Gray, George B.
1921   *A Critical and Exegetical Commentary on the Book of Job* (ICC; 2 vols.; Edinburgh: T&T Clark).
Dutcher-Walls, Patricia
1991   'The Social Location of the Deuteronomists: A Sociological Study of Factional Politics in Late Pre-Exilic Judah', *JSOT* 52: 77–94.
Dybdahl, J.L.
1981   'Israelite Village Land Tenure: Settlement to Exile' (Unpublished PhD. dissertation, Fuller Seminary).
Eagleton, Terry
1996   *Literary Theory: An Introduction* (Oxford: Blackwell, 2nd edn).
Eaton, John H.
1979   *Festal Drama in Deutero-Isaiah* (London: SPCK).
1986   *Kingship and the Psalms* (Sheffield: JSOT Press, 2nd edn).
Eichrodt, Walther
1961   *Theology of the Old Testament*, I (London: SCM Press; ET of *Theologie des Alten Testaments, Teil I* [Stuttgart: E. Klotz, 6th edn, 1959]).
Eisenstadt, S.N. and L. Roniger
1984   *Patrons, Clients and Friends: Interpersonal Relations and the Structure of Trust in Society* (Cambridge: Cambridge University Press).
Eitam, David
1979   'Olive Presses of the Israelite Period', *Tel Aviv* 4: 146–54.
Epsztein, Léon
1986   *Social Justice in the Ancient Near East and the People of the Bible* (London: SCM Press; ET of *La justice sociale dans le Proche-Orient ancien et le peuple de la Bible* [Paris: Les Editions du Cerf, 1983]).
Fager, Jeffrey A.
1993   *Land Tenure and the Biblical Jubilee: Uncovering Hebrew Ethics through the Sociology of Knowledge* (JSOTSup, 155; Sheffield: JSOT Press).
Fendler, Marlene
1973   'Zur Sozialkritik des Amos', *EvT* 33: 32–53.
Fewell, Danna Nolan and David M. Gunn
1993   *Gender, Power and Promise: The Subject of the Bible's First Story* (Nashville: Abingdon Press).
Finley, Moses I.
1973   *The Ancient Economy* (London: Chatto & Windus).
1977   'Die Schuldknechtschaft', in Kippenberg 1977: 173–204.
1986   'The Alienability of Land in Ancient Greece', in *The Use and Abuse of History* (London: The Hogarth Press): 153–60, 237–38.
Fleischer, Gunther
1989   *Von Menschenverkäufern, Baschankühen, und Rechtsverkehrern* (BBB, 74; Frankfurt: Athenäum).
Fohrer, Georg
1979   'Bemerkungen zum neueren Verständnis der Propheten', in P.H.A.

Neumann (ed.), *Das Prophetenverständnis in der deutschsprächigen For-schung seit Heinrich Ewald* (WdF, 307; Darmstadt: Wissenschaftliche Buchgesellschaft).

Fox, Michael V.
1996 'The Social Location of the Book of Proverbs', in Michael V. Fox *et al.* (eds.), *Texts, Temples and Traditions: A Tribute to Menahem Haran* (Winona Lake, IN: Eisenbrauns): 227–39.

Fox, Nili Sacher
2000 *In the Service of the King: Officialdom in Ancient Israel and Judah* (Mono-graphs of the Hebrew Union College, 23; Cincinatti: Hebrew Union Col-lege Press).

Frei, Peter
1996 'Zentralgewalt und Lokalautonomie im Achämenidenreich', in Peter Frei and Klaus Koch, *Reichsidee und Reichsorganisation im Perserreich* (OBO, 55; Fribourg: Universitätsverlag, 2nd edn): 8–131.
2001 'Persian Imperial Authorization: A Summary', in Watts 2001: 5–40.

Frick, Frank S.
1994 '*Cui Bono?*—History in the Service of Political Nationalism: The Deuteronomistic History as Political Propaganda', *Semeia* 66: 79–92.

Fried, Lisbeth S.
2001 ' "You Shall Appoint Judges": Ezra's Mission and the Rescript of Artaxerxes', in Watts 2001: 63–90.

Frymer-Kensky, Tikva
2001 'Israel', in R. Westbrook and R. Jasnow (eds.), *Security for Debt in Ancient Near Eastern Law* (Leiden: Brill): 251–64.

Gadamer, Hans-Georg
1989 *Truth and Method* (London: Sheed & Ward; New York: Continuum, 2nd edn; ET of *Wahrheit und Methode*; 5th German edn in *Gesammelte Werke*, I [Tübingen: Mohr, 1986])

Gamoran, Hillel
1971 'The Biblical Law against Loans on Interest', *JNES* 30: 127–34.

Gellner, Ernest and Waterbury, John (eds.)
1977 *Patrons and Clients in Mediterranean Societies* (London: Duckworth).

Gerstenberger, Erhard S.
1996 *Leviticus: A Commentary* (OTL; Louisville, KY: Westminster John Knox; ET of *Das dritte Buch Mose Leviticus* [ATD, 6; Göttingen: Vandenhoeck & Ruprecht, 1993]).

Gese, Hartmut
1981 'Komposition bei Amos', in J.A. Emerton (ed.), *Congress Volume, Vienna 1980* (SVT, 32; Leiden: Brill): 74–95.

Geus, Jan Kees de
1982 'Die Gesellschaftskritik der Propheten und die Archäologie', *ZDPV* 98: 50–57.

Gorgulho, Gilberto
1991 'Zefanja und die historische Bedeutung der Armen', *EvT* 51: 81–92.

Gorringe, Timothy J.
  1994   *Capital and the Kingdom: Theological Ethics and Economic Order* (London:
          SPCK/Maryknoll: Orbis Books).
Gottwald, Norman K.
  1980   *The Tribes of Yahweh* (London: SCM Press).
  1992   'Social Class and Ideology in Isaiah 40–55: An Eagletonian Reading',
          Semeia 59: 43–57.
  1993a 'A Hypothesis about Social Class in Monarchic Israel in the Light of
          Contemporary Studies of Social Class and Social Stratification', in
          The Hebrew Bible in its Social World and in ours (Atlanta, GA: Scholars):
          139–64.
  1993b 'Social Class as an Analytic and Hermeneutical Category in Biblical
          Studies', *JBL* 112: 3–22.
  1999   'The Expropriators and the Expropriated in Nehemiah 5', in Sneed 1999:
          1–19.
  2001   *The Politics of Ancient Israel* (Louisville, KY: Westminster John Knox).
Gottwald, Norman K. and Richard Horsley (eds.)
  1993   *The Bible and Liberation: Political and Social Hermeneutics* (Maryknoll,
          NY: Orbis Books and London: SPCK, rev. edn).
Grabbe, Lester L.
  2004   *A History of the Jews and Judaism in the Second Temple Period.* I. *Yehud: A
          History of the Persian Province of Judah* (London: T&T Clark
          International).
Grabbe, Lester L. (ed.)
  1997   *Can a 'History of Israel' Be Written?* (JSOTSup, 245; Sheffield: Sheffield
          Academic Press).
Gramsci, Antonio
  1975   *Quaderni del Carcere* (ed. V. Gerratana; 3 vols.; Turin: Einaudi).
Grant, Elizabeth, of Rothiemurchus
  1991   *The Highland Lady in Ireland: Journals 1840–1850* (ed. Patricia Pelly and
          Andrew Tod; Edinburgh: Canongate).
Greenberg, Moshe
  1983   *Ezekiel 1–20* (AB, 22; Garden City, NJ: Doubleday).
Gunkel, Hermann
  1926   *Die Psalmen übersetzt und erklärt* (Göttingen: Vandenhoeck & Ruprecht).
Gunkel, Hermann, and Joachim Begrich
  1933   *Einleitung in die Psalmen* (2 vols.; Göttingen: Vandenhoeck & Ruprecht).
Gutiérrez, Gustavo
  1987   *On Job: God-talk and the Suffering of the Innocent* (Maryknoll, NY: Orbis
          Books; ET of *Hablar de Dios desde il sufrimiento del inocente*, Lima:
          Centro de Estudios y Publicaciones y Instituto Bartolomé de las Casas,
          1986).
  1988   *A Theology of Liberation* (2nd edn; London: SCM Press; rev. ET of
          Teología de liberación, Lima: Centro de Estudios y Publicaciones, 1971).
Haag, Herbert
  1985   *Der Gottesknecht bei Deuterojesaja* (EdF, 233; Darmstadt: Wis-
          senschaftliche Buchgesellschaft).

Habel, Norman C.
1985   *The Book of Job: A Commentary* (OTL; London: SCM Press).
1995   *The Land Is Mine: Six Biblical Land Ideologies* (OBT; Minneapolis: Fortress).
Hamilton, Jeffries M.
1992   *Social Justice and Deuteronomy: The Case of Deuteronomy 15* (SBLDS, 136; Atlanta, GA: Scholars Press).
Hanson, Paul D.
1975   *The Dawn of Apocalyptic* (Philadelphia: Fortress Press).
Hartley, John E.
1992   *Leviticus* (WBC; Waco, TX: Word Books).
Hayes, John H.
1988   *Amos, the Eighth-Century Prophet: His Times and his Preaching* (Nashville: Abingdon).
Henrey, K.H.
1954   'Land Tenure in the Old Testament', *PEQ* 86: 5–15.
Hesiod
1988   *Theogony and Works and Days* (trans. with intro. and notes by M.L. West; Oxford and New York: Oxford University Press).
1990   *Theogonia, Opera et Dies, Scutum* (ed. F. Solmsen); *Fragmenta Selecta* (ed. R. Merkelbach and M.L. West; Oxford: Clarendon Press).
Hillers, Delbert R.
1984   *A Commentary on the Book of the Prophet Micah* (Hermeneia; Philadelphia: Fortress).
Hindess, Barry and Paul Q. Hirst
1975   *Precapitalist Modes of Production* (London: Routledge).
Hobbs, T.R.
1997   'Reflections on Honor, Shame, and Covenant Relations'. *JBL* 116: 501–03.
Holladay, J.S.
1995   'The Kingdoms of Israel and Judah: Political and Economic Centralization in the Iron IIA-B (Ca. 1000–750 BCE)', in T.E. Levy (ed.), *The Archaeology of Society in the Holy Land* (New York: Facts on File, 1995), 368–98.
Hopkins, David C.
1983   'The Dynamics of Agriculture in Monarchical Israel', in K.H. Richards (ed.), *Society of Biblical Literature 1983 Seminar Papers* (Chico, CA: Scholars Press): 177–202.
1985   *The Highlands of Canaan: Agricultural Life in the Early Iron Age* (SWBA, 3; Sheffield: Almond Press).
1996   'Bare Bones: Putting Flesh on the Economics of Ancient Israel', in V. Fritz and P.R. Davies (eds.), *The Origins of the Ancient Israelite States* (JSOT-Sup, 228, Sheffield: Sheffield Academic Press): 121–39.
Hopkins, Dwight N. and George C.L. Cummings (eds.)
2003   *Cut Loose your Stammering Tongue: Black Theology in the Slave Narratives* (2nd edn, Louisville: Westminster John Knox).
Hossfeld, Frank-Lothar, and Erich Zenger
2000   *Psalmen 51–100* (HKAT; Freiburg/Basel/Vienna: Herder).

Houston, Walter J.
 1987 ' "Today in your Very Hearing": Some Comments on the Christological Use of the Old Testament', in L.D. Hurst and N.T. Wright (eds.), *The Glory of Christ in the New Testament: Studies in Christology in Memory of George Bradford Caird* (Oxford: Clarendon Press): 37–47.
 1993a 'The Kingdom of God in Isaiah: Divine Power and Human Response', in R.S. Barbour (ed.), *The Kingdom of God and Human Society: Essays by Members of the Scripture, Theology and Society Group* (Edinburgh: T&T Clark): 28–41.
 1993b 'What Did the Prophets Think They Were Doing? Speech Act Theory and Prophetic Discourse in the Old Testament', *BibInt* 1: 167–88; reprinted in Robert P. Gordon (ed.), *'The Place Is Too Small for Us': The Israelite Prophets in Recent Scholarship* (Winona Lake: Eisenbrauns, 1995): 133–53.
 1995 ' "Open your Hand to your Needy Brother": Ideology and Moral Formation in Deut. 15: 1–18' in Rogerson, Davies and Carroll R. 1995: 296–314.
 1999 'The King's Preferential Option for the Poor: Rhetoric, Ideology and Ethics in Psalm 72', *BibInt* 7: 341–67.
 2001 'What's Just about the Jubilee?', *Studies in Christian Ethics* 14.1: 34–47.
 2003 'The Role of the Poor in Proverbs', in J.C. Exum and H.G.M. Williamson (eds.), *Reading from Right to Left: Essays on the Hebrew Bible in Honour of David J.A. Clines* (JSOTSup, 373; Sheffield: Sheffield Academic Press): 229–40.
 2004 'Was There a Social Crisis in the Eighth Century?', in Day 2004: 130–49.
Houten, Christiana van
 1991 *The Alien in Israelite Law* (JSOTSup, 107; Sheffield: Sheffield Academic Press).
Houtman, Cornelis
 1997 *Das Bundesbuch: Ein Kommentar* (Leiden: Brill).
 2000 *Exodus. III. Chapters 20–40* (HCOT; Leuven: Peeters; ET of *Exodus, III* [COT; Kampen: Kok, 1996]).
Hunter, A. Vanlier
 1982 *Seek the Lord! A Study of the Meaning and Function of the Exhortations in Amos, Hosea, Isaiah, Micah and Zephaniah* (Baltimore: St Mary's Seminary and University).
Jackson, Bernard S.
 1989 'Ideas of Law and Legal Administration: A Semiotic Approach', in R.E. Clements (ed.), *The World of Ancient Israel: Sociological, Anthropological and Political Perspectives* (Cambridge: Cambridge University Press): 185–202.
 1998 'Justice and Righteousness in the Bible: Rule of Law or Royal Paternalism?', *ZAR* 4: 218–262.
 2000 *Studies in the Semiotics of Biblical Law* (JSOTSup, 314; Sheffield: Sheffield Academic Press).
Jameson, Fredric
 1981 *The Political Unconscious: Narrative as a Socially Symbolic Act* (Ithaca, NY: Cornell University Press).
Jeremias, Jörg
 1971 'Die Deutung der Gerichtsworte Michas in der Exilszeit', *ZAW* 83: 330–54.
 1998 *The Book of Amos: A Commentary* (OTL; Louisville: Westminster-John

Knox; ET of *Der Prophet Amos* [ATD, 24/2; Göttingen: Vandenhoeck & Ruprecht, 1995])

Jobling, David
1992 'Deconstruction and the Political Analysis of Biblical Texts: A Jamesonian Reading of Psalm 72', *Semeia* 59: 95–127.

Jobling, David, Peggy L. Day, and Gerald T. Sheppard (eds.)
1991 *The Bible and the Politics of Exegesis* (Cleveland, OH: The Pilgrim Press).

Johnson, Aubrey R.
1967 *Sacral Kingship in Ancient Israel* (Cardiff: University of Wales Press).

Joosten, Jan
1996 *The People and Land in the Holiness Code: An Exegetical Study of the Ideational Framework of the Law in Leviticus 17* (SVT, 67; Leiden: Brill).

Kaiser, Otto
1983 *Isaiah 1–12: A Commentary* (OTL; London: SCM Press 2nd edn ET of *Das Buch des Propheten Jesaja, Kapitel 1–12* [ATD, 17; Göttingen: Vandenhoeck & Ruprecht, 5th edn 1981])

Käsemann, Ernst
1969 'Primitive Christian Apocalyptic', in *New Testament Questions of Today* (London: SCM Press).

Kaufman, Stephen A.
1984 'A Reconstruction of the Social Welfare Systems of Ancient Israel', in W. Boyd Barrick and John R. Spencer (eds.), *In the Shelter of Elyon: Essays on Ancient Palestinian Life and Literature in Honour of G.W. Ahlström* (JSOT-Sup, 31; Sheffield: JSOT Press): 277–86.

Kessler, Rainer
1989 'Die angeblichen Kornhändler von Amos VIII 4–7', *VT* 29: 13–22.
1992 *Staat und Gesellschaft im vorexilischen Juda vom 8. Jahrhundert bis zum Exil* (SVT, 47; Leiden: Brill).
1994 'Frühkapitalismus, Rentenkapitalismus, Tributarismus, antike Klassengesellschaft: Theorien zur Gesellschaft des alten Israel', *EvT* 54: 413–27.

Kippenberg, Hans G.
1977 'Die Typik antiker Entwicklung', in Kippenberg (ed.) 1977: 9–61.
1982 *Religion und Klassenbildung im antiken Judäa* (Göttingen: Vandenhoeck & Ruprecht, 2nd edn).
1983 'Die Entlassung aus Schuldknechtschaft in antiken Judäa: ein Legitimätsvorstellung von Verwandtschaftsgruppen', in *Vor Gott sind alle gleich: soziale Gleichheit, soziale Ungleichheit und die Religionen* (Düsseldorf: Patmos): 94–104.
1991 *Die vorderasiatischen Erlösungsreligionen in ihrem Zusammenhang mit der antiken Stadtherrschaft* (Frankfurt: Suhrkamp).

Kippenberg, Hans G. (ed.)
1977 *Seminar: Die Entstehung der antiken Klassengesellschaft* (Frankfurt: Suhrkamp).

Knierim, Rolf P.
1995 'Justice in Old Testament Theology', in 'The Interpretation of the Old Testament', in *The Task of Old Testament Theology* (Grand Rapids: Eerdmans): 86–122.

Knight, Douglas A.
1994	'Political Rights and Powers in Monarchic Israel', *Semeia* 66: 93–118.
2000	'Whose Agony? Whose Ecstasy? The Politics of Deuteronomic Law', in David Penchansky and Paul L. Redditt (eds.), *Shall Not the Judge of All the Earth Do Right? Studies on the Nature of God in Tribute to James L. Crenshaw* (Winona Lake, IN; Eisenbrauns): 97–112.

Knohl, Israel
1995	*The Sanctuary of Silence: The Priestly Torah and the Holiness School* (Minneapolis: Fortress).

Koole, Jan L.
Isaiah, III (HCOT; Kampen: Kok; ET of *Jesaja* [3 vols.; Kampen: Kok, 1985, 1990, 1995)
1997	I: *Isaiah 40–48*
1998	II: *Isaiah 49–55*
2001	III: *Isaiah 56–66*

Kovacs, Brian W.
1974	'Is There a Class-Ethic in Proverbs?', in J.L. Crenshaw and J.T. Willis (eds.), *Essays in Old Testament Ethics* (New York: Ktav): 173–89.

Krašovec, Jože
1988	*La Justice de Dieu* (OBO, 76; Fribourg: Editions Universitaires/Göttingen: Vandenhoeck & Ruprecht).

Kraus, H.-J.
1988	*Psalms 1–59* (Continental Commentary; Minneapolis: Fortress; ET of *Psalmen 1: Psalmen 1–59* [BKAT, XV/1; Neukirchen-Vluyn: Neukirchener Verlag, 1978]).
1993	*Psalms 60–150* (Continental Commentary; Minneapolis: Fortress; ET of *Psalmen 2: Psalmen 60–150* [BKAT, XV/2; Neukirchen-Vluyn: Neukirchener Verlag, 1978]).

Kuschke, Arnulf
1939	'Arm und reich im AT mit besonderer Berücksichtigung der nachexilischen Zeit', *ZAW* 57: 31–57.

Lang, Bernhard
1985	'The Social Organization of Peasant Poverty in Biblical Israel', in Lang (ed.), *Anthropological Approaches to the Old Testament* (London: SPCK): 83–99. Reprinted from Lang, *Monotheism and the Prophetic Minority* (SWBA, 1; Sheffield: Almond Press, 1983): 114–27.

Lasserre, Guy
1995	'Lutter contre la paupérisation et ses conséquences: Lecture rhétorique de Dt 15/12–18', *ETR* 70: 481–92.

Leclerc, Thomas L.
2001	*Yahweh Is Exalted in Justice: Solidarity and Conflict in Isaiah* (Minneapolis: Fortress Press).

Leeuwen, Cornelius van
1955	*Le développement du sens social en Israël avant l'ère chrétienne* (Studia Semitica Neerlandica 1; Assen: Van Gorcum).

Lefebvre, Jean-François
2003 *Le jubilé biblique: Lv 25—exégèse et théologie* (OBO, 194; Fribourg Suisse: Editions Universitaires/Göttingen: Vandenhoeck & Ruprecht).
Lemche, Niels Peter
1976 'The Manumission of Slaves—the Fallow Year—the Sabbatical Year—the Jobel Year', *VT* 26: 38–59.
1979 '*Andurārum* and *Mîšarum*', *JNES* 38: 11–22.
1985 *Early Israel: Anthropological and Historical Studies on the Israelite Society before the Monarchy* (SVT, 37; Leiden: Brill).
1994 'Kings and Clients: On Loyalty between the Ruler and the Ruled in Ancient "Israel" ', *Semeia* 66: 119–32.
1995 'Justice in Western Asia in Antiquity, or: Why No Laws Were Needed!', *Chicago-Kent Law Review* 70: 1695–1716.
1996 'From Patronage Society to Patronage Society', in V. Fritz and P.R. Davies (eds.), *The Origins of the Ancient Israelite States* (JSOTSup, 228; Sheffield: Sheffield Academic Press): 106–20.
1999 'The Relevance of Working with the Concept of Class in the Study of Israelite Society in the Iron Age', in Sneed 1999: 89–98.
Lenski, Gerhard E.
1966 *Power and Privilege: A Theory of Social Stratification* (New York: McGraw-Hill).
Levenson, Jon D.
1993 'Exodus and Liberation', in *The Hebrew Bible, the Old Testament and Historical Criticism: Jews and Christians in Biblical Studies* (Louisville: Westminster John Knox): 127–59.
Levin, Christoph
2003 'Das Deuteronomium und der Jahwist', in *Fortschreibungen: Gesammelte Studien zum Alten Testament* (BZAW, 316; Berlin: de Gruyter): 60–80.
Levine, Baruch A.
1989 *Leviticus* (JPS Torah Commentary; Philadelphia: Jewish Publication Society of America).
Levinson, Bernard M.
2004 'Is the Covenant Code an Exilic Composition? A Response to John Van Seters', in Day 2004: 272–325.
Loewenstamm, S.
1969 'Tarbit and Neshek', *JBL* 88: 78–80.
Lohfink, Norbert
1990a 'Das deuteronomische Gesetz in der Endgestalt—Entwurf einer Gesellschaft ohne marginale Gruppen', *BN* 51: 25–40.
1990b 'Die Sicherung der Wirksamkeit des Gotteswortes durch das Prinzip der Schriftlichkeit der Tora und durch das Prinzip der Gewaltenteilung nach den Ämtergesetzen des Buches Deuteronomium (Dt 16,18—18,22)', in *Studien zum Deuteronomium und zur deuteronomistischen Literatur* (Stuttgarter biblischer Aufsatzbände, 8; Stuttgart: Verlag Katholisches Bibelwerk): I. 305–23.

Lohfink, Norbert (ed.)
	1985	*Das Deuteronomium: Entstehung, Gestalt und Botschaft* (BETL, 68; Leuven: University Press and Peeters).
Longley, Clifford
	2002	*Chosen People: The Big Idea That Shaped England and America* (London: Hodder & Stoughton).
Loretz, Oswald
	1975	'Die prophetische Kritik des Rentenkapitalismus', *UF* 7: 271–78.
Loretz, Otto
	1984	*Habiru-Herbräer: Eine soziolinguistische Studie über die Herkunft des Gentiliciums ʿibrî vom Appellativum ḫabiru* (BZAW 160; Berlin: W. de Gruyter).
MacDonald, Nathan
	2003	*Deuteronomy and the Meaning of 'Monotheism'* (FAT, II/1; Göttingen: Mohr Siebeck).
MacIntyre, Alasdair
	1985	*After Virtue: A Study in Moral Theory* (London: Duckworth 2nd edn).
McCarter, P. Kyle, Jr
	1980	*I Samuel* (AB, 8; New York: Doubleday).
McConville, J.G.
	2002	*Deuteronomy* (Apollos Old Testament Commentary; Leicester: Apollos).
McKane, William
	1970	*Proverbs: A New Approach* (OTL; London: SCM Press).
	1998	*Micah: Introduction and Commentary* (Edinburgh: T&T Clark).
McNutt, Paula M.
	1999	*Reconstructing the Society of Ancient Israel* (London: SPCK/Louisville: Westminster John Knox).
Malchow, Bruce V.
	1996	*Social Justice in the Hebrew Bible: What Is New and What Is Old* (Collegeville, MN: The Liturgical Press).
Mannheim, Karl
	1936	*Ideology and Utopia* (London: Routledge; enlarged ET of *Ideologie und Utopie* [Bonn: F. Cohen, 1929]).
Marcus, Ralph
	1937	'The "Plain Meaning" of Isaiah 42.1–4', *HTR* 30: 249–59.
Martin-Achard, Robert
	1984	*Amos: L'homme, le message, l'influence* (Geneva: Labor et Fides).
Marx, Karl
	1973	*Grundrisse: Foundations of the Critique of Political Economy* (Rough Draft) (London: Allen Lane; ET of the below).
	1981	*Ökonomische Manuskripte 1857/58*, in K. Marx/F. Engels Gesamtausgabe, II/1–2 (Berlin: Dietz).
Mayes, Andrew D.H.
	1979	*Deuteronomy* (NCB; Grand Rapids: Eerdmans/London: Marshall, Morgan & Scott).
Mays, James L.
	1969	*Amos: A Commentary* (London: SCM Press).

Mein, Andrew
  2001   *Ezekiel and the Ethics of Exile* (Oxford: Oxford University Press).
Melotti, Umberto
  1977   *Marx and the Third World* (London: Macmillan).
Mesters, Carlos
  1989   *Defenseless Flower: A New Reading of the Bible* (Maryknoll: Orbis; ET of
         Flor sem Defesa: Uma Explicação da Bíblia a Partir de Povo [Petrópolis:
         Vozes, 1983]).
  1993   'The Use of the Bible in Christian Communities of the Common People',
         in Gottwald and Horsley 1993: 3–16.
Milgrom, Jacob
  1976   *Cult and Conscience: The Asham and the Priestly Doctrine of Repentance*
         (Leiden: Brill).
  1991   *Leviticus 1–16: A New Translation with Introduction and Commentary* (AB,
         3; New York: Doubleday).
  1996   'The Changing Concept of Holiness', in John F.A. Sawyer (ed.), *Reading
         Leviticus* (Sheffield: Sheffield Academic Press): 65–75.
  2000   *Leviticus 17–22: A New Translation with Introduction and Commentary*
         (AB, 3A; New York: Doubleday).
  2001   *Leviticus 23–27: A New Translation with Introduction and Commentary*
         (AB, 3B; New York: Doubleday).
Miller, Robert D.
  2005   *Chieftains of the Highland Clans: A History of Israel in the Twelfth and
         Eleventh Centuries B.C.* (Grand Rapids: Eerdmans).
Miranda, José Porfirio
  1977   *Marx and the Bible: A critique of the Philosophy of Oppression* (London:
         SCM Press; ET of *Marx y la biblia: Critica a la filosofia de la opresión*,
         Salamanca: Ediciones Sigueme: 1971).
Möller, Karl
  2001   'Words of (In-)evitable Certitude? Reflections on the Interpretation of
         Prophetic Oracles of Judgement', in C.G. Bartholomew, C. Greene, and K.
         Möller (eds.), *After Pentecost: Language and Biblical Interpretation* (Scrip-
         ture and Hermeneutics Series 2; Carlisle: Paternoster Press/Grand Rapids:
         Eerdmans): 352–86.
  2003   *A Prophet in Debate: The Rhetoric of Persuasion in the Book of Amos*
         (JSOTSup, 372; London: Sheffield Academic Press).
Morgenstern, Julian
  1962   'The Book of the Covenant (Concluded)', *HUCA* 33: 59–105.
Morrow, William S.
  1995   *Scribing the Center: Organization and Redaction in Deuteronomy 14:1–
         17:13* (SBLMS, 49; Atlanta, GA: Scholars Press).
Mosala, Itumeleng J.
  1989   *Biblical Hemeneutics and Black Theology in South Africa* (Grand Rapids:
         Eerdmans).
Mouffe, Chantal
  1979   'Hegemony and Ideology in Gramsci', in Mouffe (ed.), *Gramsci and Marx-
         ist Theory* (London: Routledge): 168–204.

Mowinckel, Sigmund
   1962   *The Psalms in Israel's Worship* (Oxford: Blackwell; ET of *Offersang og Sangoffer*, Oslo: Aschehoug, 1951).
Nakanose, Shigeyuki
   1993   *Josiah's Passover: Sociology and the Liberating Bible* (Maryknoll, NY: Orbis Books).
Nardoni, Enrique
   2004   *Rise Up, O Judge: A Study of Justice in the Biblical World* (Peabody, MA: Henderson; ET of *Los que buscan la justicia: un studio de la justicia en el mundo bíblico* [Estella, Spain: Editorial Verbo Divino, 1997]).
Nelson, Richard D.
   2002   *Deuteronomy: A Commentary* (OTL; Louisville: Westminster John Knox).
Neufeld, Ernest
   1955   'The Prohibitions againt Loans at Interest in Ancient Hebrew Laws', *HUCA* 26: 355–412.
   1958   'Socio-Economic Background of Yobel and *Šᵉmitta*', *RSO* 33: 53–124.
Newbigin, Lesslie
   1986   *Foolishness to the Greeks* (London: SPCK).
Newsom, Carol A.
   2003   *The Book of Job: A Contest of Moral Imaginations* (New York: Oxford University Press).
Niehr, Herbert
   1986   *Herrschen und Richten: Die Wurzel špṭ im Alten Orient und im Alten Testament* (FzB, 54; Würzburg: Echter Verlag).
North, Christopher R.
   1956   *The Suffering Servant in Deutero-Isaiah* (Oxford: Clarendon Press, 2nd edn).
   1964   *The Second Isaiah: Introduction, Translation and Commentary to Chapters XL-LV* (Oxford: Clarendon Press).
Oded, Bustenai
   1977   'Judah and the Exile', in J.H. Hayes and J.M. Miller (eds.), *Israelite and Judaean History* (London: SCM Press): 435–88.
O'Donovan, Oliver and Joan Lockwood O'Donovan (eds.)
   1999   *From Irenaeus to Grotius: A Sourcebook in Christian Political Thought 100–1625* (Grand Rapids: Eerdmans).
Oosthuizen, Martin J.
   1997   'Deuteronomy 15:1–18 in Socio-Rhetorical Perspective', *ZAR* 3: 64–91.
Osgood, S.J.
   1992   'Early Israelite Society and the Place of the Poor and Needy: Background to the Message of the Eighth-Century Prophets' (unpublished Ph.D. thesis, University of Manchester).
Otto, Eckart
   1994   *Theologische Ethik des Alten Testaments* (Theologische Wissenschaft 3.2; Stuttgart: Kohlhammer).
Paul, Shalom M.
   1991   *Amos: A Commentary on the Book of Amos* (Hermeneia; Minneapolis: Fortress Press).

Perlitt, Lothar
    1980   'Ein einzig Volk von Brüdern', in D. Lührmann and G. Strecker (eds.), *Kirche: Festschrift für Günther Bornkamm zum 75 Geburtstag* (Tübingen: J.C.B. Mohr): 27–52.
    1994   'Die Staatsgedanke im Deuteronomium', in S.E. Balentine and J. Barton (eds.), *Language, Theology and the Bible: Essays in Honour of James Barr* (Oxford: Clarendon Press): 182–98.

Philo of Alexandria
    1937   *Philo with an English translation* by F.H. Colson, vol. VII: On the Decalogue and On the Special Laws, books I–III (LCL; London: Heinemann and Cambridge, MA: Harvard University Press, 12 vols., 1929–62).

Pleins, David J.
    1987   'Poverty in the Social World of the Wise', *JSOT* 37: 61–78.
    2001   *The Social Visions of the Hebrew Bible* (Louisville: Westminster John Knox).

Polan Gregory J.
    1986   *In the Ways of Justice toward Salvation: A Rhetorical Analysis of Isaiah 56–59* (New York/Bern/Fribourg: Lang).

Polley, Max E.
    1989   *Amos and the Davidic Empire* (New York: Oxford University Press).

Pons, Jacques
    1981   *L'oppression dans l'Ancien Testament* (Paris: Letouzey et Ané).

Premnath, D.N.
    1988   'Latifundialization and Isaiah 5.8–10', *JSOT* 40: 49–60.

Prior, Michael
    1997   *The Bible and Colonialism: A Moral Critique* (Biblical Seminar, 48; Sheffield: Sheffield Academic Press).

Rawls, John
    2001   *Justice as Fairness: A Restatement* (ed. Erin Kelly; Cambridge, MA: Belknap Press of Harvard University Press).

Redford, Donald B.
    2001   'The So-Called "Codification" of Egyptian Law under Darius I', in Watts 2001: 135–60.

Reimer, Haroldo
    1992   *Richtet auf das Recht! Studien zur Botschaft des Amos* (SB, 149; Stuttgart: Verlag Katholisches Bibelwerk).

Rendtorff, Rolf
    1993   'Isaiah 56:1 as a Key to the Formation of the Book of Isaiah', in *Canon and Theology* (Minneapolis: Fortress Press): 181–89.

Richardson, M.E.J.
    2000   *Hammurabi's Laws: Text, Translation and Glossary* (Biblical Seminar, 73; Sheffield: Sheffield Academic Press).

Rodd, Cyril S.
    2001   *Glimpses of a Strange Land: Studies in Old Testament Ethics* (Old Testament Studies; Edinburgh: T&T Clark).

Rogerson, John W.
    1986   'Was Early Israel a Segmentary Society?', *JSOT* 36: 17–26.

Rogerson, John W., Margaret Davies and M. Daniel Carroll R. (eds.)
1995 *The Bible in Ethics* (JSOTSup, 207; Sheffield: Sheffield Academic Press).

Rowland, Christopher, and Mark Corner
1990 *Liberating Exegesis* (London: SPCK).

Rudolph, Wilhelm
1971 *Joel-Amos-Obadja-Jona* (KAT, 13.2; Gütersloh: Gütersloher Verlagshaus [Gerd Mohn]).

Schmid, Hans Heinrich
1968 *Gerechtigkeit als Weltordnung: Hintergrund und Geschichte des alttestamentlichen Gerechtigkeitsbegriffes* (BHT, 40; Tübingen: Mohr Siebeck).
1973 'Schöpfung, Gerechtigkeit und Heil. "Schöpfungstheologie" als Gesamthorizont biblischer Theologie', *ZThK* 70: 1–19. Reprinted in Schmid, *Altorientalische Welt in der alttestamentlichen Theologie* (Zürich: Theologischer Verlag, 1974): 9–30.

Schwantes, Milton
1977 *Das Recht der Armen* (Beiträge zur biblischen Exegese und Theologie, 4; Frankfurt: Peter Lang).

Schwienhorst-Schönberger, Ludger
1990 *Das Bundesbuch (Ex 20, 22–23, 33)* (BZAW 188: Berlin: W. de Gruyter).

Scott, James C.
1985 *Weapons of the Weak: Everyday Forms of Peasant Resistance* (New Haven, CT: Yale University Press).

Seenan, Gerard
2003 'Pity the Poor, Struggling Middle Classes: They've Got a Bad Case of Luxury Fever', *The Guardian*, 6 September: 3.

Seitz, Christopher R.
1989 *Theology in Conflict: Reactions to the Exile in the Book of Jeremiah* (BZAW, 176; Berlin: de Gruyter).
1991 *Zion's Final Destiny: The Development of the Book of Isaiah: A Reassessment of Isaiah 36–39* (Minneapolis: Fortress Press).

Seitz, Gottfried
1971 *Redaktionsgeschichtliche Studien zum Deuteronomium* (BWANT, 5.13; Stuttgart: Kohlhammer).

Sicre, José L.
1984 *'Con los pobres de la tierra': La justicia social en los profetas de Israel* (Madrid: Ediciones Cristiandad).

Silver, Morris
1983 *Prophets and Markets: The Political Economy of Ancient Israel* (Boston: Kluwer-Nijhoff).

Simkins, Ronald A.
1999 'Patronage and the Political Economy of Monarchic Israel', *Semeia* 87: 123–44.

Smith, Morton
1987 *Palestinian Parties and Politics that Shaped the Old Testament* (London: SCM Press, 2nd edn).

Sneed, Mark R.
1996 'The Class Culture of Proverbs: Eliminating Stereotypes', *SJOT* 10: 296–308.
Sneed, Mark R. (ed.)
1999 *Concepts of Class in Ancient Israel* (South Florida Studies in the History of Judaism, 201; Atlanta, GA: Scholars Press).
Soggin, J. Alberto
1987 *The Prophet Amos* (London: SCM Press; ET of *Il Profeta Amos. Traduzione e commento* [Brescia: Paideia, 1982]).
Soss, N.M.
1973 'Old Testament Law and Economic Society', *Journal of the History of Ideas* 34: 323–44.
Speiser, E.A.
1960 *Genesis* (AB 1; Garden City, NY: Doubleday).
Steinberg, Naomi
1991 'The Deuteronomic Law Code and the Politics of State Centralization', in Jobling, Day and Sheppard 1991: 161–70.
Stiglitz, Joseph E.
2002 *Globalization and its Discontents* (London: Penguin Books, 2nd edn).
Stulman, Louis
1998 *Order amid Chaos: Jeremiah as Symbolic Tapestry* (Biblical Seminar, 57; Sheffield: Sheffield Academic Press).
Sweeney, Marvin
1988 *Isaiah 1–4 and the Post-Exilic Understanding of the Isaianic Tradition* (Berlin: de Gruyter).
1995 'Formation and Form in the Prophetic Literature', in J.L. Mays, D.L. Petersen and K.H. Richards (eds.), *Old Testament Interpretation: Past, Present and Future. Essays in Honour of Gene M. Tucker* (Edinburgh: T&T Clark).
2003 *Zephaniah: A Commentary* (Hermeneia; Minneapolis: Fortress Press).
Tawney, R.H.
1964 *Equality* (With a new introduction by Richard M. Titmuss; London: Allen & Unwin).
Thiselton, A.C.
1974 'The Supposed Power of Words in the Biblical Writings', *JTS* NS 25: 283–99.
Thompson, E.P.
1968 *The Making of the English Working Class* (Harmondsworth: Penguin).
Tomes, Roger
2005 *I Have Written to the King, my Lord: Secular Analogies for the Psalms* (Hebrew Bible Monographs, 1; Sheffield: Sheffield Phoenix Press).
Ure, Andrew
1835 *The Philosophy of Manufactures, or an Exposition of the Scientific, Moral and Commercial Economy of the Factory System of Great Britain* (London).
Van Seters, John
2003 *A Law Book for the Diaspora: Revision in the Study of the Covenant Code* (Oxford: Oxford University Press).

Vaux, Roland de
  1955 'Les fouilles de Tell el-Fârah près Naplouse – Cinquième campagne', *RB* 62: 541–89.
  1961 *Ancient Israel: Its Life and Institutions* (London: Darton, Longman & Todd; ET of *Les Institutions de l'Ancien Testament* [Paris: Les Editions du Cerf, 1958]).
Veblen, Thorstein
  1925 *The Theory of the Leisure Class: An Economic Study of Institutions* (London: Allen & Unwin).
Veijola, Timo
  2004 *Das fünfte Buch Mose Deuteronomium, Kapitel 1, 1–16, 17* (ATD, 8.1; Göttingen: Vandenhoeck & Ruprecht).
Walzer, Michael
  1987 *Interpretation and Social Criticism* (Cambridge, MA: Harvard University Press).
Watson, Francis
  1994 *Text, Church and World: Biblical Interpretation in Theological Perspective* (Edinburgh: T&T Clark).
Watts, James W.
  1999 *Reading Law: The Rhetorical Shaping of the Pentateuch* (The Biblical Seminar, 59; Sheffield: Sheffield Academic Press).
Watts, James W. (ed.)
  2001 *Persia and Torah: The Theory of Imperial Authorization of the Pentateuch* (SBL Symposium Series, 17; Atlanta, GA: Society of Biblical Literature).
Weber, Max
  1952 *Ancient Judaism* (Glencoe, IL: The Free Press; ET of *Das antike Judentum*, Tübingen, 1921).
Weigl, M.
  1994 *Zefanja und das 'Israel der Armen'* (Österreichische Biblische Studien, 13; Klosterneuburg: Verlag Österreichisches Katholisches Bibelwerk).
Weil, H.M.
  1938 'Gage et Cautionnement dans la Bible', *AHDO* 2: 171–241.
Weinberg, Joel P.
  1992 *The Citizen-Temple Community* (JSOTSup, 151; Sheffield: JSOT Press).
Weinfeld, Moshe
  1972 *Deuteronomy and the Deuteronomic School* (Oxford: Clarendon Press).
  1991 *Deuteronomy 1–11* (AB, 5; New York: Doubleday).
  1995 *Social Justice in Ancient Israel and in the Ancient Near East* (Jerusalem: The Magnes Press/Minneapolis: Fortress Press).
Westbrook, Raymond
  1991 'The Price Factor in the Redemption of Land', in *Property and the Family in Biblical Law* (JSOTSup, 113; Sheffield: Sheffield Academic Press): 90–117.
Westermann, Claus
  1967 *Basic Forms of Prophetic Speech* (Philadelphia: Westminster Press; ET of *Grundformen prophetischer Rede* [München: Kaiser, 1960]).
  1969 *Isaiah 40–66: A Commentary* (OTL; London: SCM Press; ET of *Das Buch Jesaia, 40–66* [ATD, 19; Göttingen: Vandenhoeck & Ruprecht, 1966]).

Whybray, R.N.
　1975　*Isaiah 40–66* (NCB; Grand Rapids: Eerdmans).
　1990　*Wealth and Poverty in the Book of Proverbs* (JSOTSup, 99; Sheffield: Sheffield Academic Press).
Wildberger, Hans
　1991　*Isaiah 1–12: A Commentary*. (Minneapolis, MN: Augsburg Press; ET of *Jesaja, Kapitel 1–12* [BKAT, XI, 1; Neukirchen-Vluyn: Neukirchener Verlag, 2nd edn, 1980]).
Williamson, H.G.M.
　1985　*Ezra, Nehemiah* (WBC, 16; Waco, TX: Word Books).
　1995　'Isaiah and the Wise', in J. Day (ed.), *Wisdom in Ancient Israel: Essays in Honour of J. A. Emerton* (Cambridge: University Press).
Wisser, Laurent
　1982　*Jérémie, Critique de la vie sociale: justice sociale et connaissance de Dieu dans le livre de Jérémie* (Geneva: Labor et Fides).
Wolde, Ellen van
　2002　'Does *'innâ* Denote Rape? A Semantic Analysis of a Controversial Word', *VT* 52: 528–44.
Wolf, Eric R.
　1966　*Peasants* (Englewood Cliffs, NJ: Prentice-Hall).
Wolff, Hans Walter
　1977　*Joel and Amos* (Hermeneia; Philadelphia: Fortress Press; ET of *Dodekapropheton 2 Joel und Amos* [BKAT, XIV/2; Neukirchen-Vluyn: Neukirchener Verlag, 2nd edn 1975]).
　1990　*Micah: A Commentary* (Minneapolis: Augsburg Press; ET of *Dodekapropheton 4 Micha* [BKAT, XIV/4; Neukirchen-Vluyn: Neukirchener Verlag, 1982]).
Woodhouse, W.J.
　1938　*Solon the Liberator: A Study of the Agrarian Problem in Attika in the Seventh Century* (London: Oxford University Press).
Wright, Christopher J.H.
　1984　'What Happened Every Seven Years in Israel? Old Testament Sabbatical Institutions for Debt, Land and Slaves', *EvQ* 56: 387–403.
　1990　*God's People in God's Land: Family, Land and Property in the Old Testament* (Grand Rapids: Eerdmans/Exeter: Paternoster).
　2004　*Old Testament Ethics for the People of God* (Leicester: IVP).
Würthwein, Ernst
　1950　'Amos-Studien', *ZAW* 62: 10–52.
Yamauchi, Edwin M.
　1980　'Two Reformers Compared: Solon of Athens and Nehemiah of Jerusalem', in Gary Rendsburg *et al.* (eds.): *The Bible World: Essays in Honour of Cyrus H. Gordon* (New York: Ktav): 269–92.
Yetman, Norman R.
　1970　*Life under the 'Peculiar Institution': Selections from the Slave Narrative Collection* (New York: Holt, Rinehart & Winston).
Zimmerli, Walther
　1970　'Das Gnadenjahr des Herrn', in Arnulf Kuschke and Ernst Kutsch (eds.),

Archäologie und Altes Testament: Festschrift für Kurt Galling (Tübingen: Mohr Siebeck): 321–32.

1979 *Ezekiel: A Commentary on the Book of the Prophet Ezekiel* (Hermeneia; Philadelphia: Fortress Press; ET of *Ezechiel* [BKAT, XIII; Neukirchen-Vluyn: Neukirchener Verlag, 1969]).

Zwickel, W.

1994 'Wirtschaftliche Grundlagen in Zentraljuda gegen Ende des 8. Jh.s aus archäologischer Sicht', *UF* 26: 557–92.

INDEX OF REFERENCES

The order of biblical references and the numbering of verses are those of the Protestant English Bible.

Genesis
1.29–30 155
4.10 216
9.1–7 216
18.18–19 209
18.18–19 95
18.20 216
18.23–33 208 n. 21
19.25 208 n. 21
38.17–18 111
40.14 214 n. 38
47.13–26 17

Exodus
2.23–25 216–17
2.24 206 n. 13
3 113
3.6 206
3.7–9 202, 206, 207 n. 14, 216
3.8 207
3.9 109 n. 37
3.10–15 207 n. 14
3.10 207
3.13 207
3.15 207
3.16 207
3.17 207
4.22–3 207
5 9
6.2–8 202, 206 n. 10
11.5 207
12.48 108
20.22–23.33 105–7

20.22 106
21.1–22.20 106–7
21.1–22.17 70
21.2–22.17 170
21.1–11 29, 31, 70, 107, 186 n. 80, 197
21.2–6 104, 186
21.2 91
21.5 91
21.18–22.17 107
21.20–21 107
21.26–27 107
21.35 107
22–23 66 n. 65
22 125
22.18–23.19 70
22.21–23.12 **105–17**
22.21–23.13a 107–17
22.21–23.9 170
22.21–24 108–9
22.21–27 **107–14**, 129
22.21 106–9, 113, 216
22.22–23 109
22.23–24 70, 112–14, 124, 184
22.23 112–13
22.24 112–13, 133
22.25–27 108–14
22.25–26 109
22.25 31, 115
22.26–7 70, 104
22.26 112
22.27 70, 111–14, 124, 170, 184

22.28–31 107
22.28–30 70
22.31 70
23.1–8 **114–15**, 116–17, 216
23.1–3 108
23.3 114–15
23.4–5 108
23.6 115
23.6–8 108
23.7–8 114
23.7 115
23.8 115
23.9–12 108
23.9 107–9, 113, 216
23.10–12 **115–17**
23.10–11 116–17
23.12 117
23.13a 108
23.15 106
23.20–33 106, 207
23.24 209
23.33 209
24.3–8 169
30.11–16 171

Leviticus
6.2 68 n. 76
17–26 190–1
18–19 105
19.9–10 42, 116
19.15 102, 114, 216
19.33–34 113
19.33 108

19.35–36 69
19.35 102
25 26, 32, 102, 131, 165,
   187, 193, 227, 229
25.2–22 191–2
25.2–7 116, 117 n. 67
25.2 195, 197
25.6–7 116
25.8–55 **189–202**
25.8–34 24
25.8–13 31, 168
25.8–10 189
25.10 145, 198, 200
25.14–17 31
25.14 108, 194–5, 197
25.15–16 195
25.17 108, 193–4
25.23–55 189, 191–2, 195
25.23–4 192
25.23 31, 107, 116, 194 n.
   107, 195, 200–2
25.24–34 29
25.24–25 20, 38
25.25 182, 194–6, 214
25.28 196
25.35–43 44
25.35–8 44–5, 196
25.35 44, 110, 184, 195,
   201
25.36–7 31, 197
25.36 193
25.37 103, 109
25.39 110
25.39 195
25.39 197
25.39–43 196
25.39–46 145
25.39–55 197
25.39–47 45
25.39–43 31, 44
25.39 44
25.40 45, 196
25.41 196–7
25.42 200
25.43 45
25.44–46 216
25.46 196
25.47–9 214

25.47 195–6
25.49 214
25.54 196
25.55 200
26 170
26.14 169
26.34 198

Deuteronomy
Deuteronomy **173–89**,
   228
4.25–31 174
5.2–22 169
5.14 117
5.15 178
7 207, 209
7.1–6 210
7.4 209
7.6 209
7.16 209
7.25–26 209
8.17 174
9.1–6 208
9.3 208
9.4 208
9.5 208
10.12–11.1 210
10.14–19 217
10.14 217
10.16 217
10.17–18 216
10.18 189
10.19 113
12 176
12.29–30 209
13.6–11 182
13.12–18 174
14.22–29 **178–9**
14.23–27 176
14.28–29 168
14.29 178
15 102
15.1–18 44
15.1–11 44, 131, **179–85**
15.1–3 168
15.1–2 185
15.1 179 n.52, 180 n. 55
15.2–3 31

15.2 32, 179–81, 187
15.3 181–2, 216
15.4–8 14
15.4–6 183–5
15.4 183–5
15.5 183–4
15.6 44
15.7–11 44, 110, 123,
   175, **181–6**
15.7 181
15.9 180–1, 184
15.10 44, 125, 178,
   183–4, 189
15.11 115, 174, 181,
   183–5, 196
15.12–18 29, 31, 44, 87,
   104, 145, 179–80,
   185–7, 197
15.12–13 91
15.12 84, 179 n. 52,
   180–1, 184, 186
15.13–15 32, 186
15.15 178, 219
15.17 181
15.18 44–5, 178
16.11 178
16.12 178
16.14 178
16.15 178
16.18–18.22 174
16.18–20 168, 216
16.19–20 115
17.8–20 168
17.8–13 176
17.14–20 134, 137
17.14 137
17.15 171, 181
17.16 136
17.20 137
19.6 214
21.15–17 38
23.19–21 31
23.19–20 110, 178
23.20–21 181
23.20 109, 178
23.3–8 216
24.10–22 177–8
24.10–11 111

24.12–13 104
24.13 125
24.13 178
24.14 182
24.15 125, 178, 184
24.17a 115
24.17b 111
24.18 113, 178
24.19–22 116
24.19 125, 178
24.22 113, 178
24.6 111
25.13–15 69
24.14 68 n. 76
25.16 102 n. 9
26.12–15 178
26.13 178–9
26.14 179
26.16–19 169
28 170, 125
28.43 171
28.47–68 174
29.1 169
29.19–28 174
30 174
31.16–21 174
32.4 211

Joshua
Joshua 207
10.40 208
11.11 208
11.14 208
23.11–13 209

Judges
2.3 209
2.11–13 209
2.18 109 n. 37
3.5–7 209
4.3 109 n. 37
6.9 109 n. 37
10.12 109 n. 37

Ruth
1.2 26
1.22 42
2 123

2.2 43
2.8 214
2.10 43
3.10 43, 214 n. 38
3.12 214
4 38
4.3 42

1 Samuel
8 134, 136
8.11–18 136
8.14 164
10.1 157
10.6 157
10.18 109 n. 37
12.3 68 n. 76
16 26
16.13 157
17.12 26
22.2 110

2 Samuel
7.12–16 138
7.14–16 147
8.15 83 n. 84, 130, 145
23.1–2 157

1 Kings
2.26 83
15.12–15 83 n. 130
16.30 136
19.1–2 136
21 17, 19, 134, 136, 164
21.3 27
21.8 40
21.11 40
22.19–23 215
22.39 64

2 Kings
3.4 7 n. 28
4 39
4.1 29, 103, 110
4.13 40
7.1 20
7.16 20
8.3–6 144
12.1 38

13.4 109 n. 37
13.22 109 n. 37
16.5–9 42
21.24 38. 175
22.1 38
22.8–10 82
22.12 82
23 31
23.1–24 174
23.26 38
23.31 38
23.39 38
24.18 38

1 Chronicles
4.4 26

2 Chronicles
26.10 37

Nehemiah
5 13, 19, 78, 103–4, 110, 172
5.1–5 **29**
5.1 9
5.2–5 32, 87
5.2 29, 63, 185 n. 79
5.3 24, 29
5.4 33, 36
5.5 63, 185 n.79, 197
5.6–13 31–2
5.6 66
5.7 40
5.8 29, 45, 63
5.11 24
5.12 32
5.18 36
8 169
10 171
10.29 171
10.32–39 171
10.32–33 171
10.32 172

Job
Job **126–31**
1.14–15 223
9.13 205
20–24 126

20 125
20.5 127
20.10 127
20.15 127
20.19 127
20.23–25 127
21 127, 130
24 19
24.1–17 126–7, 130
24.1 222
24.7–12 87
24.12 222
29–31 **127–31**
29 22, 43, **127–9**
29.2–5 129
29.11 128
29.12–17 128
29.12 43, 128, 144, 215
29.13 128
29.14 128
29.15 128
29.16 43, 128, 130
29.17 128–9, 215
29.25 43, 128
30.1–14 129
30.1 129
30.3–8 87
30.5 129
31 **129–30**
31.13–23 128–9
31.13–15 129
31.14 130
31.15 133
31.16–23 130
31.16–20 130
31.18 130
31.19–20 130
31.21–23 130
31.23 130
31.38–40 129–30
31.39 130
32.10 102 n. 9
38–41 223

Psalms
Psalms 134, 211–13
2 138
2.2 138

2.6 138
2.7 137–8, 150, 158
2.10–11 219
9–10 **151–2**
9.1–4 151
9.3–6 151
9.5 151
9.12 151
9.13–15 151
9.16 151
9.17 151
9.18 151
10 216
10.2–13 151
10.2 151, 216
10.8 151
10.9 151
10.10 151
10.12 151
10.14 151
10.16 151
10.17 151
10.18 151
11.7 211
12.5 142
16.6 26
18 138, **150–1**
18.20–27 150
18.27 142, 150
18.28 217 n. 44
20 138
21 138
22.25 217 n. 45
25.16 217 n. 45
34.7 217 n. 45
35.10 142, 217 n. 45
40.17 142
40.18 217 n. 45
45 138, **150**
45.6–7 150
47 215 n. 40
49 120 n. 78
51 212
51.1 212
51.14 212
56.2–3 67
58.3 216
58.10 216

69.18 142
69.27–28 26
69.30 217 n. 45
70.5 142
70.6 217 n. 45
72 14, 44, 128, 134,
   138–49, 154–8, 160
72 (71 LXX) 153
72.1–11 140
72.1–4 140–1, 146, 215
72.1 139 n. 19, 216, 219
72.2 141
72.3 138, 140–1
72.5–17 140
72.5 141
72.6–7 138, 141
72.8–11 141, 219
72.8 141, 154 n. 66
72.12–17 140
72.12–14 139, 141,
   146–7, 215
72.12 43, 128, 135, 139,
   141, 144, 153
72.13 153
72.15 141
72.16 141–2
72.16–17 138
72.20 139
74.12–14 205, 216
74.19 217 n. 45
76.9 142
82 205–6, 215
82.2–3 216
82.2 102 n. 9
86.1 142, 217 n. 45
88.16 217 n. 45
89 138
89.3–4 138
89.9–10 205
89.18–38 147
89.25 219
89.27 219
89.28–37 138
93, 96–99 215 n. 40
94.3 216
94.6 216
96.10–13 219
96.10 205, 211

96.13 205, 211
98.6 205
98.7–9 219
98.9 205
98.9 211
101 138, **150**
101.1 150
101.2 150
101.7 150
101.8 150
103.4 142
103.17–18 212
106.42 109 n. 37
109.11 110
109.22 217 n. 45
110 138
110.3 137–8
113.7–9 219
116.15 142
132 138
132.11–12 138
140.13 217 n. 45
143.1 212
143.2 212
143.11–12 212
143.12 212
144 138
145.17 211

Proverbs
Proverbs 24, 99, **117–26**,
    129
1–9 118–9
6.1–5 123 n. 89
10–29 122
10.1–22.16 118
11.1 69
11.15 123 n. 89
11.26 120
13.23 120
14.20 120
14.21 43, 120, 123
14.31 120, 123, 125
15.16 68
15.25 122
16.11 69
16.19 119 n. 77
17.5 121, 123, 125, 133

17.17 43
17.18 123 n. 89
18.23 120
18.24 43
19.1 119 n. 77
19.4 120
19.17 12, 123–4
19.22 119 n. 77
20.16 123 n. 89
20.23 69
21.13 43, 121, 123–4
22.9 43, 123
22.17–24.22 119
22.2 120, 125, 129
22.7 102, 120
22.9 121, 123
22.16 68 n. 76, 121
22.22–23 121, 124
22.26–27 123 n. 89
23.10–11 121, 124
23.10 122–3
25–29 118
25.1 118
27.10 43
27.13 123 n. 89
28.3 120
28.6 119 n. 77
28.8 121, 123
28.11 120
28.27 43, 121, 123
29.7 121, 123–4
29.13 120, 125–6, 129
30–31 122
30.8–9 122 n. 88
30.14 120, 122 n. 88
31.1–9 144
31.1–8 128
31.8–9 144
31.8 128
31.9 122 n. 88
31.10–31 99
31.20 120–1, 123

Song of Songs
8.11–12 23

Isaiah
Isaiah **77–9**, 134, **161–3**

1–39 77, 79, 224
1 87–9
1.10–17 81 n. 124
1.15 88
1.21–6 74
1.23 78
1.26 161
1.27–28 224
3 87
3.1–7 79
3.13–15 74, 78
3.14–15 36
3.14 87, 90, 162
3.15 39, 87, 90
5 78, 87
5.1–7 74, 88, 94–5, 206
5.3 78
5.5 94
5.7 78, 94, 162, 216
5.8–10 29, 74, 78, 86
5.8 164
5.11–12 78
5.15–16 94
5.16 94
5.20 98
5.22 92
5.23 78, 92
6.1–8 215
9.2–7 77, 150, 153
9.6–7 154 n. 66
9.6 150
9.7 153, 161
10 87
10.1–4 63, 74, 78
10.1–3 35
10.1–2 91–2
10.2 87
11.1–9 77, 79, **153–7**,
    161–2, 225
11.1–5 154
11.2 154
11.3–4 215–6
11.3 154
11.4 154, 161
11.6–9 154–5, 162, 229
14.32 150
16.4b–5 153, 161
16.5 150

19.16 130
27.1 205
29.17–21 161, 166
29.18–21 161
29.19 161
29.20–21 161
29.21 92
30.12 68
32.1–8 153, **160–2**
32.1 161
32.2 162
32.5–8 162
32.7 92
32.15–20 161
32.16–17 161
32.17 163
32.19 163
33.15 91
36–37 78
40–66 210–3
40–55 76, 78, 156, 224
41.2 210
41.8 213
41.9 213
41.14 213
41.16 213
41.20 213
42.1–4 **156–7**
42.1 156–8
42.2 157
42.3 156
42.4 156
43.1 213
43.3–4 212–3
43.7 213
45.1 155–6
45.20–25 211
45.21 211
46.13 211
48.18 210
49–54 77
49.1–6 156
50.1 110
50.4–9 156
51.5 211
51.6 211
51.8 211
51.9 205

52.13–53.12 156
54.1–8 213
54.4 213
55.3 156
56–66 158
56 19
56.1 211, 224
58 79, 87, 90–1, 96, 102
58.1–12 74
58.3 87
58.6 87, 90
58.7 87
58.8 210
58.9b–12 96
59 79
59.1–2 224
59.3 89
59.15–20 96, 224
59.18 224
59.20 96, 224
60–62 77, 156
60.21 161
61 157–8
61.1–4 161
61.1–2 158
61.1 77, 145, 200
62.1 210
62.2 210
65.13–15 224
65.17–25 161, **162**
65.21–22a 162
65.21 162
65.23 162
65.25 162
65.25 162
66 77
66.3 89

Jeremiah
Jeremiah **80–4**
1–25 80
1–9 80
1.1 83
1.3 80
2.4–13 94
2.4–8 80
2.8 80
2.9–13 80

2.18–19 80
2.34 74, 81, 88
3.1–5 80
4.22 80
5.1–5 80
5.20–29 74
5.22 216
5.26 91
5.28 88, 92
6 202
6.7 90
6.12 30
6.13 91
7 89
7 95
7.1–15 81 n. 124
7.1–7 74, 88
7.3–11 84
7.3–7 84
7.6 87
7.8–11 81–2, 84
7.21–26 81 n. 124
8.7 80
8.10 91
9.1–9 80
9.3 80
9.6 80, 93
9.23 80
9.24 93
13 80
19 80
21.12 68, 154 n. 66
22.1–23.6 **134–5**
22.3 135, 144, 154
   n. 66
22.13–19 36, 74, 81, 87
22.13–17 135
22.13–16 202
22.13–15a 81 n. 120
22.13 137
22.15–16 81, 93, 135,
   144
22.15b–17 81 n. 120
22.16 154 n. 66, 155
22.17 88–9, 91
22.18 81 n. 120
23.1–4 136
23.5 136, 144

26–45 80
26.17 82
26.24 82
27–29 83
27.20 40
29.10–14 80
29.10 80
29.24–29 82
30–33 80, 84
30.20 109 n. 37
31.35–36 216
32 22
32. 6–12 38
32.7 20
32.9 20
33.15 84
34 87, 88, 95, 200
34.8–22 29, 31, 74, 91
34.8–11 145
34.8–9 83 n. 130, 145
34.12–22 84
34.14 84
34.16 84
34.17 84
34.19–20 84
34.19 39, 88
36 82–3
36.25 82
37.12 26
38.1 83
39 80
39.14 82
40.5 82
51 202
51.13 91
52 80

Ezekiel
Ezekiel **84–6, 163–6**
1–3 84
1 84, 215
1.1 85
5.13 202
7.23 90
8–11 84
9–11 84
11.14–16 85
16.49 208 n. 21

18 85, 95, **100–5**, 108,
  123, 125, 129
18.5–18 105
18.5–9 **100–5**
18.5b 101
18.6 101
18.7–8 101–4
18.7 123
18.9 101
18.10–13 100, 105
18.12 102 n. 12
18.14–17 100
18.16 104
20–23 85
22 68, 85, 87–9, 108
22.1–16 75, 85
22.1–13 95
22.5 68
22.6 88
22.7–12 85
22.7 87
22.13 91
22.23–31 39, 75, 85
22.25–29 167
22.25 85, 88–9
22.26 85
22.27 85, 88, 91
22.28 85
22.29 85, 87, 89–90, 101,
  164
25–32 84
28.18 102 n. 9
33.21 84
33.23–29 85
34 85, 87, 134, 136,
  163–4
34.1–31 75
34.1–6 86, 136
34.8–10 87
34.16 163
34.17 163
34.17–22 86, 136
34.20 163
34.22 87, 163
34.23 164
34.25–29 163
36.22 203
37.22 164

37.24 164
40–48 84–5, 161, **164–6**
43 84
44 85
44.10–14 85
44.15 85
44.28–31 164
44.28 164
44.29–30 164
45.1–12 164
45.1–8a 164
45.3–4 164
45.7–8a 164
45.8–9 86
45.8 108
45.8b 164
45.9 165
45.10–12 165
46.16–18 164–5
46.17 86, 165
46.18 86, 108, 165
47.1–12 164
47.13–48.35 164
47.13–48.29 164
47.22–23 165
48.21–22 164

Hosea
4.1–2 202
4.14 68
8.4 134
11.1–3 207

Joel
3.1–8 29
3.6 66

Amos
Amos 21–3, **53–5,**
  58–73
1.1–8 53
1.1 7 n. 28, 25
1.2 59
1.3–2.16 58
1.4–5 60
1.13–15 53
2.1–3 53
2.6–16 58, 61, 75

2.6–8 62, 64, 66, 69
2.6 23, 29, 45, 55, 61–2,
  65–7, 70, 91, 99
2.6a 53
2.7 61, 63, 66–8, 87, 92
2.8 23, 66, 70
2.9–12 53
2.9–11 95
2.9–10 94
2.14–15 60
3 64
3.1–8 53
3.1 55, 206
3.3–8 54
3.9–4.3 64
3.9–15 61, 75
3.9–12 53
3.9 35, 64, 68
3.10 66–7, 90
3.11 60
3.12 35, 64, 72
3.13–14 53
3.14–15 60
3.15 29, 64
4.1–3 53, 61, 75
4.1–2 92
4.1 35, 64, 66–8, 87
4.4–12 53
4.4–5 68
4.6–12 58
4.11 60
4.12 55, 58
5 64
5.3 60
5.4–6 53
5.5 60
5.7 61, 64
5.10–12 61, 64, 69, 75
5.10 69, 114
5.11–12 60
5.11 23, 35, 64, 66, 67 n.
  68, 69, 162
5.12 61–2, 64, 66–7, 69,
  92, 114
5.14–15 53
5.18 64
5.21–27 53
5.21–24 81 n. 124

5.24 61
6.1–6 92
6.1 35, 64
6.5 23
6.7 60
6.12–14 53
6.12 61, 92
6.13 64
6.14 60, 109 n. 37
7–9 58
7 53
7.1 36
7.8 55
7.9 55, 60, 134
7.10–17 54
7.11 60
7.14 7 n. 28, 25
7.17 60
8.1–3 53
8.2 55
8.4–7 61, 64, 69, 75
8.4–6 23
8.4 61 n. 36, 67
8.5 23
8.6 23, 66, 70, 91
8.8 53, 60
8.11–14 53
9.1 60
9.4 60
9.5–6 53, 60
9.7–15 54
9.7 205–6
9.8b-10 55
9.8 55, 59
9.10 60
9.11 59
9.13–15 72
9.14 162

Micah
Micah 23, **56–57,**
  75–6
1.1 13
1.2–7 75
1.5b-7 56
2.1–11 29, 75
2.1–5 29, 56, 86
2.1–2 75–6, 164,

2.2 68, 90–1
2.3–4 75
2.5 26, 75
2.6–7 56
2.8–9 76, 87
2.9 63, 87
2.10–11 56
2.10 75
3 87
3.1–7 56–7
3.1–4 75
3.1–3 35
3.1 57, 76
3.2–3 90
3.4 75
3.6–7 75
3.9–12 75
3.9 76
3.10 35, 76, 88–9
4 56
4.1–13 75
4.4 60, 76
5.1 56–7
5.4–6 56–7
6.1–8 56–7, 95
6.1–5 94
6.6–7 57
6.9–15 30
6.13–15 75
6.16 56, 75
7 56
7.1–10 75
7.1–7 56
7.9 76
7.18–20 75–6

Zephaniah
1.12–13 30
2.3 166
3.1–4 167
3.11–20 166
3.11–13 161,
  166–7
3.13 167
3.14–20 166

Zechariah
2.9 130

7.10 63
9.9–10 154 n. 66
13.8 38

Malachi
3.5 68 n. 76
3.8–10 172

Ecclesiasticus (Ben Sira)
38.24–34 25

Matthew
3.17 158

Mark
10.42–44 159

Luke
4.16–21 158
6.20–26 158
13.31–35 158–9
16.6–7 103 n. 16
18.7–8 158–9
22.24–29 159

John
18.36 225

Mishnah
Sheb. 10.3 181

Amenemope
25.12–13 119
26.13–14 119

Code of Hammurabi
117 104 n. 21

Aristotle
Constitution of Athens
5–6 30 n. 53
9 30 n. 53
12 28 n. 40, 30 n. 53

Rhetoric
I.2.3 65 n. 60, 141
  n. 27

Philo
de Spec. Leg. II.71–3 180
  n. 56

INDEX OF SEMITIC WORDS

Not all words are indexed, but only those that have some significance beyond a single verse. The order is that of the Hebrew alphabet.

'ebyôn 61–2, 115–16, 120–3, 128, 141–2, 151, 184
'āḥ 44, 181–5
'aḥuzzâ 196, 198
andurārum 145, 180

bêt'āb 26–9, 43, 46, 48, 63
beṣa' 91

g'l 72, 142
gō'ēl 38 n. 91, 142, 213–14
ge'ullâ 38
gzl 68, 90, 101, 121, 123, 135
gezēlâ 90, 101
gēr 46, 87, 108–9, 113, 122, 165, 182, 196–7, 201

dîn 92, 121
dāl 61, 114–15, 120–3, 127, 141, 154 n. 64, 166
derôr 145, 158, 165, 198, 200

zāqēn 78

ḥbl 66
ḥmd 91
ḥāmās 67–8, 90, 142, 165
ḥēn 43, 123
ḥnn 120–1
ḥesed 42–3, 212, 214
ḥōq 216
ḥōrîm 40

ynh 90, 101, 108, 164
yešû'â 210–2

yš' 72, 142

lḥṣ 108–9
lmlk 32

mehûmōt 68
maḥsōr 122
mkr 185
miṣwâ 107
maššā' 110–11
mišpāḥâ 26, 198
mišpāṭ 61, 92, 135–6, 139 n. 19, 150, 156, 163
mîšarum 32, 145, 180, 192, 202

nādîb 162
naḥalâ 91
nekōḥâ 69
nokrî 182
nṣl 72, 142
nś' pānîm 114, 218
nāśî 164
nš' 110–11
nōše 109–11
nešek 103, 121

sāgān 40

'ibrî 186
'āwel 102
'im 44–5, 110
'nh 109
'ānî / 'ānāw 61–2, 109–10, 120–3, 141–2, 150–1, 154 n. 64, 158, 166

ʿᵃšûqîm 68, 90
ʿāšîr 63, 120 nn. 78, 81, 122
ʿšq 68, 90, 101, 120–1, 123, 135
ʿōšeq 68, 88

prozbul 181, 187
pešaʿ 65

ṣaddîq 61–2, 66, 99, 101, 115, 121, 123–4,
    155
ṣedeq 101, 115, 128, 135, 150, 210–13
ṣᵉdāqâ 61, 78, 101, 128, 205, 208, 210–14,
    224
ṣeʿāqâ 206, 216

qāṣîn 76

rîb 129

rēaʿ 112, 137, 181
rṣṣ 87, 90, 127
rāš 120–1, 122
rāšāʿ 99, 124, 150–1,
    216
rešaʿ 150
rišʿâ 208

śār 78, 162

šōd 67–8, 90, 165
šālôm 163, 205
šmṭ 180
šᵉmiṭṭâ 145–6, 180

tôšāb 201
tarbît 103, 121
tᵉšûʿâ 211–12

Albertz, R. 83, 129, 173, 176, 177, 221
Alt, A. 27, 70, 106
Aristotle 28, 30, 65, 141
Ateek, N.S. 207
Auld, A.G. 59

Bach, R. 70
Baltzer, K. 210
Barton, J. 59, 60, 71, 79
Begrich, J. 138
Ben-Barak, Z. 27
Bendor, S. 26–9, 46, 62, 63, 65, 78, 183
Bennett, H.V. 116, 176
Beuken, W.A.M. 161, 163
Beveridge, W. 2
Bird, P. 62–3
Blenkinsopp, J. 50, 157, 160
Blum, E. 172
Bobek, H. 21
Boesak, A. 8, 10
Bottéro, J. 170
Broshi, M. 49
Broyles 138–41, 154, 158
Brueggemann, W. 126, 130, 147, 151–2, 203, 207
Buber, M. 54
Bultmann, C. 108

Calvin, J. 4, 147
Carney, T.F. 34
Carroll, R.M.D. 23, 55
Carroll, R.P. 53, 81, 82, 88, 137, 224
Carter, C.E. 24, 191
Chaney, M.L. 13, 33, 36–7, 78, 79, 146, 162
Chapman, M.D. 188

Charpin, D. 149
Chavel, S. 145
Childs, B.S. 58, 110, 115
Chirichigno, G.C. 104, 180, 185, 192
Christensen, T. 188
Claburn, W.E. 173, 176
Clark, G.R. 42, 212
Clines, D.J.A. 6, 126, 131, 169, 222–3
Coggins, R. 53
Collins, T. 53, 75
Cone, J. 8
Coote, R.B. 12, 22, 53–5, 59, 60, 72
Corner, M. 5
Craigie, P.C. 150, 151, 180, 181, 183
Croatto, J.S. 5, 10, 222
Croft, S.J.L. 138
Crüsemann, F. 106, 108, 136, 166, 168, 172, 173, 175, 176, 178, 183
Cummings, G.C.L. 220

Dahood, M. 139
Davies, E.W. 70
Davies, G.I. 7
Davies, M. 188
Davies, P.R. 134
Day, J. 138, 215
Dearman, J.A. 24, 35, 36
Derrett, J.D.M. 103
Dhorme, E. 130
Driver, S.R. 38, 130, 180, 183
Dutcher-Walls, P. 82, 176
Dybdahl, J.L. 26

Eagleton, T. 11
Eaton, J.H. 77, 137, 138, 151, 152, 156, 157

Eichrodt, W. 203
Eisenstadt, S.N. 21, 41–44, 214
Eitam, D. 30
Epsztein, L. 3

Fager, J.A. 190, 191, 194, 195, 198, 200, 201
Fendler, M. 64, 65
Fewell, D.N. 208
Finkelstein, I. 49
Finley, M.I. 28, 32, 37, 38
Fleischer, G. 20, 23, 28, 39, 61, 62, 64–8, 70, 119
Fohrer, G. 54
Fox, M.V. 118
Fox, N.S. 36
Freedman, D.N. 190
Frei, P. 171
Frick, F.S. 83, 144
Fried, L.S. 170, 190
Frymer-Kensky, T. 66

Gadamer, H-G. 6, 148
Gamoran, H. 103
Gellner, E. 41
Gerstenberger, E.S. 61, 154, 190
Gese, H. 59
Geus, J.K. de 23, 48
Gorgulho, G. 166
Gorringe, T.J. 7, 97, 98, 189, 225, 229
Gottwald, N.K. 5, 8, 9, 21, 32–5, 51, 219
Grabbe, L.L. 36, 169, 171, 172
Gramsci, A. 14
Grant, E. 110
Gray, G.B. 130
Greenberg, M. 102
Gunkel, H. 138
Gunn, D.M. 208
Gutiérrez, G. 5, 131, 203, 223

Haag, H. 156
Habel, N.C. 130, 131, 196, 198, 223
Hamilton, J.M. 44, 123, 184–5
Hamilton, C. 227
Hanson, P.D. 158
Hartley, J.E. 190
Hayek, F.A. 98

Hayes, J.H. 59
Henrey, K.H. 26
Hesiod 31
Hillers, D.R. 76
Hindess, B. 37
Hirst, P.Q. 37
Hobbs, T.R. 42
Holladay, J.S. 23, 29, 39, 47, 48
Hopkins, D.C. 19, 30, 36 37, 117
Hopkins, D.N. 220
Horsley, R. 5, 8
Houston, W.J. 1–3, 4, 10, 11, 14, 19, 23, 29, 32–3, 38–40, 54, 77, 119, 121, 126, 138, 140–1, 154, 158, 161, 179–80, 189, 192, 195
Houten, C. van 109
Houtman, C. 106, 107, 111, 114–15, 117
Hunter, A.V. 54, 58

Jackson, B.S. 107, 109, 144, 170
Jameson, F. 14, 146, 198
Jeremias, J. 55, 75
Jobling, D. 138, 142, 146, 150
John of Salisbury 148
Johnson, A.R. 138
Jonge, M. de 138
Joosten, J. 190, 191

Kaiser, O. 78
Käsemann, E. 225
Kaufman, S.A. 145
Kessler, R. 20, 25, 29–32, 39, 64, 135, 137
Kippenberg, H.G. 11, 12, 21, 24, 25–33, 35, 38, 42, 103, 172, 183, 185
Knierim, R.P. 203–5, 207, 208–10
Knight, D.A. 173, 176, 177
Knohl, I. 190
Koole, J.L. 156–7, 211
Kovacs, B.W. 124
Krašovec, J. 210–11
Kraus, H.-J. 138, 151
Kuschke, A. 121

Lang, B. 21–5
Lasserre, G. 178, 186
Leclerc, T.L. 78, 94, 224

Leeuwen, C. van 121
Lefebvre, J.-F. 38, 44, 45, 185, 190–8, 200–1
Lemche, N.P. 21, 28, 42, 145, 215
Lenski, G. 34–5, 38, 40, 49
Levenson, J.D. 100, 217
Levin, C. 181
Levine, B.A. 190, 198
Levinson, B.M. 106
Loewenstamm, S. 103
Lohfink, N. 173, 174, 183
Longley, C. 220
Loretz, O. 21, 25, 29, 186

MacDonald, N. 210, 217–18
MacIntyre, A. 132
McCarter, P.K. 136
McConville, J.G. 38, 173, 175, 180
McKane, W. 76, 120–1
McNutt, P.M. 26
Malchow, B. 3
Mannheim, K. 14, 155, 168, 191, 199
Marcus, R. 156–57
Marx, K. 5, 21, 25, 227, 229
Martin-Achard, R. 71–2
Maurice, F.D. 188
Mayes, A.D.H. 38, 179, 183, 217
Mays, J.L. 23, 61
Mein, A. 100
Melotti, U. 34–5
Mesters, C. 5
Meyer, E. 31
Milgrom, J. 44–5, 102–4, 111, 190–2, 196
Miller, R.D. 27
Miranda, J.P. 5, 6, 13, 61, 70, 94–5, 97, 101, 115, 113, 150, 203–4, 206–9, 216–17, 219, 224–5, 229
Möller, K. 54, 55, 58, 59, 65
Montgomery, J. 152
Morgenstern, J. 103
Morrow, W.S. 180, 183
Mosala, I.J. 5, 8–13, 15, 33, 56–7, 75–6, 96, 207
Mouffe, C. 14
Mowinckel, S. 215

Nakanose, S. 176
Nardoni, E. 3

Nelson, R.D. 38, 116, 173–4
Neufeld, E. 198
Newbigin, L. 226
Newsom, C. 124, 126, 127–9, 131
Niehr, R. 139
North, C.R. 156, 210

O'Donovan, J. 148
O'Donovan, O. 148
Oded, B. 39
Oosthuizen, M.J. 178, 179, 183
Osgood, S.J. 26
Otto, E. 112–14

Paul, S.M. 58, 61, 66–9, 73
Perlitt, L. 173–4, 176, 181–4
Philo 180
Plant, R. 13
Pleins, D.J. 3–4, 17, 56, 65, 77, 81, 84, 86, 97, 106, 118–19, 121–2, 126, 168
Polan, G.J. 224
Polley, M.E. 58, 59, 65
Ponet, J. 148
Pons, J. 67
Premnath, D.N. 29
Prior, M. 8, 208

Rashi 193
Rawls, J. 149
Redford, D.B. 171
Reimer, H. 55
Rendtorff, R. 78, 224
Richardson, M.E.J. 103–4
Rodd, C.S. 6, 96, 100–1, 103
Rogerson, J.W. 27
Roniger, L. 21, 41–4, 214
Rowland, C. 5
Rudolph, W. 55, 68

Schmid, H.H. 15, 205
Schwantes, M. 62, 122
Schwienhorst-Schönberger, L. 112
Scott, J.C. 9
Seenan, G. 227
Seitz, C.R. 39, 77, 78
Seitz, G. 179, 183
Sicre, J.L. 59, 65, 74
Silver, M. 20–1

Simkins, R.A. 21, 37, 41–2
Smith, M. 31
Sneed, M.R. 73, 118–19
Soggin, J.A. 62
Soss, N.M. 195
Speiser, E.A. 45
Steinberg, N. 177
Stiglitz, J. 2
Stulman, L. 80
Sweeney, M. 59, 167

Tawney, R.H. 2, 188
Thiselton, A.C. 154
Thompson, E.P. 220
Tomes, F.R. 215
Tutu, D. 8, 10

Ure, A. 220

Van Seters, J. 103, 106–7, 111, 113–15, 186
Vaux. R. de 23, 111
Veblen, T. 23
Veijola, T. 174, 179–81, 183

Walzer, M. 13–14, 187
Waterbury, J. 41
Watson, F. 16, 17

Watts, I. 152
Watts, J.W. 168–71
Weber, M. 108
Weigl, M. 166
Weil, H.M. 103, 110–11
Weinberg, J.P. 47
Weinfeld, M. 3, 32, 61, 82–3, 144–5, 173, 175, 180, 195, 217
Westbrook, R. 194
Westermann, C. 54, 87, 93, 118, 157, 210
Whybray, R.N. 87, 117–18
Wildberger, H. 29, 94, 154
Williamson, H.G.M. 50, 160
Wisser, L. 80, 81, 93
Wolde, E. van 109
Wolf, E.R. 22
Wolff, H.W. 53–4, 56–7, 59, 61, 64, 68–9, 76, 87
Woodhouse, W.J. 28, 30
Wright, C.J.H. 3, 180, 197
Würthwein, E. 70

Yamauchi, E.M. 32
Yetman, N.R. 220

Zenger, E. 139, 141
Zimmerli, W. 85, 101–2, 158
Zwickel, W. 36

Subject Index

Ahab 136
alien 108, 112–13, 165, 182, 196–7, 218
apocalyptic 224–5, 229
aristocrats 25–33, 118. *See also* ruling
    class
Asiatic mode of production *see*
    tributary mode of production
Athens 28, 30–1

bloodshed 85, 88–90
bribery 67, 115
brotherhood **181–9**, 228

Canaanites, annihilation of 8, 207–10
capitalism 1, 97–8, 226. *See also* rent
    capitalism
centralization 176–7
charity 118, 132, 200
    and justice 132
class 1, 7, 19–21, 56–7, 72–3, 96–7,
        117–22, 146–7, 162, 184, 187–9,
        197–8
    formation 47–8
    See also class society, ruling class
class society, ancient 25–33
command economy 36–7, 47
community 112, 117, 133, 176–7, 182–3,
        187–9, 230
corruption 78
corvée 89, 135
courts of law 69, 78, 92, 114–15, 130
covenant **169–71**, 206, 213–14, 217
Covenant, Book of **105–17**
    aim 106–8
    social context 106
credit *see* debt

David 139, 145, 164
    house of 59, 77–9, 143, 145, 152–7,
        161
    son of 225
    See also king
debt 22, 24, 28, 66, 102–4, 109–12, 123
    relief 13, 79
    remission 172–3, **179–85**, 202
    cancellation 30, 180–1
    security *see* pledges
    See also debt-bondage, usury
debt-bondage 22, 28, 31, 44–5, 48, 90–1,
        104, 110–11, 185–7
    release 185–7
decrees, royal 143–6, 180, 191–2
democracy 221–2, 227
dependency 22, 44, 110, 115, 117, 185–7
Deuteronomistic History 136, 144
Deuteronomists 82–3, 95
Deuteronomy
    authorship 175
    date 173–5
    social context 173–7

equality *and* inequality 2, 26–7, 47, 100,
        117, 133, 137, 165, 167, 188–9,
        196, 200, 202, 227
Exodus, the 94, 108, 133, 206, 219–20
exploitation 11–12, 22, 90–1, 110
extortion 90–1

faction **13**, 79, 83, 85, 146, 165, 167
family 26–8, 176–7, 179, 182–3, 188, 193,
        197, 200
fatherless, the 87, 108, 122, 128, 130
foreclosure 29, 37, 76. *See also* pledges

forgiveness 212
fraternity *see* brotherhood
freedom *see* liberty

Gedaliah 80, 82–3
gleaning 116–17, 178
God
  approves conduct 129
  as creator 216
  as patron 201, 213–14
  as king 215–17
  as landowner 200–2
  authority of 169–71
  blessing 178, 184, 186, 189
  justice of 16, 93–6, 130–1, 192,
    203–25, 229
    impartial 205–6, 215–17
    partial 206–14
  See also judgment, divine; knowledge
    of God
governing class *see* ruling class

hermeneutics 5–10
history 18–19
Holiness Code 101, **190–1**
  date 191
  social context 190
  values 190–1
honour 105, 114, 123–4, 127–9. *See also*
  shame

ideology 8–9, **12–16**, 53–4, 56–7, 73,
  143–7, 152, 167, 173, 175–7, 198,
  204, 218–21, 227–9
  royal 134–5, 137–8, 153
inequality *see* equality
interest *see* usury
Israel, kingdom of 19
  fall 59–60, 72–3

Jehoiachin 77
Jehoiakim 81, 89, 135, 145
Jerusalem 59, 76, 82, 84
  fall 81, 84
  See also Zion
Jesus Christ 158–9, 225, 230
Jezebel 136
Josiah 145, 175

jubilee 145, 158, 165, **189–202**, 227
Judah, kingdom of 19, 33–41, 79, 144–7,
  174–7
judgment, divine 53–6, 58–61, 80–1, 94,
  96, 105, 113, 130, 205. *See also*
  retribution

king 77–9, 83, 85, 94, 128–9, 130,
  134–59, 174, 215–17, 219
  criticism of 135–8
  as defender of the poor 135, **138–52**,
    154
  legitimacy 142, 147, 150, 152
knowledge of God 80–1, 93, 155, 162

land 21–2, **25–38**, 120–1, 130, 164–5,
  189–202
  expropriation 136, 164
  loss 22, 29–30, 48, 76, 86, 189–90,
    197
  market 20, 24, 189, 194
  redemption 142, 192
  redistribution 25–8
latifundia 29, 35, 47
law 69–71, 95, 170–1, **173–202**, 216
  apodictic 70–1, 106–7
  casuistic 106–7, 170, 191–2
  codification 171
laziness 24–5, 121
lending *see* debt
liberation theology 2, 4–5, 221–2. *See*
  also Croatto, Gutiérrez, *and*
  Miranda *in the Index of Authors*
liberty 90–1, 188, 200, 202, 227
loans *see* debt

marginalized, the 177, 179. *See also*
  aliens, fatherless, *and* widows
markets 20–21, 24, 47, 189, 194, 199,
  201, 228
Marxism 5, 8, 11–12, 33–4, 199, 221, 227
merchants 64
Messiah 152–9, 225, 230
métayage see sharecropping
mode of production 33–4
monarchy *see* king
money 24, 191
murder *see* bloodshed

Naboth 136, 199
neo-liberalism 2, 20–21, 98, 228
noblesse oblige 73, 78, 124, 127–8

officials 34, 40, 82, 92, 106
oppression 6–9, **61–71**, 81, 84, 85, 102,
    108–9
  acts of 65–9
  deliverance from 128, 141–6, 149,
    215–17
  victims of 55, 61–3, 86–7
oppressors (identity) 63–5, 87–8
  elimination of 154–5, 161
orphans *see* fatherless

Palestinians 207–8
patronage 22, **41–6**, 49, **99–133**, 178,
    185, 196, 200, 213–14, 215
peace 154–5, 162, 225
peasants 21–7, 34, 39–40, 46, 47–50, 55,
    60–1, 86, 143, 163, 165, 172–3,
    191, 199
'people of the land' 38–40, 85–6, 90,
    163–4, 167, 175–6
Persian Empire 19, 33, 50, 169–71
pledges 28–9, 31–2, 50, 103–4, 110–11,
    178
political theology 148
poor, the (identity) **61–3**, 86–7, 92,
    108–9, 120–3, 128–30, 141–2,
    166–7
  undeserving 129
power 104, 124, 132–3
  legitimacy 152
priests 83, 85, 88, 171–3, 175–6, 190–1,
    198
prophets **52–98**

redaction criticism 52–8
redistribution, economic 34–5, 41,
    46
rent 22–4, 28
rent capitalism 21–5
retribution 124–5, 126–7. *See also*
    judgment, divine
rhetoric 11, 58–61, 65, 71–3, 75–86,
    93–6, 139–42, 169–71, 181–5,
    192–4

righteousness 78, 100–5, 140–1
  as world order 205, 212
ruling class *or* governing class *or* upper
    class 21–2, 26–8, 40, 59–60, 64–5,
    73–4, 76, 78, 82, 87–8, 106,
    118–19, 166, 167, 172, 175–7

sabbath day 117
sabbath year 115–16, 198
salvation 210–13
Samaria 23, 36, 64, 68–9, 72
scribes 82, 106, 118
servant of YHWH 155–8
shame 105, 109. *See also* honour
Shaphan, house of 82–3
sharecropping 22
slavery 23, 129–30, 196–7. *See also*
    debt-bondage
slaves, African-American 219–20,
    223
social gospel 4
Sodom 208, n. 21
Solon 28, 30–1
specialization, agricultural 48
state *see* king
  exploitation by 33–40
stranger *see* alien

taxation 33, 35–8, 40, 48, 66,
    164
temple 164, 171–2
texts, social setting of 5–16
  'Book of the Covenant' 106
  Deuteronomy 173–7
  Holiness Code 190–1
  Job 126
  Psalms
  Proverbs 117–19
  prophets 73–5
  Isaiah 77–9, 155
  Jeremiah 81–3
  Ezekiel 85
  Amos 53–4, 59–60, 72–3
  Micah 56–7, 75–6
theodicy 76, **125–7, 130–1**, 178
theology 16, 203–25
tithe 164, 171–2, 176, 198
  third-year 178–9

Torah 105, 168–202
  as a whole **168–73**
    rhetorical aim 169–71
    social setting 171–2
tribute 19, 33, 143

upper class *see* ruling class
usury 4, 31, 102–3, 109–11, 177–8
utopia 14–16, 100, 155, 160, **167–8**,
    174–5, 178, 183–4, 190, 194,
    197–8, 201–2, 227, 229

violence 67–8, 154–5, 165
virtue 131–3

wages 178
war 60–1
widows 87, 108, 122, 128, 130
wisdom literature 117–33
  Egyptian 119
women 62–3, 196. *See also* widows

Zion 75–6, 77–8. *See also* Jerusalem